CW01081429

ORKNEY
WORDBOOK

Roy Long

ORKNEY WORDBOOK

a dictionary of the dialect of Orkney

Gregor Lamb

Byrgisey

Copyright © Byrgisey, 1988, 1995

First published 1988
Paperback revised edition 1995

ISBN 0 9513443 5 8

All rights reserved. Apart from any fair dealing for the purposes
of study, research, criticism or review, as permitted under the
Copyright Act, 1956, no part of this publication may be
reproduced, stored in a retrieval system, or transmitted in any
form by any means, electronic, electrical, chemical, mechanical,
optical, photocopying, recording or otherwise, without prior
permission of the publishers.

Printed by the Kirkwall Press,
The Orcadian Office, Kirkwall, Orkney.

for

Robbie o Leaquoy

farmer, fisherman,
Orcadian, Birsay man

By the same author:-

Come thee Wiz, Kirkwall Press, 1978*
Nivver Spaek, Kirkwall Press, 1980*
Orkney Surnames, Paul Harris, 1981*
Hid kam intae words, Byrgisey, 1986*
Orkney Wordbook, Byrgisey, 1988, (hardback)*
Sky Over Scapa, 1939-1945, Byrgisey, 1991*
Aviation War Diary, Orkney, 1939-1945, Byrgisey, 1992*
Naggles o Piapittem, a study of the placenames of Sanday, Orkney,
    Byrgisey 1992
Testimony of the Orkneyingar, the placenames of Orkney,
    Byrgisey, 1993
Orkney Dictionary, Orcadian-English/English Orcadian,
    (in preparation; co-author Margaret Flaws)
At the Edge of Time (historical novel, in preparation)

* titles out of print

I am fifty years of age. When I was young, about five or six old men spoke mostly Norse but they were never taught to read or write any of it for a long time before so that their words and what does remain can be but imperfect. I could wish for a (dictionary) of Norse and English which would be a key to these broken and remaining words and names . . . with a box of snuff and a bottle of ale and a dram with old folks, I'll find out more of these rules and etymologies than with all the Latin and Greek masters in England. Besides, we understand these old broken Norse words and their meanings better than any stranger can do.

George Moar, (Skelday), Birsay, 1795

Orkney Archives, D23/7/15, with kind permission.

Abbreviations used in the book:-

Cai	Caithness
Dan	Danish
dial	dialect
Du	Dutch
eModEng	Early Modern English
Eng	English
F	French
Gael	Gaelic
Ger	German
HGerm	High German
Icel	Icelandic
imitat	imitative
Ir Gael	Irish Gaelic
Lat	Latin
LGerm	Low German
MedL	Medieval Latin
MDu	Middle Dutch
MHGerm	Middle High German
ModIcel	Modern Icelandic
Norw	Norwegian (includes Nynorsk)
OE	Old English
OF	Old French
OHGerm	Old High German
ON	Old Norse
Ork	Orkney
OSc	Old Scots
Scand	Scandinavian
Sc	Scots/Scotland
Sh	Shetland
Sw	Swedish

Symbols	† obsolete
	* common use

INTRODUCTION

This Orkney Wordbook began in a small way in 1968 when, as an exile in England I found odd words and phrases from my childhood days still being used as tools in my thought processes. No longer of any value in communicating, the purpose for which they had originally emerged, they had been relegated to my private world where before long they would atrophy and disappear. To forestall this inevitable fate I captured these denizens which appeared intermittently from the deep which had become their doom. Sometimes they eluded me but after a short while I had a collection of over two hundred words.

My family slowly added to the collection. In 1974 I returned to Orkney, my senses sharpened to the idiom and vocabulary of Orkney dialect and the collection began with renewed vigour. Eight years later work began in earnest on a new dictionary of the Orkney dialect and a weekly series on dialect in The Orcadian newspaper and an appeal for words and phrases brought in thousands not only from Orkney but also from Orcadians abroad.

Four people have made an outstanding contribution to this collection. Ernest Wishart from Kirkwall made available the large collection left by his brother James Smith Wishart. James lived for many years on the island of Eday, the principal source of his collection, and he was able to record from there many words which without his enthusiasm would have vanished. Joina and Peter Leith of Stenness who have done so much to record the fast disappearing elements of the Orkney way of life provided me with their own word list. Joina in her own right, made a major contribution to the Orkney entries in the Scottish National Dictionary during its forty seven year period of evolution. David Towrie from Sanday also possess a fine collection of Orkney words and phrases and very kindly spent two winters perfecting his list for me. Norman Baldwin from Leicestershire was stationed in Orkney during the war years and in this way his interest in the language and life of Orcadians began. He has made many visits to the islands and has accumulated detailed lists both from written and oral sources. He made his researches freely available to me and the ear of the southerner has, as one might expect, captured uniqueness of idiom and word usages that might otherwise have escaped.

I have listed the names of all those who have made contributions to this WORDBOOK. Many contributors gave me lists of hundreds of words, others only a few but none the less significant. At a dance in Finstown in 1987 a jolly red-faced reveller, fresh from a spirited strip-the-willow, embraced me more out of personal support than friendship. 'Beuy', he asks, 'does thoo ken whit garoye is? I kent a owld man thit used tae spaek aboot himsel in his garoye'. To hear a word like that spoken is to have the same feelings as an archaeologist stumbling on a rare and beautiful artefact. I had seen the word written in a word list only once and here from the lips of an Orcadian came a pure Norn relic of a language which had been dead for two hundred years.

The WORDBOOK takes as its basis *The Orkney Norn* a dictionary of what Hugh Marwick considered to be the relics of the Norse language spoken in Orkney. To this has been added all other words and phrases which cannot be found in a standard English dictionary. A Shetlander should find himself very much at home with this book for we share a common heritage. Scots will find many familiar words and phrases here for it was the Scots language and not the English which supplanted Norn.

Some attempt has been made to indicate usage. An asterisk denotes that a word or expression is in common use. If the word is found only in old records, it is marked with a dagger. Of the unmarked entries many thousands are still in use but sometimes they are not universally known in Orkney. For example the word *pullies* for children is well known in Birsay but is not recorded elsewhere. The Westray word *teewhuppo* for lapwing is unknown on The Mainland. At the onset it was hoped to emphasize island and parish differences but this became impractical. Post war mobility of the population has invalidated the exercise. 'Me faither kam fae Westray and me mither fae Shapinsay and I wis born in Tankerness - I don't ken whar the word kam fae, was a not untypical response.

Wherever possible an etymology is provided for the word. Where there is a clear Old Norse connection this is the preferred entry. Failing that, connections are looked for in Norwegian dialect and in the Norwegian languages. Occasionally gaps can be filled from Icelandic, Faroese, Danish and Swedish. A sizable number of entries have no etymology. These may be words lost in the parent language Old Norse, they may be highly corrupted forms of that language or of the Celtic languages or of other languages. When an old Westray man says he is 'in his ludgy pot' meaning he is 'in the best of health', only a chance stumbling upon the Old Scots legal phrase *liege poustie*, in full possession of one's faculties, provided the answer.

I am indebted to many people and organisations for helping to make the word book a reality. Dr George Marshall, formerly Depute Director of Education for Orkney, kindly made word processing facilities available during the summer school vacation of 1985 and 1986. Anna Meadows of Gairsty in Birsay began the first draft and worked assiduously in her spare time over a two year period transferring the manuscript to disc. Without her initial help and enthusiasm it is very doubtful whether the project would have succeeded. When Anna embarked on her university course Ray Hughes of the Manpower Services Commission was able to include the *Orkney Wordbook* as part of a YTS scheme and the final drafts were meticulously prepared by Heather Craigie of Evie. Orkney folk owe a deep gratitude to these two young Orcadian girls. Heather's work was made so much easier by the freely given help and congenial company of Dr Raymond Lamb and Andi Ross with whom she worked in the offices of the Orkney Heritage Society.

Financial help came from the Community Councils of most Orkney parishes who contributed £1000 to the editing of the Orkney Wordbook and the purchase of a reference copy of the Scottish National Dictionary.

It was the writer's ambition to include within the covers of the book every written and spoken form of the dialect. This soon became a pipe dream. There are omissions. Many words from old deeds and charters have been omitted in the interest of brevity. An occasional word given to me on the street, at a meeting or on the telephone has at best been laundered, at worst been lost, mislaid or become illegible. If the reader cannot find a word, remember that since there is no correct form of the dialect, the word might be entered though not in the spelt form expected. Also a word might not be included because it does exist in English, perhaps in English slang for such words are excluded from the WORDBOOK. If omissions or errors are found, please let the writer know. No guidelines are given for phonetic pronunciation for this would add considerable bulk to the book.

I sincerely acknowledge the help of those who contributed to the Orkney Wordbook. Many have not lived to sees its completion but their effort on my behalf will not be forgotten.

Betty **Ashby**, Kelso; Olwen **Aitken**, Kirkwall; Bert **Baikie**, Rendall; Norman **Baldwin**, Leicester; Mary **Bichan**, Harray; Betty **Black**, Dounby; Laura **Brough**, Rendall; Arnold **Carter**, Shropshire; Dolly **Clouston**, Rousay; Bessy **Coghill**, Birsay; Tom **Comloquoy**, Birsay; Karl **Cooper**, Sanday; Eva **Corrigall**, Harray; Peggy **Costie**, Westray; Greta **Craigie,** Stromness; Jim **Craigie**, Rousay; Graeme **Cromarty**, Stenness, Isabell **Cromarty,** North Ronaldsay; Mrs **Cumming**, Kirkwall; C R **Davidson,** Westray; M **Davidson,** Aberdeenshire; Alister **Donaldson**, Stenness; Margaret **Donaldson**, Stenness; Babs **Elphinstone**, Shetland; George **Esson**, South Ronaldsay; Isabella **Eunson**, Deerness; Jeanie **Firth**, Stromness; Margaret **Flaws**, Wyre; Davie **Flett**, Costa; Eric **Flett**, Stromness; Molly **Foubister**, Kirkwall; Bill **Foubister**, Aberdeenshire; Robert **Gaudie**, Birsay; Mrs **Gibson**, (Brinola) Rousay; (Mrs) **Goar**, Holm; Ida **Gorn**, Holm; Janet **Grainger**, Orphir; Capt John **Gray**, Stromness; Maureen **Gray**, Stromness; Bessie **Grieve**, Harray, Ralph **Groat**, Kirkwall; James **Groundwater**, Stromness; Ronnie **Harrold**, Portsmouth; (Mrs) **Harvey**, Dounby; Randolph **Hay**, Birsay; Bill **Hourie**, Sandwick; Kate **Humphrey**, Shetland; Hughie **Inkster**, Kirkwall; W **Irvine**, Papa Westray; Margaret **Johnston**, Sandwick; Kathleen **Johnston**, Kirkwall; Alan **Kelday**, Kirkwall; M **Knight**, Evie; David **Lamb**, Edinburgh; Elizabeth **Lamb**, Birsay; Jimmy **Lamb**, Bury St Edmunds; Julia **Leask**, Aberdeen; Maggie **Leask**, Stenness; Joanna **Leith**, Stenness; Peter **Leith**, Stenness; Susan **Leonard**, Stenness; T **Leslie**, Kirkwall; T **Leslie**, Westray; Alfie **Linklater**, Stenness; Freddie **Linklater**, Stenness; Thora **Linklater**, Stenness; Sylvia **Livingstone**, Aberdeen; May **Low**, Birsay; Marion **Macleod**, Kirkwall; B.M. **McLaren**, Edinburgh; A **Macdonald**, St. Margaret's Hope; Mrs **McGibbon**, Stromness; Margaret **MacKay**, Rosshire; Mary **Maclennan**, Inverness; Margaret **Mainland**, Rousay; Doris **Mair**, Aberdeen; Jane **Manson**, Kirkwall; Alistair **Marwick**, Birsay; Kenny **Meason**, Shapinsay; Eric **Meek**, Stenness; Mina **Merriman**, Sandwick; Prof **Miller**, Stromness; Tom **Miller**, Stronsay; William **Moodie**, Edinburgh; (Mrs) **Muir**, Orphir; Christina **Muir**, North Ronaldsay; John **Muir**, Evie; Moyra **Munro**,

Wigtown; Dolly **Norn**, Kirkwall; Joan **Penny**, Perthshire; Gordon **Pirie**, N.Ireland; (Mrs) **Rendall**, Westray; John **Ritch**, Stromness; Minnie **Russell**, Shapinsay; J **Rutterford**, Edinburgh; J.T. **Scarth**, Kirkwall; Liv **Schei**, Norway; Ethel **Sclater**, Orphir; D. **Scott**, Sandwick; Harcus **Scott**, Westray; Olga **Scott**, Kirkwall; Olivia **Scott**, Glasgow; Sinclair **Scott**, Stenness; William **Scott**, St Ola; William **Scott**, N.Ronaldsay; William **Sichel**, Sanday; Edith **Sinclair**, Deerness; Jim **Sinclair**, Fort William; Jimmy **Sinclair**, Kirkwall; Betsy **Skea**, Kirkwall; Willie **Skea**, Kirkwall; Bryan **Smith**, Aberdeen; Irene **Smith**, Stronsay; Marion **Spence**, Evie; Victor **Spence**, Evie; Mrs **Stephen**, South Ronaldsay; William **Stockan**, S. Africa; Alan **Stout**, Orphir; Tom **Stout**, Aberdeenshire; Billy **Sutherland**, Stenness; J.S. **Tait**, Holm; K. **Tait**, Stromness, Bill **Taylor**, Stenness; James **Taylor**, Birsay (Leoquoy); James **Taylor**, Birsay; (Flaws); Robert **Taylor**, Birsay; George **Towers**, Selkirk; David **Towrie**, Sanday; John **Towrie**, Kirkwall; Jim **Twatt**, Kirkwall; Mary **Twohig**, Merseyside; Winnie **Walls**, Harray; Fiona **Wilson**, Shetland; Len **Wilson**, Kirkwall; M **Wilson**, Sanday; Ernie **Wishart**, Kirkwall; James Smith **Wishart**, Kirkwall; Joseph **Wood**, Rendall; Miss **Wylie**, Deerness.

G Lamb
South Waird
Marwick
Birsay

November 1987

Seven years have passed since the *Orkney Wordbook* went to press. Despite its shortcomings it has proved to be enormously popular and has helped, I hope, to contribute to a greater awareness of the dialect. It is encouraging to learn that dialect is now encouraged in schools and to learn that there is a desire in schools to have a pupil's own dictionary in which he/she can read not only Orkney words with their English meanings but also look up English words and find their Orkney equivalent. This can only be an excellent training in language, man's most sophisticated accomplishment. The use of dialect in schools is a far cry from my own school days when the use of dialect words and expressions was severely frowned on. 'No such word as *tuction*' said the headmaster drawing a bold red line through it with a flourish of his pen! Although dialect has been for me an obsession for as many years as I can remember I did not teach dialect in school because in my own experience I knew that obsession is a bad qualification for a teacher. I did actively encourage the spoken dialect however though I must admit to being a little thrown when one day I asked a pupil why he had been absent. 'I hid a right dose o the skitter' he replied! There was laughter all round but general agreement that it was much easier to spell than diarrhoea.

It was extremely fortunate that the first edition of the WORDBOOK was computerised. Although converting the original primitive data has been very time consuming, without it there would have been no second edition. The opportunity has been taken to include many words which were sent to me after the publication of the book and to revise many of the entries. In the original edition, the Norwegian compositors did not mark the sub cntrics in bold type, despite repeated instructions, the result being to make the interpretation of some entries very difficult. This has now been resolved. Many of the etymologies have been revised in the light of a greater understanding of the origin of the words which go to make up the vocabulary of our dialect.

I should like to thank the helpful staff of The Orcadian who, once again, have coped so well with this difficult assignment and a special thanks is owed to Edwin Work of 'The Leonards' who persuaded me, very reluctantly at first, to embark once more on this mammoth task. Among the many contributors to this revised edition I should like to single out for special mention William Skea of Kirkwall who read the original from cover to cover and who sent a long list of words and expressions current in Sanday when he was young. Kenny Meason from Shapinsay and Margaret Flaws from Wyre have also made significant contributions. No doubt there are many old words and expressions as yet unrecorded and many thousands which alas have been lost for ever. I hope you enjoy this new edition, that you learn something more of the dialect and, most important of all, that you continue to use it.

Gregor Lamb,
South Waird,
Marwick,
Birsay.

November 1994

A the letter *a*, pronounced *e* in the West Mainland if followed by the letter *r*, e.g. *arm* becomes *erm*; the short *a* is pronounced *ay* in Westray e.g. *apples* becomes *ayples*.

a 1 = a, indefinite article, unlike in English, generally always used before vowels, *tae boil a egg*; see AAFIL for an exception to this rule.

a 2 a contracted form of 'have', used only after 'could', 'would' and 'should'; '*He could a lost his wey*.' '*John wid a 'phoned home*.' '*You should a seen him!*' [also Sh]

a 3 in [see AE]

a-back* backward, used negatively usually, '*He's no a-back o askan*'.

a-pace* still; in peace, '*Sit a-pace beuy!*'.

aa* all. **aabody** everybody. **aathing** everything. **aa hae and aa want** alternating between having little and having plenty. **aa me born days** all my life, '*Ah'm never seen such a sight in aa me born days*'. **aa and sae**, very nearly, almost.

aaber to thrash a sheaf in such a way that some grain is left on. **aaber-tait** a wisp of aabered straw. [Norw *avberja* half-thrashed straw]

aachan swarming. [Sh *ogin*, ON *aka* to move]

aafil* 1 = awful 2 as in English, used adverbially to emphasize degree e.g. '*Hid's aafil fine he's home early noo*'; see NAAFIL for adjectival form [compare HORRIBLE]

aak* see AK 2.

aan*, ann = awn.

aanie-onyoo, anonyou white tailed eagle, at one time quite common in Orkney. [ON *örn*, eagle; words which are of Norse origin and have *r* before *n* usually lose the *r* in Orkney dialect. [see CHOIN as another example]. The form *aanie-onyoo* seems to be a rhyming duplicate; compare RIVVLE-PIVVLE, WHIM-WHAM etc.; in placenames the bird is always called the *onyo* or *unyo*; they frequented hill-top mounds which today are called *Unyo Tuacks*]

aar see ARR.

ab verb. to hinder, '*His rheumatics abbèd him a lot*'. noun. 1 a stutter. 2 a hindrance. [Norw *jabba* to stammer]

abble weak. [probably related to AB above; compare Swed *happla* to stutter]

abed land which has been under the plough for a long time. [origin uncertain]

abee heart disease in sheep causing sudden death. [origin unknown]

abersee the 27th letter of the alphabet!. In the olden days when Orcadian children repeated the alphabet, they would end with *abersee*. In Scotland the word *eppershand* was used. [corruptions of *and (per se) and* the name given to the sign & which appeared after *z* in old school alphabet books]

abical-dunkie see AP.

aboot* = about. **aboot ages*** about the same age, '*He wis aboot ages wi me*'. **aboot-gaan buddy*** a person who always seems to be visiting or going about. **aboot-hands (wi)*** in the vicinity, '*Is thee mither aboot-hands?*'. **home-aboot*** in or around the house, '*He lay home-aboot for a while*'. **in-aboot*** inside, '*Bide in-aboot, bairns, till that unkan man's by*'. **oot-aboot*** out and about, '*Willie can get oot-aboot noo the weather's warmer*'. **aboot-kast** a sudden change in the direction of the wind

abune* = above [also Sc]. **abune a** unreasonable, '*Tae ask me tae deu hid again I thowt wis abune a*.' **abune the fire** that part of the old Orkney kitchen which faced the fire. Aboondariggs, *above the riggs* is a placename in Sanday.

accorned* = according, '*Ah'll gae yi accorned tae whit I hiv*'. **accorned tae the man**, as it is said, '*Ah'll gae thee something tae weet thee trapple accorned tae the man*'.

ach an expression of annoyance '*Ach! I tellt him tae be home afore ten and just luk at the time!*'

acht verb. to own. noun. 1 possession. 2 something worth having, '*Hid's an acht tae hiv the likes o that*'. [OSc *aucht*; OE *āgan* to possess]

ackband control, *tae hiv no ackband ower*. [Sc *aweband* restraint]

Adam the dark purple orchid. [compare Sc *Adam-and-Eve*]

ae 1† in e.g. John a Toftis, Criste Aelingklaet. [ON *á*, in etc]

ae 2 one, also **ee** [also Sc.]. **ae-baest tree** the smallest plough tree, intended for use with one horse.

ae-fald simple, not cunning. [also Sc; nME *anfald* sincere]

aem see EUM 1, EUM 2.

aest 1 to envy. [? ON *oeskja* to wish]

aest 2 = east, '*A wind fae the aest is no good tae man or baest*'.

aet* 1 = eat, '*Hid'll aet afore a stone*' it is better than no food at all.

aet 2 to own, '*Whar aets that piece o grund?*' [OSc *aucht*; OE *āgan* to possess]

aff* 1 = off, '*Ah'm aff the mind o hid*' I've changed my mind. **aff-faas** the left-overs. **affgo** a strange object, '*Hid wis a queer kinda affgo standan fornent the hoose*'. **aff-pit*** delay [also Sc]. **aff-shaering butter** butter specially made for the end of harvest. **aff-shaering feast** a feast which took place at the end of harvest. **affscum** worthless people. **afftak** a lull in a storm. **aff-takkan*** ridiculing. **aff the baet** [see BAET 1.]

affens* often. [a contraction of Eng *often-times*]

1

afthanks part of a boat where the bands come together at the stem and the stern [also Sh; ON *hanki*, eye on the edge of a sail or on the side of a boat - used in a transferred sense]

afore* 1 = before. 2 over, *tae go afore the craig* to take one's life by jumping over a cliff. [ON *hlaupa fyrir bjorg*]. *pittan bruck afore the shore* tipping rubbish on the shore. [a special usage of ON *fyrir* with a great variety of meaning]

after = after. **after-burn** the last of the ale drained from the keg. [Sc *burn water*, water from a burn or stream]. **aftersuit** the space in the stern of a boat. [ON *skutr* stern]

agairy to leave service before the contract date had expired. [compare ON *gøra* to contract; see GARRA-BANNOCK]

agalis very difficult. [compare Norw *agalauss* extraordinary]

agee* of a door etc squint, *'Did anybody go agee?'* that is misplace one's trust by cheating or stealing, etc. [also Sc and Eng dial; Sc *gee* to move to one side or another]

ageldro see GILDRO.

agers greedy. [compare Norw *hegreleg* greedy]

aggle, haggle verb. to make a mess. noun. a mess. [corruption of Eng *addle*]

agildro see GILDRO.

Agist* = August [also Sc]

aglas *aglas wark* a piece of work which has turned out badly. [Norw. *agelaus*, undisciplined]

Ah* first person singular *I*, only in present tense and future tense of verb. 'to be', e.g. *'Ah'm right playsed yir comed'*. *'Ah'll hae tae go, I doot.'*

ahint* behind. An Orkney farm servant, taking a cow to the bull complained that the cow had been awkward, *'Sheu widna go afore me'*, he said *'so I hid tae go ahint her'*. [also Sc]

aichan a straw of bere or oats with the head on. [also Sc but with the narrower meaning *head of corn*; ON *ögn* chaff or husks]

aikaspire*, aikelspeckled mouldy, *'My the buddum (bottom) o me net coorteen (curtain) is aal gin aikaspire'*. [also Sc in a variety of forms; the essential meaning is *to grow (of grain)*; see AIKER; OE *spir* sprout]

aikel a hard lump found in the fat of animals. [ON *oexl* a lump]

aikelspeckled see AIKASPIRE.

aiker 1 a stalk of corn. 2 an ear of bere. [Sc *ikker*; ultimately related to Eng *ear* (of corn); OE *ēar*]

aiman adj. used as an intensive, *an aiman fool*, a raving fool [see EUM 2]

ain* adj. own, *'Luk efter thee ain bairns'*. [see NAIN]

aint, ent to look after. **ainty, enty** attentive. [ON *enta* to care for]

ainway progress, *'Thoo're no makan muckle ainway'* [? *endway*]

air 1 see ER.

air* 2, **aire, ayre** a gravelly spit. [common in placenames; ON *eyrr* gravel]

air* 3, **ere** verb. to taste. noun. 1 = air. 2 a small quantity, *'Pit a air a tea in the pot'*. [compare Sc *to get an air of* to smell something]

aire see AIR 2.

airt* a direction, *'The lum'll no draa whin the wind's in this airt'*. [also Sc; Gael *aird* point of a compass]

aisins the eaves of a house. [Sc. *easings*; OE *efesung*]

aithken, euchen a mark on a sheep to denote ownership. [ON *auðkenni* a distinguishing mark on cattle]

aitrament a mild oath. [probably ON *eitr* poison + Eng suffix *ment*]

aitran, naitran applied to fine rain, *'Hid's aitran and rainan'*. [compare Norw *eitersnjo* fine snow; the essential meaning is 'poisoning' but used here in the sense 'bitter'; compare ATTRY]

aize* to blaze. **aizer*, eezer** a roaring fire. [ON *aesa*, of fire, wind etc., to rage]

ak, aak* 1 to be about to be sick or to cough up phlegm. *akkan and spittan* spitting. [see HACKY and UIK; related forms are found in Sc. Norw. and in the Celt. languages]

ak, aak* 2 the common guillemot. **ak-swappan** catching auks by sweeping special nets through the air at the cliffs. [ON *álka* auk]

akamy 1 small 2 nasty. [ON *ögn* grain + Norw. *mutt*, grain, both with the additional meanings 'little thing']

akkéd compulsive, *an akkéd thief*. [ON *aka* to move or drive]

alaith shame. **tae think alaith** to be ashamed. [related to Eng *loathe*]

alamotti the stormy petrel. [also Sh (Foula) *oily mootie*; Sh *oily* is a corruption of Sh *oller* mud, Ork dial OOLER dirt, ODDLER sewer, Norw *aale* cattle urine; the reference is to the foul substance ejected by the bird; see MOOTIE]

alat 1 out of order, *'Hid's gin alat'*. 2 unwell [? a form of ILL-AT]

ale = ale. **ale-hurry** a recess in the wall in which ale was stored. In the ruinous house of Nether Benzieclett, Sandwick where once it is said a King of Norway stayed, there is a haunted ale-hurry. The ghost of a grey ewe appeared regularly at the back of this *hurry* where a man was supposedly murdered. [see HURRY]

alick see EELICK.

alin a measuring rod the same length as a Sc ell. [a

form of Sc *ell-wand*]

alinery† solely, in particular [also Sc]

alison a shoemaker's awl. [also ELSHIN]

aliss [also Sc] = alas.

alittie a term of condolence, '*What a pity!*' [origin unknown; compare ALOOR]

allooed 1 allowed. 2 required to, '*Thoo're alloed tae come up*'.

alonks† along. [obs Sc *alongis*]

aloor an expression of grief. [see ILL-OOR]

alwis 1 = always. 2 anyway, '*Hid wis there yesterday alwis*'.

am alum. [see AWM]

amble, ammle a ploughtree. [ON *hamla*]

amers* = embers [also Sc]

amis* 1 describing the deserved outcome of a rather irresponsible action, usually preceded by 'weel', '*Hid wis weel amis that I called thee in whin thoo chappéd*' this was said to the writer by an old lady who, expecting a friend to knock, unwittingly invited in a complete stranger. 2 **amis bairn** a child whose father had died before he/she was born. **an amis ting o bairn** a sickly child. [Sc *amos* alms; ON *ölmusa-barn* orphan]

amiskopft see INSKEYFT.

amiter of a person or animal, weak. [ON *úmáttigr* infirm]

amly see EMLY.

ammer goose see EMMER-GOOSE.

ammers 1 cross-beam of a roof. 2 a beam of wood from which pots are suspended over a fire. [possibly related to Danish dial *hamar* cross-beam but more likely from an original form *rammer/rammel/rammel* with loss of initial *r*; see REEMER and RAMMLE(-BACK)]

ammle see AMBLE.

ample = 1 adj. ample. 2 noun. more than enough, '*No more tatties for me, I hiv ample.*'

amsho a mild oath. [ON *and-skoti* fiend or devil]

and = and, used in the idiom, '*Watch and no....*'* '*Watch and no fa on the brigstones for they're ferfil slippy*'. [Eng *Watch you don't...*]

andoo* 1 to row a boat against wind or tide so that it keeps in position for fishing etc. [also Sh]. 2 to stroll. [ON *andoefa* to keep a boat in position by rowing]

ane* see EEN.

ang see AAN.

animal = animal. **animals*** cattle, '*Me son only works wi sheep, he doesna hiv any animals*'. [compare BAEST]

anker a measure of spirits, [Dutch word used generally throughout NoEurope, including Scotland: MedLat *anceria* a small vat]

ankerskeeto a kind of cuttlefish. [see SKEETO;

compare Norw *ankartroll* a type of cuttlefish]

anmark of animals troublesome. [ON *ann-marki* a blemish]

ann see AAN.

anner head see HINNER HEAD

annoyed 1 = annoyed. 2* worried. A non-Orcadian can be upset to be told by a host, '*I was annoyed when yi didna come last night*'.

anonyou see AANIE-ONYOU.

anse to take aim at. **ansees** intentionally. [ON *anza* to pay attention]

answer* to obey, 'That thing o bairn'll no answer'. [ON *anza* to pay attention]

anteran* odd in the sense of occasional, '*Hid's December noo and we just git a anteran egg fae the hens*'. [also Sc; ME *aunter* chance; ultimately from Lat *advenire* to happen]

anunder* underneath. [probably = in-under]

anywey* anyhow. [compare SOMEWEY]

Ap-helly-day† a feast held at the end of January. [Sh *Uphellya*; OSc *uphalie day*; ON *uppi* at an end + *helgr* holiday]

ap* = up. **apacailie-dunkie, abical-dunkie** a seesaw. [appears in a great variety of forms in dial; Sh *hederkandunk* a see-sawing or a thump; for second element see DUNK a thump]. **ap-settan** having airs and graces. [= setting oneself up]. **ap the spoot** offended. **ap-trow**† apparently an old nickname for an inn or ale house. [see DOON-TROO]

apae* = upon.

aplicot* a common pronunciation of *apricot*. [included here because it shows the common inter-change of *l* and *r* in Ork dialect, a feature of the Indo-European languages]

appasill an invitation to eat up at table. [= *Help theesel*, Help yourself]

appiegiest a fool. [Sh *attikast* probably from an assumed ON form *aptrkast* something thrown away]

arasees tricks. [perhaps related to ON *oerr* mad, furious]

arboo maggots in an animal's back. [see VARBO]

arby the sea pink. [Marwick suggests the name is related to ON *haerbúa* mat grass; ARVO may be a related form]

ark 1 = ark. 2 a chest or box. 3 something huge, *a ark o a hoose*.

arkamy, erkny a large seal. [ON *örkn* seal]

arl 1 to tell an exaggerated story, a common preoccupation in Orkney at one time! [perhaps a metathetical form of Norw *ralla* to talk]

arl 2 a woman fishgutter. [a word used in the North Isles in the early part of this century; ME *erles* indenture]

arr, aar to feel revulsion at a certain food, '*Me stom-*

3

ach arred at it'. [see VARR]

arrf, erif † inheritance. **arrfhouse**† the house where the division of a deceased's property was made. [ON *arfr*]

arroo* a pullet: *arroo eggs* pullet eggs. A story from Evie in the 1920s is that a lady collecting for Earl Haig's (Fund) was, through a misunderstanding, offered *arroo eggs*! [Gael *eireag*, young hen]

arvo, ervo common chickweed. [ON *arfi*]

as 1 = as. 2* than, *better as his*. [compare Sc. *or*]

asee the angle between the beam and the handle on the rear side of a plough. [ON *áss* a beam]

aside* = beside. [compare ATWEEN]

ask drizzle, small particles of snow. [compare EESK]

asly *to lay in asly* to bring together things which are essentially separate, eg horses from different farms might have worked *in asly* to finish an operation quickly. [perhaps ON *slaegja* profit]

asoond in a faint. [also Sh; a form of OSc *aswoon* = *a* + *swoon* as in Eng *asleep*]

ass = ash [also Sc]. **assie-cairt** the old name for the refuse vehicles used in Kirkwall and Stromness. **assie pattle** 1 a lazy person who stays at home and pokes in the ashes. 2 a nickname for someone from Sandwick, Orkney. [compare Ger *Aschenputtel* and ON *kol-bítr*]. **assie pow** in old Orkney houses the fire was in the middle of the floor. The removal of ashes invariably meant the removal of earth from time to time so that eventually the hearth was a hole. [Sc *pow* pool]

asticle* = astragal, one of the bars holding the panes of a window.

astie wait!, hush! [perhaps a form of *wheesht-thee*; see WHEESHT]

astrees the beam of a plough. [ON *áss* a beam + Sc *tree*, beam]

atfares business, behaviour, *queer atfares* . [ON *atferð* conduct]

at-pitten* annoyed. [see PIT]

at* 1 that, *'I tellt him at I couldna come'*. [ON *at*]

at 2 = at* , *'Whar are we at noo?'* Where are we?

atgauns ongoings. As Marwick says 'more specifically the results of an individual's behaviour'.

atgeung* approach *'He hid a queer atgeung wey o deuan hid'*. [*at* + *?going*]

atgong bad behaviour. [a form of ATGAUNS]

atifer shame. [compare Norw *gjera attyver seg* to do something which one comes to regret]

atlyan of a person who overstays a welcome, *an atlyan thing*. [the story is told of a neighbour who, when visiting, persistently stayed sometimes until 2 a.m; this pattern ended when the host, in despair on one occasion, got up and said to his wife, 'We'll hiv tae go tae bed lass and let this man get home.'! [compare Sh *tae lay anesel at* to be unwilling to rise]

atteal† a type of duck. [also OSc; probably a form of TEAL]

atter to crave after. [origin unknown]

attercape an ill-thriving hen. [ON *eitraðr* poisoned, confused with ETTERCAT]

attry 1 of weather cold, bitter. 2 ugly. [ON *eitr* poison; also Sc; compare AITRAN]

atween*, awheen = between, *a day atween weathers* a mild day between stormy days.

atyun no good. [origin unknown]

aukaspeed malt overgrown. [a form of AIKERSPIRE]

auld* = old. **Auld Nick*** the devil. **auld farrant*** [also Sc.] old fashioned. **Auld New Year's Day** 13th January. **Auld Hallowmas** 1st November.

aumrie a cupboard. [found in a variety of spellings; also Sc; ultimately from Lat *armarium*; compare Fr *armoire*]

aund† to breathe. In a 17th-century trial it was said of a witch that she, *aundit in bytt* she breathed (into a vessel) [ON *anda* to breathe]

ava* at all, *'There wis nobody there ava'*. [Sc = *of all*]

aval used of an animal on its back. [Sc *avald*]

avalis weak. [ON *aflauss*]

avar an exclamation of surprise [corruption of *beware*]

avildro see VILDRO.

awa away [also Sc]. **awa way't**, dead

awheen see ATWEEN.

awm, am alum. **awm-skin*** an animal skin dressed with alum.

awrige† the sharp angle of the ridge made by ploughing. [OF *areste* a ridge]

ax* = ask. [a metathesis of *ask* found throughout Sc. but in Ork only heard in the dial of the tinkers; OE *ascian* or *axian* to ask]

axe* 1 = axe. 2 a North Ronaldsay sheep mark.

axes† the onset of an illness. **axes grass** the reed *juncus effusus*, the pith of which was used as the wick of the cruisie lamp; it was also used for medicinal purposes. [compare Sh *eksis girs* 1 dandelion, 2 devil's bit and Ork ECCLE GRASS butterwort; OSc *axes*; Eng *access* the onset of illness]

aye* 1 always, *'He's aye gaan there'*. 2 *Hello* in a greeting but more generally **aye aye**. 3 yes, *aye wid he etc* he certainly would. [also Sc; ON *ei*]

aynig, ayning† possession; [ON *eign* possession]

ayre see AIR 2.

ayrkskifft† a division of inheritance [ON *arfskipti*]

B the letter B pronounced as in English, frequently omitted in pronunciation after M eg. rumbled = *rummled*.

ba* = ball. **The Ba**, the traditional ball games held in Kirkwall on Christmas Day and New Year's Day. **ba o the leg** the calf of the leg. **baa-piece*** a piece of thick leather put on the sole of a shoe to compensate for wear [referring to the ball of the foot]

baa-piece see BA.

baa*, bo, bod a submerged rock. **baa o the tide** the ripple made by the tide running over a submerged shoal. **baa haggies** ripples in a tideway. [ON *boði* a shallow, literally a warner; also common in Orkney placenames].

baak*, bawk 1 a rafter, usually COUPLE BAAKS or TWART-BAAKS. 2 a hens' roost. [also Sh]. 3 a rope from which nets are hung. 4 the long line from which hooks are suspended. 5 a seat in a boat. 6 a ridge in ploughing. 7 a division between lands. [see GARBOU]. 8 a low partition wall in Orkney houses. **baak huins***, **buckheuns** to be *in the baak huins* to be out of sorts or offended. [the essential meaning is to stay on the perch like a sick hen. [see HEUN; ON *bjálki* a beam or *bálkr* a partition]

baakie* 1 the great black-backed gull. 2 the razor-bill. [Faroese *bakur*]

baaltick a rubber boot. [from an old trade mark *Baltic*]

bab-at-the-bowster an old Scottish dance, once performed in Orkney. It is a ring dance with a *bowster* or bolster placed in the middle, usually the last dance at an old wedding [also Sc.]

back-steys '*The sun is settan his back-steys*' said when sunbeams can be seen in the clouds. [a nautical metaphor]

back-stane the stone set at the back of the hearth to protect the wall [also Sc.]

back treat* a party for all those who helped with the organisation of a wedding.

back-come an expression of regret or disappointment.

back-door trot see BACK.

baffle a trifle. [also Sc; origin uncertain]

baffling the flattening of crops by wind and rain. [a form of BAFFIN]

bag = bag. **bags*** the scrotum (vulgar)

bagse 1 to struggle with difficulty through mud etc. 2 to stride clumsily. '*Here she is bagsan up the road*'. [a variant of BUCKSE]

baillie† a parish official earlier known as the UNDERFOUD. [OF *bailli*]

bailyament a state of prosperity. [originally the district under a BAILLIE]

baim-flooers flowers in bloom. [OE *beam* a beam, later a ray of light]

bain see BEND.

bairn* 1 a child [also Sc]. 2 used metaphorically in Birsay of a small hill on which a fisherman took his bearings. **bairns*** used to address friends of any age in this sense, '*Weel bairns Ah'll hae tae go*'. [also Sh., the exact equivalent of familiar Eng '*folks*']. **hairns, hairns!*** equivalent of Eng '*What's the world coming to!*' and usually accompanied by a slow and deliberate shake of the head. **bairny*, bairnly** childlike, used of immature behaviour. [ON *barn*, child with extended meaning 'people']

baist to beat. **baisting** a thrashing. [also Sc and Eng dial; ON *beysta* to thrash (corn)].

bait 1, bite pasture. [ON *beita*]

bait 2 to shoo animals away. [ON *beita* to set (dogs) on]

baiver to get blown about in the wind. [ON *bifra* to shiver]

bakbord† the port side of a vessel [ON *bak-borði*]

baldos a lead used to sink a handline. [compare LEAD LUSS; Sh *boltastone*; Norw *bulti* a chunk of wood]

ball to throw (especially stones). [also Sc and Sh; ON *bella* to hit or strike]

baloo the long-tailed duck. [also known as the CALOO; imitat]

baltioram 1 a scolding. 2 a noisy party. 3 destruction, havoc. [origin uncertain]

bambo a rag doll. [doubtful; compare Ital *bambino* a baby]

bamf to call in a loud voice. [? imitat]

bamlet a blow. [compare Eng dial *bammel* to beat]

band 1 to lay a long stone across (a wall) to bind both sides together. [a form of BIND]

band 2* = band. '*I could eat that tae a band playan*' I could eat any amount of that.

band 3 a hinge. [OSc *band* hinge etc]

bane = bone. **bane shacklin*** a cruel way of restraining a sheep. One leg was pushed through the other to prevent the animal jumping over the hill dyke into the crop.

banffie a kind of kite flown by Kirkwall children in the 1920's. [origin uncertain]

bang 1 = bang. 2 to jump with fright. 3 **bang on*** to jump on something quickly, '*He banged on the horse*'. [Sc *bang up* to jump quickly]

bangry *to win the bangry* to get the best share of something. [see VANGER]

bank*, bangse 1* = bank, especially a peat bank face from which the peats are cut. [also Sc and Sh]. 2* the coastline or edge of a loch eg *The Lyliebanks* along the shore of the Loch of Skaill, Sandwick.

bann an interdict. [ON *bann*]

Banna feet see BARNIFEET.

banno-corn a little stack of corn. [a form of BAIRN + corn]

banno-hive see BANNOCK.

banno-disty bad-tempered. [ON *barn* a child and *dust* a tilt or fight; essentially behaving like a child]

bannock*, **banno**, **binnack** a flat cake of flour, oatmeal or bere-meal, '*A misty May and a laeky June, is sure sign o a bannock soon*', i.e. will provide ideal crop growing conditions. **banno-hive*** a facial and body rash supposedly caused by eating bannocks made with freshly ground meal. [Sc *hives* a skin eruption; origin unknown; OE *bannuc*]

banstickle, branstickle, brandie, bruntie the stickleback. [also Sh; compare Icel *brandastikill*; ON *branda* a little trout]

banyar only in the phrase *banyar days* hard times. [obs Eng *Banyan Day* a day on which no meat was served on a ship]

bar-end the end of the sheaf with the grain. [?Sc *bar* to thrash]

bare = bare. **bare handed*** empty-handed, '*He's no bare-handed*' he's well off. **bare naked*** stark naked [also Sc]

bark 1, hillbark tormentil. [roots were used to bark or tan leather; they were also boiled in milk and used as a cure for diarrhoea; compare Faroese *börka* tormentil root]

bark 2 1 = of a dog etc to bark. 2 to give a hacking cough.

barkéd* bruised or filthy dirty, '*His feet wis just barkéd*'. [also Cai; compare Sc *to bark* to encrust; to bark = to tan]

barkloves barefoot. [ON *berr* bare; *klauf* cloven foot]

barlo-brock, barley play, barrels truce in children's games. [related to Eng *barley*; Eng *byrlaw* local law]

barm* yeast or the froth of fermenting ale. [general in Eng dial]. **barman*** seething with anger, foaming or barming at the mouth. [also in Eng dial; OE *beorma* yeast]

barn = barn. **barn-closs** two stone walls built out from the barn door to direct the wind for winnowing.

Barnifeet, Bannafeet a Stronsay goblin. [ON *barnafótr* child's foot]

baroot used in the sense **baroot corn**, bere grown in land in which bere had been sown the previous year. [ON *barr* bere; ON *rót* root, literally bere root]

barrels see BARLO-BROCK.

barsgerd covered in dirt. [? a form of BARKÉD]

batt a sudden gust of wind. [OSc *bat* = stroke or blow]

batter* stiffness in new linen, cotton, etc., '*Wash the tea tooal and tak the batter oot o hid*'. [Sc *batter* paste etc made by beating]

bavall an ungainly, clumsy man. [see BIVVAL]

bawk see BAAK.

bawkie a ghost. [ON *bokki* a he-goat; compare Norw *bokke* a big man; Sc *bogle* and Eng *bogey* (man)]

bawkie-blindie = blindie-bawkie, blind-man's buff. [compare Norw *blinde-bukk*]

bawns 1 a fuss. 2 a person full of tricks. [probably ON *bunsa* to drive violently]

bayl* see BEEL.

be 1 = to be. *tae let a'be* to let alone. The present tense of the verb *to be* is used for the perfect tense in Ork dial eg, '*Ah'm been*' I have been', '*Wir done hid*' 'We have done it'. [notice the subjunctive form of *be*, '*If thoo bees good Ah'll gae thee a sweetie*'; also Sh]

be† 2 in the direction of, *be-north, be-sooth* etc. [also Sc]

bear = bear (to carry). **bearin skin** a sheepskin worn to protect the clothing when carrying a caisie of dung etc.

bear (afore) appear as a vision to. [ON *bera fyrir*]

beard = beard, '*Yi canna draa a strae across his beard the day*' he's in no mood for teasing. **beardie-stick** a shaving brush.

beat see BAET 2.

bed 1 = bed. **bedfast, bed-lyan** bedridden. **bedseck*** a chaff mattress, made of sack-cloth.

bed 2 to lay flat a growing crop of corn. **bedded** of crop, flattened. [Norw *bada* to crush down]

bedyow a lazy woman. **bedyowy** of a woman, lazy. [ON *beðja* a wife; compare WHANG]

bee 1 = bee. 2 a fly, especially of the large variety. [see FISHY BEE]

beefling a battering [compare BAFF]

beek a pile of tangles built up to dry out. [origin uncertain; compare Norw *bøkja* to dry partially]

beel 1 to enclose (cattle). [ON *boela*]

beel* 2, **bayl** to fester. [also Sc; origin obscure]

been-hook† a cottar, duty-bound to help a farmer at harvest time. **been-plough†** a man who could be called upon to help with ploughing. [OE *bēn* a request; compare MEng *boon work* an unfixed amount of ploughing which a steward could demand; Eng *hook* a sickle]

beer to complain, *beeran and greetan* crying or fretful. **beerin** querulous. [OSc *bere*; OE *gebaeru* conduct]

bees-wid = be as it would, however.

bees-will* = be as it will, however.

beesmilk*, beestie-milk the milk of a cow newly calved. **beesmilk cheese*** a rich pudding made from beesmilk. [also Sc; OE *beost*]

beet 1 to repair (a boat). **beiting** repairing. [ON *boeta* to repair with influence from Sc *beet* to mend]

beet 2 equalising price in a barter, '*Hoo much beet'll I get*' [ME *beete* to correct etc]

beezer* something really big or fine, *a beezer o a car.* [also Sc principally by children; origin unknown]

begin = begin. past tense **begood**†

beglan walking in bow legged fashion. [compare Faroese *bekla* to walk crookedly]

begood see BEGIN.

beguggled destroyed or spoiled by mud or slime [see GAGGLE]

begunk disappointed [also Sc origin uncertain]

behadden = beholden

beiting see BEET.

belanter to delay. [see LANTER]

belky to drink a great quantity. [OE *belgan* to swell]

belkie see GRUELLY BELKIE.

bell cluster of leaves on a tangle. [compare Icel *bjalla* root of edible tang]

Bellia a Stronsay goblin. [origin unknown]

belly the bag in which a foal is born, formerly used as window panes. [ON *belgr* bag]

Beltane*, Beltan an ancient Celtic fire festival held in May when bonfires were lit on many hills. **beltan tirls** a period of bad weather at Beltane. [also Sh and Sc; Gael *bealltuinn;* see TIRL]

belya the pollack, a type of cod. [probably ON *belgr* bag, from its shape]

belyve speedily. [also Sc; Eng *by life* with movement]

bemilded lacking the energy to get up and go. [origin unknown]

ben* *to go ben* to go into the best room of a house. **ben-end*** the best room of a house. [also Sc; OE *binnan* within]

bend, bain thick leather for the soles of boots. [also Sc; related to Eng *band* in the sense of that which binds]

benk see BINK.

benlin stone the stone which anchored the straw rope used to hold down the thatch on old Orkney houses. **benlins** that part of a stack where the straw ropes were tied. **bennle** to tie down with straw ropes. **bennel** the waist of a corn stook or belt. [ON *bendill* a cord]

benner *as dry as benner* very dry, like clothes freshly aired. [? a form of Sc *bennles* things dry and brittle like reeds; related to Eng *bent* coarse grass]

bennle, binnal to tie down with straw ropes. [see BENLIN STONE]

bent = bent (grass). **benty bugs** small insects found in bent grass.

bere = bere, a type of barley grown in the north of Scotland, common throughout Europe at one time. **bere-bannock*** a bannock made from ground bere. **bere-whin** a bere-bannock, so called because of its tendency to go hard very quickly. [see WHIN]

berge* 1 a piece of wood projecting from the bottom of a door to prevent rain water being blown in, usually called a **water berge***. 2 the stones at the base of a chimney underneath which the thatch is fixed. [also Sc; origin uncertain, perhaps OE *beorgan* to protect]

bergel, bergilt(o) 1 the wrasse. 2 a stout person. [also Sc; compare Norw *berg-gylta* wrasse]

berkimal a large tangle. [origin uncertain but compare BIRK 2]

berkiny short and dumpy. [origin uncertain; compare Sh *bjarki* little, insignificant]

berry a rock. [ON *berg*]

bert, birt a back eddy in the tide. [ON *burðr* a bearing]

besom*, bisom 1 a coarse long handled brush. 2 a reproachful term for a woman. [also Sc; both forms probably from OE *beseme* brush]

besprent scattered. [OE *besprengan* to sprinkle]

best = best. **best-end*** the best room in the house. **bes/best kens*, bes/best knows*** Goodness knows, '*Whar he is noo, best kens*'. '*Best bliss thee*' bless you. [best = 'he who is best', i.e. God; compare Eng *God knows!*]

beswell, beswid see BEES-WID, BEES-WILL]

better* 1 = better. 2 more, '*He hid better or a pail*', '*I waited and I better waited*' I waited a long time. **better-like*** better-looking, '*He's better like the day*'. [also Sc]

beu* 1 the sound made by a cow. 2 the roaring of the wind. [imitat]

beufsie, bufsy clumsy. [Norw *bufsa* to run clumsily]

beul 1, buil verb. to pen animals. noun. a place of shelter for animals [a *naut's beul* existed at one time across the valley from the Dwarfie Stone in Hoy]. 2 a division in a stable. **beul stone** stone which formed the division between one animal and another. **beulding pin** in those days of common pasturage it was the job of one household to pen the animals for the night, the custom being to pass a stick (*beulding pin*) from house to house daily to indicate whose turn it was. [Ice. *ból* animal pen]

beul 2 a metal neckband for a cow. [see BOOL 3]

beuss *tae mak a beuss o something* to mess something up. [? ON *beysta* to thrash (corn)]

beuy * = boy. 1 an expression of surprise, not necessarily addressed to a male. 2 a form of greeting used when addressing a familiar male of any age '*Weel beuy whit's deuan the day?*'. **beuysa beuysa*** goodness me. [only in the vocative or exclamatory form is *boy* pronounced *beuy*, otherwise *boy* as in English]. **boyo(s)*** a

7

congratulory remark (not necessarily sincere) addressed for example to a child showing his skill or to a friend in a new car.

beyo† a kind of scythe. [probably a form of ON *bugt* a bending; compare Sc *bay* to bend and Eng *reaping* hook]

beyogit of stockings, knitted in a pattern of rings of different colours [also Sh: ON *baugr*, a ring]

bi = by. **bi-ordnar** extraordinary, especially, *bi ordnar good*. **bi time*** early, '*We got wir crop in bi time the 'ear (year)'.*

bide* past tense **bade** to stay. [also Sc; OE *bidan*]

biff a dent, especially in the side of a cap, hat etc. [Sc *baff* a blow; OF *baffe*]

biffle to knock something against something else carelessly eg a shoe. [see BIFF above]

big 1* to build. **bigging** 1 a building. 2 anything built. [also Sc; ON *byggja*]

big 2 = big. **big end*** the room in the Orkney two-teacher school in which the bigger children are taught. [compare PEEDIE END]. **bigoos*** an estate house, *the bigoos o Binscarth*. **bigsy*** conceited [the *sy* is a Sc adjectival suffix]

big 3 barley. [ON *bygg*]

bikko 1 a she-dog. 2 a dog made of straw at harvest time. [ON *bikkja* a bitch]

bilbows† to put, *in the bilbows* to tie the two thumbs together, set the person on his haunches, put the hands down over the knees then put a stick through the elbow joints and under the knees. [Eng *bilboes* a bar with sliding shackles]

bildro see VILDRO.

bilge = bilge. **bilge-kod** a strap of wood used to protect the bilge of a boat. [ON *koddi* a pillow]

bimmy feeblick see MIMMY-FEEBLICK.

bind = bind. **binder** in wall building, a large reinforcing stone passing from one side of the wall to the other.

bing* 1 a heap. 2 a bin. [also Sc and Sh; ON *bingr* a heap]

bingjaveeniknik a word used by tinker children in the Finstown area in the 1930's. [the meaning of this word has not been ascertained]

bink a bench, generally of stone. [also Sc; OE *benc* bench; see SAE-BINK]

binkle to bend (tin etc), '*Binkle hid and hid'll deu*'. [Sc *bink* to bend]

binnack, binnock see BANNOCK.

binnal see BENNLE.

binnaly of well baked bread hard or firm or of a stocking knitted too tightly. [perhaps related to BENNER]

birk 1 a birch timber, especially, *Hielan birk*, Highland birch, frequently used as roof timbers in old Orkney houses.

birk 2 outer skin on big tangles. [same word as Eng *bark*; ON *bjork*]

birkie* 1 *bonny birkie* said for example, to a child with a dirty face. [*birkie* was used in Scots for a *smart* boy and in Westray the sense was *high* spirited boy]. 2 a nickname given to tbe people of the Sandwick district of South Ronaldsay. [it is possible that we have two words here of completely different meaning. Norwegian *bjørka* to excite, might explain the complimentary forms; the others may be related to BARKÉD; many of these parish nicknames are extremely old - as early as the 16th. century - and a good number are uncomplimentary].

birl* to spin around, '*Me head wis fairly birlan*'. **birlo** a school game for boys. [also Sc and Sh; imitat]

birn to smart with the cold, literally to burn with the cold. **birny*** 1 cold weather with low humidity and usually with wind. 2 of land dried up. 3 of clothing, coarse. [ON *brenna* to burn]

birr* to turn with a rapid motion. [also Sc; compare BIRL]

birsable see BISS.

birse 1 see BISS.

birse 2 see BRIZ.

birstle = bristle, the stubble on an unshaved chin.

birt se BERT.

bismar† an old Orkney beam balance which was used for weighing small quantities up to approximately 12 kg. [ON *bismari* believed to have come from Turkish *batman* entering ON through Russian *bezmen*]

bismore the fifteen spined stickleback. [so called because its appearance resembled the BISMAR]

bisom* see BESOM.

biss*, birse bristle or bristles, *tae get somebody's biss up* to anger someone. **bissy** easily roused to anger. **birsable** hot tempered. [ON *bust*]

bit = 1 bit. 2 a measure of degree, *a good bit awey*. **bits** a North Ronaldsay sheepmark. **bit a ting*** a term of sympathy and endearment used for a child ('bit of thing' in English is a nonsense; the phrase seems to be pure Norse; compare Norwegian *bitte liten*, very tiny and *lite ting* an endearing little child].

bitch 1 1 = bitch. 2 **The Bitch** harvest. [from the old custom of making a straw dog at harvest time with the last corn to be cut]

bitch 2 *a two faced bitch* a joiner's mash.

bite 1 see BAIT.

bite* 2 1 = bite. 2* dinner, *a bite o dinner*, '*We'll go fur a bite o dinner noo*'. **biter** a sea term for a knife. [such taboo names were extremely common]

bito a small piece or quantity. [*bit* + dimin]

bivval, bavall a big person or animal. [related to

Norw *bøvel* monster]

bizzie, bizzie stones the stones on which an animal rests. [ON *báss* stall in a byre; see also BOSS 2; also in Sc and Sh]

bla* = blow. *a bla o dirt* a boaster. *tae bla up* of the wind to rise. **blawn** of meat or fish putrid. [the original sense is dried (in the wind and without salt), hence blown]

blab* to tell tales. [also Sc; ME blabbe]

blabberan see BLAGGERAN.

black = black. **blacked coffin** a pauper's coffin, blackened with boot-polish. **blacken** to darken, '*Never blacken me door again!*'. **blackety** a mild oath, '*Tak the blackety thing oot*'. [*Black* or *Blackie* seems to have been used for the *devil* though not specifically recorded as such]. **blackie*** a blackbird. **blackie-lendid** absolutely nothing, '*Whit did yi find in the box?*', '*Blackie-lendid!*' [a corruption of BLACK ILL-ENDED]. **black ill-end!** an oath. [see ILL-END]. **black oo**, '*He pays no black oo for that*' It's born in him. **Black Peter** an Orkney playground game also known as Horny. [both terms are synonymous with *devil*]. **blacksight** a curse, '*Blacksight hid's owerweel*' said by someone who was making a temporary repair. [*sight* is a corruption of ON *sótt*, sickness, therefore *blacksight* =black sickness =Black Death =plague ='Plague on you!']. **black steen** idle, very idle. **black weet** rain.

black oats a small kind of oats which will grow on very poor soil, almost the wild oat

blad weakly, *a blad o a man* [also Sc OE *blaed* ON *blað*, a leaf]

bladderskate*, bletherskate someone who talks nonsense. [also Sc; ON *blaðra* nonsense; the *skate* element is probably a contemptuous term for a person; compare SKATE-RUMPLE; ON *skata* skate (fish)]

bladdoch buttermilk. (Gael. *blathach*)

bladds a disease like smallpox [also Sh; Swe. dial. *bladda*, a lump of dirt]

blaggeran*, blabberan, blatteran flapping in the wind. [ON *blakra* to flap]

blaithin a lobster or crab with a soft shell. [ON *blautr* soft]

blame = blame. **blamedy ting** nothing at all. [compare FEENTY]

bland water with a handful of oatmeal in it used as a refreshing drink. [ON *blanda* a mixture of two fluids, especially whey mixed with water]

blandick a vessel used to hold milk until it is churned. [origin uncertain]

blarno very thin porridge. [origin uncertain]

blash 1 watery drink. 2 continual rain. **blue blash** skimmed milk. **blashy*** of weather very wet.

[also Sc *blash*, imitat.]

blate shy, used negatively, '*Thoo're no blate!*'. [OSc *blate*]

blatho buttermilk. [Gael *blathach* buttermilk]

blatteran see BLAGGERAN.

blawn fish half dried fish [OSc *blawe* to blow]

blaze 1 = blaze. 2 to heat up ale by immersing a red hot poker in the cog.

bleb see BLIBE.

bleck shoe polish. [OSc *blek*; a deriv of BLACK]

bleesh weak tea. [imitat; compare PLEESHY]

bleesk of a gun, to blast; *tae hiv a bleesk at a rabbit* [see BLEESTER]

bleester 1 to make an exploding noise, *to bleester and shoot*. 2 to flicker. [ON *blástr* to blast]

bleib see BLIBE.

blen a mark, '*There's no a blen o sea on the day*' in other words the sea is calm. [used also in Sh in a similar sense; ON *blána* to become blue]

blessy pale. [ON *blesi* the blaze or star on a horse's head and Ger *blass* pale]

blest having a white spot on the head. [ON *blesóttr*; see BLESSY]

blether* to talk nonsense. also Sc. [ON *blaðra* nonsense]

bletherskate* see BLADDERSKATE.

blett a spot or patch. [compare Icel *blettr*]

bleupsy* fat. [BLIBE + common Sc adjectival suffix *sy*]

bleusk* *a blue bleusk* a blue flash. [imitat; compare Sc *flisk* sudden movement]

blibe*, bleb, bleib a little blister. [Sc *bleb*; OE *blāwan* to blow]

blide* happy, '*Ah'm blide thoo're come*'. '*Blide am I tae see thee!*' used to be the warm greeting accorded a visitor. **blide-meat** food provided for visitors at a house where a child has been born. [Eng *blithe* or ON *blíðr*]

blin to doze off. [Sc *blind the ee* to sleep; (blind the eye)]

blind (rhymes with *wind* in the sense *gale*) = blind. verb. to bind the stone in a road with clay. **blind daa*** see DAA. **blinding clay** used to finish off a road. **blind oats** oats affected by smut. **blind pap** a blocked teat. **blind window** a built up window.

blinder* (rhymes with *cinder*) to blind with an especially bright light, or with fine snow. **blindroo*** a blinding snowstorm. [*blinder* = to blind: *oo* is a common Orkney dialect nounal suffix]

blindie-bawkie see BAWKIE-BLINDIE.

blink* 1 = blink. 2 a moment, '*Ah'll just bide a blink*'. **blinkie*** a dimin of BLINK. [also Sh and Sc]

blinks* see WEATHER BLINKS.

blinsieve a basket or tray for carrying grain etc. [*blind*

9

+ *sieve*]

bliss* = bless, '*Bliss me!* Good bliss me!**' Goodness me! **blissings*** '*Blissings on thee*' You have my blessing. '*Blissings be wi thee*' a parting greeting. [ME *bliss*]

blitter* to work in water. [more commonly PLITTER; related Sc forms]. **blittero** having a muddy consistency. [ON *bleyta* mud or mire]

blokie-blindie see BAWKIE BLINDIE.

blood sooker, bloody sooker = blood sucker, the horse fly [see KLEGG]

bloodwit† a fine for bloodshed. [OE *blōdwite* through Sc]

bloody pudding*, bluidy pudding black pudding [also Sc]. **Bloody Puddings*** a nickname for the people of Stromness.

blooro a slight disagreement. [origin uncertain]

blooter 1 a wet mess. 2 a heavy shower. [see BLITTERO]. **blootered** very drunk.

blot* the water in which anything is washed. '*Luk whit kam oot o the first blot efter I washed me coorteens.*' **soapy blots** dirty soapy water. [ON *blautr* wet; also Sc]

bloupéd tripped, '*He bloupéd on the step*'. [compare Sc *blupt* overtaken by any misfortune which might have been avoided by caution]

blouster a gale. [related to Eng *blustery*; ON *blástr* blast]

blout 1 something soft, eg cow dung. 2 metaphorically a person. [ON *blautr* soft]

blow the blade of a tangle. **blowry** used to describe the big blades of tangles. [ON *blað* leaf]

blue blash see BLASH.

blue-nild* mould. [also Sc and Sh; sometimes also GREEN-NILD; origin doubtful; compare Faroese *nál* sprout of grain; see AIKASPIRE]

bluidy puddin see BLOODY PUDDING.

bluster of a light to flicker. [see BLEESTER]

blutter nonsense, *a lot o blutter*. [see BLETHER]

bo see BAA.

boaley a marbles game. [OSc *boull*; Fr boule *ball*]

boar see BORT.

boare† see BORE.

bobo a louse. [probably has the sense *lump* as in ME *bobbe* bunch; see GUBBOES]

bock* to retch or vomit. [also Sc; onomat.]

bod 1 a wave breaking on the shore. [see BAA]

bod 2 a bid at an auction sale etc. [ON *boð*]

boden fitted out. [also Sc; ON *boðinn* ready, prepared for service]

bodle 1 a 17th Century Scots coin. 2 savings or a nest egg. [OSc *bodle*; of obscure origin]

bodom* bottom. [also Sc; see BUDDUM]

bogie 1 a bag made from the dried stomach of a whale. [see BOGY]

bogie 2 see BOGLE.

bogle* 1 of cattle to bellow. 2 of children to sob loudly, especially, *boglan and greetan. boglan and singan* singing tunelessly like a drunk man. [compare Cai. *bugle* of bulls, to bellow and Sc *bugle* of a cock to crow, literally to make the sound of a bugle]

boglo the outside peat on a peat-bank. [Faroese *torvbøkil* lump of peat]

bogy, bogie a skin bag. [ON *belgr* the skin of an animal taken off whole and used as a bag; see OILY BOGIE]

bokie see BAWKIE.

boll to start again, *tae mak a boll*. [origin doubtful; see also BOUL]

Bollick a Stronsay goblin. [origin unknown]

bollocks = bollocks. **bollock naked*** stark naked, vulgar)

bomer something big, *a bomer o a baest*. [also Sh; related to Norw *bumba* a fat woman]

bomo* a coot. [perhaps a deriv of ON *boppa* to wave up and down, relating to the movement of the bird's head as it walks]

bonie, bonny 1 a prayer, but found only compounded. **bonie-hoose** a church. **bonie land** heaven, '*He's gin tae the bonie land*' he has died (only to children). **bonie-man** a priest. There was a Bonnyman's House near Langskaill (now vanished) in Birsay-be-South in 1595. **bonie-words*** a child's goodnight prayers:-

Gentle Jesus meek and mild
Look upon a little child
Fain I would to thee be brought
Gracious Lord forbid it not.

an earlier pre-Reformation prayer, also known in Shetland, was recorded in Stromness at the beginning of this century:-

Mary mither had thee hand
Roond aboot wir sleepan band
Had the lass and had the wife
And had the bairnies a their life.

bonny* 2 1 = bonny. 2 dreadful, '*That's a bonny mess yir made*' '*Yir a bonny like sight!*' **bonny fine hid** that's all very well by me. **bonnykin** a large amount.

bonsper, boonspal* in a hurry to do something, *in a bonsper*. [Eng *bound* with a metathetical form of SPRET as suffix]

bonxie* the great skua. [also Sh; ON *bunki* a heap; the reference being to its size]

booick*, booa, buack, buo a large pimple. [Sh *bulek*; probably a dimin related to Norw *bola* a blister; compare Gael *buicean* a pimple]

book bulk, especially of the body. [ON *búkr* trunk]

booking night* the night on which intimation of a wedding was given to the session clerk or church officer.

10

bool 1 of fish to play on the surface of water. [Icel *bulla* to bubble]

bool 2 a large rounded rock. [ON *bolle* a ball]

bool 3 a circular hinged piece of iron, fixing cattle in the byre. (also BEUL). **bools*** the handle of a bucket or a three-toed pot (the essential meaning is 'bent'). **boolsy** bent or crooked especially of the legs. [compare Norw *bøyle* hoop]

booliver large object. [? a form of Eng *bulwark*]

booman a good fairy supposed to help at Yule by threshing corn while the household is asleep [also Sh: ON *búi*, a fairy (only in compounds such as *haug-búi*, *berg-búi* etc.) + *man*]

boona 1 harness for a horse. 2 equipment generally. 3 sex organ, '*Mercy Ah'm cut the ram's boona*' said when shearing the animal. **boonie** verb. 1 to dress oneself. 2 to mend. 3 to put right. noun. a garment made and laid by to be worn when the occasion arises (compare Norw. *bunad*, national costume) [ON *bunaðr* equipment; Sc *bouney*]

boondie 1 a dunlin. 2 a common sandpiper. [ON *bundil* a bundle; compare BONXIE where the deriv may be more easily understood]

boonie 1 a young boy about 12/13 years of age. [see BOUNDAE]

boonie 2 see BOONA.

boons the bounds of a district. [OF *bonne* boundary]

boonspal *see* BONSPER.

boonta = bounty, a voluntary fee or gift.

boonvara applied to cattle wandering. [the first element is probably Sc *boon* boundary; Sh has *varg* a wandering animal; ON *vargr* wolf; Faroese *vargur* a wild sheep]

boon† a crofter or poor farmer. [ON *bóndi* farmer; see also BOUNDAE; it is interesting to note how this perfectly respectable Norse word became degraded to 'poor farmer' with the arrival of the Scots; compare BEDYOW]

boordly stout, substantial [OSc *burely*]

boorticement shelter. [see BOURTISEMENT]

boorwid* (tree), bourtree the elder-tree. [Sc *bour-tree*; also known as the *bown-tree* in Northumberland; may be 'boundary tree' from Eng *bound* or *bourne* boundary]

boos see BUSS

boosam see BOWSOME.

boose to bustle about. [Norw *buse* to be precipitate]

boosy broo see BUSS 2.

bootie a piece of cloth or flannel used formerly as a head wrap. [ON *bót* a patch of an old torn garment]

boovil to beat or thrash. [see BAFFLE]

borag*, borick, brog a bradawl. [see BORY]

bore 1, boare† a wave or tidal race eg the Bore of Papay. [same as Eng *bore* as in the Severn Bore;

ON *bára* a breaker]

bore 2 = bore, '*Bore a holie, bore a holie, bore a holie*' when tickling a child. [see WHUMMLE]

borick see BORAG.

borrow = borrow. **Borrowing Day** the third of April. One could keep anything borrowed on this day! [see TAILY DAY]. **Borrowing Days** the last days of March which, if fine were 'borrowed' from April or the first days of April which if stormy were 'borrowed' from March.

bort, board to split (stones), *to bort a flag*. [related to Norw *braeda* a flake; ON *bryða* to chop up; compare Sc *brod* and *boord*]

bory* a bradawl. [ON *borr*]

boss 1 1 a cupboard, in a wall recess, also known as a **boss press**. 2 of a turnip etc frosted, hence soft. [OSc *bos* hollow]

boss 2, buss 1 light chaff. 2 litter in bird's nest. [Norw *bos* bedstraw; see BIZZIE STANES]

bottle = bottle. **bottle of play*** truce, in children's games in Shapinsay as late as the 1950's. To return to a game a child had to say, '*Bottle's broken and whisky spilt*' [*bottle* is a corruption of *barrel*, in turn a corruption of BARLEY PLAY; see BARLO BROCK]. **bottle nose*** a nickname for the puffin [a reference to the bill]

boul an attempt. [a form of BOLL]

boundae† Jo Ben who wrote on Orkney in the 16th century said the common greeting on meeting was, '*Goand da boundae*', 'Good-day fellow.' (The use of BEUY today in exclamations and greetings may be a relic of this usage. Ben's transcription appears to indicate that 16th century Orcadians spoke with a nasal accent.). [an extension of use of ON *bóndi* farmer; see BOONIE 3]

bouney materials. [see BOONA]

bour-tree* see BOORWID.

bourtisement, boorticement a windbreak to keep west wind spirits from entering the house. [a metathesis of Eng *brattice* with a *ment* suffix found in standard Eng; compare Eng *bartisan*]

bout* 1 once up the field and once down the field with a plough (compare WUP). 2 anything bent; used in placenames referring to coastal features.

boute/bought enclosure for sheep. [ON *bugt* a bending; Norw *bug* bay; see BUGHT]

bovval to thrash or beat. [see BAFFLE]

bow 1 a large farm. **bowman*, buman** a farm worker who had a separate house yet had his food provided by the estate; the farm labourers' cottages at Elsness in Sanday are called Bowman's 1, 2, 3 etc. **bow-teind** a tax paid to the minister from the produce of each cow. [also Sc; ON *tíund* a tenth part; ON *bú* farm]

11

bow 2 (rhymes with now) to bend at the waist, '*He wis bowan and workan at the back o the hoose*'. **bow-legged***, **bowsy legged*** bandy legged. [OSc *bow* to bend; OE *búgan*]

bow 3 diarrhoea in animals. [only recorded as GREEN BOW; ON *bogi* a spurt as from a fountain or vein]

bow 4† 1 a wall, specifically a tunship wall. 2 land enclosed by a wall. **bowed quoy†** a quoy with a wall around it. [Marwick believed this word to be related to ON *boer* farm but it is probably an abbreviated form of ON *bálkr* a balk; compare the Garbo/Gerbo farms of North Ronaldsay and Sanday both of which are built on old walls and originally recorded Gerbak]

bow* 5 a measure of grain etc just over 62 kg. [also Sc; ON *bolli*]

bowan of a dog, barking. [imitat]

bowsie device for adjusting the rigging on yoles or model boats

bowsome, bowsum, boosam of a woman = buxom, handsome, pleasant, agreeable etc.[also Sc]

bowtang bladder-wrack. [compare Norw *butang* a kind of seaweed which cows will eat; in Deerness, *bowtang* was known as PADDY TANG, pig tang]

bow-teind see BOW 1.

box = box. **box bed*** a bed the three sides and top of which were made of wood. The back of the bed was always divided in two horizontally to assist in transport since the bed was always considered moveable property.

boyo(s) see BEUY.

Boys' Ba see BA.

braa* 1 = brave. 2 fine. [also Sh]. Speaking of the morning weather, an old man said, '*Hid's makan a braa sook on the hilltops bit hid's kinda slestry in the valleys*'. **braaly*** adj. well. [also Sh]. **braws** fine clothes. [see BRAVE]

brace the part of the chimney immediately above the fire. **brace steen** a stone behind the old open fire, also known as the BACK STANE. [OSc *brace*, reinforcing stone or timber]

brachins wooden hames for a horse collar. **brechins** a frame on a sheep's neck to prevent it going through a fence. [Sc *brechim*; NoME *bargham*]

brack* = break, *tae brack somebody's gird* to steal a boyfriend or girlfriend, literally to 'break the hoop'. *tae brack the back o (something)* to make real progress. **bracken** poor quality peats. **bracken road** a rough farm road. **bracken water** choppy sea. **brack oot*** to bring new land under the plough.

brad, brod to jerk a line as soom as a fish bites. [ON *bregða* to move swiftly]

brae* hillside or mound. [also Sc]

braeth* = breath, '*He cam tae the door wi his braeth on his lip*' out of breath.

braid* see BRAITHIN.

brail 1 intense heat. [compare Icel *braela* to burn]

brail 2 of fish to play on the surface of the water. [Norw *braela* to caper]

braithe to melt down (chiefly fish livers) into oil. [ON *braeða]*

braithin, braid the band round the top of a cubby. [ON *bregða* to twist; Eng *braid*]

brakes see BRECKS.

bram, brammo a mixture of milk and meal, eaten uncooked. [this may be a variation of Gael *dramag* foul mixture which gives Sc *drammach*; with the same meaning as Ork BRAM]

brander 1 of an animal to be in heat. [also Sh *brind*; ON *brundr* heat]

brander 2 the cross piece of the legs of a chair. [similar usages in Sc; ON *brandreið* a grate]

brandie, bruntie see BRANSTICKLE.

brandiron a gird iron on which oatcakes were baked. [see BRANDER 2]

brandit striped, chiefly of cattle. [also Sc; compare Icel *bröndóttr* a brindled ox]

brangle of a horse entangled in its tether, to struggle or twist. [obs Eng *brangle* to wrangle or brawl; Fr *branler*]

branks* 1 a bridle [also Sc]. '*He his the branks on him noo*' he's engaged to be married. 2 an iron girdle for the head which restricted speech; used up until last century as a punishment for an up offender. 3 mumps. [OF *bernac* which had the additional meaning barnacle; the idea of holding, restraining seems to be behind the word; compare Du *prang* fetter]

branstickle* see BANSTICKLE.

brat*, bratto a coarse apron. [also Sc and Sh; Gael *brat*; OE *bratt*]

brats the scum on boiled whey. [Sc *brat* scum; ON *breyta* to change or transform]

bratto* see BRAT.

brave† '*Brave day!*' a fine weather greeting. Already so rare in the 1940's that a gentleman who consistently used this greeting was nicknamed *Owld Brave Day*. [see BRAA]

braws see BRA.

bread 1 = bread. 2 bannock but only in compounds BERE BREAD*, OAT BREAD* etc. '*They're no eaten the bread o idledom*', They worked hard for a living.

brechans see BRACHINS.

breck a slope, a common Orkney placename element. [ON *brekka* a slope]

brecks, brakes* uncultivated land. [OE *braec* uncultivated land between fields; related to the verb 'break' in the sense of a division]

12

bred-band see BRIDTH-BAND.

breeds a membrane eg the diaphragm of an animal. [probably related to Norw *braeda* a thin flake or plate]

breef see BRIEF.

breeket see BREEKSED.

breeks the roe of the cod or similar fish [also Sc from their resemblance to trousers]

breeks*, **breek†** trousers. **breek-band*** trouser band. **breek leg*** the leg of a pair of trousers. **breek brithers** rivals in love with one girl. [also Sc; OE *brēc* breeches]

breeksed*, **breeket** stiff from exertion, '*Wan day in the paet hill and Ah'm breeksed*'. [origin unknown]

breekyinees trousers. [related in some way to BREEKS; perhaps a dimin]

breenge *tae breenge aboot* to bustle about. [also Sc; origin obscure]

breer* verb. of corn to sprout. noun. *in breer* with the shoot just showing. adj. full, '*Tak me a breer basket o neeps*'. [OE *brerd* edge]

breese† a game of football which formerly took place at Deerness school between the boys of the east of the parish and the boys of the west. The game was played at the end of December and the winning team had the sole use of the ball on New Year's Day. [origin uncertain; perhaps OSc *brusche* violent rush or impact; *breeze* was applied to a race at Old Scottish weddings the prize being the bride's handkerchief]

breest* verb. to mount a horse by placing one's breast on the horse's back. noun. 1 = breast. 2 the gable of a house. **breest stone*** the lintel stone above a fireplace. **breesting-stone** a mounting block.

breeze of a sow to be in heat. [Norw *braesna*]

breezo a heather fire. [ON *brísingr* a big blaze]

breid = broad. **the breid o the back** the flat of the back

brelky of a person short and stout. [compare Sh brolki a lump; see BROLTY]

brent to spring. [ON *bruna* to advance quickly]

bresso charlock. [related to Lat *brassica* charlock but how the Lat name of this weed entered the dialect is puzzling; see TISHALAGO for another illustration of this]

brett-baler a baler of straw ropes, an occupation recorded in a late 19th century Shapinsay record [see BRAID; baling straw rope could hardly have been a full time occupation]

brett* *tae brett up the sleeves* to roll up the sleeves. *tae brett up tae somebody* of a small person challenging someone bigger than himself/ herself, '*Good, he fairly bretted up tae him*'. [ON *bretta* to turn upwards; Icel *bretta* to roll up the sleeves]

brew = brew. **brewing stane** a stone regularly used in brewing malt. Its function was to hold down in the KAG the sheaf which acted as a strainer.

bride's cog* see COG.

bridth-band, bred-band side by side. The story is told of a Sandwick man who tricked his neighbour by placing two rabbits in one snare. The old man was very surprised when he saw this, '*Good they must hiv been runnan bridth-band!*' he said. [breadth + band]

brief, breef 1 = brief. 2 self-assertive, voluble.

brig* bridge. [also Sc]

brigde the basking shark. [also Sh; ON *bregða*]

bright-eye eye-bright [an example of many reversed couplets found in the dialect; compare OOTSIDE-IN, NETTING WIRE etc.]

brigstones* a stone pavement in front of a house. [also Sh; Norw *brusteinn* influenced by Sc *brig*]

brim of a cat to be in heat. [ON *breyma köttr* a she cat in heat]

brime to haul a boat partly up a beach. [ON *brýna*]

brimman* of a bucket etc full to the brim. [compare LIPPAN and BREER 2]

brinn 1 a cold biting wind. [see BIRN]

brinn 2 see TEEBRO.

brinno a heather fire. [ON *brenna* a fire]

brinny water water poured on SOOANS to keep it fresh. [burn water though perhaps through ON *brunnr* spring]

brisk* cartilage. [ON *brjósk*]

bristle* to roast hastily. [Sc *birsle*; recorded in 16th century Eng *brissill*]

britchin* part of a cart horse harness which passes round the hinder part of the animal. [see BREEKS for deriv]

briz, birse to squeeze. [OE *brāsan* to crush]

broch* 1 any fortified place or, more specifically a massive circular Iron Age tower. 2 a halo round the moon. Such a broch was a portent of bad weather, the number of stars in the broch being the number of good days to come before the weather broke. [ON *borg* a fortification; in general use throughout the North of Scot]

brochan gruel. [Gael *brochan*]

brod 1 see BRAD.

brod 2 a mother goose. [also Sh; OSc *brude* offspring]

brod 3 the cover of a book. [a form of BOARD; also Sc]

broddened impudent, insistent. [also Sc; OSc *browdin* embroidered]

brog* 1 a sarcastic hint. [probably a form of PROG, hence a sharp remark]

brog 2 see BORAG.

broglie untidy. [related to Sc *broggle* to botch]

broken-for-neb* of an egg cracked and just about

13

to hatch. [compare Faroese *brostið fyri nev*]

brolty, broltie*, brolkie a stout fellow. **brolty-teeting** a corn bunting. **skitter brolty** 1 a corn bunting [see SKITTER]. 2 a diarrhoetic calf or cow (apparently a transferred meaning) [Icel *bolt* a bundle; compare Cai *bolty* lavro corn bunting: see BRELKY]

brooa-brinkie the forehead, used to children. [Sc *brinkie-brow*; ? ME *brent* steep; compare obs Norw *brink* cliff, bluff]

brook 1 to enjoy. [also Sc; OE *brūcan* to enjoy]

brook 2 rotting piles of seaweed on the beach. [ON brúk]

broom 1 = broom. 2 whin (in the Dounby area formerly).

broonie* 1 a bannock or scone made of bere-meal. [compare Norw *bryne* a slice of bread or cake]

broonie 2 the guardian spirit of the old Orkney home. [Sc *brownie*; the original (Celtic) name of this Orkney spirit was *Luridan*; the Sc form of which was *Lurdane*]

broonie 3 see AFTER-BURN

brooser of a face red and rosy, *a brooser o a face.* [compare Norw dial *brøselig* plump]

brose* seasoned oatmeal on which hot water has been poured. [also Sc; origin uncertain]. **Brose Day** Shrove Tuesday:-

> First hid comes Candelmas Day
> An than the new mune
> An than hid comes Brose Day
> If it ever wis so sune
> An than there's forty days
> Atween Brose Day an Pase Day
> The forty days o Lent'

brosie faced fat faced. [also Sc.]

brosom active, perhaps officious. [origin uncertain; ? a corruption of Sc *boosam* vigorous; Eng *buxom*]

brother = brother. **brother part†** (of land) a term used in old records. In UDAL law a brother inherited twice as much as the sister in addition to the principal dwelling house.

browst a brewing of ale. [also Sc; a deriv of BREW]

bruck* 1 rubbish. **bruckly*** of stones easily broken. **bruck hole***, **bruck quarry*** a hole or quarry where rubbish is dumped. **brucky hoose*** an old building where rubbish is kept. **brucky roo** a rubbish dump. [see ROO; OSc *brok* broken or small pieces]

bruck 2, brucks to potter around. [compare Icel *brák* to toil]

brucking* a severe bruising. [see BRUCK 1]

brucks see BRUCK 2.

brucksy 1 dishevelled in dress. 2 untidy in work. [see BRUCK 1]

brudge 1 to chop up finely of eg vegetables. 2 to bruise. [ON *brytja*]

brullye, bruil commotion [also Sc]. **brulyack**, '*The poor owld horse gid doon in a brulyack at the door*'. [a northern form of *broil* from Fr *brouillier* to trouble]

brulya* a sudden burst of heat in the morning. [OSc *brulze* to burn or broil; OF *bruillir* to burn]

brulyack see BRULLYE.

brumplo a small ebb fish known in Eng as the *rockling*. [origin doubtful]

brunt = burnt [also Sc]. **bruntie** an old nickname for a blacksmith. [the Scots called a blacksmith *brookie*]

bruntie see BRANDIE.

brunyo see BROONIE 1.

brute = brute. **brute-fu** very drunk.

Bu found frequently as a placename in Orkney. In old records incorrectly spelt Bull. [ON *bú* estate etc]

buack see BOOICK.

bubbles* 1 = bubbles. 2 nasal phlegm [also Sc.]

buck to hunch the shoulders while laughing. [origin uncertain]

buckheuns see BAAK.

buckie* 1 the common periwinkle (*litterina litterea*). [also Sc with the sense 'large whelk'; compare Lat *buccinum* shellfish; see also BRESSO and TISHALAGO for Lat words in Orkney dialect]. 2 a nickname for an inhabitant of Gairsay.

buckse*, bux to walk through a muddy mess '*He kam bucksan through the iper*' [Norw *baske* to dabble in water]

buddo* a term of endearment, addressed to a child or a lady. [Eng *bud* (as in *rose-bud*), also used as a term of endearment + *o* diminutive]

buddum*, bodom noun. = bottom. verb. *tae buddum* of a boat, to ground. **buddum moss** the lowest peat in a peat bank. [also Sc]

buddy* a person [also Sc]; '*This buddy cam oot o the hoose*'. **poor buddy** an ailing person. **man buddy** a man. **wife buddy** a woman [Eng *body* as in somebody etc]

bufsy see BEUFSIE.

bugget a big clumsy fellow. **buggety** of a man stout. [compare Sc *bullgit* a large unshapely mass]

buggy of the sky dark. [initial *m* is often substituted by *b* in Orkney dialect, hence a variation of Eng. *muggy* see MUGGROFU]

bught† to pen sheep [see BOUT]

buik = book, *far i the buik* well-read, learned, clever.

buil see BEUL 1.

build a heap of drying tangles. [Eng *build*]

buile† appears in old records in the form **head-buile†** principal farm. [ON *bøl* farm]

builos good things to eat. **buily** a feast, a feast of good things. **bullwant** good to eat. [compare

14

Dan *bolsje* sweetmeat, dainty]

buirk to belch. [also Sc; imitat; compare Eng *burp*]

buiss mess, especially in *tae mak a buiss o something*. [probably a form of Eng *bush*]

buist† '*Dat buist been afore me time*'. [common in old dial writing; a form of Eng *must*; see BUGGY for explanation]

buithy, buivy a sca caisic. [related to ON *bytta* a bucket; see BUTTO]

bulder* 1 noisy, rough movement, '*The calfs wir coman in a bulder through the door*'. 2 nonsense, *just a bulder o dirt*. [Norw *bulder* din; also Sh]

Bull see Bu.

bull* = bull.(rhymes with 'lull'). *bull hid in yi* an unsophisticated remark usually from a male to a child ordering him to eat up his food and not to be so particular.

bullan a heap of peats or tangles. [ON *bolungr* a pile of logs]

bullwant see BUILOS.

bulwand* the dock. [ON *bolr* a tree trunk but used here in the sense stem; Eng *wand*; *bulwands* were used in making CUITHE CUBBIES]

buman* a farm worker. [see BOWMAN]

bummack see BUMMO.

bummand* a spasmodic conversation. [Sc *bummle* to speak carelessly]

bummer the chief organiser of a feast. [unlikely to be the same as Sc *heid-bummer* overseer (but in a contemptuous way); see BUMMO for better interpretation]

bummie see BUMMO.

bummled 1 = bumbled. 2 confused or perplexed

bummo, bummock a small wooden bowl. **bummie** a one handed cog. **bummack**† an entertainment anciently given by tenants to a landlord. **bummock** ale. [Norw *bomme* a wooden box]

bund 1 = bound. 2 fixed, eg of an earthfast stone. **bund-Sunday** a Sunday worked by servants (feeding animals only). **in-bund** hemmed in, especially of houses.

bung* to throw something carelessly into some receptacle etc., '*Bung hid aal in the shed min afore hid gets weet*'. [also Sc; a form of Eng *bang*]

bungse to wrap up well. [also Sh; ON *bunki* a heap]

bungy a young seal. [related to ON *bunki* a heap]

bunnon a form of BANNOCK used in Westray

bunstal of a child short and stout. [Sh *bungset*; ON *bunki* a heap]

bunter a woman of loose reputation [also in English dial.]

buo see BOOICK.

burbendle see GARBENDLIN.

burd* 1 the young of a fowl. 2 a young seal. **burded*** of an egg having a chick inside. [ON *burðr* offspring]

burden = burden. **burden caisie** a straw basket which would hold 64 kg of grain. A stout straw rope was fastened to one side with both ends and a loop went over the shoulders. [see CAISIE]

burekens a native of a district. [compare Norw *burekkja* cattle track; see KLOGANG and SUILKIE for similar usage]

Burgh School the old name for Kirkwall Grammar School.

burian a mound. [a common placenames in Orkney where it appears in the form Burrian; also Sc; ON *borg-in*, fort]

burly = burly. **burly hoose** a sea-term for a church.

burly, burlo, burloo a crowd. **in a burlo** in a mix up. [compare Eng *hurly-burly*]

burn 1 see AFTER-BURN.

burn* 2 a stream. [also Sc; OE *burna* a brook or spring; ON *brunnr* was used in the sense spring or well]

burnchadis bronchitis. [the form *broonchadis* is found elsewhere in Sc]

burrow a kind of coarse grass growing in clumps. [compare Norw *burra* gnarled, dwarf tree]

burry see BURROW.

bursn easily out of breath, panting. [also Sc; Sc *burs(t)en* burst]

bursteen grains of bere heated until dry then ground, the resultant flour being mixed with buttermilk and eaten. **bursteen lumps** a nickname for Eday people. [? Sc *bursten* burst; compare Eng *pop-corn*]

busk to dress oneself. [also Sc; ON *búask* to prepare oneself]

buss 1 see BOSS.

buss 2* 1 = bush. 2 a kind of seaweed which grows in the Stenness Loch and in brackish water generally. When driven on to the beach it is called *buss*. It is for this reason that the mouth of the Stenness Loch is called The Bush. 3 a lump or tuft; a *buss o gress*, '*Beuy thee oats are growan in busses*'. a **buss o pens** a feather duster. **bussie-broo, boosy broo** the native Orkney sheep so called from the tuft of wool on its forehead. **busso** a tuft of grass.

buss 3 to shake the oats out of poor straw. [ON *beysta* to thrash corn]

buss 4 to potter around, '*I wis bussan aboot in the shed and I noticed me tins hid been knockéd doon*'. [? Eng *busk*]

bussie-broo see BUSS 2.

busslin guts the small intestines of a sheep used for making puddings. [related perhaps to ON *posi* a small bag]

busso see BUSS 2.

but-end* the main living room in the house. *to go but* to go to the but-end. [also Sc; OE *butan* without]

butter = butter. **buttergams** nonsense. [compare Sc *buttery-lippit* smooth tongued; Norw *gamsa* to jest or play]

butties false oat grass also known as SWINE BEADS or POOTIE BUTTIES.

butto a small wooden cog with a lid. [ON *bytta* a pail or tub; see AUND for an old usage]

butty part of entrails of an animal. [Norw *botn*]

bux see BUCKSE.

buznakan lingering over a job. [origin unknown]

by = by. **by the hand** in reserve, at one's disposal, available. **by-begotten*** illegitimate. [compare MERRY-BEGOTTEN]. **bye-pit*, by-pit** something temporary, *'No need fur a belt, this piece o binder-twine 'll deu as as a bye-pit'*.

byre* a cowshed. [also Sc; OSc *byre* cowshed; a form of OE *būr* dwelling or Eng *bower* with its original meaning of cottage]

byrne one piece garment for a boy or girl. [ON *brynja* coat of mail]

byrth a term used to denote the size of a ship. [ON *byrðr* burden (of a ship)]

bysk tainted or sour. [ON *beiskr]*

bytt a small container for liquids. [see BUTTO]

C the letter *c* normally pronounced as in English. A hard *c* is sometimes pronounced *ch*, eg *cake* becomes *check*. When an old Rousay lady was told that her grand-daughter had received a £25 cheque as a wedding present her reply was, *'Mercy hid'll tak them a while tae aet (eat) that.'* She had understood the wedding gift to be a 25lb. cake!

caa* 1 = call. 2 to drive sheep or whales. 3 to drive a nail. **caa ower*** to knock down: *'Yi can caa me anything as long as yi don't caa me ower'*. **caa tae***: *'Caa the door tae'* close the door. **caa teu** a fuss. [compare Eng *set-to*]. **caa the tae (in)*** to trip, immortalised in the Old Sanday rhyme:

> *Maggie Snoddie puir buddy*
> *Caa'd her tae in a curly-doddie*
> *Ap she got*
> *Doon she fell*
> *Caa'd her tae*
> *In a cockle-shell!'*

cack, keech excrement. [also Sc; OSc *cawk*; Lat *cacare*]

cackers steel protectors for the heels of footwear. [Eng *calk*]

caddie* 1 a pet lamb. 2 a call to a lamb. 3 a spoilt child. [Eng dial *cade* pet lamb]

caddis a kind of lint. After frequent use, woollen underwear collected *caddis* which was scraped off with a knife as part of the old domestic laundry routine! [also Sc; OSc *caddas* cotton wool; OF *cadaz* the tow or coarsest part of silk]

caes* = because. **Caes why!** Because I felt like doing it!, a child's impertinent reply to the question, *'Why did you do it?'*.

caff chaff. **caffy hoose** chaff store [OE *ceaf*]

cairn* a heap of stones. [also Sc; Gael *càrn*]

caisie, kaisie, kazy a basket usually made of heather but sometimes grass or reeds. [OSc *cassie*; ON *kass* case]

Caitness see KETNES.

calgered entangled. [origin unknown].

callow to calve. [also Sc; OSc *callow*]

caloo the long-tailed duck. [imitat; compare BALOO]

cam*, kam see COME.

campshious, camsho of an awkward fighting nature. [a corruption of Eng *captious*]

camsweevil see CAPSWEEVIL.

can 1, canne an old measure equivilent to 1/48 of a barrel. [OSc *can* a can, a container, metal or otherwise]

can* 2 = can, to be able*: *'He'll no can tae get aboot noo wi his bad leg'*. He won't be able to etc. **canless** not having the knack. [compare Sc *can* skill]. **canna** cannot.

canne see CAN 1.

cant* 1 = slope. 2 side: *'He has a fine cant tae him'*. 3 humour: *'He's in a good cant the day'*. 4 chance: *'I wid go if I hid a cant'*. **cantled** in an unusual mood. **cantlie** unsteady, leading over to one side.

canteelams see KANTEELAMS.

canteer to improve in health. [origin unknown]

canty* cheerful. [also Sc; compare LoGer *kant*]

capsweevil, capsweevle, camsweevil, kapsweevil, kipersweevil to turn upside down by accident: *'I hopp I don't capsweevil wi this eggs'*. [probably Sc *coup* + ON *sveifla* to turn]

carkid see KARKET.

carl-doddy see CURL DODDY.

carmas see KIRMASH.

carval a large nail or a spike used for building *carvels*, light boats [also Sc]

carvey* caraway (seed). Formerly it was common for little bushes of *carvey* to be grown near the door of the Orkney house and used for seasoning food. [Fr *carvi*]

cash *a big cash o a man*. [origin uncertain; ? a form of CLASH 2]

cassen see CAST.

cassied* of stones, set on edge like cobbles. [Sc *cassie* a causway; ME *causé*; LLat *(via) calciata* trodden way]

cast, cuist verb. past part CASSEN. 1 = cast. 2 to don or doff clothes. [also Sc] 3 to spread peats flat out on the heather to dry. 4 to abort. **cast up*** to taunt by raking up the past. **tae cuist tail at** to argue with. **cast aboot** of the wind, to veer. **cassen** turned sour. **cassen awa** lost at sea. **cassen loop** in knitting a dropped or double stitch. noun. (expressing degree), *a good cast o wind*, a favourable wind.

cat 1 = cat. 2 something very small, *a cat o a ting*. [compare *Catty Geo* a small indentation in the Birsay Coast]. **cat gut** sea lace (*chorda filum*). **cat lick** a tuft of hair which persists in lying in the wrong way, also known as COO LICK. **cat loup** a short distance [compare COCK STRIDE]. **cat's fur*** a nonsense reply given to someone (usually a child) who asks what an adult is making: '*Whit's that for?*' '*Cat's fur*'. **cat's lick*** a quick wash [also Sc]. **cattanow** a disturbance [see NYOW]. **cattie-buckie*** the dog whelk (*nucella lapillus*). **catty face, catawhissie, kata face, cata face** the short-eared owl. **cat-wa** a dividing wall in a house [on which the cat sat]

catharrows a difficult time, used in the sense: '*My he's been through the catharrows this last peedie while*'. **catharled** very badly dressed: *a catharled thing*. [also Sc; OSc *to draw the catharrows* to draw different ways, to thwart each other]

catyugle see KATOGLE.

cauld* = cold. **Cauld Kail** the nickname of an inhabitant of Evie parish. *Cauld kale warmed up is no very good*, a recommendation not to renew a relationship with a member of the opposite sex.

certy* indeed! [also Sc; ME *certes* assuredly]

cess see SESS.

ceuf 1 a clumsy person. 2 a useless person. 3 a coward. **ceufsy** badly dressed. [Sc *coof*; origin unknown]

ceul 1 a puff of wind. 2 clouds in the sky. [ON *kul* a breeze]

ceut-meut *oot o ceut-meut* out of order. [origin unknown]

ceutos see KUITOS.

ceuts see KUITS.

chaar see CHAR

chabble choppiness in the sea. [compare Sc *jabble*]

chackie, chuckie the wheatear. [imitat]

chad 1 a difficult mare. 2 a hussy. 3 a fellow '*He's no a bad chad*'. [ON *jalda* a mare; compare Sc *jaud*]

chaddery land full of rotten stone. [Sc *chaddy* gravelly]

chaddy guts the largest of the intestines. [compare Sc *jaudie* stomach of a pig; OF *chaudum* tripe]

chaest* = to chase, past tense CHAESTED*

chaet = cheat: **no chaet for*** having more than one's share of something: '*He's no chaet for lugs*' he's got big ears.

chaffy sek a big sack to collect and air the chaff which went into the chaff mattress. [Eng *chaff* + *sack*]

chak the groove cut in the main timbers of a boat into which the boards were fitted. [Sc *chak* a cut, a hack]

chalder*, chaldro, chaldrick an oyster catcher. [ON *tjaldr*]

chamer, chaumer a small stone house, sometimes an addition to a house for a relative. [also Sc; through OSc *chambre*; Lat *camera* a vaulted room]

change = change. **change (hoose)**† an ale house [also Sc. (where horses were changed), compare Eng *post house*]. **change ale** home brewed beer. **changey** of the weather etc changeable.

chansh see SHANCE.

chant* of a native Orcadian, to talk to another native speaker in an affected fashion using English pronunciation and phrases and avoiding use of dialect e.g. saying, 'I shan't know till tomorrow when I'm returning,' instead of the expected, 'Ah'll no ken till the morn when Ah'm gaan back.' [Eng *cant*]

chanty* a chamber pot. [also Sc; origin unknown]

chap* 1 to knock [also Sc], '*He chappéd fower or five times at the door and got no reply.*' 2 to mash potatoes: '*I like me tatties chappéd*'. 3 to chop wood: '*Ah'll go and chap twa three sticks for the fire*'. **chappan and changan*** constantly changing: '*He's always chappan and changan the hoose*'. **chapping tree** potato masher. [OSc *chap* to strike; a form of chop]

chapse* to eat noisily: '*Stop chapsan on yir maet*'. [imitat]

char, chaar a bad egg, especially one which a hen etc has been hatching and has proved to be infertile [ON *karr*, slime on a new born animal, Norw. *kjerr*, bog, Sc. *jar-hole*, cesspool]

chard, shard 1 a hollow in sandy links. 2 a ridge in sandy links. [ON *skarð* a notch; see MESGAR]

Charlie rake a large rake, four or five feet across pulled manually over a field to collect the last of the hay or straw. [also known as *Satan* and *The Devil* presumably because it was a *hellish* task]

charl pin the pin which acts as a hinge on a wooden *kist* or chest. [OSc *charnel* a hinge]

charve headstrong, fearless. [ON *djarfr]*

cheeg-a-lee see CHEEKASIDE.

cheek 1 = cheek. 2* the side of something eg a fireplace. **cheek for chow** side by side. [Eng cheek by *jowl*]

cheekaside, cheeg-a-lee, cheekily squint. [ON *keikr* bent backwards; but compare Norw *skakkset* squint]

cheem 1 1 to throw, especially, *tae cheem a stone*. 2 to aim in the sense of align: '*Cheem hid in the hole noo*'. [related to Norw *kima* to swing]

cheem 2 that part of a barrel which projects beyond the bottom and top. [Eng *chime*]

cheemings the jowls. [origin unknown]

cheep verb. 1 = to cheep. 2 of grain to sprout. noun. a sound or mention*, '*Ah'm no heard a cheep fae him fae he left*.' [also Sc]

cheese = cheese, '*Never say cheese*' don't mention it.

cheeter* 1 **cheeteran and laughan** laughing in a muffled way, like children in a classroom. [a form of Eng *titter*]

cheeter 2, cheeto 1 a small fish. 2 a young coal-fish. [ModIcel *kóð* the young of a fish]

cheman watching without appearing to take notice. [origin uncertain]

chemois† principal house of an estate. [OSc *chemis*; OF *chemois* chief mansion]

chickers* = checkers, draughts.

chieler see CHILDER 2.

chigaleerie, jigaleerie crooked or askew. [origin uncertain; compare CHEEKASIDE; *leerie* is a Sc suffix; see FITKALEERIE etc]

chiggo a well built girl. [Norw *tjukka* thick set]

childer 1 see CHILTER.

childer 2, childers, chieler children, [Sc childer; OE *cildru* children]

chilter*, childer, cholder, of moving liquid in a stomach or in a bad egg, to make a noise. [imitat; compare SWILTER]

chilto a young girl. [Norw *tulta*]

chimley*, chimla chimney. [also Sc and Eng dial]

chimp, jimp verb. to eat in dainty way through embarrassment. adj. neat. [also JIMPIT; Sc *jimp* to curtail, to give short measure]

chincough† whooping cough. [also Sc; Eng *chink* to catch or draw the breath in laughing or coughing]

chingaring an old children's game. [Sc *jingo-ring* a singing game]

chingle* = shingle [also Sc]. **chingly stone*** a small pebble.

chinnal hard boulder clay underneath a soft surface. [? a form of CHINGLE]

chinner see GENNER.

chinnery used of flaky weathered sandstone, especially *chinnery braes*. [related to Eng *chine*; OE *cinu* cleft]

chinning a narrow gap: '*Open the window a chinning*'. [see CHINNERY]

chirlywheeter see SKIRLYWHEETER.

chirpan* soaking wet. '*Me feet's chirpan*' i.e. so wet that they are making a noise in the shoe! [imitat; compare Sc *chirk* and *chorp*]

chocks jaws. [also Sc and Eng dial; OSc chouk; ON *kjálki* jaw bone]

chocksband the rope of a halter which passed under the neck of an animal [see CHOCKS]

chocksy cow parsnip. [similar forms are found in Norw, Wel and Lat; Lat *cicuta* hemlock]

choggle 1 = joggle. 2 a short awkward swell in the sea.

choin 1 a large pool of water. 2 a marshy hollow. [common in placenames; ON *tjörn* pool; *r* before *n* is often lost in dialect]

chold to cover in a variety of senses. [compare ON *tjald* tent]

cholder see CHILTER.

choldro* an infertile egg. [see CHILTER]

chollop a mix-up. [origin uncertain]

cholty a small squat keg. [origin doubtful]

chomheed a stupid fool. In an argument in Shapinsay in the 1880's, a man dismissed three generations of his neighbour's family in one sentence: '*Min thoo are a chomheed and so thoo are and so wis thee faither afore thee and luk at thee son Willie, whit a chomheed he is*'. [Sc *toomheid* fool, from OE *tom* clear]

choop, joop a kind of jumper formerly worn by men and children. **jupsie** ill-fitting. [perhaps Sc *jupe* but compare ON *hjúpr]*

chootch a fool: '*Yir a right chootch!*' telling someone off. [compare Sh *chouskie* knave]

choots*, jutes dregs, lees. **chootie*** of water cloudy. [Sc *jute* dregs]

chow, jow a lump of something such as earth. **chows** small lumps of coal. [also Sc; origin uncertain]

chucket† a blackbird. [onomat]

chuckie see CHACKIE.

chuffsie fat in the face. [Sc *chuffy* chubby]

chulder see CHILTER.

chull, jull a big lumpy object. [also Sh; compare Norw *dult* a bundle]

chummle* 1 = jumble. 2 to disturb a liquid and bring up sediment from the botton. In the olden days one had to be careful not to *chummle* the water in the well in the summer time.

chund, jund of solids or liquids large in size. **chundery** of a poor coalfish with its head out of proportion to its body. [Sc *junt* a form of joint]

chupp a high headland. [compare Norw *kup* hump; OE *copp* hill]

cla see KLA

claes* clothes [also Sc]

clag* to stick. **claggy*** sticky. **claggy thistle** some unascertained plant with a bur, hence with a tendency to stick to the clothing. **claggered** thickly coated with something sticky. **clagum** toffee. [also Sc; eModEng; compare Dan *klag* clay]

claik* verb. 1 of a hen to make a loud noise (more frequently KLANK). 2 to gossip. [imitat]

clair 1 = clear. 2 ready or prepared '*Dinner's clair*'.

clamjamfry *the whole clamjamfry* the whole lot, but in a disparaging sense. [also Sc; origin uncertain]

clams a leather worker's vice, often made of two barrel staves. [Sc *clams* a vice]

clank* see KLANK.

clap, klap = verb. to clap. noun. uvula, *the clap o the hass*. **clappit** close together, '*His cheeks are fairly clappit*' he is thin in the face. **claps** the jaws.

clapshot* cooked potatoes and turnips mashed together, a traditional Orkney dish. [also Cai; origin uncertain; first recorded in Cai in 1916 but John Firth in *Reminiscences of an Orkney Parish* hints that the name was known in Orkney in the 19th century. [see KLEPP a lump of something soft and SHODDO]

clart* to spread something on thickly, especially: *clarted wi gutter (mud)*. [also Sc; compare ME *biclarten* to defile]

clash* verb. 1 = clash. 2 to gossip. 3 **tae clash doon** to throw oneself down on a seat: '*Don't clash thee doon here*'. **tae clash neeps** an operation undertaken 2/3 weeks after tall weeds like RUNCHO were removed before '*waterfurring*' for the winter [also Sc]. noun. 1 a heap. 2 a large woman [also Sc], *a clash o a wife*. 3 a chat. 4 a heavy shower, *a clash o weet*. **clashmaclavers** idle talk [also Sc]. **clash-pie*** a tell-tale.

clat, klat a big scraper used in a byre. [also Sc; ? related to KLA; see KLOORO for a similar development of meaning]

cleck see CLAIK.

cleg see KLEGG.

clemel see KLEMEL.

clep see KLEPP 1.

clepp see KLEPP 2.

clerp a resounding slap. [onomat]

clett see KLETT.

cleuks claws. [also Sc; OSc *cluke*; see illustration of CLEUKS under DIGGIE-DOO]

clibberbrods see KLIBBER .

click* to snatch: '*He clickéd hid oot o me hand*'. [Sc *cleek* to snatch; OSc *cleke* to snatch]

clim to climb [also Sc]

climmer, klimmer to climb (in a scratching way). [Eng *clamber*]

clink 1, klink to become less swollen or to diminish. **clinkéd*, klinkid** used of anything eg a person or a stack which has become less in bulk or weight. [also Sc; compare LoGer *klinken* to compact]

clink 2 money. [also Sc; imitat]

clinker a measure of degree, '*That wis a clinker o a dinner*' the very best of its kind. [Sc *clink* a blow, sudden fall; compare CLASH]

clinter see KLINTER.

clip, klip 1 = clip. 2 a gaff for landing fish [also Sc]

clipe* 1 to tell tales. [also Sc; ME *clepe* to call]

clipe* 2 verb. to strike. noun. 1 a blow. 2 a leather belt formerly used by teachers to punish children, more usually called TAAS. [compare coll Eng *clip*, a slap]

clipper the special seat used by the AK-SWAPPERS. [see AK SWAPPAN; ON *klyf-beri* pack saddle]

clite falling apart, *gin clean tae clite*. [Sc *clyte* a dirty mess]

clivoo see KLIVVY.

clock a black beetle. [also Sc and Eng dial; compare Swed dial *klocka* earwig or beetle]

clod* 1 = a clod. 2 a lump of hard peat* '*Pit twathree clods on the fire*'.

clog 1 = clog. 2 a special type of wooden snow skate with metal base and tied to the shoe, common in the West Mainland of Orkney up until the 1960's when the practice of putting grit on the roads in winter made skating impossible. This type of skate was brought to Orkney in the late 19th century by an Icelander who worked in a Stromness boatyard.

cloor* see KLOOR

cloorer a masonry chisel. [also Cai; Sc *clour* to deal a blow; origin uncertain]

clooro see KLOOR.

cloot*, kloot 1 a cloth. 2 the sail of a boat. *a tongue that wid clip cloots* said of a sharp tongued individual. [OSc *clout*; OE *clut*]

closs* a narrow passage between two buildings. [Sc *close*; ultimately Lat *clausum* an enclosed space]

cluck* of a hen to brood. **cluckan hen*** a broody hen. **clucksmither** a hen with chickens. [compare Sc *clocking* hen; Norw *klukke*]

clumbung see KLUMBUNG.

clump*, klump to walk with heavy steps. [compare Eng *clomp*; Norw *klampa*]

clurgis a mess. [CLURT + GIS]

clurt* a big lump, *a great clurt o a thing*. [see CLART]

clyres, klyers glands in the intestinal fat of an animal. [also Sc; MDu *cliere* gland]

coat 1 = coat. 2 jacket*.

19

cock 1 = cock (bird), '*The cock that goes cryan tae bed'll rise wi a watery head*' a cock crowing at bed-time is a sign of rain. **cockaletty** a hermaphrodite hen. [cock-a-lady?]. **cock and pail** the bung of a brewing churn. **cocks and hens*** birds foot trefoil [also Sc]. **cock loft** the side loft in a church. **cockstride*** a short distance: '*The sun goes a cockstride along the hill every night*'.

cockalowrie a daisy. [also Sh; Norw *kokul* cluster + LEERIE; see FITKALEERIE]

cockstride see COCK.

cockle to totter. **cockly*** liable to fall. [also Sc; compare Far *kongul*, a lump of peat; the essential meaning is *roundness* hence liable to roll; see KOOGLIE]

cod*, kod a pillow. [also Sc; also known as a *head-cod*]. **codlin** a triangular shaped stone, awkward to use in building. **cod up** in carpentry to insert a packing wedge. [ON *koddi* pillow]

cog* 1 a small cask, especially **bride's cog*** a wooden vessel with upright handles filled with a special home brew and used at a wedding reception. 2 the contents of such a vessel: '*Feth that's a good cog*'. **cogs** school toilets. (see also PISS 2) [OSc *cog*; ON *kaggi*]

colasheen a fight with tongue or hands. [Sc *collieshangie*]

cole* 1 to pile hay into the small stacks in the field, part of the drying process. 2* a small stack of hay. [also Sc; origin uncertain]

cole hill (the)† the peat hill. [ON *kol* coals or charcoal]

colly see KOLY.

colozal = adj. colossal. noun. a great number or quantity, '*There wiz colozal o folk there*'. [compare NORMOUS]

come past tense CAM, KAM, perfect tense COMED. 1 = come. 2 of clothes, to get softer, of meal to become finer etc. **come at*** 1 improve especially of health: '*He's walkan withoot his stick noo, he's fairly coman at*'. **come at** 2 used negatively *He didna come at me*, he didn't succeed in hurting me with his taunt. **come against*** 1 *a naafil come against kinda cratur*' abrasive in manner. 2 of food disagreeable. **come intae words*** (only in past tense) '*Hid kam intae words*' we got around to talking about .'. **come keek** a fad or an invention: '*Oh hid's just anither come keek*'. **come on end**, to make a start, *He'll no come on end tae luk for a wife.* **come thee wiz*** literally 'come thy ways', a familiar invitation to a friend to enter the house and used in other similar situations [this expression can be found in Shakespeare]

comper the fish, the fatherlasher, known in Sanday as JOHNNY MAINLAND [also Sc origin unknown]

concord = concord. **concordedly** in a composed manner.

concother happy. **fu concother** of two people happy to be together. [origin uncertain; but compare COTHER]

concurrence occurrence

condoberties, condubadies '*I widna hiv any condoberties wi him!*' I wouldn't have any dealings with him. [origin uncertain; ? Sc *curbawdy* the art of seeking a quarrel]

congle see KUNGLE.

constant constantly, always.

conter = to counter.

coo*, koo = 1 cow (plural **kye**) 2 a shellfish like a large cockle, called *koo* by children who used them in farm games. **coogil, koogild**† in old records, a cow's grazing. [ON *kúgildi* cow's value]. **coolick*** a tuft of hair sticking up on the head. [Eng *cow-lick*; the hair of a cow stands up in this way when licked]. **coo's keep** the right of a son or daughter otherwise disinherited to keep a cow on the family holding. **coo's plirt** see PLIRT. **coosworth, kowisworth**† a proportion of odal land, 1/16 of a penny land. [Eng *cow's* + *worth*; compare ON *kú-gildi*]

coof see CEUF.

cookie* a small leavened slightly sweet bun. **cookie shine** a social evening or party [also Sc]

cool see COOLIE.

coolick see COO.

coolie*, cool a woollen cap. [Eng *cowl*]

coolter-back, koolter-back the razor bill. [see COOTER-NEB]

coolter-neb, koolter-neb see COOTER-NEB.

coom*, koom dust, especially mill dust. **tae lay in coom*** to shatter. **tae coom ower** of the sky to darken. [OSc *cowm*; ON *kám* grime]

coom-ceiled*, cumsiled of a ceiling lined with boards. [an Orkneyman, many years resident in New Zealand was visited by his elderly granny who made a special trip out to see him. When looking over the new house he was building, he was much amused when granny looked at the unfinished ceiling and remarked, 'Bit thoo'll be cumsiling hid.'! [also Sc; OSc *cumseil* to make an arched ceiling; Sc *coom* arch]

coop* see COUP.

coor 1 = cower. 2 to hide.

coorse = 1 coarse. 2 of weather, rough '*Hid's a coorse day, min.*'

coosworth see COO.

cootch '*Stoop-cootch!*' shut-up!'. [Sc *cooch* a command to a dog to lie down; a development of Eng *couch*]

cooter-neb razor bill. [OSc *coutar* etc the coulter of

20

a plough]

cooticans see KUITS.

coppie a small stool. [the sense is *a small block*; compare Norw *kubbestol* chair carved from a block of wood]

corbie 1 a rook. 2 a raven. [OF *corbin* from Lat *corvus* crow]

corn 1 used specifically of the crop *bere* in Orkney*. 2 a small quantity*. [also Sh; see GRAIN]. 3 **corn-huggie, korn-huggie** the hole left in a stack after a few sheaves have been removed. [ON *högg* a breach or gap]: '*He'll no get a corn fork tae his erse*' He's well bred.

coronoy see COTANOY.

corrie-handed, corrie-jouket left handed. [Gael *cearr* left hand; Sc *jouket* cunning]

cors, kors† a cross. In Orkney a *cors* was formerly passed round from house to house as an indication that an assembly was about to be held. Such a signal was used elsewhere in Britain, sometimes burning crosses being used. [found in placenames in the form *Corse*; compare Norw *kors* cross]

cose to exchange or barter. [Eng dial *corse*; origin unknown; before the days of pedigreed hens it was very common to *cose a setting o eggs*]

cost† an old term signifying duty payable in kind as distinct from cash. [ON *kostr* goods]

cotanoy, coternoy, coronoy 1 a mix up. 2 annoyance. [*cat* + NYOW]

cother 1 kindly, affectionate. 2 warm and snug. **couthersome** 1 cuddly. 2 of a woman, loving. [NEng dial *cowther* to comfort]

counsel-man see ROITH.

coup*, coop, cup to tip or spill [also Sc]. **cuppan*** pouring with rain. **coup-cairt** a cart which tips. [OSc *cowp* to upset]

couples* rafters. **couple-baaks** the cross beams in a roof. [see BAAK; also Sh; OSc *coupill*; ME *cuppil*]

Court Book a book containing the records of a court of justice in the 16th and 17th centuries.

coust see CUIST.

couthersome see COTHER.

couthie friendly. [also Sc; OE *cuði* known, probably with the sense *known as a friend*]

cow see COO.

cowe* a large piece of heather pulled up by the root, usually *heather-cowe* . [also Sc in the sense *bunch of twigs* or *broom*; origin uncertain but perhaps related to Norw *kolla* to dock and Sc *cow*]

cowld* = cold. **cowld-bitten*** always feeling the cold.

craa*, kra verb. = to crow. noun. 1 a crow. 2 the mussel (because of its resemblance to the black wings of a crow when opened). [ON *kráken-skel*]. **the craa's on the stab** used metaphorically as a portent of death e.g. relatives gathering at a house where someone is very ill. **craamill** a large rattle used to frighten cows [also Sc]. **craa poke** the skate's egg case. **craas feet** Ordnance Survey bench-mark. **to be among the craas** to be involved in trouble through bad associates.

crab = crab. **crab-staff** a hook for cutting creel ropes.

crack 1 verb. 1 = to crack. 2 to talk. [general throughout Eng dial; compare CLASH and CLAIK]. noun. a slap: '*Shut up or Ah'll gae yi a crack*'*. [imitat]

crack 2 *a crack o a ting*, a person who has arrived at maturity but is of very short stature [also Sh compare Du. *krak(ke)*, a broken down horse]

crackie only in the phrase: '*My Crackie!*' goodness me!

craew to crush: '*Beuy he just craewed the bones atween his teeth*'. [origin uncertain]

cramp† a word used in Sanday formerly for artificial (probably burnt) mounds. **cramps** iron hard pan. In Birsay also used for *cinders* because of the resemblance. [Norw *krampa* to press or squeeze (together)]

cran 1 a crane. 2 an iron upright with a projecting arm used to suspend a pot etc over an open fire.

crankie 1 = crankie. 2 of a boat, unstable.

cratur 1 = creature. 2 a cow: '*We'll hae to pit the craturs oot at the end o the month*'. [in common use in Birsay at the beginning of this century]

creepie* a small stool. [also Sc; the essential meaning is *bending*, which probably refers to sitting down as in Gael *crub* to sit; Eng dial *cricket* a small stool is probably likewise related to Eng *crouch* and Sc *currie* a small stool from *coor* to cower]

creesh a mixture of whale oil (or hen fat) and tar rubbed on wool to make it more pliable before it is woven. [OSc *cresche*; OF *craisse*; Lat *crassus* fat]

creetle see KREEKLE.

creu* see KRO.

creukal see KRUIKLE.

crinchy of an old person, bent. [Sc *crine*; Cai *krin* to shrink with age; Gael *crúon* withered]

cringle see KRINGLE.

cringled see KRINGLE.

cringled-teu see KRINGLE.

cringlo see KRINGLE.

crome see KROME.

crooels running sores. [also Sc; Fr *ecrouelles*, scrofula]

croopan see CRUPPAN.

croopen see KROPPEN.

croopened see KROPPEN.

croose merry or high spirited. [also Sc *crouse*; NoME *crus*]

croot to pronounce the letter *r* with a burr. [Sc *croot* to croak; compare ON *kretta* to murmur]

crootle to walk slowly and painfully, especially: *crootlan and creetlan*. **crootled doon** especially: *crootled doon wi rheumatics* going in a bent fashion. [Sc *croodle* to crouch; see KREEKLE]

cross = cross. **crosses on** the middle and index finger crossed as a protection against evil (children's game).

crub to confine. **crubbit,** cramped [also Sh; see KRUBBAN]

crubban see KRUBBAN.

crud of butter to curd, that is to form lumps as the cream is being churned. [also Sc; ME *crudde* curd, a good example of metathesis; see KITTLE for comparision]

cruggle see KRUGGLE.

cruik* see KRUIK.

crump to have difficulty in sounding the letter *r* properly [see KROM and CROOT]

cruppan the body, especially the body of a fowl. [ON *kroppr* body]

crusie* a small open iron lamp with a rush wick. [often OILY CRUISIE; also Sc; LaLat *crucibulum* a light burning before the cross]

cruttle see KRUTTLE.

cry 1 = a cry. 2 to proclaim banns in a church. **taen (taken) cryan** to be in labour. [Sc *crying* labour]

Cubbie Roo*, Cubbie Row a legendary giant who lived in Orkney, his name being invariably associated with big stones. [supposedly derived from *Kolbein Hrúga* a Norse chieftain who lived in Wyre but perhaps ON *koppu-rá* block marking a boundary]

cubby*, kubby a woven straw basket for holding peats etc. [compare MidDu *cubbe* a basket; Norw *kupa* fish basket]

cuist see CAST.

cuit see KUITS.

cuithe see KUITHE.

cuithin see KUITHE.

cullya*, kolyie a seagull. [imitat]

cullyawhummlie se KAILWAMPLE.

cullye to cuddle. [OSc *culze* to caress]

cumareen a loud noise such as the sound of the grouse (see MOORHEN) or the sound of a number of voices arguing. [imitat; compare Sc *curmur* low rumbling sound, purring of a cat]

cummel a large sea-worn stone on the beach. [see KUNGLE]

cumsiled* see COOMCEILED.

cundy-hole a conduit. [also Sc; corruption of *conduit* + *hole*]

cungle 1 see KUNGLE.

cungle 2 to argue. [Sc *cangle*; Norw *kjangle*]

cunjer cunning. [ON *kunngir* wise]

cunnin, kunnin a rabbit. **kunno** 1 a straw rabbit used in a game played round stacks in a cornyard. 2 the game itself. [Sc and Eng *coney*; Fr *conin*; Lat *cuninculus* rabbit]

cunningair a rabbit warren. [also Sc; obs Eng *conyger*; OF *conniniere*]

cunyo a corner. [OSc *cunz(i)e* corner of a wall]

cup 1 1 = cub. 2 conceited or ill-mannered youth. 3 a strange fellow.

cup 2 see COUP.

cuppo a small depression in a field etc: common in placenames as *Cup* or *Cuppin* [O.N. *koppr*, (a) hollow]

curl 1 = to curl. 2 to roll: '*Curl the ball tae me min*'. **curl-dodie* curly dodie*, carl doddy** curly clover, especially of the red variety (*trifolium pratensis*). [also Sh; see DODD]. **curlie** the *plate* of the old living room stove.

currie-currie Oh dear me! [ON *kurr* a murmur]

currivan, kurrivan a slight disagreement. [also used in Cai, compare similar Sc forms *curry-shang, currie-wurriein, carfuffle* used in the sense uproar and KURRMULYO below; the prefix in these instances is Gael *car* a turn or a twist; compare Gael *caramasg* confusion, literally *turn-mix*]

currmulyo, kurrmulyo confusion. [see KURRIVAN above for first element; *mulyo* is Sc *mell* to join in a fight; from OE *meller* to mix]

cursit* accursed: '*Hid's a cursit thing o bairn that*'.

custel-penniet the bailiff's commission on the goods of a deceased person. [ON *kostr* expense; ON *penningr* money]

cut* 1 = cut. 2 humour [also Sc], '*He's in poor cut the day*'. 3 a measure of wool, 1/12 of a hank. [also Sc]

cuthin see KUITHE.

cutty, cutto, cuttack noun. 1 a half grown individual. 2 a dumpy thick oat bannock, sometimes baked on hot embers. **cuttack, cutto** a vole. **cuttie** only in *clay-cuttie* a clay pipe with a broken stem. adj **cutty** 1 short. *a cutty piece* quite a distance. 2 little, *the weather's a cutty bit better the day*, [compare DAINTY; the essential meaning is short; compare Gael *cutach* bob-tailed; *cutag* a little dumpy girl]. **cutty slap** a hare's nest. If a pregnant woman stepped over a hare's nest it was believed her child would be born with a hare lip. [a corruption of Sc *cutty's clap* a hare's nest; Sc *cutty* a hare + *clap*]

cuttel a measuring rod equal to a Sc ell. [origin unknown]

cutty dance a sort of dance performed squatting on one's haunches [? related to KUITS: compare FITKALEERIE]

D the letter *d* pronounced as in English. Formerly *d* was pronounced *th* in certain words eg *lathy* = lady, *a bothy* = everybody.

da, dae† definite article *the*. [still current in Sh but obs in Ork though it remains fossilised in some placenames eg *Aboondariggs* (above the riggs) in Sanday]

daa*, dawfish the small spotted dog-fish. [also known as the BLIND DAA; Gael *dall* blind and *dallag* spotted dogfish; fishermen believed the fish was blind]

daater see DOTIR.

daaver see DOVER.

daawurt a day's work, used as a measure eg: *a daawurt o paets* the amount of peats cut by one man in one day. [Sc *darg*; ON *dagsverk* a days work]

dab 1 fine, misty rain. [see DAGG]

dab* 2 just right: *'Beuy that bit o wid is just the very dab'*. [OE *gedafen* suitable]

dabal, dybal a wet piece of land. [Norw *depel* a muddy hole]

dabchick the little grebe. [general throughout Eng dial]

dacher to nod off to sleep. [perhaps Sc *dacher* to hesitate etc but compare DAAVER]

dachin to abate [also Sh: origin unknown]

dack, deck an interval between showers. [also Cai; Norw *daka* to go slowly]

dad* verb. to move noisily, *tae dad like a sinloo* to roll on the ground in anguish like the sandlark when anyone approaches its nest. noun. a blow: *'Gae the shovel a dad and tak the sharn off hid'*. [also Sc; imitat]

dae 1† = the. [see EMLY-AMLY for this old usage]

dae 2* = do.

daeth = death. *at daeth's door** very ill.

daev see DAIVE.

daffins cords used to attach nets to the rope from which they are hung. [also Sc; origin unknown]

daffo 1 a small wooden tub. [also Sc; Gael *dabhach* a large vat]

daffo 2 a sloppy meal given to sick animals. [see DAVVO]

dagg drizzling rain. [also Sc; compare Norw *dogg* dew or fine rain]

daggon a lump of something (eg cheese). [Sh *daggen*; origin unknown]

dagsy bow-legged; *a dagsy kinda waak (walk)*. [origin uncertain]

daidly an apron. [also Sc; the essential meaning is *rag* as in BRATTO; see DUDDS and DALDO for related forms]

dainty 1 = dainty. 2* considerable, *a dainty piece tae walk. a dainty nappy* an old term for a boy entering his teens. [see NAPPY]

daisket*, deeskit exhausted. [ON *dasast* to become exhausted]

daive, daev to deafen: *tae daive at someone* to deafen them. **davesam** noisy. [ON *deyfa*]

daiversome: noisy [see DAVESAM]

daldo*, dido* *'He's me daldo'*, he's quite a character. [the essential meaning is *ragged*; compare Sh *dildos* ragged clothes; see DILDER 2 and TALDERS]

dale = to deal. [Sc *dale* to divide or distribute; ON *deild* a share]

dammle*, dimmle to lower a bucket into a well or pool in order to fill it. [Norw dial *damla*]

damp the end of a piece of line, especially a long line. [Norw *tamp*]

dander 1* verb. to stroll. noun. a stroll. [also Sc and NoE; origin uncertain]

dander 2 temper: *'His dander was up'* he was in a bad temper. [a form of TANDER]

dang see DING.

danyel, denyel a wet patch of land. [related to Norw *dyngja* mire or ooze]

dar to stir (eg in a fire) too much with a poker. [related to Norw *darra* to vibrate]

dare 1 = dare. 2 to make an impression, *'The metal wis so hard the file never dared on hid.'*

dark = dark. **darn** = darken: *'Never darn me door'* don't visit me. **darkening** twilight.

darkavised having a dark countenance. [also Sc; *dark* + Sc *avise* manner, fashion]

darn 1 1 to hide, eg of a bird or animal in the heather. 2 to nestle down to sleep. [also Sc; OE *diernan* to hide]

darn 2 see DARK.

darro 1 a fishing line. 2 a little wooden frame round which the line is wound. [also Sc; ON *dorg* angler's tackle]

darrowas a scolding. [origin unknown]

darsha* = dare say: *'I darsha thoo doesna hae a penny thoo could lend me?'* [*s* following *r* in Orkney dialect is pronounced *sh*]

daughter see DOTIR.

davesam see DAIVE.

davvo, duivo a large lump of something. [see DIVOT]

Davy Dascal a playground game played in Sanday [orgin unknown]

dawdoswang a heavy swell in the sea. [origin uncertain; ? DAD + *swing*]

daw-fish see DAA.

day = day: *'Hid'll be the day afore hid'* an indication that something has to be postponed: *'I wis gan tae deu the washing bit I doot hid'll be the day afore hid'*.

dayfelly white mist lying in a depression. [? ON *dögg-fall* dew fall]

dayset evening. [ON *dagsetr*]

dead man's fingers a sea sponge [it looks like a hand! see TROW GLOVE]

deadman's liver the early purple orchis (*orchis mascula*). [Sc *dead man's thoom(s)*; *dead man* is applied to many plant names in Sc]

deaf = deaf. **deafie** a deaf person.

dealer a ladle. [Eng *deal* with the original sense of sharing or distributing; OE *daelan* to share]

deck 1 1 dough [also Sc]. 2 a badly baked bannock. Also known as a **deckie bannock**. [Norw *deig* dough]

deck 2 of the weather to improve. [see DACK]

deckie bannock see DECK 1.

dee 1* = to die. past tense DEED. perfect tense DINED: '*He wad dined if I hidna gotten a rope tae him*'.

dee 2† an old form of pronouncing THEE, immortalised in a story from Harray. Two old ladies had an argument about the ownership of a pigeon: '*Dat's no dee doo Dora, dee doo deed*' That's not your pigeon Dora, your pigeon died.

deeal a wet patch in a field. [ON *díli* a spot]

deean a marshy spot. [Norw *dynn* mire or mud; the real meaning is *quagmire* from ON *dýja* to shake]

deed* 1 a clipped form of indeed, especially: '*Oh deed aye*' Oh yes indeed. 2 see DEE 1.

deemster, dempster† a judge. [the word is still used in the Isle of Man, ME *dempster*]

deen to fit or suit. **deenin** what is necessary: '*Hid wid deen thee better tae bide at home*'. [Du *dienen* to serve]

deeskit see DAISKET.

deezy *a bit o deezy plough* used of the old plough. [Norw *disa* to potter about]

deil* = devil. **deila thing, deily thing*** nothing at all. '*Deily bit o me!*' I certainly won't. **deilblickets, deily-blicket** nothing at all. [a corruption of Sc **deil-be-licket** devil be punished, a mild oath]. **deil-scaithe** well-deserved, '*Hid wis deil-scaithe they were catched.*' [see SKAITHE]. **deil's burdeen** such a large load that some is certain to fall off (the folklore of Britain if full of stories of the devil dropping some of his huge load of stones or earth): *as scared as the devil for broken gless* very scared. '*He wid eat the deil dipped in tar*' he has a voracious appetite.

dell* = delve. **dellow** a small patch of ground, a patch to be dug.

demmle a commotion in the sea, a splashing. [see DAMMLE]

demooricky of a jersey etc dull in colour. [Sh *dumbet*; ON *dumbóttr* dark misty colour of cows (combined perhaps with MOORIT)]

dempster see DEEMSTER.

demption pouring rain, *a demption o rain*. [ON *demba* + Eng *ion* suffix; compare TUCTION]

dent very thin BEND leather [a form of DINTLE]

denyal see DANYEL.

depoperat impoverished. [OSc *depauperat*]

desk 1 = desk. 2 a seat or pew in a church.

desstance damage or trouble, '*There's no much desstance along the shore road efter the gale*'. **tae wirk desstance** to make mischief. [origin uncertain; compare Norw *deise* to topple or tumble]

deualess*, deuanless good-for-nothing *a kind a deualess critter*. [also Sh; ON *dáð-lauss*].

deukoo a doll made from a shawl, a string tied round to form the neck. [ON *dúkr* cloth]

deurk big, heavy or unweildy. [see DURK]

devo a large round field stone [see DAVVO]

dey a female servant or dairymaid. [ON *deigja*]

diacle a small dial or compass. [OSc diacle]

dian stone, darrow stone a piece of stone usually red or brown in colour with a small hole in it hung on the sunward side of the old Orkney plough as a charm or carried by a fisherman on a string round his neck; at the other end of Britain, in Weymouth, Dorset, fishermen used to hang in the bows of their vessels, for luck, a small flint-stone with a naturally bored hole in it [? Gael *dán* fate, luck, Gael *darrag*, small stone]

dickans punishment: '*Thool get thee dickans!*' [Sc *dichen*; see DIGHT]

dido see DALDO.

die a big wave. [related to Icel *dýja* to move to and fro]

die flooer ragwort. [? *weed* flower; compare Norw *dåe* hemp-nettle and Sh *okerdu* a type of weed]

diet = 1 diet 2 meal, repast.

differ 1 = differ. 2 difference* [also Sc]. '*Hid maks no differ whit wey yi go*'.

different 1 = different. 2* a number of different (people etc): '*Different folk wir sayan he's bankrupt*'. [Eng *people were saying* etc]

dig = 1 dig. 2 plan or determination. 3 rhythm '*He just works awey at his own dig*'.

diggie-doo, dikkie-doo a game of hide and seek around the stacks in a cornyard. [Sh *skutamillaskroo*; ON *dik* a run + DOO 1]. The catcher in this game often spoke this little verse:-
> *I warn yi once, I warn yi twice*
> *I warn yi oot o Glowries eyes,*
> *If Glowrie gets yi in his cleuks*
> *He'll grind yi as small as fower and*
> *twenty sillock heuks*

dikko the pursuer in a game of DIGGIE-DOO.

dight 1 to clean: '*Gae the floor a dight*'. 2 to gut (a fish). [also Sc; OE *dihtan* to arrange]

dikkie-doo see DIGGIE-DOO.

dikko see DIGGIE-DOO.

dilder* 1 to shake, '*He wis just dilderan wi the cowld*'. 2 to dangle. 3 to bounce e.g. a child up and down on the knee [Norw *dildra* to shake]

dilkie lazy or slow. [see DRILTY]

dill 1 of the wind, a fire etc to die down. 2 of a pain to ease. 3 to pass from memory [also Sc and nEng; nME *dillen* to render dull]

dillowan the dock plant. [origin uncertain; the first element may be the same as the *dill* of DILLSOWY, hence *ragged*, a reference to the plant's appearance in winter; compare Sh *dill rags*; *owan* may be a curtailed form of DOWHAN]

dillsowy tattered. [compare Sh *dillbells* matted wool hanging from sheep; related to DILDER above and TALDER]

dim darkness [ON *dimma*, darkness: see RIV]

dimmle to scoop up a small quantity of liquid with eg a bowl *tae dimmle a bowl* . [see DAMMLE]

dind off white in colour. [? a form of DUN]

dined see DEE 1.

ding*, dang, past, perfect tense **dung** verb. to bang or knock. noun. a knock, '*He gid me a right ding*'. [also Sc; general in Eng dial; ON *dengja* to bang]

dint '*Ah'm heard no dint o hid*' I've heard no mention of it. [Sc *din* rumour = Eng din]

dintle thin bend leather. **dintle rivlings** shoes of untanned hide made from thin leather. [also Sh; ON *dindill* the tail of a seal, the essential meaning being 'to swing or bend', hence thin, supple leather]

dip 1 = to dip. **dippings** gravy.

dip 2 to sit down [also Sh Norw. *dippa*, to bend down]

dippers a rig for a boat. [? a dipping lug sail]

dird to bump along the ground: '*Me feet gid fae me on the ice and me head just dirded on the grund*'. [also Sc and Sh; a clipped form of Sh *dirdle*; ? a metathesis of DILDER]

dirl verb. to spin round. [when it was proposed to close rural schools in the West Mainland and transport all the children to Dounby, an angry Sandwick parishioner remarked to Education Department officials at a public meeting, '*Yi'll aal be in yir beds still when wir bairns are dirlan roond the pairish*.] 1 a blow: '*Whit a dirl he got on the side o the head*'. 2 a toy windmill. [compare BIRL, TIRL, SKIRL etc]

dirr to quiver. [compare Norw *dirre*]

dirt, drit 1 = dirt. 2 the dung of fowls, dogs, cats etc. 3 nonsense: '*Dirt wi thee. Thoo're a blether o dirt, a freck o dirt* etc. 3 a mild expletive today,

'*Ah dirt, Ah'm no gaan*' but formerly must have had the force of present day '*Ah shite, Ah'm no gan*'. [ON *drit* dung of fowls]

dirty aulin the Arctic Skua. [Sc *Dirty Allan*; ON *drit* bird dung; Norw *aale* dung ooze; see also SCOUTIE ALLAN where *scoutie* means *faeces*]

dirvin a lump of something. [origin uncertain]

dis* = 'tis. **dissat*** indeed it is. **disso** 'tis so. [HID + is, that, so]

dishwashings* dishwater; BLOTS is more common

disjaskit neglected or in disorder. [also Sc; origin uncertain]

dismal = dismal. **dismal bonny** really attractive. [compare HORRIBLE]

diss* a small stack. [ON *dys* cairn; found in Orkney placenames]

dissat see DIS.

disso see DIS.

dist a small particle. [Eng *dust*]

dister fine rain. [Norw dial *dustra* to drizzle]

dive to argue. [origin unknown]

divert verb. = to divert (i.e. to entertain or amuse). noun. a happy-go- lucky person.

divot* a piece of turf. [also Sc; OSc *devat* turf]

divso of a woman, untidy. [Norw *tafs* poor wretch]

dizzen* = dozen, '*He'll be aboot a dizzen*' He is about twelve years old.

do verb. = do: '*Hid does me*'* I am satisfied with it. noun. = a joke* '*That wis a right do on him*'. **done** 1 = done. 2* finished: '*Is yir tea done?*' [also Eng dial]. **do-ap** a telling off.

dob to stab or stub; '*I dobbéd me finger on that nail*' I caught my finger on that nail. [also Sc; Eng *dab*]

dochan*, dowhan the plant the dock. **no worth a dochan** useless [Sc *docken*; OE *doccan* docks]

docher rough usage. [Gael *dochair*]

dodd a matted lump (of eg wool). **dodie** only in CURLY DODIE. [also Sh; Norw dial *dodd* a tuft or heap]

dodge jog, trudge along. [also Sc; a form of DAD]

dodgel something large of its kind, eg 1 a lump. 2 a clumsy person. **dodshal** clumsy. [Sc *dodgel* large lump: ? related to DODD]

dog = dog. **dog-dreel** *to be on the dog-dreel*, said of a young man who calls on his lady friend and spends the night with her. [ME *trollen* to wander; compare EF *trollerie* aimless wandering of dogs]. **dog feenkle** yarrow. **dog flooer** dandelion. **dog too, doggy too*** a clump of grass where dogs urinate. A nickname for a hovel in the olden days (presumably a turf house) now fossilised as placenames eg in Shapinsay. [ON *þúfa* mound]. **dog's peas, dog's piss** the meadow vetchling. **dog thistle** the sow thistle.

doggets sheep dung. [see DODD]

25

dolder* 1 to shake. A gentleman who used this word to describe the movement of millstones was nicknamed *Dolders*. 2 to amble along. [see DILDER]

dolders the scrotum [see TALDERS]

doliment see TULLIMENT.

Dollick a Stronsay goblin also known as BOLLICK. [origin uncertain]

domaless having no energy. [? a running together of Sc *dowless* unhealthy; OE *dugan* to be able, with some Norse word related to Norw *dåmlaus* colourless]

dome† judgement. **domismen†** members of a judicial body. [ON *dómr*; ON *dómsmenn*]

donafeing† an old legal term, the confiscation of property. [ON *doema fé* to adjudicate goods belonging to someone, pursuant to a judgement]

done see DO.

Dons a nickname given by Westray people to those islanders whom they believed, because of their colouring, to be descendants of shipwrecked Spanish Armada Sailors. [*don* the Span title *Sir, Mr* etc]

doo 1† the old pronunciation of *you* familiar. [Eng *thou*; *thoo* is now universal though it too is receding fast; compare DEE]

doo 2 a pigeon. **doo-cot** a dove cot. [Sc *doo*; Eng *dove*]

doofie = bottom, '*Ah'll scud yir doofie*' I'll smack your bottom. [ON *düf*]

dook* verb. to drive wooden wedges into a wall to hold nails. noun. a wooden wedge driven into a wall. [also Sc; compare Friesian *douk* a spigot]

doolshie a child's cart. [origin unknown; may fall into that group of very old service terms which have entered dial; Hindi *dolti* is a box borne on poles on men's shoulders; Eng *doolie*]

doon 1 = down. 2 light chaff, especially the light meal deposited round the edge of a millstone. [ON *dúnn* bird's down].

dooncome see DOWN.

dooncoming see DOWN.

doondie, dundie 1 a saithe or coalfish in its third or fourth year or a big thin cod. 2 a nickname for an inhabitant of Papa Westray. [origin uncertain; Norw *dunt* bundle; Gael *duntag* squat]

doonfa-seekness see DOWN.

doonie see DOWN.

doon the gates see DOWN.

doontroo see DOWN.

doop, dup 1 the thick end of an egg [also Sc]. *tae die in the doop* of a chicken to die just before hatching. 2 the backside: '*Ah'll scud thee doop for thee if thoo doesna watch oot*'. [ON *döf* rump; LGer *dop* a shell]

door = door. **door sole** threshold: '*Luk whit's raised wir door lintel the day*' look what has arrived. [*sole* = sill]

doos* of an animal to butt. [also Sc; Norw dial *dusa* to hit violently]

doosit matt black. [related to Norw dial *dysjutt* dark coloured]

doot 1 = to doubt. 2* to be certain: '*I doot thoo'll nivver see thee £5 again*'.

dore to pester: *deil (devil) dore thee!* an old curse. **doreen*:** '*A doreen on thee!*' Confound you! (but in a mild sense). [Old Norse *dár*, dumbfounded]

dort* verb. of a bird, to shun its nest after its eggs have been touched, '*The eggs are cowld, I doot she's dorted*'. Also used of a ewe which forsakes its lambs or of a dog which is fussy about its food:-

A dortan dog wis niver fat
The more he dorted
The less he got

noun. *tae be in the dorts*, to sulk. adj. **dorty** 1* of a plant or vegetable slow in growing. 2 of a child sulky:

Dorty dorty doon da brae
Canna say his A B C

[Sc *dort* to sulk; notice the old pronunciation of *C*].

dose 1 1 = dose. 2 a large number*, '*Whit a dose o folk wis there*'.

dose 2 to stub the toe. [see DOOS]

dosy Marwick quotes this word from Hoy in the phrase: '*Dosy apae thee*' where he says it means '*Blessings upon you*' but he may be wrong in this. [Sc *dozen* to stupefy and Sc *dazen* damn; see DORE, DOREEN and DOZE for related forms]

dotir, daater a boil. [spelt *daughter* by Marwick; related to OE *dott* head of a boil and OHiGer *tutta* nipple; Eng *tit*]

dottle ash etc in a smoker's pipe. [also Sc; related to Eng *dot* small speck]

dovened 1 to be numbed with cold. [also Sc; related to DOVER below]. 2 of a green plant withered. [ON *dofna* numb or insensible]

dover, daaver to fall into a light sleep. **doverless** lifeless, lazy. [also Sc; related to DOVENED above].

dowhan see DOCHAN.

dowie* of a calf etc: *tae luk (look) dowie* to be sickly. [also Sc; origin unknown]

down = down. **dooncome*** a fall in social position [also Sc]. '*Hid wis a right dooncome tae them when Willie hid tae go tae the coort!*'. **dooncoming** a sloping path or road: '*I met him in the dooncoming*'. [OSc *douncome* descent]. **doonfa-seekness** epilepsy, a cure for which was cutting off the patients' fingernails and a lock of hair while he was having a fit. The hair and nails were then buried where the sufferer had fallen. **Doonies, Doon the Gates** originally those who were born to the north of the cathedral in Kirkwall, those who lived *doon the gates*, down the path(s); the Watergate is the present street to the south of the cathedral. **doontroo†** an old nickname for an ale-house; **ap-trow** was used in a similar sense. Hugh Marwick cleverly recognised this connection in 'Ap-trow' an old ale house near Quoys of the Hill in Birsay be-North. He explained that name as 'up-through'. 'Doon-troo', now Breck Cottage in Marwick Birsay was also an ale house and Doon-trow was an old house which lay between the Barony and Kirbister in Birsay but nothing is known of its history. [compare Sc *doon-bye* in, '*I'll go doon-bye (to the ale house)*']

doy '*Doy! Doy!*' to a child, '*Blessings upon you!*' [? DU-OY]

doze 1 dose. 2 stupefy, stun [see DOSY]

drabelly, drabellies holes bored through the timbers of a boat along the ship's inner keel to drain bilge water to the plug-hole. [= *draw* + *belly*]

drabie untidy or slow in action. [a form of Eng *drab*]

draibly *draibly lukkan*, untidy with clothes dragging on the ground. [related to Eng *drabble*]

draigelt see DROCK.

drail* to trail behind. [related to Norw dial *drala* to saunter]

draipsy, dribsy ill-kempt or untidy. [see DRABIE]

drap* 1 = drop. 2 a quantity, not necessarily a small quantity, '*Thoo'll tak a drap o whisky*'.

drawing sheaf a sheaf of straw selected by drawing straw.

dredyou, dredya marshy or swampy ground. The old name for the piece of marshy ground lying between Laxhowe and Madras, Harray, also known as '*Da Muckle Mire*'. [ON *drit* dung + ON *gall*, bile, used here in the sense *marsh*]

dreebits and drabbits = dribs and drabs.

dreed = dread: '*I dreed hid's no gan tae be much o a day*'. [compare *fear* used similarly in Eng]

dreef* 1 = drift. 2 a crowd of people or large number of animals*.

dreel* 1 = drill. 2 a row or heaped up ridge of plants such as potatoes or turnips: '*Twa three dreel o tatties will deu me fine*'. **dreel-dunged** of turnips with dung applied to them in open drills. [the plural of *dreel* is *dreel*; compare HORSE in this respect]

dreesh to order around in a peremptory way, used especially of a mother with a number of children. [see DROOSE]

dress 1 = dress. 2 to iron: '*I must go and dress the*

claes'. [also Sc.]

dribbit, drivvit a fall or the blow sustained from such. [Norw dial *dribba* to bump against something]

dribsy see DRAIPSY.

driddle to trail behind. [also Sc; related to DRITTLAN]

dright 1 = draught (of a boat). 2 the path along which a boat is drawn up the beach.

drighty see DRILT.

drill to dawdle. **drilly** dawdling. [see DRAIL]

drilt* 1 to carry something so heavy that one's progress is impeded. 2 to loiter. **drilty** one who comes last. *the drilty load* the last load of sheaves brought into the farmyard. [Norw dial *drilta* to walk slowly]

drim verb to loiter. noun the tail end: *the last drims o the tide*. **drimmy** lacking energy. [related to TRIMSE with the meaning *dangling, end* etc.]

drimp *tae drimp aff tae sleep* to nod off. [ON *drúpa*, to droop]

dringle to trail behind. [Norw *drigla* to loiter]

drink = drink, '*Three drinks o the May flood turns a sillock intae a cuithe*'. [it is possible to catch coalfish after three high tides in May]

drip to collapse. [Norw *dryppe* to drop]

drissie always late. [OE *drusian* to be sluggish]

drit dirt. [ON *drit;* the placename '*Puldrite*' (dirty pool) in Rendall shows this form; see DIRT]

drittlan walking with dragging feet. [also Sh; Norw *dritla*; to '*drittle*' would seem to be a metathesis of '*to drilt*'; in Sc the form is *druttle*]

driv* fine rain, typically a **weet driv***. [ON *drífa* a fall of snow with the essential meaning *spray*]

drive = drive. *tae drive swine/pigs* to snore loudly.

drivel verb. to trail through mud. noun. a lazy, slovenly fellow. [Norw *drivla* to loiter]

drivis force or energy. [related to '*drive*' perhaps through ON *drífa* to drive]

drivvit see DRIBBIT.

drock* *a drock o swaet*, saturated in perspiration. **drockin*** a drenching. **drockit, drookéd, drookled, draigelt**: *like a drookled rat* very wet, drenched. [related to ON *drukna* to be drowned]

drompie lacking animation. [see DRIMMY]

droo, droor a kind of sea-weed (*chorda filum*). [ON *þrádr* thread]

drookéd see DROCK.

droor see DROO.

droose to push, *tae droose off* to frighten off. [Norw dial *drussa* to rush at]

drooth* = drought, also Sc. '*Hid's makkan a lot o drooth*' a drying wind is blowing. **droothy 1*, droothy** noun. a drunkard. adj. addicted to drink.

droothy 2 the devil, only recorded in the phrase *Whitna droothy is this?*' What the devil is this?

27

[an ancient Norse relic in the dialect; the placename *Knowes o Trotty*, Neolithic mounds in the parish of Harray, also preserve this name; compare ON *Þrúðr*, the daughter of Thor, German *Drude*, an evil fairy]

drootsie slow or slovenly. [a variant of DRISSIE]

drop* a let-down: '*Whit a drop he got when his wife left him*'. [also in other Eng dial]

dross 1 = dross. 2 afterbirth of a cow.

drouthy see DROOTH.

drow the devil. [obs Norw drolen; see TROW]

drucken* drunk. [also Sc; ON *drukkinn* past part of drekka to drink]

drugg 1 a drizzle. **druggly** drizzly. [Sh *drogg*; Sc *drow*; origin unknown]

drugg 2 verb. to work laboriously. noun. a drudge [Norw dial *drugga*]

drugger a strong wide boat used for ferrying animals. [? related to DRUGG 2]

drulty tree a bar across the end of a box bed reputed to play a part in intercourse. [also Sh; compare Sh *drult* to move clumsily; *drult* may be a lost verb 'to have intercourse'; compare FOOTER for a similar development of meaning]

drumman a small fat inshore cod. [ON *þrömmungr* a kind of fish, (mentioned only in the *Edda*]

drunt 1 to swear in the sense of using bad language. **druntin** a curse which in very strong language meant, '*Away with you!*' [Druntin = Trondheim, hence the phrase meant '(Go to) Trondheim' but the writer has argued elsewhere that *trond* is a lost word for the 'devil'. 'Trondheim' in this sense would be the equivalent of Old Norse 'Alfheim' or 'Jotunheim'].

drunt 2 to fart. **drunyan** bellowing like a cow. [ON *drynja* to roar]

drush a great number. [Norw dial *drose* a flock, shoal etc]]

dry 1= dry. a **dry biscuit*** a plain biscuit without butter. **dry blows** an exchange of blows which does not draw blood.

dry 2 the natural weaknesses/cracks in flagstones in quarrying [origin unknown]

dud 1 an article of clothing. [OSc *duddis* poor ragged clothes]

dud 2 a gusting wind, especially a **snowy dud*** which heralds the onset of snow. [Sh *dod*; imitat; compare TUD]

dudded, duddled of a cow polled. [ME *doddyd*]

duff lazy, inactive. [Sc *duff* to refrain from exerting oneself]

duffies a name current until the 1960's for the toilets at Stromness Academy. Also recorded (rarely) in Scotland where it takes the alternative form *yuffies*. [? Gael *dabhach* a large vat; Ork DAFFO a small wooden tub; see COGS for parallel development of meaning]

duivo see DAVVO.

dull a boundary stone. [also Sc; Eng dial *dool*; ON *deilis-steinn* boundary stone; ON *deila* to divide]

dumraw† disregard of court (in old documents) [ON *dómrof* disregard of judgement for which a fine was payable; the word was also applied to the fine]

dunder a loud noise. [Norw *dunder* a banging]

dundie see DOONDIE.

dunk* bang or thump, '*Whit a dunk he got*'. [ON *dynkr*]

dunky damp, moist. [Norw dial *dunken* moist, sultry]

dunshie short and squat. [Sc *dunchy*; Gael *duntag* plump]

dunt* verb. to strike. noun. the blow from such a strike. [also Sc; ON *dyntr*]

dunter, dunter-goose 1* the eider duck. 2 the dolphin. [compare Norw *dynta* to move with a bobbing motion]

du-oy great grand child. [Gael *dubh-ogha* a great-grand child; see OY]

dup see DOOP.

durk, deurk of a thing or person, thick in size. [also Sc in a variety of similar forms; Gael *durc* fat person]

dusso-crab a female crab. [Norw dial *dussa* thick, squat woman]

dwam* *in a dwam* in a swoon. [also Sc; OE *dwolma* confusion]

dwang* a cross bearer used in the construction of an interior wall. [ON *þvinga* to constrain]

dwarry back a stunted or deformed animal. [first element is probably ON *dvergr* dwarf + back]

dybal see DABAL.

dyelro see GELDRO.

dyoard see GORD.

dyst 1 a heavy blow 2 the sound of a heavy weight falling [also Sc: OSc *dois*, a violent impact]

dyuivo a depression or hollow in the land. [ON *djupr* deep]

28

E the letter E pronounced as in English.
ear* year. plural **ear** if directly preceded by a numeral e.g. *a hunder ear* but *hunders o ears* . [ON *ár* year]
earsky see LUGSKY.
eatch see EETCH.
ebb 1 1 = ebb. 2 the foreshore*. **ebb maet*** shellfish, mcat from the ebb.
ebb 2 a corner of the house where odds and ends are kept. [a corruption of ON *egg* edge]
eccle grass butter-wort. [Sh *ekel girs*; see AXES]
Eday Men mucus in the corner of the eye. [origin uncertain; ?perhaps *Evie* Men is intended? ON *efja*, mud or ooze; compare Eng *Sandman*]
edgar the grain from which BURSTEEN is made. [Sc *aigar*; see AIKER]
edyan keen. [ON *íðinn* steady or diligent]
ee 1 of ale to ferment. [ON *iða* to move restlessly]
ee 2, ae one, '*Ee day and every day*' every day without fail.
eech, owch the *ch* is pronounced as in Sc *loch*, '*Whit did she say about the coo when yi wir ower?*' '*She never said eech or owch*,' She didn't mention it. [Sc *eechie* or *ochie*]
eek *to eek a bit on* to add a bit on, **eek oot** be sparing with something and make it last longer. [ON *auka*]
eel ale. [OSc eill]
eeld fire. [ON *eldr*]
Eelick a Stronsay goblin. [origin unknown]
eelo an eel. [*o* is a dimin]
een* 1 = one [also Sc]. **eens*** used as a pronoun for things or people, especially, '*eens fae aff*', non-Orcadians resident in Orkney.
een 2 old plural of *eye*; compare SHOE. [OE *eagan*]
eenigar not well, not thriving. [origin unknown]
eens see EEN 2.
eens errant *tae go eens errant* to go specifically for something. [also Sc; a corruption of *aince errand* once errand]
eerie-orms, veery-orms, ornamentation, especially in wood carving. [Sc **fleerie-orms**, Lat *variorum* various; Sh retains the Latin original!]
eerie-oye a great grandson. [also Sc; Gael *iar-ogha*]
eerisen a short prayer. [Eng *orison* prayer]
eeseral, esral useless eg of silly talk, *a lok o eeseral rubbish*. [origin unknown]
eesk* 1 of a door, mouse, new shoes etc to squeak. [imitat; also WEESK]
eesk 2 to drizzle. [compare Sw *åska* thunder, Ice *aska* snowstorm; see ESKE]
eeskyie common sense or decency, '*He didna hiv the eeskyie tae apologise*'. [ON *oeskja* to wish]
eetch, eatch a big smithy-made hoe. [Sc *eetch* = adze; see FITEETCH]
eeteral of an animal, sickly looking. [origin

unknown]
eezer see AIZE.
egg = egg. **eggy money** income from the sale of eggs, **aff ane's eggs** 1 mistaken. 2 nervous, *kept like a egg on a sae-tree* kept very carefully.
eggalourie a dish of eggs and milk boiled together. [see COCKALOURIE]
eggle 1 to incite. 2 of weather to threaten, '*Hid's egglan up in the east*'. [Eng *egg* + *le* suffix]
either drizzle. [see AITRAN]
ek a whiff of some foul-smelling substance. [compare Norw *øgja* to feel squeamish; se AK]
ekk sound, '*I could hear the ekk o their voices*'. [origin unknown]
elded burnt. [see EELD]
elf = elf. **elfbelt** a belt worn in 17th century Orkney as a protection against elves. **elfies** cut-down rubber boots. **elf shot** a flint arrowhead. [from the old belief that it was used by elves]
ellwand see ELT.
else 1 = else. 2 already [also Sc]
elshin an awl. [also Sc; ME *elsyn*]
elt 1 to toil at something, especially to knead dough. 2 to tease. *as dugged as eltit clay* very stubborn. **eltan** wading. [also Sc in a variety of meanings including to become dirty]. **eltit** filthy dirty. [ON *elta* to pursue; to knead dough; Norw *elta*]
ellwand a measuring rod one ell in length. **(The) Lady's Elwand** Orion's Belt. **elwin** a device used by spinners for winding wool. **elwin skud** head over heels, turning over like an ELWIN.
emauded hemmed in. [see IMALDED]
emby indoors. [ON *í bae*, Sc *in-by*; the *n* is changed to *m* by the following *b*; compare *Doomby*, the local pronunciation of *Dounby*]
emly-amly† walking with great difficulty, only in the old nursery rhyme:-
Kent doo hoo
Da dogs gaed tae da mill
Trill trill trill
Ap aboot da clappers
And doon aboot da happars
Da dogs gaed tro da mill
First in dis man's mael pock
And dan in dat man's mael pock
An in da miller's mael pock
An hame again
Emly-amly emly-amly
Fill, fill, fill.
[Norw *amle* to struggle; *emly-amly* is a rhyming duplicate; compare AANIE-ONYOO]
emmer goose* the great northern diver. [also Sc; ON *himbrin;* the word goose is used loosely in local dial; compare DUNTER-GOOSE eider duck]
empy* = empty.
end = end, *tae lay up an end* to think of getting

29

married. **end rigg** that part of a field ploughed last. **end riggs** the dregs.

Englishman 1 = Englishman. 2 a nickname in Westray for the velvet swimming crab. [origin unknown]

engral of animals, greedy. [origin unknown]

ennis a dilapidated house. [Eng *inn-house* probably used pejoratively]

ent, enty see AINT.

enyafoo out of sorts. [see ININYAFOU]

equalman† umpire. [ON *jafnaðar-maðr* fair (impartial) man]

er *'Hid's er o the night yet'* It's early yet. [ON *ár* early]

erd(d)rift drifting snow. [also Sc; see YERTDRIFT]

ere see AIR 1.

erestreen the night before last. [Eng *ere* yester evening]

erif a court. [see ARRF]

erkny see ARKAMY.

erra small. [see UIRRY and related forms]

errans* = 1 errands 2 shopping purchases, *'Ah'll hae tae go tae the toon for twa three errans.'*

erse* verb. to move, *'Erse along a bit min'*. noun. 1 = arse. 2* part of the trousers which covers the bottom, *'He's spret the erse o his breeks'*. 3* bottom of a bucket, bag etc, *'Guid seks the erse is gin oot o me message bag'*. **erse-aboot-face*** back to front. [Eng *arsy-versy*]. **erse ahint*** to be last, *'He's always ersan ahint on the the ferm'*. **erselings*** with the backside first, *'I could only win oot erselings through the window'*. [old suffix *lings*, in the direction of]. **erse-rubber** the last sheaf to be brought into the corn yard. The last person to bring in such a sheaf had his trousers removed and his backside was rubbed with the stubble end! **ersy crab** the crab which walks backwards or *erselings* and buries its head in the sand.

erseland see URISLAND.

ervo see ARVO.

eske 1 light spots of rain before a heavy rainstorm. 2 to exude matter. [probably the same word as EESK 2]

esral see EESERAL.

etherin a rope on a stack, load etc at right angles to the main ropes. [also Sc; Eng dial *edders* willow woven to form the top of a fence]

ettamon punishment, *'Thoo'll get thee ettamon yet beuy'*. [? ON *agi* punishment with Eng suffix]

ettercap a spider. **ettercaps** cobwebs on hedges and in ditches visible on dewy mornings. [OE *atorcoppe* a spider, literally 'poison head'; Eng dial *ettercop* an ill-natured person]

ettercat a troublemaker. [? a corruption of ETTERCAP]

ettle to irk *'Hid's been ettlan him for a while'*. [also Sc with a variety of different meanings; ?English *nettle* with loss of initial *n*]

euchain poor condition. [Sh *eken*; ? a form of AKAMY]

euchen see AITHKEN.

euchie see YEUK.

eum* 1 see UIM

eum* 2 mad, used of animals only and frequently with the word *clean* prefixed, *'The bull gid clean eum'*. [ON *ólmr* wild]

eun* see UIM

Eve the pale mauve orchid. [see ADAM and PULDERY]

every = every, *every noo and again** every now and then.

eye = eye. **Thing wi the wan (one) Eye** an Eday monster who would catch any naughty child [compare the less fearsome TAMMY O TIRLYBRAES] *'She wid be laughan wi wan eye and greetan wi the ither'* she was very emotional.

eyrisland see URISLAND.

ezer see AIZER.

F the letter *f* pronounced as in English.

fa 1 see MOOSEFA.

fa 2 verb. 1* = fall. 2 to obtain, *'A dizzen (dozen) eggs if yi can faa them'*. noun. something obtained [also Sc]

faa the internal organs of a slaughtered animal. [ON *fall* the body of a slaughtered animal]

faaick *brakkan faaick* making ready the ground for sowing bere. [Sc *fauch*; OSc *faulch*; OE *f(e)alh* ploughed land]

faa-ing feet of a woman about to give birth, *'She's just at faa-ing feet'*. [ON *fall* childbirth]

faasan fawning, especially of an animal. [Sc *fause* to flatter; Eng *false*]

faater, fauter a criminal [Eng *defaulter*]

faavaless lazy. [see FAVILLO]

face = face. **face-washing*** a telling-off. **facie*** a small cliff or bank. **facings*** boards round a door or window [also Sc; Eng *architraves*]. **in a face** systematically e.g. *'Tak hid in a face'*, an instruction given to a fellow worker e.g. to take sand from a pit in a systematic manner.

fae* 1 from. 2 since, *'He's been coman here fae he wis a boy'*, *'There comes he fae'* a Westray idiom

'That's typical of that family'. **fae the hoose**, '*Ah'm gan fae the hoose*' I'm going away.
faer fear. **fur faer** out of fear, '*He widna deu hid fur faer o hurtan himsel.*' **faerd*** afraid. **faerd for himsel/hersel** someone persistently concerned about health. **faerdy** a taunt to a coward [also Sc and Eng dial; Eng *feared* obs. afraid]
facy doomed to die. **fai-a-fa me†** an expression of surprise and annoyance. [ON *feigŏ* forboding of death; compare STOON ME]
fag of a boat to drift. [ON *vakka* to stray]
faid to frown. [also Sh; origin unknown]
fail* a turf or sod. **faily-dyke*** a wall made from turf. [the name commonly applied to the tunship wall]. **faily-fight** an old game among boys in which they kicked turfs up with their boots and threw them at an opponent. [in ON times a similar sport called *torfleikr*, turf play, existed; Gael *fál.*]
fain to be fond of. **fainfu** fond or affectionate. [Eng *fain* in its archaic sense; compare ON *fagna* to rejoice]
fair 1 = fair. 2* good, '*He got a fair price for his kye*'. **fair tae middling*** slightly above average. **fair faa thee buddo** a greeting. [also Sc *fair (luck) befall you*]. **fairly** = 1 fairly. 2* entirely, '*Thee tyres are fairly done*'. 3* quite, *fairly fairly* quite so. 4* really, used as an adverb of emphasis, '*He can fairly run*'.
fairing as the carriages returned from the Lammas Market before the 1st World War, country chidren who had been unable to go to the market would wait by the roadside and call '*Fairing!*' and if they were lucky they might have been thrown some sweets. [also Sc *what has been obtained at a fair*]
fairnteckle* a freckle. [also throughout Sc and Eng dial; the original meaning of this word is *fern seed*; freckles supposedly resembling them]
fair-weather a taboo term for thunder [Icel *fárveŏr* gale]
fall = fall. '*Hid fell afore me*', it suddenly came into my mind
fand 1 see FANG 2.
fand 2 see FIND.
fang verb. 1 to catch or capture. noun. anything of value found which the finder might appropriate. 2 a half-hitch on a rope. When tethering horned cattle it was customary to put a loop round the horns and a fang on one ear to prevent it pulling the stake. [*fang* here is used in the sense *hold*; compare Sc *fank* a noose which appears as *phang* in Shakespeare; ON *fanga* to capture]
fangs to search for food. [a deriv of FANG]
fann* verb. 1 of powdery snow to blow around. 2 of the aurora to dance around (a metaphorical use).

noun. a snowdrift. [ON *fann* snowdrift; ON *fenna* to cover with snow]
fanty an oath. [see FEENTY]
far* = far. *far awey wi hid** used of someone in his/her dotage.
farder* = farther.
fargis, pargis a confused heap, especially of clothes etc. [essential meaning is a *mess*; ON *verga* to soil + GIS]
farly, ferly a novelty. [Sc *ferly* a wonder; ON *ferligr* monstrous, dreadful]
fart = fart. *fartan fill* absolutely stuffed with food.
fas, faze flattery. **fasit** flattered. [Sc *fause*; Eng *false*]
fash to trouble. **fashious** fastidious, '*She is so fashious to work wi I canna manage tae playse her*'. [also Sc; OF *fascher* to annoy]
Fastern's Een† Shrove Tuesday. [also Sc; a corruption of *Fastens Evening*; *fastens* the genitive of OE *faestenes* fast]
fatifu 1 = faithful. 2 affectionate.
fauld 1 1 = fold. 2 a strand of rope.
fauld 2 1 = fold (an enclosure). 2 the milking of cows.
favillo a lazy person. [ON *fífill* fool]
favour = favour. **for any favour!*** for goodness sake!
fay-nits, fay-nix truce in children's games. [Fr *faineance*, i.e. *faire* (to do) + *neant* nothing]
faze see FAS.
feck 1 to pay attention to, '*A hairst sky's no tae feck*' a harvest sky looks worse than it is. [ON *vaegja* to yield, to comply with]
feck 2 a long line used for fishing. [related to Eng *fake* a coil of rope; Sc *fake* to fold]
feckie a kittiwake. [ON *vöku-skarfr* the kittiwake]
fee = fee. **feeing market** traditionally the first Mondays in May and November. These were the only holidays for farm workers to give them an opportunity to change jobs. If a worker had not been asked to stay by the time of the *feeing market* it was an indication that his services were no longer required.
feeblo scentless mayweed. [ON *fífl* a dandelion]
feedy an oath. [a form of FEENTY]
feefle see FUFFLE.
feefly foolishly clumsy. [see FEEFLE above]
fee-fue to procrastinate or dawdle. [see FIG]
feefy see FUFFLE.
feak a whim or fancy [= Eng *fake*]
feel = feel. *to feel a duck* to examine by touch whether or not a duck is about to lay an egg.
feeman pouring out, of blood etc., '*The blood wis just feeman oot o the gash on his airm*'. [Eng *foaming*]
feenk, feich a stink. [ON *fnykr*]
feenty*, fanty, feedy relating to the devil. **feenty-bit*, feenty-thing*** nothing or not at all. [ON *fjánde* enemy; Eng *fiend*; compare Eng *devil-a-*

31

bit]
feering* the furrow drawn out to mark the *rigs* before ploughing. [OE *fyrian* to make a furrow]
fisk to bungle or fail through lack of skill [origin unknown]
feesk to smoulder. **feesowy** drizzling. [Norw *fisa* to float in the air like smoke or to go up in smoke]
feesked* of food, rotten (eg cheese). [Icel *feyskinn* rotten]
feester to drift through the air like smoke. *Festie Geo* on the Black Craig, Stromness is so called because of the spume which rises from here. [see FEESK]
feet 1 = feet. [see also FIT]. 2 a foot. [the singular form is not used in Orkney; a visitor to the islands who was told that her host had sprained his *feet* remarked that she had never heard of anyone spraining both feet at once!]. 3 a footstep [also Sc] '*Ah'm no gaan wan feet*'. 4 socks, '*I think Ah'll change me feet*'. **feetoes** old stockings used as slippers. **feetstep** = footstep. **feetick** a padding of straw in a boot. **feetspur** footrest in a rowing boat. [ON *sperra* a spar]
feeyeo a fissure or crack. [origin unknown]
fegs* faith, '*Weel, fegs Ah'll hae tae go*'. [also Sc; a contracted form of Eng *faithkins*]
feich see FEENK.
feint 1 a triangular piece of cloth in women's clothing. 2 the three cornered part left over when ploughing a field which isn't square. [OF *fente* split]
feird, ferd old form of *fourth*. [ON *fjórdi*]
felkyo the name of a witch who used to live in the Hillside district of Birsay. **felkyied** tired looking (the sense is *bewitched*; compare TROWIE). [ON *fjölkyngis-kona* witch]
fell 1 = to fell. 2 to stun.
feltry see FYOLTRY.
fence = fence. **fence a court†** to open a public assembly. Originally it probably meant *to mark off the area in which the assembly was held*, the area in question becoming temporarily sanctified. **fence the tables** to prepare for communion in the church.
fend to provide. **fendan*** of a hen searching for food. [a form of Eng *defend*]
fendless weak. [also Sc; obs Eng *fend* to defend + *less*]
fer = far. *fer oot aboot* remote, out-of-the-way.
ferd see FEIRD.
ferfil* very, especially *ferfil fine*. [Eng *fearful* used in the same odd way as Eng *awfully*]
ferky to jerk. [ME *ferk* to whip or beat; OE *fercian* to proceed]
ferly a fanciful notion. [see FARLY]
ferokerly† for the most part. [origin unknown]

ferry = ferry. **ferry-louper*** someone who is not a native of Orkney, someone who arrives by ferry [see LOOP]. **ferryman** the Patagonian daisy (Westray). [origin unknown]
ferty agitated or excited. [see FERKY]
fesgar, fesgal 1 the reinforcing band round the top of a CUBBY. '*He hid a fesgar o hair aboot the face o him*' he had a full grown beard. **in a fesgar** of a scarf, in a twist. [compare Sc *fas* knot; related to WAZZIE; ON *gyrða* to gird with a belt; see also BRAITHIN]
fest 1 = fast (firm). 2 to tether, '*Fest the sholt fornent the hoose*,' tether the pony in front of the house.
festan 1 = fasting. 2* starving hungry.
feth* 1 = faith. 2 indeed, '*Faith Ah'll baet (beat) him yet*'.
fettle the strap of a caisie. [ON *fetill* a strap; also Sc]
feuls flocks of gulls feeding at sea and indicating good fishing. [ON *fugl* bird]
feuly* foolish, *a feuly thing o boy*. [a form of Eng *foolish*]
feutries see FROOTERY.
fey 1 uncannily knowing before hand. [OE *faēge* doomed].
fey 2 unchanged (eg in personality). '*As for Robbie, he's just fey*' [origin uncertain]
Fiars Prices† the price of grain fixed yearly in the Sheriff Court. It was in this way that SKAT values were converted to cash. [also Sc; OF *feur* fixed price; from Lat *forum* market]
fickle 1 = fickle. 2 difficult [also Sc]
fiddle 1 = fiddle. 2 in rope making a kind of comb to keep the strands separate. [? from its resemblance to a fiddle bridge]. 3 a hand-machine for sowing grain [from its resemblance to a fiddle].
fidge see FITCH.
fidro a child's game. [perhaps related to Norw *fidra* to rush around or to play]
fierdy in good condition. [Sc ferdy; ON *ferðugr* ready; Ger *fertig*]
fig to fig and feu to rush around doing trifling jobs. **figgerin** a snowflake. [ON *fjúka* to be blown by the wind; ON *fjúk-renningr* drifting snow]
fikie painfully particular about details. [a curtailed form of Eng *finicky*]
fill* 1 = fill. 2 full, '*Mak sure the bucket's fill*'. **filler*** a funnel for filling oil lamps etc.
filloo, fulloo* = fellow.
filty = filthy. **Filty Man** the devil.
fimister see FIMMIS.
fimlar crab a kind of crab. [see FIMRO below for posssible explanation]
fimmis a state of excitement. **fimister** excitement through fear. [ON *fimr* agile]
fimro the velvet swimming crab. a fast moving crab. [ON *fimr* quick]

find past tense FAND. perf tense FUND. = find.

fine = fine (end). *tae come tae fine* to make a final decision.

fineer = veneer.

Fin-men, Finfolk legendary characters from Orkney folklore. **Finfolkaheem** the winter home of the Fin-folk. [ON *Finnar* the Finns]

finnigal the angler fish. [Eng *fin*; for *gal* see BERGAL]

finolickies adornments. [metathesis of Eng *finical* fussy; Sc *finicky* intricate]

fintan 1 of a dog sniffing about. 2 trying in an underhand way to get information. [Eng *feint* to make a deceptive movement]

fintow a short piece of rope with an eye spliced on one end made fast to the lobster creel and attached to the buoy rope. [ON *taug* rope; the first element may be a form of FANG]

fircer to get a boat ready for the sea. [origin uncertain]

fire = fire. **fire hoose†** the main living room in the old Orkney house, later called the BUT-END [a direct translation of ON *eld-hús*]. **fire stane** a hearth stone.

fire* to throw, '*Fire yir byke on the cairt and Ah'll gae ye a lift*'. '*I widna trust him as far as I wid fire him*' I wouldn't trust him at all. [ON *fyrir* to throw]

firned in bad condition through age, '*The vaporiser o me Tilley lamp wis aal firned ap*'. [see FURN]

firry angry, furious. [Sc *firr* a state of agitation; compare Eng *whirr*]

fish = fish. '*He's a fish that's lain too long aboot the shore tae be catched*' he's a confirmed bachelor. **fish matlo** see MATLO. **fish meeag** see MEEAG. **fisho** the blenny, a small fish found at the shore. **fishy bee*** the gad fly or blue bottle. [*bee* is commonly used for *large fly* in Orkney]

fiss 1 a call to a cat when it is where it shouldn't be!. [more commonly KIS]

fiss 2 drizzle. [see FEESK]

fissies chilblains. [origin doubtful unless it be related to Sc *fease* an annoyance or inconvenience]

fist attempt. [also Sh where it is a variant of *frist*; ON *freista* to attempt]

fit = foot. '*Fits thee*' move out of my way. **tae tak (one's) fit in (one's) hand** start off, take one's leave. **fitago-mash** another name for the game of FITKALEERIE. **fitband** a rope by which two sheep were tied together by their near front legs to control their movements. **fitkaleerie, fitakaleerie** a dance performed in a sitting position with an ale cog in the hand. [Sc *leerie* suffix; see COCKALOURIE]. **fitlan** walking with a very short step. **fitless cock** when making giblet soup, after stuffing the neck and other

skins with beremeal, blood, pepper, salt etc, the remains of the stuffing was made into a dumpling, and boiled in the soup. This dumpling was a *fitless cock*, footless cock. **fit-trees** treadles. *foot-boards*. [*tree* is used here in the sense of board, beam etc; see SWINGLE-TREE].

fitwazzy a footstool. [ON *vasi* a sheaf; the stool was made of twisted straw; Sc *fassag*]

fitch move slightly or restlessly, edge along. [a form of FIDGE]

fiteetch*, fiteitch 1 a carpenter's adze. 2 a hook for TAILING turnips (East Mainland). [see EETCH; Sc *fit* foot, the long handled adze being held in position by the foot]

fittock the foot of an old stocking cut off and worn as a shoe or as an extra sock or drawn over a boot. [see FEETOES]

fitty-gomash a method of warming the feet; two people stood face to face gripping each other's shoulders and striking first one foot and then the other against the opposite foot of the partner in a sort of dance [compare FITKALEERIE]

flaa 1 verb. to tell a lie. noun. a lie. **flawan** telling lies. [Sc *fleg* a lie]

flaa 2† a strip of grass. [also Sc in the form flaw; ON *flá* strips of meadowland]

flachter, flauchter *flachter spade* a spade for cutting turf. [related to ON *fletta* to flay; see FLEETER]

flackie a woven straw mat. [ON *fletta* to braid or plait]. **tae baet flackie** [see FLEUKS]

fladgan walking in a clumsy manner. [compare Sc *flodge*; imitat]

flae*, flay = flea.

flagan a piece of thin flaky worthless material [Norw *flagna* to flake off]

flaighter to shoo away. [also Sc; see FLEG]

flail = flail. **flail-huid** literally flail *hood*. The piece of leather joining the two parts of a flail.

flam a great state of excitement. [compare ON *flaumósi* rushing heedlessly on and ON *flan* a rushing]

flamp limp or exhausted. [compare Eng dial *flimp* limp]

flan* verb. to gust, '*The wind's in a bad airt, hid's flanan doon the lum*'. noun. a gust. [ON *flan* a rushing]

flanning flannel. **flannings** flannel trousers. [also in Eng dial]

flap* 1 = flap. 2 trouser fly.

flash the name given to shallow dew ponds common in Orkney until the early part of this century when an earth tremor cracked the clay seals. [ME *flasshe*]

flat 1 = flat. 2 the skate (fish). 3 a side plate (Westray) [also Sc] **flattie*** a small flat bottomed boat.

33

flatch verb. to flatten. adj. anything large and flat. [a form of Eng *flat*]

flauchter see FLACHTER.

flawan see FLAA.

flay* 1 1 = flay. 2 to trim the turf off the top of a peat bank. *tae flay a bank.* **flaymeur** turf removed from a peat bank. **flay-the-cat** an old sport in which a boy would grab the *twart-backs*, swing his feet up and through his arms, then drop to the ground.

flay 2 see FLAE.

fleckit* applied to an animal with a coat of different colours. [ON *flekkóttr*]

fled see FLEE.

flee* past tense FLED. verb. to fly, '*Hid's weeng wis broken, hid just couldna flee.*' '*I fled tae Aberdeen and than I tuk the train*'. noun. a fly.

fleemister a state of excitement. [ON *felmta* to be in a state of fright or alarm]

fleenk 1 to take on a strong flavour, '*The butter's fleenkéd*'. [the essential meaning is *to turn*; ? related to Eng *flinch*]

fleenk 2, flink verb. to kick the heels up in the air like a young lamb. noun. *tae hiv a fleenk* to carry oneself in a dignified, almost supercilious manner. [a form of Eng *fling*]

fleep* verb. to turn a garment etc. inside out (a Rousay minister who admitted that his wife was not very pretty stressed that she was beautiful inside. This drew the reply 'Thoo'll hae tae fleep her.'!) noun. 1 an anxious state (a turning inside out). [Sc *flipe*]. 2 a loose flap of something, especially skin or cloth. 3 a good-for-nothing or a coward. Sc *floop*]. 4 a light slap. 5 an anxious state. *fleepsy* stupid. *fleepy* clumsy. [compare Norw *flipe*, Eng *flip*, *flap*]

fleerie-orms a form of EERIEORMS used in South Ronaldsay.

fleero of material etc light or unsubstantial. [Sc *flird*]

fleest an explosion. [see BLEESTER and BLEUSK for related forms]

fleester 1 a slight shower. **fleestery** as in *fleestry cloods* light rain clouds. [Sc *flistin*; OSc *flist* a puff]

fleester 2 verb. to strip off something eg thatch from a roof. noun. a rag, especially a rag hanging from someone's clothing. [ON *flysja* to split]

fleet a piece of a large fish cut into the shape of a smaller and used as bait. [? related to FLEETER]

fleeter* 1 something flapping or dangling, *a great fleeter o skin came off his hand.* 2 *a fleeter o land* an extent of land. **fleetery** hanging in rags. [ON *fletta* to flay]

fleg* verb. to frighten. noun. a fright. [also Sc; OE *flecgan* to put to flight]

flep an unpleasant individual. [see FLEEP]

flesh† butcher meat. **flesh payment** payment by giving one's labour to a creditor. [OSc *flesch*]

flet 1 see FLYTE.

flet 2 a straw mat. [ON *fletta* to braid, plait]

fleuk, fluik 1 a flounder. 2 a large sticky snowflake. 3 a nickname for Flotta people. [see also BAET FLEUKS]. '*Hid wis a fleuk's head*' it came to nothing. [OE *floc*]

fleuks see FLUIKS.

fleunk a useless individual, '*Whit's that muckle fleunk o a boy lyan home aboot for?*'. [the essential meaning is bending; related to Eng *flinch*]

fleuter *tae fall in a fleuter*, to collapse. [also Sc *flutter*]

fligest a scarecrow (Rousay). [see FLYGEIST]

flightan '*Hid's no use flightan wi me*' its no use being angry with me. [OE *flītan* to argue]

flinderkin, flinderskin see FLINTERKIN.

flink see FLEENK 2.

flinterkin, flinderskin noun. 1 a very dry cow pat. 2 a light smow shower (also **flinterkins**). adj. of a garment thin and shoddy. **flinderkin** a weak person or thing. [also Sc; related to Du *flenter* rag; Norw dial *flindra* a splinter]

flipper = flipper. verb. to walk in such a way that the hands are moving independently like flippers, *a flipperan wey o walkan.*

flirrup the sound made by thick cream being poured from a jug. [imitat]

flit* 1 to move house. 2* to move a tethered animal, '*Ah'll hae tae go and flit the coo I doot*'. **flitting stane** a large stone used to hammer in the stake by which an animal was tethered. **flitting terms** in olden days refers to 20th May and 28th November when people who were under contract to a farm could move house. [also Sc; ON *flytja* to carry and ON *flytjandi* moveables]

flitterchack the ring ouzel. [the element *chack* is probably related to CHACKIE + Eng *flitter*]

flitting and furing† in old leasehold agreements. [ON *flytja* to convey and ON *foera* to convey; the combined phrase meaning *to transport household goods*]

flix verb. to frighten. noun. a state of excitement. **flixed** 1 nervous. 2 frightened. [a metathesis of Sc *flisk* quick movement; compare GLUFF]

floo, flood the core of an animal's horn. [a corruption of SLOO; the form *flood* may be related to ON *sludda* a clot of mucus]

flooer *tae flooer the cargo*, to finish off a meal with something special [the metaphor is not understood]

flooster = fluster, hustle, bustle.

floosy smooth or shining [? *flashy*]

flooty a straw mat. [compare Icel *flatta* a layer of straw]

floss 1 chaff or husks. 2 the common rush. **flossbands** cord made from rushes, used in strawwork. [ON *flysja* to split; chaff splits from the grain whereas the rush was split and used as lamp wicks]

flourish 1 = flourish. 2 embroider.

flowins butter refuse left on top of the KIRNMILK after the bulk of the butter has been removed. [Eng *flow*]

flucht a fluttering, flapping (of birds wings etc). [OSc *flocht* a flutter]

fluik see FLEUK.

fluiks* *tae beat fluiks/flackie* to warm one's hands by swinging them towards, then past, each other and striking the upper arm or chest of the other side of the body [to beat the arms in the manner which a FLEUK (flounder) propels itself; dial FLACKIE is a mat which is confused with FLUIK in this expression; to BAET SKARFS is also used for this beating action; the SKARF can often be seen beating its wings to dry them since, unlike most diving birds, its feathers are not well protected by natural oils]

flure-bands the bands that secure the bottom boards of a boat to the keel [*floor* + *bands*]

fly 1 = to fly. 2 the front part of a *mutch*. [compare Sc *flee-cap*]. 3 sly, a *fly-cup* a cup of tea etc between meals. [related to Eng *fly* shrewd]. *flyan storm* a real gale.

flygeist, fligest scarecrow. [Sc *fley* frighten + Sc *gest* ghost]

flyte to scold. past tense FLET. [OSc *flyte* to scold; OE *flitan* to contend]

foal, fole a small bannock baked with the last of the dough and given to a child. [Sc *bonnach faaly*; Gael *fallaid* dry meal put on cakes]

foard to improve in condition. **foardin** feeding, '*Gae the coo a foardin min*'. [Sc *forder*; OSc *forther* further]

fodal see FORDAL

foeless careless [origin uncertain]

foggage grass growing after the first hay. [OSc *fogage* winter grazing]

foggy* mossy or spongy eg of a poor quality peat or a frosted turnip. [OSc *fog* moss]

fola-fot† a taboo term for an oar used on the port side of a boat. [ON *fola-fótr* foal foot; compare HORSE LEG BEEN]

fold see FOUD.

fole see FOAL.

follow* accompany, '*Ah'll follow thee home wi a torch*'. [also Sc; compare ON *fylgja* to accompany]

fonyaless lacking any spirit, limp. [ON *afföngum* to the best of one's power]

fool-fleg a scarecrow. [ON *fugl* bird; see FLEG]

fooshonless* useless, especially of material. A lady who found that her curtains had rotted where they were exposed to the sunlight said '*That's just fooshonless stuff*'. [also Sc *funceless*; OSc *foysoune* plenty; OF *fu(i)son* an outpouring]

foosk scaly dandruff material in horse's hair. [also known as SET; Norw *fusk* scaly material]

foosty*, fousty musty. [also Sc; obs Eng *fust* mustiness; OF *fust* a wine cask]

footer* verb. 1 to work clumsily. 2 to impede or hinder. noun. a clumsy person. **footered*** confounded. [also Sc; OF *foutre* to have intercourse]

footh, fouth a quantity. [Sc *fouth* full; the word has collected a *th* suffix as eg in *breadth*]

footho a cuttle fish. [ON *fuð* female genitalia; the significance of the name is uncertain; see FUDDY]

for*, fur = for. 1 '*Why for no ?*'* Why not? '*Whitna for a man's that?*'* What man is that? 2 used to express intention or direction, '*I gid in for tae see him*'. '*The cat's for in, will I let her?*'* '*He wis for gaean me a took oot o his bottle bit I wisna for hivin that*'*. **for whitna** see WHITNA FORA. **for why** = why, '*That'll no work and Ah'll tell yi for why.*'

forbuth† front shop. [Eng *fore* + *booth*]

forbye* 1 besides. 2 than '*Hid's better forbye the owld wan*'. [also Sc and Eng dial; found in Spenserian Eng in the form *foreby* besides]

forcharved of an animal, ailing. [ON *fordjarfað* disgraced; Norw *fordervad* sick]

forcop† a tax. [ON *fararkaup*]

fordal, fodal verb. 1 to hold back in reserve. 2 to hinder. noun. an extra, '*He hid a horse and a fordal wan*'. [OSc *fordell*; ME *fordele* advantage]

fordo to get a move on. [see FOARD]

fore* = fore. **tae the fore** alive and well, '*Oh yaas his brither's still tae the fore*'. **forebreist** the front (seat) of a cart. **foregill** part of the beam of the old Orkney plough. [compare Norw dial *kjøl* keel and bottom part of a plough]. **forenent*, forenenst** opposite. [also Sc; an abbrev form of Sc *foreanent*]. **forenoon*** before midday [also Sc]. **foresuit** the space in the bow of a boat. [*suit* is a corruption of ON *skutr* literally a projection but recorded only as the *stern* of a ship]. **forgen** opposite or in front of. **formak†** preparations for an event. **forsal** 1 to saddle and harness. 2 to spread butter, dung etc. [? *fore* + ON *seli* harness]

forespoken see FORSPOKEN.

forestem the prow. [OSc *fo(i)rstam*]

forestoop the front leg of a chair [OSc *stoup*, post]

forfochten, forfochen exhausted. [also Sc; ME *forfoughten*]

35

forkie-tail* an earwig. [found throughout Eng dial]

forlegen exhausted. [also Sh; compare Norw *forlegen* perplexed]

forrow see FORROWHAND.

forrow dyke a generic name in the North Isles for a boundary wall which runs down to the low water mark. [see FURVO]

forrowhand, forrow in reserve and ready for use. [ON *fyrir höndum*; *fyrir* on its own as an adverb in ON, can mean *at hand*; the addition of *hand* is a mere reduplication]

fors, furs see FURS.

forskal a porch. [ON *forskáli*]

forskin, furskin a protective wall built in front of a house. [Icel *forskygni* shelter]

forspoken, forespoken bewitched. [also Sc to *forspeak* to bewitch; *for* (against) + *speak*]

forstaa to understand. [also Sc; ON *forstanda*]

forswifted to be in a great hurry. [OSc *forswiftid* swept away]

fortam 1 a piece of fishing line. 2 a mooring line. [Norw dial *fortaum* the snood of a fishing line]

fortig = fatigue

fortune = fortune. **fortune bone** a wish bone.

forty-feeter centipede [also Sc]

fother = fodder, food for cattle and horses.

foud a sheriff. [Norw *foguti* an early Norse borrowing from Lat *vocatus*; literally *called*; also Sc; Faroese *futi* sheriff]

found* foundation of a building [also Sc]. **founding pint** a good luck drink given to workmen after laying the foundation of a building.

founeral letter† an invitation by letter to a funeral.

foure-areyn† a four-oared boat. [also Sc; ON *feraeringr*]

fousty* see FOOSTY.

fousum nauseating. [also Sc; OSc *fulsume* offensive, loathsome]

fouth see FOOTH.

foy a party or other entertainment originally to wish one success on a journey. **Johnsmas Foy** a short programme of readings, folk music etc presented at the time of the St Magnus Festival, a revived use of the word. [OF *voie*; Lat *via* a journey]

fozie* spongy, as for example a turnip which has been exposed to hard frost. [also Sc; compare Norw *fos*; Du *voos*]

fraets superstitious observances [related to FROOTERY]

frag a bargain, prize or treasure. [also Sh; origin uncertain]

frame 1 = frame. 2 a square or hoop of wood hung from the shoulders on which to carry pails.

frankle *in a frankle* of a rope twisted. [Sc *frample* of uncertain origin]

frapp* mixed up like a coil of rope. [related to Sc *frample*]

frassie a hermaphrodite, animal or human (Westray). [compare Sc *faizart* used of a hen or a man; origin obscure]

frathinfurth† [a corruption of *from thence forth*]

freck* a pampered child, '*Don't bother wi him he's just a freck*'. **freckéd** of a child, spoiled *a freckéd thing o bairn*. [also Sc; Eng *freak*]

freesk a *pretended smile*. **freesky-faced** having a laughing face. [origin uncertain]

freevalous 1 = frivalous. 2 delicate, sickly, weak

freight = freight. *a freight o watter* two pails of water carried together.

frem, frend 1 strange. [also Sc; compare Sh *da fremd* outsiders]. 2 estranged, '*He's frem fae the sea noo*', He doesn't go sea fishing any longer. [OE *fremde* foreign; compare Norw dial *fremmende* strange]

fren wild, used of the sea or the wind. [Sc *frenn* to rage]

frend see FREM.

freutery see FROOTERY.

Friars prices a corruption of FIARS PRICES.

frim-frass when a parent was making anything new and the daughter enquired what it was, the reply would be, '*A frim-frass tae tie on the tail (tae stick up the erse) o a speeran lass*'. [see FRIM-FROY; Sc *frim-fram* trifle]

frim-froy a reply given to an inquisitive boy. [see FRIM-FRASS]

frock a sailor's or fisherman's knitted jersey.

frootery, freutery, feutries superstition. [ON *fróðr* knowing or learned; compare ON *fróð-leikr* magic or witch-craft]

frost = frost. **frosty pillar** an icicle (Westray).

frothe a new born child. [origin doubtful; compare Norw *fro* fish fry]

frugal plentiful. [also Aberdeenshire; a strange inversion of meaning of Eng *frugal* sparing]

frugsy untidy. [? a form of FUIGSY]

frush easily broken. [also Sc; OSc *frusch* to break in pieces; OF *fruis(sier)*]

frutt a superstitious notion [see FROOTERY]

fry 1 = fry. 2* a small quantity of fish sufficient to fry in a pan, '*There's a fry tae thee fur thee dinner*'.

fudds feet. [compare Sh *fudin* tabu word for a cat from ON *fótr* foot]

fuddy of a person or a bannock thick and dumpy. [compare Sc *fud* tail of an animal]

fudsho meadow vetch. [Sc and Eng dial *fitch* and *fetch*; Lat *vicia*]

fuff 1 a puff of smoke. 2 a small explosion. 3 a short involuntary laugh. **strae-fuff** a wisp of straw. [imitat; compare Eng *puff*]

fuffle, feefle to work clumsily. **feefy** foolishly

frample]

clumsy. [also Sc; OSc *fuffil* to handle roughly]

fuggis a choking smoky atmosphere. [compare Eng *fug*]

fuggsie see FYAKSY.

fuglin a bird, especially a seagull. [ON *fugl* bird; suffix uncertain unless it is the definite article - *inn*]

fuiany poor quality seaweed. [ON *fuínn* rotten]

fuichle *tae fuichle aboot* to walk as if infirm. [related to Norw dial *fukla* to shuffle]

fuigsy see FYAKSY.

fuilteran to drag (eg of a skirt near the floor). [see FYOLTRY]

fuirce of an animal etc difficult to restrain. [related to Norw *fors*]

fulloo see FILLOO.

fumice excitement. [see FIMMIS]

fun 1 fun. 2* a joke, '*Hid wis a right fun on him*'.

funceless weak. [Cai *funseless* without savour or substance; a form of FONYALESS]

funder 1 = founder. 2 of an animal to drop dead.

funk, funkis thick smoke. [also Sc; OF *funkier* to raise smoke; Lat *fumicare*]

funko *as fast as funko* very fast. [Sc *like funkie* violently; ME *funk* a spark]

fur 1* = for. [see FOR]

fur 2 the deep trench which separated one rig from the other in the old system of land tenure. **furscam** the second horse on the right when four horses were used abreast in ploughing. [ON *skammr* short, relating to the length of the yoke; ON *for* ditch, OE *furh* furrow]

furkan melting the oil out of fish liver. [ON *farga* to squeeze; liver oil originally being squeezed out]

furkin willing. [also Sh; ON *forkunni* eager]

furn to form mould as in the inside of a badly washed churn. [ON *forn* old or rotten; compare FIRN]

furrow a cow which is not in calf. [also Sc; OSc *ferrow*; MDu *varwe-kowe* a cow past bearing]

furs, fors† 1 a waterfall. 2 a dam. There is a trout trap on the burn near the farm of Tormiston at Stenness and many years ago when an old man

was asked how the trap worked he replied, '*We made a bit a furs in the burn and the troots cam doon through the trootie house....*'. [ON *fors* a waterfall]

fursaclue an old form of trap for trout made of the stalks of the dock plant. [ON *fors* a waterfall; the second element is ON *klofi* literally a cleft but also a trap eg *verða í klofanum* to be caught in a trap; see FURS above]

furscam see FUR 2.

furskin see FORSKIN.

furskyo a protective porch built in front of a door. [ON *skjáli* a hut; *for* is found in ON *for-dyri* porch]

furthy forward in manner. [OSc *forthy* foreward]

furtiver* '*Hid'll no work furtiver*' no matter how it's done. [Eng *for whatever*]. **furtiverways*** a corruption of *for whatever ways* i.e. 'at any rate', sometimes heard in the form **furtiverways or no**, '*Furtiverways or no me mither pat on the pot*'.

furto chopped up limpet bait thrown on the sea to attract coal fish etc. [origin uncertain]

furvo, forrow dyke a boundary wall running down to the low water mark (North Ronaldsay). [ON *forve* beach]

fushenfu strong or powerful. [see FOOSHONLESS]

fusome stupid. [? OSc *fulsume* offensive, loathsome]

fussy-punds a kind of grass, *Yorkshire fog*. [ON *pundr* a kind of grass; fussy is Eng *fuzzy* a description of the head]

fuzebla excitement. [ON *fysan* to hurry; *bla* may be a metathesis of Sc *ball* bustle]

fyafly of a person or animal weak. [see FEEFLY]

fyaksy, fuggsie, fuigsy careless in appearance or work. [related to Norw *fjask* a wretch]

fyffly 1 supple 2 weak in movement [see FEEFLY]

fykan picking at one's food. [related Sc form; ON *fíkjast* to be restless]

fyoag cheery, *a fyoag o a laugh*. [Norw *fjaag*]

fyoltry, feltry 1 tattered. 2 unsteady or tottering like a poorly built peatstack. [Far *pjöltur*, rag, hence dangling, hence unsteady; see PELTER]

G the letter *g* when soft is pronounced *chee* and cannot be distinguished from words beginning with a natural *ch* sound or from words beginning with *j*, hence *cheap German jam* in dialect is *chaep Cherman cham*. *G* may also be pronounced *d* as in *deo* = geo or *y* as in *mudyard* = mudguard.

ga 1 = gall. 2 gall bladder, '*Everybody his a ga bit a stebmither his twa*' (but a step-mother has two) - an old saying!

gaa* a mock sun or the stump of a rainbow. [Eng *weather-gall*; ON *gýll* sun-dog; Sc *gow*]

gaad see GID-GAD.

gaadie a shadow picture on a wall made by hands and fingers. [compare Eng dial *gaud* a trick or a plaything; Lat *gaudere* to be glad]

gaa knot a tight knot. [related to ON *gall-harðr* very hard]

gaalo a kittiwake. [imitat; ON *gala* to scream]

gaamans appearance or sign, *That's no a great gaamans*. [origin unknown]

gaathoo 1 a gully in the landscape. 2 a deep cut eg in the finger. [origin uncertain; possibly a corruption of an unrecorded form *gaavoo* hence related to DYUIVO]

gab*, gob verb. to gossip or talk. noun. mouth. *gab tae the heels* very talkative. [also Sc; origin uncertain; compare ME *gabben* to chatter]

gabloo*, gavlo a crawling insect, specifically a largish black beetle. [Sc *gavelock* earwig; Gael *gobhlach* an earwig; Gael *gobhlach* forked; a reference to the tail of the earwig; see FORKIE-TAIL]

gad see GID-GAD.

gadge = gouge.

gae 1* past tense GID. perf tense GIN/GEEN. 1 = give. 2 feed, *gae the kye, hens, cats* etc. [Sc *gie* = give; compare ON *gefa göltum* to feed the pigs]

gae 2* see GO.

gae back see GO.

gaenaboot see GO.

gaether 1 = gather. 2 rake, *gaether the fire* rake the fire.

gaff a laugh. [also Sc; OSc *gawf(e)* a guffaw]

gafs, gavse verb. to eat hungrily. noun. a deep bite in an apple etc. [Norw dial *gafsa*]

gafter see GLAFTER.

gagg verb. to make a mess. noun. a mess. **gaggie** muddy. [see GAGGLE below]

gaggle* verb. 1 to make a mess. 2 to work clumsily and carelessly. noun. careless work. [ON *gogli* mud or ooze]

gaikly see GECKLY.

gaip to gut fish, especially herrings or sillocks. **gibbéd** gutted. [Eng dial *gip* or *gib*; Norw dial *gipa* to make an opening]

gaipy hairbrained or foolish. [Norw dial *gap* a fool]

gair to compel. [Sc *gar*; ON *gera* to make, do]

gaivaless, gevelous 1 awkward at work. 2 drawling in speech. [ON *geifla* to mumble]

galeyway jumping around or frivolous. [ON *gola* to howl + dialect adjectival suffix *away*; compare NORNAWAY]

galder a strong breeze. **galdery** a big barn like building. [also used in Sh; *Gauldry* is the name of a house in Sanday; Sh *galder* of the wind, to bluster]

gallows 1 = gallows. 2 a rascal. **gallow bread** a person doomed to be hanged.

galt see GOLT.

gamfer* see GANFER.

gammons legs and thighs. [OF *gambe* leg]

gamo the human foot. [related to GAMMONS above]

gams the area round about the mouth. **gamsy** having a protruding jaw. [also Eng dial; compare OE *goma* the palate but in plural 'jaws']

gamse of a dog to bite playfully. [related to GAMS above; Dan dial *gamse* to bite playfully]

gamsmyre clamour or pandemonium. [origin uncertain]

gan* 1 to stare at in a vacant manner. [ON *gana]*

gan* 2 see GO.

gandiveese 1 1 a whim. 2 an imaginary illness. [compare Sh *gandigo* with a similar meaning; *gandiveese* is a reversal of WHASSIGO; both elements mean to blow (of the wind) as in Eng *windbag*; see GANTER]

gandiveese 2 to stare at something in a bemused way [see GAN 1 and VEEZE 1]

ganecall† revocation [in old records, also Sc]

ganezeall† recompense [in old records, also Sc]

ganfer*, gamfer, gonfert 1 ghost. 2 shadowy features in the sky eg a GAA or BROCH. *a ganfer for snow* a fine close white dry mist coming down from the hill tops in winter and believed to be a sign of snow to follow. [ON *gandr* spirit, ghost, witch; ON *far* travel; compare ON *gandreið*, witches riding at night on wolves or broomsticks; see GANSPELL]

gang, geong a row of stitches in knitting. [ON *ganga* a course or *gong* a passage]

gangaboot see GAENABOOT.

ganner = gander.

ganners a disease in the mouth of cattle and horses [also Sh and Cai.: Norw. dial. *ganer*, pimples in the mouth of horned cattle]

gansey* a jersey. [also in Eng dial; originally from the island of *Guernsey*]

ganspel a trick. [ON *gandr* spirit, ghost, witch; Sc *speal* game; essentially 'magic trick'.]

gant to yawn. [also Sc; OE *ganian* to yawn]

ganter *a big ganter o a hoose* a big cold and uninviting house. [related to GALDERY; Sh *gander* is a high roaring wind]

ganz to prepare a fishing hook by fixing a short length of line to it which can be subsequently and more quickly fixed to a longer line. [may be related to Eng dial *gange* to twist fine wire round a fishing line to prevent fish biting off the hook]

gapie thoughtless or mindless, rash. [see GAPPUS]

gappus, gappis* a fool. [also Sc; ON *gapuxi* a gaping fool]

gappy a foolish person. [ON *gapi]*

gaps *the gaps o May.* [Sc *gabs o May]* the blustery storms which frequently come at the end of April; origin unknown; may simply mean May talking; see GAB and BORROWING DAYS for another reference to April weather]

garbendlin a straw rope used in thatching a house. The *garbendlins* were laid lengthwise on the roof unlike the other SIMMONS. [ON *bendill* a straw rope; the element *gar* is also found in FESGAR]

garbick see GARBOU

garbou 1 a strip of grass between fields 2 a muddy

ditch with little water in it. **garbick** a pit or hole.
garbick o the stomach the pit of the stomach
[ON *garð-bálkr*, wall in the sense of turf boundary wall but here it also has an opposite meaning in the same way that Eng *dike*, a ditch and
Sc *dike*, a wall are related]

garit striped. [also Sc; Norw *geiri* a stripe]

garoye see GOURAYE.

garpal big or stout. [compare Sw *gårbälg* fat paunch;
see GIRBELTIN for other examples]

garpie a tall, lean, scraggy, usually stupid, individual.
[origin uncertain; ? a form of GAPPY]

garr verb. to jumble up. noun. filth or mud [see
GURR].

garra-bannock a quantity of meal given to a farm
servant on expiral of his contract. [see
BANNOCK; *garra* is probably a deriv of ON
gøra to contract; see AGAIRY]

garra-scones a particular type of pancakes usually
sticky to the touch. [see GARRO]

garrick a dimin of GEYRO.

garro sticky mud. [ON *gormr* mud; Norw *gorr* mud]

garron nail a large nail. [perhaps from OF *jarron*
branch of a tree, hence a nail for use with such
timbers]

garry sticky. [see GARRO]

garse to fondle overmuch, '*Stop garsan that cat min*'.
[ON *gersta* to annoy]

garvis a large amount of something. [Norw *gyrva* a
mass]

gat see GOLT.

gate a path. **gate-end** place, district. [common in
placenames in the form Messigate (church path);
ON *gata* path]

gather = gather. **gathering hoose** a house where,
pre 1940, the young of the district gathered.

gauger an excise man. [also Sc; OSc *gadge* to gauge]

gavaless stupid. [see GAIVALESS]

gavel*, **gavel (end)*** gable. [ON *gafl*]

gavellous see GAIVALESS.

gaviot a windbreak. [see GIVO]

gavlo see GABLOO.

gavs playful bite of a dog. [see GAMSE]

gavse* see GAFS.

gavvy a look or an approach, '*Git oot o me road till
I get a gavvy at hid*'. [? ON *gauma* to heed]

gealding vat see GEEL.

geckly, gaikly of a warm disposition. [? for *gait-ly* =
mannerly]

gee* (pronounced with a hard *g*) mood or frame of
mind, used disparagingly. [also Sc; ON *geð*
mood or temper]

geed see GO.

geel ale or beer in the vat. **geelgawkie** the second
brewing of beer. **geeling vat, gealding vat** a
brewing vat. [Norw dial *gil* fermenting beer]

geelum a plough plane. [also Sc; ultimately Fr
Guillaume William]

geen see GO.

geen away land see GO.

geepie-gawpie a shadow picture on the wall. [prob-
ably from Eng *gape* or *gawp*]

geese-geese a call to pigs. [also Sc; Norw *giss*; compare PEESE]

geifoo a lean-to shed. [see GIVO]

gel see GELL.

gelder* see GOLDER.

geldro 1*, **gyeldro** destruction, '*The hoose is gin a-
geldro*'. [also VILDRO; from an assumed ON
gvelder, of the wind, to blow; compare Sc
skailwind and *windrift* with similar meanings]

geldro 2 to be in a silly state of mind. [see GOLDER]

gelfa ale when it will not take barm. [ON *gil* ale + *fa*
fall]

gell, gel of wood to split when exposed to the sun.
[also Sc; in Eng dial *geld*; origin uncertain]

gem 1 scurf in a horse's hair. 2 the scaly material in
new wool on a sheep's back. [origin unknown;
? perhaps Eng *gemma* bud etc]

gemple to cope with or manage. [? perhaps ON
geyma to watch or mind]

genner the gravelly soil left after the peats have been
cut. [see CHINNER]

geo*, **gue** a ravine; common in placenames. [ON *gjá*
chasm]

geong see GANG.

gersty†, gorstie† the old earthen wall which formed
the boundary of the toon or district. [found in
placenames; ON *garð-staðr* site of a wall]

gertins* garters [also Sc]

geskafoo pleasant in manner. [ON *goezku-fullr* full
of goodness]

getroth indeed! [*good* + *truth*]

geudie, goodie a grandmother. [compare Sc *geudam*
good-dame; formed on the same principle as
guidwive etc; see GEUTCHER below]

geud-wirds prayers [*guid* = good compare BONIE/
BONNY WORDS]

geup* verb. to make a fool of someone. noun. a fool.
[see GAPPY]

geupin* see GUPPEN.

geutcher grandfather. [also Sc *good-sire*; in Sc and
Ork dial an *s* following a *d/t* is pronounced *sh*]

geuth see GOTH.

geuther grandfather [clipped form of Sc *guidsire*.]

gevelous see GAIVALESS.

gevels the lines to which the sinkers of a net are attached. [Sh *kavli* is closely related; ON *kafli* is a
float or buoy for nets]

gey* very, '*Hids gey bad*' it's very bad. [also Sc; a
special development of meaning of Eng *gay*; Eng
pretty has developed in the same way, compare

Eng *pretty bad*]

geyar see GYRE.

geyr, geyro 1 a small, often angular piece of field. 2 a piece of field which cannot be cultivated eg because it is too wet. [Eng gore; ON *geiri* a triangular piece]

geyral a big-female. [ON *gýgr* giantess]

geyran standing staring. [Norw *gira* to stare]

geyro see GEYR.

Geyro Night celebrated up until thirty years ago in Papa Westray in the month of February when adults dressed up as witches and chased chidren, hitting them with a rope or tangle; in the Celtic domain this was done at Hallowe'en. [ON *gýgr* witch or troll woman]

gibbéd see GAIP.

gibbie *a horn gibbie* a big horn spoon. [see GIBBOCK]

gibbock a bone needle used for knitting shoes. [Sc *gibble* tool or instrument; origin unknown]

gibby* a tom cat, especially a castrated male. [also Sc; a shortened form of *Gilbert*]

gid* 1, geed* see GO.

gid 2 see GAE.

gid-gad*, giddy-gad*, giddy-goo, gad* an expression of disgust eg when looking at a meal which does not appeal to one. [Eng *Good God*]

gild† of full value. [ON *gildr*]

gilder* to giggle, especially, *gilderan and laughan*. [see GOLDER]

gildro an old trick in which two people were joined together so that they could not separate themselves. [ON *gildra* a trap]

gillie, gillo see GULLO.

gilpid bitter. [see SHILPIT]

gilt a long shaped haystack. [also in Cai and Sh; metaphorical use of ON *gyltr* a young sow]

gilwheevy a cheat. [Sc *gill-wheep*; Sc *gill* to fool; Eng *gull*; origin of *wheevy* uncertain]

gimmer* a young ewe. [also Sc; ON *gymbr*]

gimmer shell* the scallop. [related to Eng *gimp* to scallop]

Gimp† a Stronsay goblin. [? Sc *gymp* small and neat]

gimse verb. of a person or a horse, to toss the head noun. a lively horse [Norw. dial. *gimsa* of a horse, to toss the head]

gin 1, geen see GO.

gin 2 if; '*See gin yi deu that?*'; '*Gin a buddy meet a buddy*'. [Sc *gin* if; origin uncertain]

ginn† wild oats which were common until about 1840. **ginnowy** of oats poor. [compare ON *ginhafri* a kind of oats; *owy* is a dialect adjectival ending: see NORNAWAY]

girbeltin a beast or person with a big belly. [related to Eng *gorbellied*; the correct form should probably be *gorbelchin*; compare Sc *belch* a fat person or animal; Icel is *gor-vömb*; originally a foul expression, meaning 'shit-belly' and probably applied to a child as the German word *Gör* applied to a little brat suggests; English *girl* (applied to boys too originally!) is probably derived in this way; see GRUELLY BELKIE, PURDY and KIRRABAG]

gird a hoop for a barrel. [ME *gird* to fasten with a hoop]

girdifuff a brawl. [Sc *gird* to strike; Sc *fuff* an outburst of temper]

girn 1 a trap. [OE *grin* snare]

girn* 2 to complain in a whining way. **girny*** of a child, whining [also Sc], especially *girnan and greetan*. **girny-gow-gibby** a peevish child, '*Girny-gow-gibby the cat's guid mither*' a taunting phrase used to such a child. [ON *grenja* to howl]

girnal* 1 a meal chest. [also used for *granary* in Ork as it was in Sc but now obs; OF *grerniere* with *l* substituted for final *r*; ultimately from Lat *granarium* granary; the Earl's storehouse in Kirkwall was called *The Girnal*]

girnal 2 lump in the armpit. [compare Sc *girran* a boil; Gael *guirean* a pimple]

girse grass. **girseen** a small piece of grass; *no worth a hen's girseen* worthless. **girse heuk** the hooked metal cross-stay between shaft and blade of a scythe. [also Sc; OE *gaers* or *graes*]

girth a sanctuary. [also Sc; an old name for the round church of Orphir was the *Girth Hoose*; ON *grið*]

-gis 1 found only in compounded forms in Orkney dial always referring to a mess of some sort (see GLURGIS, LURGIS, HAGGIS, MURGIS etc). [related to Norw *gysa* ooze]

gis* 2 only negative, '*He his no gis at aal*' he is inept. **gisless*** inept. [Sc *guise* a way of doing something]

git = get. **gittan*** getting. Often placed at the end of a sentence, '*Hid's a big cat noo gittan*', it's becoming a big cat. '*Are you gittan?*' a question frequently asked by Orkney shopkeepers and meaning, 'Are you being attended to?'

gite* see GYTE.

gitelan a weak, laughable style of walking, *a gitelan ting o boy*. [origin uncertain]

gitteral low, mean, despicable. [see KITERAL]

givo, geifoo, gaviot a protective wall in front of a door. **givo** is also used of a partition wall. [Norw *gylve* a roofed passage]

gizzened* 1 dried up, especially of a barrel or tub so that there are gaps between the staves. 2 thirsty. [also Sc; ON *gisna* to become leaky]

glab* verb. to snatch, used pejoratively e.g. '*He'll glab aal he can get his hands on*'. noun. a snatch. **glabberan** impulsive. [imitat; compare GLAM

40

2, GLAMSE, GLAP etc]

glad see GLED.

glaer of a woman in men's company, bright eyed, *'Luk at her she's just glaer'*. [ME *glaren* to stare]

glafter, gafter loud laughter [also Sh]. **glaftery** silly in the sense of loud and noisy. **glafteran** giddy or vain [see GLUFF 1 for a related form]

glagse a sticky mess, *'Me dumpling's gin in a glagse'*. [see GLUGG]

glaggy soft and sticky [also Sh: see GLAGSE above]

glaip* to gulp down. [ON *gleypa*]

glaize open weave material. [Norw *glesen*]

glam verb. to snatch. noun. 1 a snatch. 2 the hand. [in Sh the form *glomek* is recorded; see GLAMSE]

glamer 1 to talk loudly. [ON *glamra* to jingle]

glamer 2 hurry, *'He wis always in a glamer'*. **glammeran** hurried. [ON *glymja* to dash noisily]

glampsie see GLAMSE.

glampy of the sky watery. [related to ME *gloumbe*; Eng *gloom*]

glamse 1 of a dog to snap. 2 to make a noise with the lips when eating. **glamsy** applied to a person or animal looking round quickly. [Gael *glamhsa* a snap by a dog but Dan dial *glamse* also means to snap (of a dog); ON *glefsa* to snap at]

glamsy of the sky showing dazzling parts and betokening rain. [see GLAMPY]

glangoir† in the report of the trial of the witch, Katherine Craigie in 1643: *'Quhat glangoir war ye doing in that ill weather?'* [Sc *glamour* witchcraft; see GRAMOWRIE]

glap 1 a sudden attack of illness. 2 a chill eg eggs might get *a glap o cowld* (cold) if the hen leaves the nest too long. *'Wrap up weel in case thoo gets a glap'*. **glapéd** of an egg, infertile. [the essential meaning is quick movement; compare Sc *gliff* sudden sensation]

gleckit, glekit* foolish. [also Sc; origin uncertain; perhaps ON *gletta* to make fun of]

gled, glad 1 gleaming, of a coal in the fire. [ON *glaðr* bright]. 2 a live coal. [ON *glód* embers]

glee 1 to shine, especially of fat on the top of soup. 2 an oily patch in the sea caused by throwing out mashed limpets to attract SILLOCKS. **gleean** *'That iron's just gleean'* it is red hot. [ON *gljá* to glisten]

gleed 1 set far apart as for example vegetables in a garden. [Sh *gled*; see GLIDE]

gleed 2 to burn slowly [also Sc OE *gled*, live coal]

gleer to peer. [Norw *glire*]

gleetin of a wound, weeping before it heals. [Eng *gleet* transparent discharge; OF *glette* flux]

glegg having sharp senses. [ON *gleggr*]

glekit see GLECKIT.

glenkit hurried. [Sc *glent* to gleam or to move quickly]

glesgend, glesgin of a dog, greedy. [Sc *glisk* a short brisk movement literally a *flash*; a reference to the speed it eats its food]

gless = glass. **glessie** a narrow space about 25 cms between the gable ends of the houses in Kirkwall, so called because it was here where all broken glass was thrown. **glessie hole** a corner in Stromness where broken gless was deposited. **casting the gless(es)** a method of fortune-telling using egg-white.

glett 1 a bright patch in the sky or a lull in a storm. 2 of sheaves in the harvest field, to dry up. [Norw *glette* bright patch in sky]

glide*, gleed squint eyed. [in Sc takes the form *gleyed, gleed, glee* etc; essential meaning is set apart or separated; ON *gleiðr* standing with ones legs wide apart]

glim a glimpse. [related to Eng *glimpse*; compare Swed dial *glim*]

glimp = glimpse. [also Sc; Du *glimp* a glimpse]

glimpsan thirsty, with the lips dry and sticking together. [see GLAMSE]

glimro a phosphorescent glow seen in peat moss. [Eng *glimmer*; see also LIMRO]

glinder to peer, *tae go glinderan aboot*. [also Sc; Norw dial *glindra* to blink]

glinted light headed or flighty. [Sh *glant*; Norw *glant* frolicsome]

glisk a glimpse or a short space of time. [also Sc; related to ON *glis* a glimmer; the sense being a 'flash']

globéd to be infatuated by somebody. *'He's just globéd in her'*. [origin uncertain]

gloggo [see GLUGGO]

glomer to feel after with the fingers. **glomer-fu** a handful. [Sh *glom*; see GLAM and GLAMSE, related forms]

gloomins unpleasant rumours. [Eng *gloom* to look sullen or dejected]

gloondie, glundge a glutton. [see GLUNT, GLUNK]

gloop*, gloup a blowhole in a cliff top caused by the collapse of a cave roof. [ON *gljúfr* chasm; Norw *glup* ravine]

gloot, glut mucus or bile brought up in vomiting. [Sc *glet* from OF *glette* earthy slime or mucus; compare GLEETIN]

glose to strike violently. [origin uncertain]

gloss a light sleep or to sleep lightly. [? related to GLISK]

gloup see GLOOP.

glouster of the weather or of a person to storm violently. [also Sc; a form of GOUSTER]

glovan anxious to get or obtain something but used in a disparaging way. [related to Dan dial *glovven* greedy]

glower = glower. **Glowrie** an evil spirit with glaring eyes who terrified children.

gloy straw used for basketwork etc. **gloystane** a stone projecting from the barn wall. The sheaf was knocked against this stone to produce gloy. [also Sc; probably through OF *glui* straw for thatching but the word *gloy* meaning rye straw is also found in MDu]

gludge a muddy pool. [see GLUGG]

gluff 1 a sudden blast or puff of wind. 2* a fright. [also Sc; Sc *gliff* where it has the other meanings 'glimpse' or 'moment']. **gluffis** noun. a noisy, rash person. adj. noisy, rash; of a horse easily startled. **gluffus** *hairy gluffus* an unknown disease of horses. A man with veterinary skill was called to Anderswick in Stenness to attend to a sick horse, '*Hairy gluffus*' said the man '*an hid's no known cure for hid*'. **gluffy** nervous. [see GLAB for related forms]

glugg slime on fish skin. [compare Sh *glagg* sticky]. **gluggo** a thick mixture of oatmeal and buttermilk. **gluggy** slimy. [a metathesis of ON *gogli* mud; see GAGGLE]

gluip see GLUPP.

glumse to be surly and give a rude reply [also Sh see GLAMSE 1]

glundge see GLOONDIE.

glunk, glunt to swallow liquid rapidly and noisily or the sound made by such swallowing. [Eng dial *clunk*; imit]

glupp, gluip* to gulp '*Stop gluppan yir maet*'. [ON *gleypa*]

glurgis a thick unpalatable mixture. [related to Sc *glaur* a mire; see also LURGIS and GURGIS]

glush slushy snow. [related to GLOOT in the sense *sticky mess*]

glut see GLOOT.

gluthery of the sky, unsettled and with a rainy appearance [Sh *glodret* ? muddy coloured, related to GLOOT]

gly a cast in the eye. **glyan** squinting [see GLY]

go, gae past tense **gid, geed**. perf tense **gin, geen** = go. **tae go fae the hoose** to go visiting. **tae go on the night** to go courting at night but in a special sense. Formerly (pre 1940) young men would visit their girlfriend's house after the parents had retired to bed [see DOG DREEL]. **go with*** to court. **gae back** to deteriorate. **gaenaboot, gangaboot** a tramp, hawker. **gan, gaen** going, '*Whar are yi gan?*' **geen-away land** the land of the dead, '*Hid's gan three o clock*' it's coming up for three o'clock, *gin tae the back o the day* gone to ruin.

gob* mouth. [see GAB]

goblet 1 = goblet. 2 a saucepan [also Sc]

gock see GOKK.

god a loaveen goodness me! [*loaveen* is a reduced form of Sc *lovnentie* an exclamation believed to be a clipped form of *Lord defend thee*]

godick, guddick a little rhyme with a double, usually sexual meaning. [also Sh; see TINNIE for an example; ON *gata* riddle; with dimin; OE *gyd* riddle]

godless* awful, '*She wis a most godless sight wi that hat on her head*' [also Sh]

godsend 1† a shipwreck. 2† a drove of CAA'IN WHALES, nowadays used of any apparent divine intervention, '*Hid wis a godsend I wis home when hid happened*'.

goind of an animal thin looking. [Sh *gant* a tall man; Sc dial *gent*; Norw dial *gand* a tall man or a thin stick]

gokk 1, gock verb. to stare stupidly. noun 1 a trick. 2 someone fooled by a trick. On April Fool's Day in Orkney '*Gokk gokk*' or '*Hinty gokk*' (*hint da gokk* or 'hunt the fool') was jokingly said to the person who had been fooled. **Gokking Day** April Fool's Day. **Gokk Days** the first three days of April. On April 1st in Orkney, as elsewhere in Britain, a variety of tricks could be played on someone. On April 2nd, the specific trick was to pin a tail on someone (this is done in parts of France on April 1st). On April 3rd one could borrow money with no intention of paying it back. These days were called TAILY DAY and BORROWING DAY respectively. [Sc *gowk*; Norw *gauk* fool]

gokk 2, gowk, gouk a cuckoo. [ON *gaukr;* see also HORSE-GOKK]

golach see HORNY GOLACH.

golder*, gelder, gulder verb. 1 to laugh loudly 2 to giggle. noun. a laugh *a great golder o a laugh*. [compare Dan *gjalde* to yell and ON *galdr* song; see SKOLDER with a related meaning]

goldrick the plaice. [from its colour]

goliment a state of high spirits. [ON *gola* to howl; see GALEYWAY]

gollan see GULLAN.

gollamus large, ungainly [also Sh; origin unknown]

gollishay a hubbub, hilarity, excitement. [see COLASHEEN]

gollow a friend or chum. [see GULLO]

golt, goltie, galt, gat a male pig, used only of old gelded pigs or of young male pigs. [ON *galti*]

gomeral*, grummeral 1 a fool. 2 a projecting lower jaw. [also Sc; see GUMERAL]

gonfert see GANFER.

goo, gue a stink of any kind especially the smell of rotten fish [also Sc: see GUFF]

good 1 = good. 2* a clipped form of Goodness me! '*Good, hid's here somewey*'. 3 *gan good-o* go-

ing very well. [compare Eng *billy-o*]. **goodly*** 1 holy or devout, especially *a goodly buddy*. 2 at least, *'He wis there a goodly meenit (minute)'*.
goodie see GEUDIE.
goon = gown. **goonie*** a nightdress [also Sc]
go on the night see GO.
goosrin the gizzard. [OSc *guisserne*]
gorback an old earthen wall. [ON *garðr* fence; ON *bálkr* a balk; there are Gerbo placenames in Sanday and North Ronaldsay]
gord a small field. [ON *garðr* enclosed space or yard]
gore-vellye the autumn battle which was fought between two mythical creatures of Orkney folklore, *Terran* and *Mither o the Sea*. [ON *gormanaðr* was the first month (*manaðr*) of winter; Sc *vellye* tumult; related to ON *vella* to boil with the sense turning over and round]
Gorie, Great Gorie an exclamation [also Sc a form of *God*]
gormless* stupid. [also Eng dial; ON *gaumr* attention]
gornick = gurnard, a type of fish.
gorstie see GERSTY.
goshawk the hen-harrier. [also improperly applied to the peregrine falcon and buzzard in Eng dial]
goth, geuth god. *Bi geuth* By God!. [ON *goð* god]
gott see TARA GOTT.
gouk see GOKK 2.
gouraye, garoye *in his full gouraye* in his heyday. [ON *goð-raðr* giving good counsel; compare BAILYMENT a direct translation of this word]
gously, gousy 1 of the weather blustry. 2 of people, precipitate. [Norw *gosa* a breeze]
gouster, guster verb. 1 to speak loudly. 2 of the wind, to gust. noun 1 a sharp breeze of wind. 2 an outburst of language. 3 a loud noise. [ON *gusta* blast]
gousy see GOUSLY.
gowan see GULLAN.
gowdy duck the golden eye duck. [Sc *gowd* gold]
gowk see GOKK 2.
gowl verb. of a person to bellow, especially *gowl and greet*. noun. a bellow [also Sc; ON *gaul* to bellow]
gowpin, gowpen see GUPPEN.
graand see GRAND 1.
graavit see GRAVIT.
grabbit vexed at having missed something. [see GRIPÉD]
grain 1 = grain. 2* a small quantity, *a peedie grain*. Also used of space: *'Just move hid a grain'*. [common in Eng dial; literal meaning *a grain of corn*; in Sh *corn* is used as exact equiv of *grain* in these senses; see also Ork LIFE-CORN]
grait† *rait and grait*, right and proper. [ON *rétt ok greitt*]

graith, graithe verb. 1 to put in order. 2 *to graithe fish* to clean them. noun. 1 fishing gear, harness etc. 2 a lather for washing clothes. **graithing riddle** a riddle for winnowing corn. [ON *greiða* to make ready]
gramels a punishment. [origin unknown]
gramowrie witch's power. [Sc *gramarie*; OF *gramaire* a book of sorcery]
gramse verb. to grab. noun. a grab. [Norw *gramse* to snatch]
grand 1†, graand† a rocky spit. [ON *grandi* a strip of beach above water at ebb tides]
grand 2 1 = grand. 2* used instead of Eng *great* to indicate a second degree of relationship e.g. *grandbairn, grand-niece* etc [also Sc]. **Grand March*** the first event at an Orkney wedding reception dance, a kind of ceremonial walk.
grat, gret* see GREET.
grave boonie grave clothes [see BOONA]
gravis of an animal, to root about. [ON *grafa* to dig]
gravit*, graavit a scarf. [Fr *cravate* from the *Cravates*, Croatians from whom the cravate came in the 17th century]
great grand* splendid or very fine, *'He kam in his great grand car'*. [compare Eng *great big*]
gree 1 reconcile (persons), settle (matters). **greement** agreement, harmony.
gree 2 fat [also Sc; a back formation from *grease* which was considered plural]
greek break of day. [in Sc takes the form *greiking*; OE *greg* grey, a reference to the night sky becoming lighter in colour; see GREY 3]
greem to screw up the face through pleasure or unhappiness. [ON *grína* to twist the face]
greemit having a spotted face. [Norw *grimet* striped in the face]
green 1 to long for. [ON *girna* to desire]
green 2 = green. **greenbean** the fish, the viviparous blenny = green bone. **green-bow** diarrhoea in animals. [also Sh; a reference to the green *arc* formed by the diarrhoea as it is ejected; see BOW 5]. **green-gate** a grassy path. [ON *gata* path]. **greenhead peat** a quality peat with a turf top. **greennild** mould, particularly on cheese. [see NILD]
Greenland Dove the black guillemot. [this bird is called *dove* or *pigeon* throughout Britain because of its affectionate behaviour; the significance of *Greenland* is not known]
greet* past tense GRET, GRAT. perf tense GRITTEN. to weep. [also Sc; OE *gretan*]
gref the bottom of a peat-bank [O.N. *gröf* a pit]
gren a lobster's hole. [ON *gren* animals lair]
gret see GREET.
grey 1 = grey. **the grey o the morning** dawn. **grey back** the hooded crow. **grey-bulwand** see

BULLWAND. **grey-fish** the coalfish in its second or third year. **grey-goose** the shelduck.

grey 2 a gentle breeze. *tae grey ap* to rise, of the wind. [ON *graeða*]

grey 3, groo verb. to dawn. noun. dawn. **greyin** dawn. [ON *grýja* to dawn; *grýjandi* dawn]

grice 1* a young pig. [also Sc; general throughout Eng dial; ON *griss*]

grice 2 the sand gaper shell or SMERSLIN (*mya arenaria*) so called because it is shaped like a pig's snout.

griff see GRUFF.

grim dawn, *grim day*. [see GRIMLINGS below]

griminagerous of a face, hideous. [ON *gramendr* fiendish; the suffix is Eng as in *cantankerous*]

grimlings*, grimplings dusk. [Sc *grim* grey + *lings*; compare Sc *darklings* twilight]

grind† gate. [common in Orkney placenames where it usually refers to the position of a farm near a gate in a tunship wall; ON *grind* gate]

grink, grunch to make a noise when exerting effort at something. [probably a form of Eng *grunt*; Sc shows the forms *gruntle* and *grunkle* to grunt; see GRONASY]

grip 1 = grip. **gripper** a midwife.

grip 2 = grip (a ditch). 2 a mill lade. 3 a deep cleft in the rocks [also in Eng dial. OE *grype*]

gripéd vexed or disappointed. [related to Eng *gripe* pain; Eng *grip* to seize]

gripper see GRIP.

grist = grist, strength or power. **gristed** *weel gristed* of a bannock having a smooth well baked appearance. [also in West Yorkshire dial]

grith sympathy or understanding. [ON *grið* sanctuary; see GIRTH]

gritten see GREET.

groatie buckie see GROTTY BUCKIE.

groby the common mugwort. [Norw *gråbu*]

gromo the equiv. of Eng *pinch* of salt but applies to the use of four fingers rather than two. [also used in the form KROMAK and KRUMMO; ON *kremja* to squeeze; ON *kreppingr* a handful is closely related]

gronasy groaning. [related to Sc *grounch* to grunt; see GRINK]

grond of a child or fish, small. [ON *grand* a grain]

grono thick oatmeal cake. [ON *grjón* groats; compare Faroese *gron* food baked from grain]

groo 1 of the wind to blow up, '*Feth she's grooan*'. [ON *graeða* of the wind, to rise; compare GREY 2]

groo 2 frightful. [also Sc and in other Eng dial but usually as a verb; related to MLGer *gruwen* to shiver with fear; Eng *gruesome* is from the same root]

groop, gruip a ditch. [OSc *grup*; Eng *grip*]

groot 1 sediment. 2 a mess. **grooty, grotty, grutty pig** a jar for holding groot where *groot* has the special meaning oil from fish livers. [this usage is found in Sh and Sc]. **grotty lavro** the corn bunting [see LAVRO and SKITTER BROLTY]. **grotty saep** soft soap formerly bought in tins, a poor quality soap. [ON *grautr* groats; OE *grut*]

grootle to bend and look eg in a bag. **grooty** *a grooty job* one which requires a lot of bending. [see CREETLAN]

grop 1 coarsely ground grain. 2 muesli. [Norw dial *grop* coarsely ground meal]

groppen a handful. [see GRUPPENFU]

grotho sorrow. [ON *groeti*]

grots big grains left after meal has been hand ground. [see GROOT]

grotti the nave of of the lower millstone. [also Sh; ON *grotti* a mythical handmill]

Grotti Finnie, Grotti Minnie an ogre or hag. [ON *grjót-öld* people of the Stone Age; *Grjót-unn* name of a giantess; see FIN MEN and LUCKY MINNIE]

grotty see GROOTY.

grotty-buckie* a small cowrie shell. [originally *John o Groats buckie*; see BUCKIE]

grotty lavro see GROOT.

grotty pig see GROOT.

grotty saep see GROOT.

ground bauk the weighted rope at the bottom edge of a fishing net [see BAAK]

grovel to grope as if in the dark. [ON *grufla* to grope]

growing 1 = a growing. 2* a seed potato sprout.

growthie of vegetation growing fast, luxuriant [Eng *growth*]

Groy a proper name applied to a grey horse. [compare ON *Grána* a grey mare]

groyn to groan, especially of an animal in pain. [obs Eng *groin* of animals to grunt]

gruel 1 = gruel. 2 porridge.

gruelly-belkie 1 a fat person. 2* a nickname for someone from Sanday. [*gruelly* is a foul nickname, most probably originally a nickname for a child, a corruption of Norw *gor-ål*, literally 'shit-shooter'; German *Gör* urchin and English *girl* are similarly derived; *belky* is a form of BELLY from ON *belgr*, bag; in Shetland, *gruelly-bag* is the nickname given to a native of the Whiteness district; compare GIRBELTIN, PURDY and KIRRABAG]

gruff, griff *i gruff* or *apae gruff* lying flat on one's stomach. **grufflings** '*He wis doon on his grufflings*'. [ON *liggja á grufu* to lie face down; compare Eng *grovelings* prostrately]

grugs verb. to mess about. *tae grugs in the gutter (mud)*. noun. a mess. **gruggie** wet, unpleasant weather. **gruggsy** dirty or slatternly. [ON *grugg*

44

mud or dregs]
gruigo a little ditch. [has the meaning *muddy* ditch; see GRUGS]
gruip see GROOP.
gruito a small channel eg for draining a midden. [see GRUIP and GROOP]
grullyan a giant or monster. [ON *gryla* ogress]
grumfie a pig [also Sc imitat.]
grummel, grummlins dregs or rubbish. [also Eng dial; Norw *grums* sediment]
grummeral see GOMERAL.
grummlins see GRUMMEL.
grumsy grumpy. [the suffix is Sc as in BIGSY]
grunch see GRINK.
grundit grey and white colour, especially of geese. [ON *grá-rendr* grey striped]
grunt = grunt. **gruntie** a pig [also Sc]
gruntle, grundle to poke in the earth. [OSc *gruntil* snout (of a pig etc)]
grunk see GRINK.
grunyasie ugly. [OSc *grunz(i)e* snout (of a pig etc)]
grunyie a reef. [common in placenames; ON *grunn*]
grunzie full of dregs [also Sh; Eng *grounds*]
gruppenfu handful. [Sc *gruppen* to grip influenced by *guppen*]
grutty pig see GROOTY.
gub, gubs a muddy piece of ground. [origin uncertain; compare GUG]
gubboes lice. [origin unknown; compare BOBO]
gubs see GUB.
gudably possibly [also Sh *guid*, good + suffix]
guddick see GODICK.
gue 1† marshland [metaphorical use of ON *gall* gall with the sense *bitter* or *sour*]
gue 2 see GOO
guest 1 = guest. 2 an object thought to foretell the arrival of a stranger. [also Sh where observation of the fire was often used for this purpose; in Orkney a TAND from the fire was believed to betoken the arrival of a stranger]
guff* 1 verb. to grunt or bark. noun. 1 a grunt or bark. 2 a puff of wind. [imitat]
guff* 2 an unpleasant smell. **guffy** smelly. [ON *gufa* vapour]
gug slime on fish. **guggy** sticky. [ON *gogli* mud]
guggle to work with the hands among any soft substance [also Sh ON *gogli*, ooze]
guid 1 to manure the land. **guidin** = natural manure. [also Sc; ON *goeða* to enrich]
guid 2 1 = good. 2 God, *Guid bliss me* goodness me! **guid-horn** a liberal glass of whisky. **guidmither, guid-fither** etc, mother/father in law. **guideed** = indeed, '*Guideed he wis here a meenit ago*'. [Eng *in good deed*]. **Guid's weather** thunder, 'God's weather'. **Guid's ert** a church yard.
guil the corn marigold.

guip see GEUP.
guirt verb. to belch. noun. a belch. [Norw *gurta* the sound made when one is vomiting]
gulder see GOLDER.
gullan, gollan, gowan, gull flooer the ox-eye daisy. [Sc *gowan*; essentially, yellow flower]
gullo, gullie, gulloa, gillie, gillo an old affectionate form of address, '*Weel gullo, hoo are thoo the day?*' In Birsay a man was addressed as *gullie* and a woman as *gullo* [compare ON *gildr maðr* worthy man]
gully* 1 a big knife eg a carving knife. [compare Gothic *gilða* a sickle]
gully 2 of persons or things, praised or agreeable. [see GULLO above]
gulsick, gulso jaundice. **gulsick girse** woodsage. It was used in Orkney as a cure for jaundice. [ON *gulu-sót*]
gulup to swallow greedily. [ON *gleypa;* see GLUPP]
gumeral a projecting lower jaw. [ON *kinnar-kjalki* jawbone]
gump of a horse, the rump. [ON *gumpr* rump]
gumpick an umbrella. [a form of Eng *gamp*]
gunnar 1 the neigh of a horse. 2 a loud boisterous laugh. [? imitat; compare Norw *gungre* to boom]
gunner a person who shoots game for sport [this word is found in the well known Orkney *Selkie o Suleskerry* ballad]
Gunni a hobgoblin. **Gunni's Hole** the name given to gaps in hills (in Iceland and Norway, trolls lived in such landscape features). [Sh *gonni* goblin; Swed dial *gonnar* goblins (only in the plural)]
gunwales = gunwales, *fill (full) tae the gunwales** unable to eat any more.
guppen*, geupin, gowpen a double handful. [ON *gaupnir* the two hands placed together to form a bowl or, alternatively, a double handful; also Sc in a variety of written forms]
gur see GURR.
gurgis a sticky mess, particularly of mixed up food. [ON *gor* cud in animals + *gis*; compare GURGIS]
gurl a strong breeze. [also Sc; compare Norw *graela* a moderate, unsteady breeze]
gurr*, gur, garr 1 slime on fish. 2 mucus in the corner of the eye or wax in the ear. **gurry** of the eyes having mucus in the corner. [ON *gor* cud in animals]
gushel 1 a sudden prolonged breeze of wind. [ON *gjósa* to burst out; Eng gust]
gushel* 2 1 verb. to work carelessly. 2 to walk with little apparent control of the feet. noun. careless work. [Eng *gush* + *el*]
guster see GOUSTER.
guthaland the Holy Land. [ON *goða-land* literally

45

land of god; *goða-land* is not recorded in ON but is a feasible word; compare *goða-hús* heathen temple]

gutcher grandfather [also Sc from an original *guid sire*]

gutter* mud. [also Sc but only in the plural; a specialised development of Eng *gutter* a channel for conveying away water; from OF *gutière* a receptacle for drops of water; *gutter* in Ork placenames is sometimes combined with a Norse element e.g. Gutterpitten in Rendall; this suggests Norw *gytje*, mud, which is from a different root]

gy* common sense. [see GIS 2]

gyeldro see GELDRO.

gyeung to go. **gyong-hoose-atween** someone who is always visiting [see ON *ganga* to go]

gyre, geyar a mythical monster or ogre. **gyre karl** an ogre. [also Sc; ON *gýgr* witch; ON *kerling* an old woman which in Sc. *carlin* acquired the additional meaning 'witch']

gyte*, gite crazy, frequently *clean gyte*. [also Sc; origin unknown]

H English *h* pronounced *itch*. In initial position the *h* is lost in the word *hospital* (also Sc) and in certain instances where *hoose* (house) is qualified [see BIGOOS, WIROOS, etc]. The *h* of *hid* (it) and *his* (us) is lost if preceded by a consonant e.g. *Tak id oot*.

ha = hall. Found in placenames in the sense of *a large house* or *a cottage*. [both usages also found in Sc; Eng *hall*]

haaf† deep sea as in *haaf fishing*. [also Sh; ON *haf*]

haafers* halves. *go haafers wi me*. [Sc *haavers*; children's claim to half of anything; *half* + *er*]

haain, hawin, haawie, haawin, haenan, howin careful with money or goods. [ON *hegna* to protect; Sc *haining* thrifty]

haant† a flock (of sheep); recorded in Rousay in the 1800's [perhaps ON *hagan* management, with an intrusive *t*; compare the similar *t* in the Birsay placename 'Huant', a variation of 'Howan']

haavie a knee shape piece of wood fitted to the stern end of a boats keel to fix it to the stern post. [Norw dial *hav* handle]

haawie see HAAINN.

haawin see HAAINN.

haayez a contemptuous name for someone or something. [origin uncertain]

habber-galyo uproar or confusion. [see HABBER-GLABBER and GAALOO]

habber-gaws blunders in reading. [also Sc; Sc *habber* to stutter]

habber-glabber impetuous. [see HAMMER-GLAMMER]

habble perhaps, '*Habble I will*'. [origin uncertain]

hack 1 1 = hack. 2 to cut very short crop using a hook. **hackéd*** having chaps in the skin, '*His hands wir aal hackéd*'.

hack 2 the footrest on a tusker. *up to the hack* to be inextricably involved in something. **hack spade** a flaying spade. [Norw dial *hake* a hook or spade]

hack 3* to cough up phlegm. **hacky*, hacky-tooh*** coughed up phlegm. [Eng *hawk*]

hackamuggie a fish dish. The belly of the fish was stuffed with chopped livers and oatmeal. [also Sh; see HACK 1 and MUGGY]

hackened ravenous for food. [see HOCK]

hacksey lukkéd coarse looking. [see HACK 1]

hacky see HACK 3.

hacky-tooh see HACK 3.

had 1 verb. 1 = hold. 2 to protect. A pre-Reformation BONIE-WORDS prayer runs:-

Mary Mither had thee hand
Roond aboot wir sleepan band
Had the lass and had the wife
And had the bairnies a their life

[in line 1 *had* is *to hold* but in the other lines it means *to protect*]. 3 to stay or remain, '*The coo widna had*' i.e. it would not stand for the bull. 4* continue [also Sc]. '*Had gaan then*' Off you go then but only in the sense 'against good advice'. *Had aff!** be off!. noun. shelter, *tak had fur the shooer* take shelter from the shower. [Sc *haud*]. **hadden** held [also Sc]. **tae had on** 1 to continue a journey. 2 to annoy.

had 2 of an animal, condition; *in good had* [a form of HOULD]

hae* past tense HID, perfect HIN. have. **hae and heal** health and wealth

haedalt a frivolous person. [see HEEDAL]

46

haenan see HAAIN.

haep = heap. **a haep o*** many, '*A haep o folk don't like this new regulations*'. [compare PILE]

haffits the temples. '*Ah'll bake thee haffets*', I'll give you a box in the ear. [also Sc; ON *höfud* head]

hag to hinder. [Icel *hagga* to put out of order]

hagger, hoger, hugger a heavy drizzle. [also Sc where it means *a fine drizzle*; ? an extended use of Sc *hagger* to cut]

haggies water breaking over a shoal. [only recorded in BAA-HAGGIES; Sh *hakk* choppy sea; Eng *hack* to cut]

haggis* a mess, especially, *tae mak a haggis of something*. [Sc *hag*, a moorland water hole; see GIS]

haggle see AGGLE.

hags a mess, '*Whit a hags yir makkan o cuttan that loaf*'. [an abbreviated form of HAGGIS]

haif-wraik what is washed ashore. [ON *haf-rek;* see HAAF]

hail 1 in a game, the goal. [also Sc and Eng dial]. **hail-doors** *coman near the hail doors* coming to an end. [*hail* was the cry as the ball approached goal]

hail 2 = to hail. verb. **haily-puckle** to hail, '*Hid's fairly haily-pucklan*'. noun. **haily-puckle***, **haily-buckie***, **haily-picko*** a hailstone

hailse, hels see HAIL.

hain to save, '*Be hainan on the butter noo*'. [see HAAIN]

hair = hair. *to hair butter* to pass a knife through farm butter in all directions to remove the hairs. '*Ah'm niver seen a hair o him fae that day tae this*' - I haven't seen him at all.

hairst* harvest [also Sc]. **hairst blinks** distant flashes of lightning at harvest time. *a hairst sky is no tae feck* a harvest sky isn't always as bad as it looks. **hairst knot** a corn dollie given as a token of love.

haith (by my faith). '*Haith Ah'm no gan furtiver*'. The story is told of someone who visited an old lady who shared her living room with a variety of fowls. During the visit, a drake appeared from under the bed, uttered '*Haith!*' and disappeared again! [also Sc; a corrupt form of *faith*]

hakie nervous. [origin uncertain]

haley stone the name given to small rounded quartz pebbles in the belief that they had fallen from the sky and were therefore sacred; they were often concealed in the walls of Orkney houses for good luck; see DIAN STANE [ON *helgi* holy]

half = half. **halfie*** a half-bottle of whisky, '*He wis no sooner in the hoose than oot comes the halfie*'. **half-lade** 1 a straw basket hung on each side of a horse's back. 2 a meal sack. [Sc *half-load*]. **halflings*** half, '*I wis halflings oot o the win-*

dow when I stuck'. [also Sc; *half* + *lings*; compare BACKLINGS]. **half-web** grey phalarope. [a description of its feet]. **half-yoke** a snack. [a refreshment between *yokes*; see YOKE]

halfers see HAAFERS.

halk hen, hawk hens† hens had to be provided for the king's falconer to feed the hawks.

hallan* a hen's perch. [also Sc with a great variety of meanings, the essential sense of which seems to be a dividing balk; Norw *hjell* a loft of loose boards in a barn; the form *halland* was originally recorded in Sc where the *and* suffix probably represents the gerund, hence dividing]

hallet, hallety light headed. [a form of Sc *hallock*; origin unknown]

hallow a large bundle of straw tied by a SOOKAN. [related to Norw *halge*]

hallowel the rubbing STRAIK on a boat. [the second element is *wale* as in Eng *gunwale*; first element unknown]

Hallowmass the first week in November. [compare Eng *All Hallows*]

hat see HIT

ham to hoard food for a baby. [Sc *hamse* to eat noisily; OF *hancher* to snip at]

hame-fare, heemfare 1 a feast given on the occupation of a new home. 2 a feast to celebrate a bride's homecoming. [ON *heimferð* a return home]

hameower 1 of speech homely, simple. 2 of habits and manners plain, simple, natural, without reserve. 3 of food plain, homely. [Sc *hameart*; ON *heimoll*]

hammel to remove the awns from bere. **hammeler** a device used in the *hammeling* process. [Norw *hamse* to shell]

hammer 1 a crag jutting out from the hillside. [common in placenames eg the *Hammers o Syraday* in Firth; ON *hamarr*]

hammer 2 = hammer. **hammer-men**† an old association of craftsmen which existed in Kirkwall. **hammer-baeten** *a hammer-baeten sky* a mackerel sky:-

A hammer-baeten sky
Is nither weet nor dry

hammer-glammer see HABBER-GLABBER.

hammer-head see HINNER HEAD.

hammer-men see HAMMER 2.

hamper hinder, restrain, confine etc.

hamsy 1 1 slovenly. 2 of woollen thread, badly spun. [Norw *hamsutt*]

hamsy 2 of a person or the weather blustery. [Norw *himsa* to behave boisterously]

hand 1 = hand. 2 a handful. [*hond* is used similarly in the Faroes]. **tae hand** at hand. **hand birt** inept [origin uncertain]. **hand bint** bound; [see HANDLESS]. **hand-doing** '*Hid's his own hand-*

47

doing' said for example when a disaster occurs through inaction. **handigrip** a handhold in a boat for pulling it up the beach. [may be Eng but compare Norw *handgrip* a handle]. **handless*** inept, *'He's a naafil handless cratur'*. [also Sc; compare MOOTHLESS]. **hand-staff, hand stay** the handle of a flail, approx. 95 cm long and 4 cm in diameter. **hand's turn*** *'He'll no deu a hand's turn'* He won't do a thing. [general throughout Eng dial]

handband† a term found in old records. a pledge. [ON *handaband* handshake]

hand birt see HAND.

handigrip see HAND.

handle* 1 = handle. 2 hand of a clock [also Sc]

handless see HAND.

handling 1 = handling. 2 an unpleasant experience, an ordeal.

handsel, hansel† a gift. **handselde**† to make a bargain by a handshake. **Handsel Monday** the first Monday after New Year which was traditionally a time for giving gifts in Scotland. **handsel wife**† the woman who gave out gifts at a wedding [also Sc]; in Orkney the gift consisted of a piece of bread and cheese. [ON *hand-selja;* common in Sc and Eng dial; ? ON *handsal* a handshake but OE records *handselen* a gift]

handskouse, hansho† a glove, recorded in a witch trial of 1640. [ON *hanzki*]

hang-how see HIGH HOW.

hangse to trample (eg growing crop). [related to Icel *hangsa* to dawdle; Sc *hainchil* has a similar meaning]

hank the *quarter* of a boat, part of side next the stem or stern. [compare Sc *hank* the lee side of a boat; ON *hank* ring on a sail or side of a boat transferred to *boat* generally]

hansel see HANDSEL.

hansho see HANDSKOUSE.

hantle some or several, *'Here's a hantle a stamps for yir album'*. *'There's few better, a lot worse and a hantle sic like'* an old saying. [also Sc; a clipped form of *handful*]

hap to cover, especially, *'Hap me back'* tuck me in. [also Sc and East Anglia; origin unknown]

happar = hopper (of a mill).

happy-kindunky a see-saw. [*kindunk* represents the sound of the see-saw hitting the ground; *happy* is probably a form of UP; compare APACAILY-DUNKY; Sh has the form *hederkandunk*]

har* 1 = her. 2 a female, *'Is the bairn a him or a har?'*. 3 the female part of the wooden hinge of an old Orkney door (?a play on *hjarri,* hinge)

harbeen, harbo, harber, hardiback a coalfish three years old or older. [*hard-bone*; the significance of the name is not understood]

harbilly of a woollen garment near the skin, prickly. [Dan *harvebul* harrow beam, must have meant *harrow* in Ork and in Sh; compare Sh *harrabel* an emaciated animal or person; see HARROW 2 and HARROBLE]

harbo see HARBEEN.

hard = hard. **hard-heid** a dogfish.

hardiback see HARBEEN.

hards flax. [see HARN]

hark to whisper, *'Whar's that?', he harkéd on the sly.* [Norw *harke* to clear the throat]

harl 1 to walk dragging the feet. 2 to rough cast with lime and small stones. [OSc *harl* to drag]

harle the red-breasted merganser. [Sc and Sh *herald duck*; OF *harle* a kind of sheldrake]

harm 1 to complain constantly. [ON *harma* to bewail]

harm 2 1 to imitate. 2 *tae harm after* to hanker after. [ON *herma* to repeat]

harn 1 coarse linen. *a harn sark (shirt) and a half croon (15p)* were the HERDIE BOY's (or lass's) fee for a summer's herding [OE *heordam*]

harn 2 to roast on embers or to harden before the fire. [a form of Eng *harden*; compare *darn* for darken]

harns brains. **harnpan** the skull [ON *hjarni* brain]

harp that part of an old mill which separated the dust of the grain from the SHILLING. **harp stoor** mill dust. [also Sc; from the fancied resemblance to a harp]

harpo the scallop, a kind of sea shell. This big shell was used as a meal scoop in a GIRNAL. It was excellent for scraping out the meal which had been packed hard in to keep out mites. [also *harp shell* in Eng; ON *hörpuskel*]

harroble the bar of a harrow. [ON *herfi* harrow; ON *bolr* trunk of a tree; Dan *harvebul*; compare HARBILLY]

harrow 1 the groove for the back-band on a horses saddle. [origin unknown]

harrow 2 = harrow, *as poor as a harrow* of an animal or person very thin.

harsh rancid [see HARSKET below]

harsket, herskit heartburn. [related to ON *herstr* harsh; compare Swed *harskhet* rancidity]

harskin, herskin 1 rough, especially to the skin (eg of tweed material). 2 of land, dry and hard. [ON *herstr* harsh]

harva-kuithe a third year coalfish. [ON *harðr* hard; see HARBEEN; see also KUITHE]

hasan† a young seal. [see TANG-WHESSER]

hasfang a dog fight. [ON *háls-fang,* literally 'throat grip']

hash* a quantity, *'Whit a hash o cars is aboot that hoose'*. [also Sc; a special development of *hash* chopped up meat]

48

hass* the neck but more particularly the throat, '*I hid a fish bone stuck in me hass*'. **hass-boils** boils on the head. [also Sc with both meanings; ON *hals* neck]

hasso = hassock.

hassens the bottom boards of a boat next the stern [also Sh: Norw. dial *hals*, the forepart of the boat next to the stem]

hat 1 a scum on fermenting ale. [Eng *head*; *hat* is also used in Sh; Norw has the form *fraud-hatt* froth hat]

hat 2 to ill treat. **hatted** ill-thriving. **hattapol** ill treated (compare HECKAPOLO). [see HATTER 1]

hatter 1 to hinder. **hatteral** a mess. [OSc *hatter* to batter; *hettir* a confused heap]

hatter 2 = hatter. *tae work like a hatter* to work hard.

hauss-spang an iron clasp which secured the handle to the beam of the old Orkney plough. [ON *hals* neck; ON *spöng* a clasp]

havers nonsense. [also Sc; origin unknown]

havie, plout-havie a bag net used to catch trout in a stream. [ON *hafr;* see TROOTIE HOOSE]

hawance carefulness, used negatively, '*He his no hawance in his hand*' he gives liberally. [see HAAIN]

hawin see HAAIN.

hawk-hen see HALK HEN.

hayve* to throw a heavy object. [probably a form of Eng *heave* but compare ON *hefja]*

haze, heeze, heisk, heysk, hysk verb. to travel quickly. noun. a state of excitement. [ON *eisa* to rush forth; see AIZE]

he = he. The pronoun *he* is sometimes applied to the weather, '*Beuy he's cowld the day*'. [also in Norw dial]

head, heed, heid 1 = head. 2 hair [also Sc], ' *I must wash me head*'. *tae go heid stoop* to go head over heels. **headie craa** 1 black headed gull. [*craa* refers to the call of the bird though usually used only for the call of the crow and the cock]. 2 a bonnet or other headgear. [? related to HEEDIE CRAA 1]. **heads and traas** all mixed up. [Sc *heads and thra(w)s*]. **head bow†** 1 the principal wall enclosing a tunship. [ON *bálkr* a balk]. **head bow†** 2 a principal farm. [ON *bú* homestead]. **headlight*** = light-headed. [also Sc; such reversals are common in Ork dial eg OOTSIDE-IN, NETTING-WIRE etc].**headlings*** headlong. [Eng *head* + *lings*; see HALFLINGS]

hear = hear, past and prefect tense **hard. hear tale o*** to hear of, '*Ah'm never hard tale o him fae he gid tae Canada*'.

heather = heather. **heather ale*** a drink brewed from heather, hops, barm, syrup, ginger and water.

heather berry crow berry, the most common berry bearing small shrub in Orkney. **heather bleater** the common snipe [also Sc]. **heather-cowe*** see COWE. **heather lintie*** the twite. [*lintie* is a form of LINNET]. **heathery brottick** hairy caterpillar found in the heather. [? a form of BROLTIE]

heather-blether vanishing islands. A mirage frequently seen in the North Isles of Orkney in the summer; see under HEAD [Norw *hildring*; *blether* is a rhyming duplication]

heck 1 to walk in a feeble manner. [Sh *heckle*; compare ON *hoekil-bjúgr* bowed in the knees; Norw *høkla* to go with bent knees]. **hecken** shivering with cold, literally hunched or *hooked* to keep warm. **heckabirnie** a lean feeble creature. [Sc *birny* cold; the essential meaning seems to be 'hunched up because of the cold']. **heckapolo** a poor worthless creature. [see PALLOWY]. **heckapooris, heckapurdy** a poor worthless creature [Ork dial *purdy*, diarrhoea, from the tendency of a sick animal to make a mess].

heck 2 to grab. [the same as Sc *hake* to kidnap; the essential meaning is to *hook* with the fingers; compare Sc and Eng dial *hake* a hook; ON *haki* hook]. **heckéd** linked tightly together (eg in a fight). **heckéd tullyo** a hand to hand fight. [see TULLYO]. **hecko** close combat.

heck 3 a barred container for feeding (hay/straw) etc to animals. [OE *haecc* related to Du *hek* gate]

heckabirnie see HECK 1.

heckapolo see HECK 1.

heckapooris see HECK 1.

heckapurdy see HECK 1.

heckéd see HECK 2.

hedal see HEEDAL.

hed stennis† head courts. [ON *stefna* appointed meeting with Eng plural and Eng *head* in the sense of *principal* but compare ON *höfud-þing* chief meeting]

heed see HEAD.

heedabo 1 reckless in behaviour. 2 head over heels. [compare Norw *hita bul* an impulsive person]

heedal, haedalt, hedal 1 a disease in sheep, bladderworm in the brain which affects their behaviour; known in English as *sturdy* or *gid*. 2 of a girl, giddy, i.e. behaving like such a diseased animal. [Sc **head-ill** jaundice in sheep]

heedie see HEAD.

heedie craa 1 see HEAD.

heedie craa 2 see HEAD.

heel* 1 1 = heel. 2* the end of a loaf of bread. [also Sc where it has in addition a variety of *end* meanings]. **heelsdro, heelster-gowrie** head over heels. **heels ower head*** head over heels. [also Sc; an example of many reversed phrases found in Ork dial; compare HEADLIGHT]

heel 2 the footrest on a TUSKAR. [ON *haell* peg or pin]

heeld 1, hield to incline to one side, '*Heeld the boat ower a bit*'. [OE *hieldan* to slope]

heeld 2 to sit down, '*Heeld thee doon*'. [see WHEEL]

heelsdro, heelster-gowrie see HEEL 1.

heels ower head* see HEEL 1.

heemfare see HAME-FARE.

heeshal*, hussel 1 a crowd of people. 2 a herd of cattle. 3 a heap on the floor. [Sc *hirsel*; ON *hirzla* a storage container]

heesk dry in the throat especially after drinking alcohol. [a form of Eng *husky*]

heeskéd high strung or hysterical. [see HAZE]

heesnakwee, heesnie see HEEZEN.

heestee hurry! [Eng *Haste you!*; compare LUSTOO and SISTOO; see SKINT for an ON example]

heestyie see EESKYIE.

heevie, huivy, huvie a straw-woven basket carried on the back. [Sc *haev* a fisherman's hand basket; related to OE *hyf* a hive and ON *háfr* bag net; see also HAVIE]

heeze see HAZE.

heezen to shiver with the cold. **heesnie, heesnakwee, histened** shivering with cold. [Norw *isne* to shiver; for *akwee* suffix see NORNAWAY]

heft 1 a fisherman's gaff. [a form of Eng *haft* a stick]

heft 2*, shaft* to raise a clenched fist. [ON *hvata hnefa at*]

hegg shabby in appearance, *tae go heggan aboot*. [seems to be a form of HECK 1]

heid see HEAD.

Heids o Norway the mountains of Norway which, in exceptional weather conditions, can be seen from the North Isles of Orkney. This is a type of mirage. [*heids* = heads = cliffs]

height = height. '*That's aboot the height o hid*'* 'That's all' or 'Everything accounted for' eg after gathering potatoes, or at the end of giving a list of one's requirements, for example in a shop. **Heighty** God.

heisk see HAZE.

helier† a cave into which the sea flows. [ON *hellir;* common in placenames]

hellar† in the old Orkney house, a small room off the living room. [see SALOR]

hellio a stone with a ring of clay round it used in parching corn for bursting. [ON *hella* a flat stone]

Helly Boot an old name for the island of Damsay. [ON *heilagr* holy; ON *baeta* to be restored to health (there was an old chapel on Damsay dedicated to the Virgin Mary)]

hellyie, hellyiefer a downpour. [compare Icel *helliskur* a pouring shower from ON *hella* to pour; origin of last element uncertain]

hellyiefyoll a scolding in the sense an out pouring of words. [ON *hella* to pour + ? ON *fjöl-* much]

helmin† a half part. [ON *helmingr;* see also HEMLIN]

helty bit not a bit! [see ILL-HELTY BIT]

hels see HAILSE.

hemliband a forked tether to which two animals can be attached. [ON *helmingr* half; ON *band* a cord]

hemlin, hemlock a sheepmark, a slice cut diagonally from the ear. [a form of ON *helmingr* half part]

hemlins the ledge inside a corn drying kiln on which the cross-beams rested. [see also TRAMINS; related to Sc *hemmel* a stage on posts to support fodder for cattle]

hemlock see HEMLIN.

hemskt active, quick [see HENKS]

hen = hen. **hennie-hoose*** = chicken house. **hen-pen** see PEN. **hen pen dirlo** a toy, a potato with feathers stuck into it thrown into the wind. [see DIRL for *dirlo* element]. **hen-toed** pigeon toed. **hen-toomal** a chicken enclosure. **hen-tree** a chicken perch. **on hen back** out of sorts (see entry under BAAK)

hench* hip. [Eng *haunch*]

hengst anxious. [ON *angist* anguish]

henks, henksie hurried in manner or movement, '*A henks thing o lass*'. [see HENGST above]

hennie-hoose see HEN.

hen pen dirlo see HEN.

Henry-Noddie* sleep in the eye. [Sh *Tammy-Noddie*, a form also recorded in Ork; Eng *nod* to sleep]

henskly hurriedly. [see HENGST]

hen-toed see HEN.

hen-toomal see HEN.

hen-tree see HEN.

herd = herd. **herdie-boy, herdie lass, hirdie boy, hirdie lass** children who in olden days were permitted to finish the school year on May 12th. so that they could herd cattle. They continued to herd the cattle till harvest-time. This special dispensation severely disrupted education in the rural schools. **herdsman**† a nickname for the Great Skua at the time when it used to drive the white tailed eagles away from the lambing grounds.

here-meed native in origin, applied to simple poetry etc. [Eng *made here*]

herrie to exhaust the fertility of land by removing the topsoil. [a form of Eng *harry* to spoil]

herse = hoarse, *a herse trapple* a sore throat.

herskin see HARSKIN.

herskit see HARSKET.

hert = heart. **hert(e)nin** encouragement, strengthening (with food etc). **herto** a pet name for a cow, especially for a cow with a white patch (heart) on its forehead. **hert rug** a strain on the emotions. **hert's care** anxiety, deep worry.

hesp a bundle or hank of thread, usually tangled. [ON *hespa*]

hess a little hill in the North Faray rhyme:-
Quoy, Cott, Doggerboat
Hammer on the hess,
Leaquoy, Windywa,
Holland on the ness
[ON *háls* ridge or hill; it used to be common to make rhymes about adjacent farm names; similar rhymes are found in Norway]

hettan hurried. [origin unknown]

heudins that part of a boat where the sides are secured to the stem [OSc *hude*, a head covering]

heuk see HUIK.

heukened see HUIKENED.

heuld, heuld horn see HUILD.

heuldry see HULDER.

heun see HUIN.

heuty craa a rough sheep shelter. [Eng *hut*; see CREU]

heuved overeaten. [see HOVED]

hey a fine achievement or a great success. [also in the form HEYS or HEYST; see HEYS below for possible interpretation]

heys, hise a tossing about, '*He'll git a good heys on the Pentland (Firth) the day*'. [Sc *heeze* with a variety of spelling and meanings; a variation of Eng *hoist*]

heysk extremely excited or nervous. [see HAZE]

hiblin a cormorant. [compare Faroese *hiplingur*]

hiblin-band see HEMLIBAND.

hickse* see HIX.

hid* **1** 1 it. 2 there (is), '*Hid's a gren more in the bottle*' There's a little bit more in the bottle. [compare Norw *det er* there is; literally *it is*]. 3 *hid* is also used as an intensive, '*Whit a time o hid wir hin*'. '*He's some lad o hid*'. [OE *hit* it; *hit* died out in England in the late 1500's]

hid* **2** see HAE.

hide 1 a seal (North Ronaldsay). [probably a taboo term; Eng *hide* skin]

hide 2 = to hide. **hidie-hole** a hiding place.

hie the command for a horse to turn left. [see WHEESH]

hield see HEELD.

highameat the last food an animal eats before it is killed. [Sh *hellamet*; ON *heilagr* holy; ON *matr* food; a relic of Roman Catholic religion where the meal was probably considered as part of the last rites]

high-how, hang-how unplanned. [compare Eng *anyhow*]

high picko see PICKO.

hild to take a rest. [ON *hvíld* rest]

hildaland the summer residence of the FINMEN. [see HILDERBOGIE]

hilder see HULDER.

hilderbogie a fool. [the original meaning must have been *troll*; compare ON *fífl* fool or troll; *hilder* is fairy as in ON *huldu-folk* fairies; Eng *bogie* spirit]

hill 1 = hill. 2* the peat hill. *in the hill** working peat e.g. '*The men's been in the hill aal day*'. **hill-anes** fairies. [*hill-ones*]. **hill chack** the ring ouzel. [imitat]. **hill-dyke*** a turf wall dividing the arable land from the hill pasture land in the old system of agriculture. **hill-sparrow** a meadow pipit. **hill-trow** a fairy who was supposed to live in the hills. **hilly cuttack** a vole.

hillbark see BARK.

hilligo silly. [see HALLETY]

hilter-skilter = helter-skelter.

him 1 = him. 2* a male e.g. enquiring of the new baby, '*Is hid a him or a har?*' 3 the male part of the wooden hinge of an old Orkney door [see HAR] '*The mither o him wis never home*'. [contemptuous form of the possessive HIS]. **him-har*** a hermaphrodite, used of a person or an animal. **him-sel, hi-sel** = himself. Taboo name used at sea by Sanday men for the *halibut* or *turbot*.

himlan see HUMMLAN.

himlest see HINMOST.

himp 1 see HOOM.

himp 2 to hurry. [see also IMP; Eng *hump*]

himps 1 to shrug the shoulders in an offended fashion. 2 to sulk. **himpy** in the sulks. [see HUMPSIE]

himsel see HIM.

hin see HAE.

hind the thin film under the shell of an egg. [ON *hinna* a skin]

hinder = 1 hinder. 2 a hinderance, obstruction, cause of delay.

hinderend* *in the hinderend,* in the end. *Although he promised faithfully, in the hinderend I hid tae deu hid mesel.* [Eng *hind end*; Sc *hinderin* at the close, in the end]

hine far or at a great distance. [Eng *hence*]

hine say agreed! [a form of Eng *even so*, used as an expression of agreement with what has been said]

hines metters a clipped form of ILL-HAWANCE (metters). [see also HAAIN]

hing* verb. = hang, *hing on a (lang) face* look glum or doleful. **hingan taegither** very ill. noun. a slope, '*There's a right hing on that field*'.

hink to twist, '*Ah'm gin an hinkéd me back*'. **hinkapulican** ailing [see HECKAPOLO] [a nasalised form of ON *húka* a twist]

hinmost*, himlest = hindmost. **hinmost bird** last of the brood: '*Deil tak the hinmost*' devil take the last.

hinner head, hammer head poorly filled ear of grain. [ON *agnar* genitive case of ON *ögn* chaff or husks]

hinnie see HONEY SPOT

hinnery nervous or excited. [origin unknown].

hinsho a sum of money. [see HANSHO; literally a *glove* but with the sense of *handful*]

hint 1* verb. 1 to gather, especially potatoes or stones. 2 gather and transport, '*Hint aal that toys ben bairns*'. [also Sh]. noun. a gathering together of objects [ON *hentan*, to grasp]

hint 2 to disappear quietly and quickly. [also Sc; related to Norw *himta* to glance or gleam]

hint-side foremost back to front. [a form of Eng *hind*; compare AHINT]

hinty gokk* the name called to an April fool. [Sc *hint-a-gowk, hunt-the-gowk*, hunt the fool; compare other Sc games *hunt the thimble, hunt the hare*, etc]

hip = hip. **hiplocks** the coarse wool which grows on the hips of sheep. **hipping** a nappy [also Sc]

hipple to limp. **hipple-scotch** = hop-scotch. [see HIRPLE]

hippuck a metathesis of HICCUP.

hirdie-boy*, hirdie lass see HERD.

hirdmanstein† one of the old Orkney head-courts. [also known as HED STENNIS; ON *hirðmannstefna* a meeting of the king's men]

hirlo a heap of stones. [origin uncertain]

hirple*, hipple to walk as a cripple. [OE *hyppan* to hop]

hirroo a box or chest. [ON *hirzla* from *hirða* to keep in a chest]

hirsally see HIRST 1.

hirst 1 1 the top of a slope e.g the *Hirst o Deealt* in Stenness 2 a rough patch of land in a cultivated field. 3 the floor where millstones were laid. **hirsty, hirsally** of a field, rough (compare HARSKIN). [also Sc with a variety of meanings; ON *hrjóstr*, barren place; OE *hyrst* hill]

hirstened the throat dry and rough through having a cold. [see HARSKIN]

his* 1 us, '*Whit aboot his, can we no come?*'. 2 me, (after imperative), '*Gae's hid*' Give me it.

hise* see HEYS.

histened see HEEZEN.

hit = hit, past tense HAT, perfect tense HITTEN, '*Ah'm hitten him ever so many times and he'll just no answer.*'

hitten see HIT

hitty-kitty over sensitive. [origin unknown]

hivvet a lump of earth etc. [ON *höfuð* literally '*head*']

hivvle to fit with thongs (especially the old

RIVLINGS). [related to ON *hefill* a noose fastened to the edge of a sail to help furl it]

hix*, hickse 1 to hiccup. 2 to laugh uncontrollably. 3 to weep loudly, *hixan and greetan*. [ON *hixti* to hiccup]

ho, hoe 1 the dogfish. 2 a nickname for an inhabitant of Birsay.

ho-egg the egg case of the dogfish. **ho-mither** basking shark. [ON *hár* shark]

hoadge, hodge 1 to move jerkily. 2 to walk with a kind of jerky motion eg as if using a crutch. [also in Sc and Eng dial; Eng *hitch*; ultimately from OF *hocher* to shake]

hoag of footwear fitting badly at the heel to slip. [probably related to HOADGE above]

hobble = hobble. **hobble-clog** a small stick approximately 20cm long and 5cm thick; a notch was cut on one end to slip on to the leg of a goose and a pin was put through the wood in front of the leg to hobble the bird.

hoblin a small heap of peats. [related to Eng dial *hobling* a haystack; a form of heap with the OE suffix *ling*]

hoch *tae hoch an oar* to rest the handle of the oar under the thigh [OSc. *how*, the shin]

hock* to dig out, '*He wis sittan on the dyke hockan at a neep*' he was scraping bits out with his front teeth. **hockéd*** having a gaunt appearance, '*His cheeks wir just hockéd*'. [a form of Sc *howk*; earlier *holk* related to LGer *holken*]

hocky '*My hocky!*' 'Goodness me!'. [a form of Eng heck!]

hode punishment, '*Yir mither'll gae yi hode when yi get home*'. [origin unknown]

hodge see HOADGE.

hodry a large kind of dogfish. [ON *hár* dogfish; meaning of suffix uncertain unless it is ON *drit*, dirt]

hoe see HO.

hoerot wet miserable drizzly weather. [? HOGER + REEK; compare Sc *hos-reek* mist, drifting snow]

hog 1 a mound which a fisherman at sea used as a mark. [ON *haugr* mound]. **hogboon** an elf who lived in a mound. **hog-boy** 1 an elf 2 a giant; the huge finger-print stone which lay near the present Millquoy in Stenness was allegedly thrown from Hoy by a *hog-boy* [ON *haug-búi* mound dweller]

hog 2 a hole eg in a stack made by removing sheaves. [ON *högg* a breach]

hogar to walk around heavy footed. **hogars** heavy boots [origin unknown]

hogboon see HOG 1.

hoger see HAGGER.

hogs to eat greedily. [ON *hakka*]

ho-kettle large dogfish. [Sh *hokel* shark; corruption

of ON *há-karl*]

hole* (*vulgar*) the rectum. [compare Ger *loch* used for hole and rectum, Eng *arse-hole*]

holm* a small island. [common in placenames; ON *hólmr*]

holster to get underway in the sense of *getting up*. [compare Sc (Banff) *hulster* a lift on to the back; probably a form of Eng *hoist*]

holyiny a big boned man. [Sh *holgin*; Norw *halge* bundle; see HALLOW]

holyo probably the lesser dogfish. [ON *hár* dogfish; compare HODRY and HULLION]

home 1 to make a temporary top on a stack. [see WHUMMLE]

home 2 = home. **home-aboot*** at home, '*He always bides home-aboot noo*'.

homelshow a mix up. [see HUBBERSHEU]

homelie-ugly see HOMERY.

homer a large kind of dogfish. [ON *hámerr* large shark]

homery in poor condition with the bones showing. **homelie-ugly** very ugly looking. [ON *humarr* lobster]

ho-mither see HO.

honey = honey. **honey-ware** a sweetish tasting tangle.

honey-spot a piece of wood fitted to fill up the angle formed by the converging gunwales at either end of a boat. [ON *hyrning* corner; ON *spotti* a bit or piece]

hoo* how?

hood the night. **stan hood** the middle of the night. [see HUID 1 and STAN]

hoodgear the pirn and fly of the spinning wheel which takes in the thread.

hoodgiekapiv = thingamabob. [origin unknown]

hoodie* the hooded crow [also Sc]

hook to bend down. [see HOOKERS]

hookatie-crookatie on the haunches [see HUIK]

hookers* *tae sit on ane's hookers* to squat. [related to ON *hokra* to go bent; compare Du *hurken* to squat]

hook-seal the self-heal plant. [origin uncertain]

hoolan a strong gale. [probably a form of Eng *howling*; compare Eng *howling* gale]

hoom, himp, huim to grow dark. [ON *húma*]

hoomin twilight. [see HOOM above; compare Norw *hymning* twilight]

hoonk to bend down or over. [probably a form of Eng *hunch* to bend the back]

hoop* = to hope, '*I hoop he'll be the morn*'. [still common in Sandwick and Birsay]

hoopéd married. [a metaphorical use of *hoop*. to *brak a man's gird* was to break up a relationship between him and his girl; really to break his hoop]

hoor* 1 = whore (*vulgar*) 2 '*Whit a hoor o a size*'

'*Whit a hoor o a day*' expressing excessive degree (vulgar).

hooran a disgust. [? HOORING; see HOOR]

hoorious unwelcoming, *Hid's no use gaan tae that hoose wi' yir collecting tin - the folk there are kinda hoorious*. [origin unknown]

hoosamil a road among or between houses [ON *milli*, between]

hoosaget *tae go hoosaget* to go visiting. [assumed ON *húsa-gata* literally *house path*; compare ON *húsa-ganga* visits]

hoosamenyie an uproar. [HOOSE + Sc *menyie* a noisy festival]

hoosavel 1 the field next the house. 2 refreshment served out to workers in this field. [ON *í húsa-velli* (in) the house field]

hooscanna a shelter built on the commons. [ON *hús* house; ON *skygni* shelter; *Skinhouse* was an old house in Firth]

hoose = house. '*He wis a good hoose moose*' said of a man always on the look out to bring home fish etc for the larder. **hoose-ateen** between houses. **hoose-room** the amount of room in a house.

hoosie see HOOZE.

hoosked moody. [? Norw *huskutt* sickly]

hooze, hoose to lift a child up and down in the air. [Sh *hus*; related to HEYS]

horax a small extension to the back of a dwelling house and roofed at the same pitch. It measured approximately 2.7 m by 1.4 m and held a box bed. [see HURRY]

horn 1 a drinking horn. 2 the horn-like projection at the side of an anvil. 3 the metal tip or tags on laces or thongs. 4 of a boat, the continuation of the stem. [also Eng; ON *horn;* see HEULD HORN]. **horn-gibby** see GIBBY. **horny** a children's game in which the devil (or devils) take their place in the middle of a playground or field and others try to run from one end to the other without being caught. If caught, the catcher becomes a devil. [Sc *Auld Horny* the devil; see BLACK PETER]. **Horny** a Stronsay goblin.

horny golach an earwig [also Sc. see GABLOO]

horra-goose the barnacle goose. [ON *hroðgas;* Sc *horie goose*; Sc *hurrock* brent goose]

horrible = horrible. Used as an intensive in Westray and in parts of the East Mainland of Orkney e.g. *a horrible bonny bairn* a very pretty child.

horro an expression of excitement on seeing some activity. [compare Eng *hurrah*]

horse 1 = horse (it does not change in the plural. 2 the moveable part of the rope-making gear which controlled the main sheet or jib sheet on old sailing models/yoles

horse-gokk* 1 the common snipe 2 the sound made by the snipe as it power-dives in display flight.

[in Sh the bird is called *snippack* but the sound is called *horse gokk*; in Norway the bird is called *humre-gauk* where *humre* is to neigh and it is also known as *horse-gauk* where Norw *horse* is mare; the smaller jack-snipe, rare in Orkney but common in Scand makes a distinct *clippety-clop* call in display flight; the snipe is also known as the MIRE-SNIPE and WATER-PLEEP, hence the riddle:-

The horse-gokk, the mire-snipe
and the water-pleep
That three birds runs apin twa feet.

[ON *hrossa-gaukr* common snipe]

horse gornick a large variety of gurnard. [see GORNICK]

horse-leg-been 1 = horse leg bone. 2 a taboo term for the port side oar in a boat. [compare FOLA-FOT]

horse-lok a wisp of straw with the ends folded in and laid by, untied, for giving to horses. [ON *lokkr* lock of hair]

Horseman's Word the password of the Horseman's Society, a secret society which included blacksmiths among their number and was found at one time all over Britain. [the sign of the horseman, an additional punchmark, can still be seen on old horse shoes]

horso, hoso, hosif, hussif, husho a type of shellfish, the Banked Wedge Shell, found in Oyce of Firth. [corruption of Eng *horsefish*]

host* of an animal or a person to cough. [ON *hosta* to cough]

hot-house* a green house.

hould condition (especially of cattle). [ON *hold* fatness (especially of cattle)]

houp = hops, as used in brewing. [OSc *howpe*]

hoved, heuved *hoved up* swollen. [ON *hevja* to swell]

hover to wait a little. [also Sc; ME *hoveren* to linger]

hovy bread which has risen well. [Norw *hov* rising of dough]

how* hollow, *'The neep wis clean how'*. [Sc *howe* related to Eng *hole*]

howa† one who frequented mounds etc. for supertitious reasons [ON *haugr* cairn; probably originally *hauga-mann*; compare EDan *höghoemen* unbaptised, heathen children]

howaness the smallest particle, *no wan howaness in the hoose*. [see HAWANCE and HAAIN]

howdie a midwife. [also known as a GRIPPER; also Sc; origin uncertain]

howe a mound, common in placenames. **howe-bakkéd** of a sea stormy, *'There's no muckle lee wi a howe-bakkéd sea'*. **howijib** a choppy sea, tidal race etc. [see CHABBLE; common in

placenames; ON *haugr*]

howin see HAAIN.

howstramp a stumble, *'Good I tuk a howstramp fornent the door'* [OSc *howe* a hole + STRAMP]

howther to raise, *'Howther hid up a bit min'* [origin uncertain]

hoy to hail, summon. [from the call *'Hoy!'*]

hubbersheu an untidy girl. [Sc *hubbleshew* disorder]

hubbet† a salt water lake. [found today in placenames; ON *hóp* bay with Norse neuter definite article *it* as suffix]

hubble a heap of seaweed piled above the beach. [see HOBLING]

hubby a kind of loose vest formerly worn by females. [ON *hjúpr* a doublet]

huderon empty. [origin unknown]

hudgans large number or quantity. [Sc *hudge*; a form of Eng *huge*]

hugal a stout ungainly person. [see HUIGGLE]

hugger see HAGGER.

huid 1, hood, heuld, huild verb. of the seasons, to get darker, *Wir in September and hid's fairly huidan noo.* noun. the middle of the night. **heuld horn** a midnight drink (taken from a *horn* originally. [the *l* forms suggest ON *hulda* a cover but may be a form of Sc *hood* with intrusive *l*; compare ON *gríma* night, literally *hood*]

huid 2 to nod off. [*huid* = head]

huidie a sun-bonnet worn by field workers. *pu the huidie on* to cap, top.

huidins the junctions of the side-boards of a boat and the stern posts. [Sc *huidin* a fastening; related to HOOD]

huidit craw the hooded crow.

huif a short strong boat-hook. [Norw dial *hov* a pot hook]

huiggle to sit or move in a huddled up fashion. [Norw *hulka*]

huik*, heuk = hook. **heuk-butter** butter made specially for harvest when the heuk or hook was used to cut crops. **huiketty-kruiketty** in a crooked fashion, in the old riddle:-

Huiketty-kruiketty whar rins thoo?
Clippét tail every year - whar speers thoo?
Answer: a stream and its bank (the meadow grass was cut from the bank every year)

huikened, heukened sitting in a bent position. [ON *húka*]

huild see HUID.

huilders see HULDER.

huily gently. [ON *höf-liga* moderately]

huim see HOOM.

huin 1 the ridge of a house. [also Sh] 2 a hen's perch. *tae be on the baak-huins* to be out of sorts. [*baak-huin* must mean hen's perch though not recorded as such; a hen which is out of sorts roosts all day and does not go outside the hen-house; see BAAK 2; combining two words of similar meaning to produce a new word is not unusual in Ork dial; see SPULLYIEREEF; ON *húnn* a knob with transferred senses; *top of a mast* hence top]

huinka, hunka to loiter about, especially of young boys after girls at night. [ON *hinka* to hobble, hence *to delay*; compare *hinkr* loitering]

huins *tae be on the heuns o* to be on the mind of doing something. [? ON *hugan* a minding]

huiv rich growth of grass or clover. [compare Norw *hov* a second mowing]

huivy see HEEVIE.

hulder, hilder *hulder o bones* a thin person. *tae go in a hulder* to stoop in walking [also Sh]. **heuldry** thin and bony. **huilders** a big clumsy person. [the sense is the noise of rattling bones; compare SKOLDER]

hulet† the eagle owl. [Sc *howlet* related to Eng *howl*]

hull a skin or covering. [Eng *hull* a husk]

hullcock a fish, the smooth hound. [origin unknown]

hullion the lesser dogfish. [see HOLYO]

hulster to make ready for departure. [Sc *hulster* to put a load on one's back]

hum and hae see HAE.

humbug 1 = noun. humbug. 2* verb. to inconvenience, *'Ah'll go an no humbug thee'*.

humelsho see HUMMLE 2.

hummel of farm animals, naturally hornless. [OSc *hommill* hornless]

hummelsho see HUMMLE 1.

hummlan, himlan used as an intensive, *hummlan hot, hummlan cowld* etc. [Eng *humbling*]

hummle 1, hummel to chew in a partial way. [see HAM]

hummle 2 to overturn, *'Hummle the barrel min and git a gren more'*. **hummelsho** great confusion or turmoil. [see WHUMMLE]

hummleband an oar-thong. [ON *hamla* to restrain; ON *band* band]

hump = hump. **humpy backéd*** humped backed.

humpsie sulky. [Eng (slang) *hump* sulks with Sc *sie/sy* adjectival suffix]

hunch 1 = hunch. 2 to heave or shove with the shoulder.

hund 1 a dog. 2 a scoundrel. [ON *hundr*]

hundamess, hundamis 1 a great quantity of dirt. 2 much ado about nothing. [ON *hundr* dog + MESS]

hundan of a dog or person roaming around ravenously. [ON *hundr* dog]

hunder = hundred. There were two measures of a hundred used in Orkney, the *big hunder* or *long hunder*, 120 or 6 score (a measure common to all Teutonic peoples) and the *sma hunder* which

was 5 score. **hundersgrund** ground in which it is possible to plant a hundred and twenty cabbages. [*hundred* here is the *long hundred*]

hunka see HUINKA.

hup-hover a dilemma. [origin unknown]

hupp to hobble a horse. [Eng *hopple*]

huppidy-drolty see HUPPIDY-KRA.

huppidy-kra* to carry someone *huppidy-kra* on one's shoulders. [probably Sc *apae da craigs* that is on the neck though this phrase is not recorded in Sc; there is no *craig* form of neck in ON but the word exists in Norw *krage* and similar forms exist in Du and Ger; **huppidy-drolty** to carry *huppidy-drolty*, over the back in fireman fashion; the essential meaning of *drolty* is hanging down as in Norw *drolde* something of a cylindrical shape hanging down]

huppo a toad. **huppo-stuil** a toadstool. [compare Norw *hopp* a frog or a grasshopper; the final *o* is a common Orkney dimin]

hurkle to make a gurgling noise in the throat. [Norw *hurkla*]

hurl 1 a noise in the throat caused by phlegm. [also Sc., a wheezing; see HURKLE above]

hurl 2 verb. 1 = hurl. 2* to wheel a barrow etc. 3 to wheel something in a barrow. (When, during the war, an old man was told that the enemy had been hurled back from the front he remarked that, had he been in charge, he would have made them walk!). noun 1* a ride, *'Wid yi like a hurl in me barroo?'* 2 a quick movement or action, *'Gae the kettle a hurl o a boil'*. **hurl barrow** a wheel-barrow.

hurn a lobster's hole. [ON *hyrna* a nook]

hurr to make a sound like a top or a cat purring. [also Sc and Eng dial; compare Norw *hurra*]

hurry 1 = hurry. **hurriedly** suddenly, *'He died hurriedly'*.

hurry 2 a hole or corner. **ale-hurry** a corner of the house where ale was kept. **hurry-timmer** the small fitted timber at the bow or stern of a boat. [see HONEY SPOT; Sh *horek*; ON *hyrning*]

husband† found in records with the sense of the original ON *húsbondi* householder.

hushle a strong, gusty, dry wind of short duration. [also Sh; echoic]

husho see HORSO.

husky stormy (weather). [Norw *husken* of weather bleak]

huskyan, hustyan strength or power. [compare Norw *husk* might]

hussel see HEESHAL.

hussif see HORSO.

hussy a pocket case for holding needles, thread etc [? *housewife*.]

hustlan rustling eg of sheaves in a drying wind. [see

HUSHLE]
hustyan see HUSKYAN.
hutheron a stupid person. [? a form of HUDERON empty]
huvie see HEEVIE.
hwinkle faced lantern-jawed [origin uncertain]
hydrin a layer or a sprinkling. [origin unknown]

hyeukin shivery and cold. [essentially *in a bent position*; see HUIKENED]
hypéd bad tempered. [compare Eng *hipped*]
hysk see HAZE.
hyveral a lazy person. [Sc *haiveral*]

I usually pronounced as in English but there are certain exceptions e.g. *the weeked keeng wis seek in a baseen*, (the wicked king was sick in a basin). There are many examples of this and there is no obvious rule governing such pronunciation. Notice these differences too. '*Ah'm gan tae the fishing fur I like fishan,*', '*Ah'm gan tae deu me knitting noo fur I like knittan*'. The older people on the island of Burray did not make this distinction as in this example, '*Ah'm gan tae the fishan fur I like fishan.*'
i a common contraction of *in*, '*Go i the hoose*'.
icerd see ISITT.
ilk† each. [also Sc; OSc *ilk*]
ilkin a curse, '*Muckle ilkin tae thee!*' spoken when grudgingly giving someone something. [Eng *ill-gain*]
ill* 1 = ill. 2 = bad. 3 very, as an intensive. 4 used with the negative to convey the idea *pleasant enough* especially, '*He's no a ill fullo (fellow)*', '*Hid's no a ill day*'.
ill-anseran* of a child refusing to behave, '*That's a ill-anseran thing o bairn that*'. [ON *anza* to pay attention]
ill-at clumsy. [see below]
ill-at-gaan clumsy. [ILL-AT + GAAN (going)]
ill-avised see ILL-DIVVISED.
ill-beggit ill natured. [ON *bágr* to thwart]
ill-belkifood of a horse etc., uncompliant. [compare Norw *ill-bellug*]
ill-benyied see ILL-VENGIED.
ill-benyiefood a form of ILL-BENYIED.
ill-best the best of a bad lot. [compare Faroese *ill-bestur*]
ill-bisted, ill-birted bad tempered. [ON *byrstast* to show anger; literally *to bristle up*; see BISS]
ill-casten untidily dressed. [see ILL-UPSHAKKEN]
ill-contriven awkward. [Eng *contrive*]
ill-divvised, ill-divished, ill-tivished of forbidding or untidy appearance, slovenly. [see TIVISY and DIVSO, both words relating to untidiness; *ill* has the sense 'very' here; see ILL]
ill-end literally *bad ending*. Used as a curse, '*Ill-end apin thee!*' or as a substitute for *the devil* in the example, '*Whit ill-end can he be wantan here the day?*' **ill-endfu** most ill-endfu pain an unbearable pain.
ill-fain to dislike, '*Ah'm right ill-fain o this weather*'. [ON *feginn* glad]
ill-fardie hasty. [Norw *ferðugr* ready, prepared hence *badly prepared*; see FIERDIG]
ill-faured shabby. [a form of Eng *ill-favoured*]
ill-feld fearsome looking. [the essential meaning is *ragged*; see FYOLTRY]
ill-fossered untidy or slovenly. [Marwick suggests that this is a form of *ill-fostered*]
ill-gaet of an animal, unwell. *The coo gid ill-gaet apin me* [ON *gata*, path Sc *gate*, direction]
ill-grossened ill-humoured. [Sc *groosie* fat and awkward; related to Eng *gross*]
ill-hammsied morose or in a bad mood. [see HAMSY]
ill-haversed untidy in person. [ON *haefa* of clothes to fit]
ill-helt ill-health, a curse, '*Ill-helt tae thee!*' **ill-helty bit** not a bit.
ill-herskind 1 rough to the touch. 2 disagreeable. [see HERSKIN]
ill-hertit of a turnip etc hollow in the middle. [Eng *heart + ed*]
ill-himpid awkward or annoyed. [see HIMPS]
ill-hivered see ILL-HYVERED.
ill-hymed in a bad mood. [related to Norw *himutt* dusky and ON *huma* to grow dusk; see HOOM]
ill-hyvered, ill-hivered of forbidding appearance. [see ILL-HAVERSED]
ill kamered ill natured, forbidding. [ON *kám* dirt]
ill keestered see KEESTER.
ill-kyeltered badly woven. [see KELTER]
ill-less devoid of malice
ill-luckéd* unlucky.
ill-minted mischievous. [also Sc; see MINT]
ill-nettered = ill-natured, *as ill-nettered as seut (soot)* very perverse.
ill-oor a curse, '*Ill oor tae thee!*' Ill-hour to you. [compare ILL-END]

56

ill-run cantankerous. [Eng *run*]

ill-scathe a curse, '*Ill-scathe tae thee!*'. [ON *skaði* harm]

ill-set angry. [a special use of Eng *set*]

ill-snored, ill-snorted angry or ill-tempered. [the essential meaning of *snored* is *twisted*; compare Norwegian *snur* which means *knot* or *quarrel*]

ill-snuikct ill-humoured. [compare Norw *snøkk* whim]

ill-sweelt in manners, rough.

ill-swilded unwieldy. [ON *svella* to swell]

ill-thraan* awkward. [ON *þrá* to be obstinate]

ill-tivished see ILL-DIVVISED.

ill-treeskiferd, ill- treested ill-tempered. [ON *þjrózkufullr* refractory]

ill-tricket mischievous. [Eng *trick*]

ill-trifty-bit not a bit!. [Eng *thrift* in the obs sense *prosperity*; *ill-trift* must have been an old curse; compare ILL-HELTY BIT and FEENTY BIT]

ill-twartened ill-natured. [ON *þverr* across; compare Eng *cross* angry]

ill-twirned awkward, bad to live with. [a form of ILL-TWARTENED]

ill-twisterfu 1 difficult. 2 twisted. [Norw *tvist* conflict, dispute]

ill-upshakken untidy, someone who looks as if his clothes had been thrown at him [seems to be a special use of Eng *shaken up*]

ill-vedyid see ILL-VEEKIT.

ill-veed see ILL-VEEKIT.

ill-veekit*, ill-vedyied, ill-veed mischievous or bad humoured. [ON *vikja* to turn; used here in the sense of *twist*]

ill-veetrit argumentative. [probably a form of ILL-VEEKIT]

ill-venyied, ill-benyied ill-disposed. [ON *venda* to turn; compare ILL-VEEKIT; compare the use of *turn* in Ork dial, '*He has a fine turn wi him*']

ill-vilshed ill-willed.

ill-visked nasty or awkward.

ill-ways feigning sickness.

ill-yatto-coman said to someone who has arrived at an inopportune time. [ON *illa ert ðu kominn*]

ilta 1 *in an ilta* excited. [probably a development of ILTA 2]

ilta 2 sorrow at one's own conduct. [a form of ON *illr* evil, bad; compare Norw *ilde*; the Norn form of the Lord's Prayer formerly used in Ork included the phrase, *delivra vus fro olt ilt* deliver us from all evil]

ilta-kilta out of order, *oot o kilter*. [see ILTA 2 and KILTER]

ilted angry, displeased. [see ILTA 2 above]

ilty anger, ill-nature. [see ILTA 2]

ilty-fu full of evil or hatred, *Ilty fornirr the cat's guidmither* an expression of exasperation = *ilty-*

fu nirr etc. [compare Sh *nurri* a pet name for a cat; see ILTA above; the final element is *full*]

imalded buried. [literally IN-MOLDED]

imbian a native, '*He's a imbian o Evie*'. [ON *innbúandi* inhabitant; the *b* changes the preceding *n* to *m*; compare *Dounby* in Ork pronounced *Doomby*]

imby see EMBY.

ime* soot, on the bottom of a kettle or in the chimney. [ON *ím* dust or ashes; Norw *him*, membrane, N Eng *hime*, hoar frost]

immer-goose see EMMER-GOOSE.

imp 1 the part of the fishing line to which the hooks were made fast; it was spun of hair and fastened to the line at regular intervals. [also Sc; OE *impa* a graft]

imp 2 to hurry. [a form of HIMP]

imse, impse 1 to get going. 2 to be excited. [Norw *imsa* to stir]

imy of the weather, not clear, '*Hid's kinda imy the day*'. [see IME]

in = in. **in life** alive. verb. **to in** to bring in, especially harvest crops. **in-aboot*** inside, '*Bide in-aboot bairns till that man goes by*'. **in anunder*** underneath. **in-bow** certain articles which a tenant had to leave behind when he vacated a farm. [ON *bú* farm; see STEEL-BOW]. **in-breck** a portion of infield pasture land newly broken up. **in-bund*** of a house etc., hemmed in. [Eng *bound in*]. **in-by*** 1 the main living room of the old Orkney house had a central stone pillar against which the fire was built, that part of the room facing the fire was the *in-by*. 2 the fields surrounding a farm. **infield** land within the hill dykes. **in-haeing** a MUCKLE SUPPER [see HAE; also known as IN-TAKKING]. **in-pit** a wedding to which guests were required to bring food and drink. **inshot** of the tide a landward setting spurt of the tide, literally a *shooting in*. **in-takking** a feast held when all the grain crop was built in the yard [also known as IN-HAEING]. **in-time*** the end of break time in some Orkney primary schools. **in-toed*** pigeon-toed.

indright 1 purpose. 2 reception, '*He didna get muckle indright there*'. [Norw *idrag* expectation with the essential meaning a *drawing into*]

inees a peat bog. [Gael *innis* riverside meadow; Sc *insh*]

inganafou ailing. [see also ININYAFOU; Sc *ingang* deficiency with suffix *ful*]

ingnail variant of HANGNAIL.

ingral see ENGRAL.

ininyafou tired or listless. [see INGANAFOU]

innerly kind hearted. [also Sc; compare Dan *inderlig* kind]

innigar see EENIGAR.

innis 1 see ENNIS.

innis 2 a nasty smell. [see EUN 2]

inskeyft† a piece of land not in the run-rig system but belonging to one proprietor. [the last element means *a division*; OE *skiftan* to divide; ON *skipta* to arrange; ON *engjaskipti* division of meadow lots]

inteepidfu argumentative. [perhaps related to ON *teppa* to obstruct]

iper* midden ooze. [Gael *eabair* slimy mud or mire; Gael *òpar* mud on trouser legs]

iree see IRON-EERIE.

iron dyke a volcanic *dyke* several examples of which are found on the Birsay coast.

iron-eerie brown water coloured by iron-ore in the ground. [a form of Eng *iron-ore*]

irpid spiteful. [apparently NIRPÉD with loss of initial *n*]

is* 1 see HIS.

is* 2 me. '*Gae's a gren*', give me a small quantity, '*Ah'm seen is gittan up at five on a bonny morning,*' I have seen me get up etc. [seems to be the equivalent of Eng 'royal we']

is* 3 used instead of ARE in the 3rd person plural e.g. '*Dances is no whit they used tae be.*' [also Sc]

I'se common formerly, '*I'se warran*', I warrant, in the sense of '*I'm sure*'. [*I'se* is a form of *I shall* and is found throughout Sc and Eng dial where the present tense would be more appropriate]

isitt, icerd the letter Z

ither 1 1* other. [also recorded as TITHER]. 2* else, '*Whit ither could a body deu?*' **nothing ither** said by a shopkeeper when he means '*Would you like anything else?*'. **nothing ither fur 'id** no other course of action, '*When me car broke doon, there wis nothing ither fur 'id bit tae go an git me bike.*' 3* either, '*Ither yi tak hid or lave (leave) hid - that's yir choice*'.

ither 2 udder

ithy an eddy alongside a tideway. **ithysteen** an anchor-stone, such an anchor was used when fishing. [ON *iða*]

J English *j* pronounced *chy* in the alphabet, otherwise *ch*. *A cheelie-chug is the same thing as a chum-char*, is the approximate pronunciation of 'a jelly-jug is the same as a jam-jar'.

jabble choppy sea motion. [also Sc; ? imitat]

jack to skin a seal. [origin uncertain; compare Sc *chack* a cut or hack]

jackie a jackdaw. [common throughout Eng dial]

jag the motion of a carriage. [a form of Eng *jog*]

jalouse to guess or infer, '*I jalouse thir gittan merried*'. [also Sc; a special development of *jealous*]

jeck a large mug, usually made of tin. [Sc *jack* a leather pint mug; drinking mugs were formerly called by personal names such as *Jug, Jill, Jack*; *Jeck* is the Ork pronunciation of Jack; see MUTCHKIN JECK]

jee to align, '*Jee hid in the hole*'. [Sc *jee* to move to one side or the other; Eng gee]

jeelie = jelly. **jeelie-jug** a jam jar. **jeelie-piece** a piece of bread spread with jam [also Sc]

Jenny-hunder-legs centipede. [also known as MAGGIE-HUNDER-LEGS and FORTY-FEETER]

jigaleerie crooked. [see CHIGALEERIE]

jimp 1, jimpit see CHIMP.

jimp 2 a trick. [origin unknown]

jing-bang only in the phrase, *the whole jing-bang* the lot. [also Sc; origin unknown]

jird a sudden push [also Sh imitat.]

jockteleg, jocktullie a large knife or a large pocket knife. [also Sc and Sh; *Jock* + *leg*, the original knives being leg shaped]

joggle see CHOGGLE.

Johnny Mainland A fish, the father-lasher. Name used by Kirkwall boys early this century and still used in Sanday. [*Johnny* is a nickname as in Eng *John Dory*; *Mainland* probably refers to the Orkney surname Mainland]

John-run diarrhoea [also The RUNS]

Johnsmas Foy see FOY.

jole see JULL.

jospan a coarse loose coat. [a form of Eng *jupon*]

joukerie-packerie* dirty work in the sense of underhand dealings. [also Sc; the verb to *jouk* meaning *to dodge or duck*; *jouk* is a corrupt form of *duck* where a *j* comes to be substituted for a *d*; see JUBISH below for another example]

jow see CHOW.

jubish doubtful about something. [Sc *jubious* dubious; the Sc verb *to jubish* means *to suspect*]

jull, jole see CHULL.

jund 1 a heavy blow. 2 a big push. [OSc *joundie* to jostle]

jupsie having a large head. [see CHUFFSIE]

jutes see CHOOTS.

58

K usually pronounced as in Eng. Formerly in certain parts of Orkney e.g. in Rackwick, *k* before *n* as in *knob* was pronounced. *K* before *n* was pronounced in Eng too at one time and the practice continues in the Teutonic languages. A *y* is often inserted behind a *k*, '*I kyen hid fine*', '*Pit on the kyettle mither*', '*Best kyens for I kyinno*'. (Goodness knows for I don't know); *K* is sometimes pronounced *t*, the best example being *Ortney*, the regular pronunciation of Orkney.

kab see CAB.

kabby a small cod. [compare Norw *kabbe* block of wood, stump, etc]

kace see KES.

kaddy the call to a pet lamb. [see CADDIE]

kae a jackdaw. [also Sc; Norw *kaie* with similar forms in MDu and Dan]

kag, cag a keg, especially a brewing keg. **kagsy** squat like a keg, '*Min that is a kagsy calf.*' **setting the kag** the operation in which part of a sheaf and the brewing stone were placed in the keg in readiness for the water and other ingredients. [ON *kaggi* a keg; see COG]

kaiko see KECKO.

kail 1 borecole, especially the curly variety. 2* cabbage [also Sc]

kailwample a number of people fighting together. [the first element is also found in Sc *cullishangy*; for second element see WHUMBLE; in the testimony of Kit Huntling in the book, *Orkney Peat Fires*, she allegedly used the word CULLYAWHUMMLIE which is a variation of the same word; a story using similar words is told in Caithness so the accurate reporting of the testimony is in doubt!]

kaily-creu see PLANTI-CREU.

kailyflee see KALYFLEE.

kaimer see KAME.

kaisie see CAISIE.

kaivy *to kaivy ower* to fall asleep through exhaustion. [also Sc; compare ON *kefja* to founder]

kaka, kako see KECKO.

kalwart of the weather, chilly. [also Sc; compare Norw dial *kalvor(d)en* coldish]

kalyflee, kailyflee a butterfly. **kailyworm*** a caterpillar. [OSc *kaill* a form of Eng *cole*]

kam 1 a mould used in metal working. [refers to the KAMSHELL which was (and still is) used in moulding]. **kamshell** the bone of the cuttle fish which is often found on the Orkney shore. [also Sc in the form *caumshell*; Sc *camstane* white limestone or clay]

kam 2 see COME.

kame 1, kaimer 1 of a horse to rear. 2 of a wave to swell up into a ridge. [related to ON *kambr* a crest]

kame 2 a hilltop but only in placenames eg the Kame o Hoy, the Kame o Corrigall. [ON *kambr* a ridge or crest]

kammo a blow on the head. [? an extended use of Sc *cammock* a crooked stick]

kan a sea mark. [ON *kenni* mark; compare AITHKEN]

kanless see CAN 2.

kant see CANT.

kanteelams especially, *to cast kanteelams on somebody* to recall an old story in order to discredit someone. [related to Sc to *cant* to tattle or gossip; the suffix is not understood unless it be a form of *lings*; the OE suffix, hence *canteelings*]

kappaskift† a division of land (in a 17th century Court Record). [Norw *kappe* to cut; see also SKIFT and RAPASKIFT]

kappiestone a stone sinker for a net. [also Sc; ON *köppa* boulder]

kapsweevle, kapsweevil see CAPSWEEVIL.

karket, karkid, carkid the ox-eyed daisy. [? used for making a *carket* (Sc flower necklace)]

karl the male partan. [also Sc; ON *karl* man; compare Sc *carl-cat* a tom-cat] **karlin** 1 an old woman 2 a witch [Sc *carline*]

karm state or condition of things. [Norw *karm* a frame or setting]

karmash see KIRMASH.

karr 1 a big strong man. [a form of ON *karl* man]

karr 2 a hard bed of rock. [compare Yorkshire dial *carr* a rock; from the Celtic languages; compare Gael *carraig* a rock]

kassen see CAST.

kast see CAST.

katabelly, katabella the hen harrier. [ON *katt-belgr* cat's skin; compare Icel *kattarskinn* an owl]

kataface see CAT.

kathy see CADDIE.

katogle the owl, applied to all types of owls. [compare Norw *kattugle* tawny owl]

katoo see CAA.

katoosh a great disturbance [variant of CAA TEU]

katrisper a strong gale. [ON *rispa* to scratch; it is said that a cat scratching a post etc is a sign of a gale to come]

kattanow see CAT.

katty-wa see CAT.

katty-whelk see CAT.

kavelse to take the hook out of the mouth of a large fish with a small notched stick. [Sh *kavel*; see KEVEL]

kavit† a pannier bag for a horse. [origin uncertain; compare Sc *cabbie* a type of pannier]

kazy see CAISIE.

keagle a stout clumsy person. [see KEGEL]

keb*, kib a sheep tick. [Sc *ked*; origin unknown]

keck to make a noise like a goose. A stomach also *kecks* when it is hungry. [imitat]

kecker '*He's a kecker*' he's dead, a goner etc. [Sc *keck* to faint]

kecko, kaiko, kako, kaka the cow parsnip and similar plants. [also known as CHOCKSY; related to Lat *cicuta* hemlock; related forms are found in the Scand languages; Eng *kex*]

keech see CACK.

keechy poops see POOPS.

keek to peep, '*I saa her keekan at the window*'. [Norw *kikke* to peep]

keel* 1 1 the back, especially, *on the keel o the back* flat on the back. 2 a ridge e.g. Keely Lang, a long hill ridge straddling the Firth/Orphir boundary. 3 a brand on a ewe from a ram and by extension the dye on the ram to mark the ewe. [ON *kjölr* keel, back of book, ridge etc]

keel 2 noun. kale. '*I got me keel through the reek fae her*' I was thoroughly told off. verb. **tae be keeled** '*Yi'll be keeled through the reek for that*'. **keel root** a sea term (taboo) for the starboard oar in a boat [*kale root*, see HORSE LEG BEEN]

keel 3 *tae go through the keel harrows*. [a corruption of CAT HARROWS]

Keelbrae a Stronsay goblin. [origin unknown]

keel draught a runner on the bottom of a boat. [Norw *kjøldrag*]

keelie† a boy's game of marbles. [origin unknown]

keelie-whablo a roar, uproar. [compare KAILWAMPLE]

keelin a large cod. [also Sc; ON *keila*]

keem see KAME.

keeng see KING.

keep, kyeep, tyeep = 1 keep. 2* with regard to health, to fare '*Hoo are thoo keepan?*' a common greeting to an elderly person [also Sc and Eng dial]. **keeping*** *tae hiv a keeping on something* wishing to hold on to something for sentimental reasons, '*Na, Ah'll no gae thee that brooch, I hiv a keeping on hid*'*.

keero the native Orkney sheep locally known as the North Ronaldsay sheep. [Gael *caora* sheep; compare Sc *keerie* a call to a lamb or sheep and *kairy* a small breed of sheep; see the interesting hybrid word KERSEY]

keeso, kyso 1 something bulky. [also used of a person; compare Sc *keessar* a big ugly woman]. 2 to carry a large burden in the arms. 3 a drooping posture. [Norw dial *kis(e)* a bulge]

keester unpleasant trait, '*He his queer keesters in him*'. [origin uncertain]

kegel, keagle 1 an unshapely lump. 2 a stout, clumsy person. [ModIcel *koggul* a lump]

kek a twitch [ON *keikja*, to bend the upper part of the body backwards]

kelder a well. [common in placenames; ON *kelda*]

kelks cod roe. [also Sc; compare Swed dial *kalk* pith in wood]

kelpie a water monster. [also Sc; Gael *cailpeach* bullock, colt]

kelp-ware fine soft fronds of seaweed which come ashore with the spring tides. Formerly used as a kind of catalyst in the kelp making process.

kelter 1 coarse homespun cloth. [also Sc; Gael *cealltair* broad cloth]

kelter 2 to tumble. [Sc *kilt* to overturn]

kemp 1 verb. to struggle. noun. a struggle. [also Sc; ME *kempen* to fight]

kemp 2 ragwort. [also Sc but refers to *ribwort plantain*; Norw *kampe* is also *ribwort plantain*; the Sc and Norse are the correct forms; the Orkney form shows a transference of meaning; in the children's game of *kemp* (used in Scotland in this sense) one child holds a ribwort plantain stalk horizontally and the other tries to knock the head off by hitting it with his/her stalk; see KEMP above and SOLDIERS]

kemperman a champion. [see KEMP 1]

ken*, tyen to know [also Sc]. **kenning** a small bit or quantity. **kenno*, kinno, kyinno, tyinno** '*I kenno*', (I) do not know. [ON *kenna* to know]

kep to catch. [also Sc; a form of Eng *keep*]

kep-sweevle see CAP-SWEEVLE.

kerseckie 1 a cloth bag carried on the back. 2 a soft knitted padded garment under a jacket. [Sc *carsackie*; Eng *cassock*]

kersey the native sheep. [Gael *caora* sheep + ON *sauðr* sheep]

kes, kace, kest 1 a heap of tangles. 2 a dunghill or cess pit. 3 a large person. [ON *kos* heap]

Ketnes old pronounciation of Caithness. [ON *Katiness*]

ketter see KYETER.

kettle* 1 of a cat or a rabbit, to give birth. [Norw *kjetla*; Sc *kittle*]. **ketling*** a kitten or the young of a rabbit. [ON *ketlingr*]

kettle 2 = kettle. **kettle corner steen** the first stone laid in building a chimney bed.

kettling an irritation. [see KITTLE]

keuf* see CEUF.

keuffy see KUIVY.

keufsy see CEUFSY.

keul *a keul o wind* a puff of wind. [also Sh; ON *kul*]

keuller see KUILLER.

keult a heavy burden. [see KYOULT]

keulter see KYOLTER.

keuvy see KUIVY 1.

kevel a wooden gag put in a horse's mouth. [ON *kefla* to gag a lamb; a deriv of kefli a stick]

kevie see KAIVY.

kib see KEB.

kich* verb. to void excrement. noun. excrement (used with children only). **kichy-poops*** excrement (used with children only). [forms of this word are found throughout the Indo-European languages; compare Lat *cacare* to defecate; ON *kúkr* excrement; see CACK]

kid a coaxing term to a sheep or lamb. [see CADDIE]. **kiddy-baes** a nickname for Gairsay folk [*baaing sheep*]

kie to show or appear, '*Sae weel hid kies on*', That shows him in his true light. [Sc *kythe*; OE *cyðan* to show]

kik a twist, especially of the neck. '*Ah'm gin me neck a kik,*' [ON *keikr* to bend backwards]

kil = kiln [also Sc]. **kil crack** a flaw in glass, crystal etc., a crack induced in the firing process in a kiln. **Kil Corner** the meeting point of Harbour Road and Junction Road, Kirkwall where a kiln was at one time situated. **kil rusket** over-dried on a kiln. **kiln-ais, kiln-laece** the main beam in a kiln to support the cross pieces. **kil hogie** the fire place of a kiln. [a corruption of *kiln logie* where *logie* is Gael *logan* a hollow or pit]

kilder to totter. [Sc *kilter*; related to OE *tealtrian* to totter]

kile to hasten. [Norw *kile på* to hasten]

kil hogie see KIL.

kilt to tuck up a skirt etc to prevent it getting soiled. [also Sc; OSc *kilt* to tuck up]

kim bed. [Sc *coum* or *coumit-bed* a type of wood lined box bed; see COOMSILED]

kimp, kimse to toss the head through pride. **kimsey** proud. [Norw *kimse* to toss the head]

kimse see KIMP.

kin = kin. *tae coont kin* to relate one's pedigree, formerly a common occupation among Orcadians. **kin-redder** a person able to give his pedigree in detail and to tell of the whereabouts of his surviving relatives.

kinda* colloquial Eng *kind of*, to some extent, a very common expression in the dialect, '*Hid's kinda weet the day*'. **kinda middling*** in fairly good health or condition. **kindaweys*** after a fashion [also Sc], '*Are yi feenished wi the hoose?*' '*Kindaweys.*'

kine see KYNE.

king, keeng = king. **Kingdom o Lee** a children's game not unlike HORNY but the devil in this instance is a king. [also played in Sc where it is known as 'King o Cantland']. **king's land** land formerly in possession of the crown. **laa o keengs** the law of male succession.

kinlit of the wind, fickle. [a special development of Eng *kindled*]

kinno* see KEN.

kinshy stylish, proud. [? Sc *kinchie* merry, cheerful]

kinuver to play tricks. [Eng *connive*]

kinyal† poor (people). [origin unknown]

kip 1, kippack, kippis 1 a bundle. 2 a small number. 3 a lock of hair. [ON *kippa* bundle]

kip 2 to pull. [? ON *kippa* to snatch]

kipersweevil see CAPSWEEVIL.

kippack see KIP 1.

kippacks natural clover. [? perhaps since it grows in bunches; see KIP 1]

kippis see KIP 1.

kirk 1 verb. to tug. noun. a tug. [Norw *kjerka* to struggle with something difficult]

kirk* 2 church. '*Ye can mak a kirk or a mill o hid*' Do what you like. *the nearer the kirk the further fae grace* an irreverent saying about regular church goers. [also Sc and NE dial; ON *kirkja*]. **kirkyard*** graveyard. **kirkin feast** about ten days after the wedding a return feast was given to the bride and bridegroom by the young men who attended the wedding. [also known as a BACK TREAT]. **kirking plaid** a plaid of fine material worn by the bride on her first visit to the church after the wedding. **kirk-haken** eager to go to church. **kirkéd** the newly married couples' first visit to church, '*We were kirkéd on the last day o May*'. **kirk-marked** hare lipped. **kirk sookan** the neckband of the joggs or pillory [see SOOKAN]. **kirk sookened** belonging to a church district. [Icel *kirkjusókn* parish].

kirmash, karmash, kirmas, carmas 1 a mix up. 2 a crash. [origin uncertain]

kirmew the tern. [also Sh; onomat]

kirn* a butter churn. **kirmilk*, kirnmilk*** butter milk. **kirncap** a wooden bowl for lifting butter out of a churn. **Kirner** a nickname for an inhabitant of Deerness. **Kirnlicker** a nickname for an inhabitant of Stenness. [ON *kirna* a churn; ON *kjarna-mjölk*]

kirr 1 diarrhoea. **kirrabag** a pet name for a child, *a peerie kirrabag o a boy* (compare PURDY). [ON *kar* slime (on the skin of a newly born calf etc.)]

kirr 2 a sound made to soothe a hen, '*Kirr kirr noo!*'. [ON *kyrr* quiet]

kirr-bed *on kirr-bed* sick. [Sc *care-bed* perhaps conflated with ON *leggya í kör* to lie ill]

kirr-karr the ruffling of the sea caused by two contrary gusts of wind. [ON *kari* in a reduplicated form]

kirshen to christen; **kirshning** christening

kirsow see KREESO.

kirsty-kringlick a long legged hill spider. When a child found one he would place it on his hand and say this rhyme:-

Kirsty kirsty kringlick
Gae me nave a tinglick
What shall ye for supper hae

Deer, sheer, bret an smeer
Minchmeat sma or nane ava
Kirsty kringlick run awa!
[*Kirsty* is the personal name; *kringlick* shows
the dimin *ick* suffix]. **kirsy-kringlo** a daddy-
long-legs. (through confusion with the long legged spider) [ON *kringla* a circle; a reference to
the rounded shape]

kis, kiss see KIZZ.

kishyfaik† the kittiwake [see WAIKO]

kiss 1 see KIZZ.

kiss 2 used to taunt a little child especially when it is
naked, '*Kiss, kiss, kiss!*' [compare Norw *kiss* a
call used to attract cats, calves etc]

kist* 1 verb. to place in a coffin. **kisting** (the) the
laying of a dead body in its coffin. noun. a chest
or box. **kist o whistles** a church organ. [also Cai;
ON *kista*]

kist 2 see KIZZ.

kit 1, kitt, kittie, kitto, kitta* a term used in calling
hens. [imitat; compare TEKK and TIKKIE]

kit 2 a bucket, '*Get a kit oot o the ubby*'. [OSc *kyt* a
kind of pail; Du *kit* a tankard]

kit 3 the cry of the red grouse, *kit kit kit kit, kabow
kabow*. [imitat; see KITTY-COME-HOME]

kitchal 1 paunch 2 a man with a paunch. [compare
Eng *kite* belly; see KITPOCK]

kiteral a filthy little child. [compare OSc *ketterel* a
term of abuse]

kithuntling a monster. Kit Huntling was a legendary character who lived in Harray. [Sh
keddhontla a kind of ogress; from an assumed
ON *kettu-hyndla* cat-dog]

kithy-wind a whirlwind. [form of Eng *giddy*; compare LATHY]

kitpock the stomach of a fish. [*kit* related to
KITCHAL above; ON *poki*, Sc *pock* bag]

kitta see KIT.

kittedly nimbly. [? a metathesis of *kittledy*; compare
Sc *kittle* (adj) excitable and *kittle-leggit* nimble
(in dancing)]

kittick, kittiwacko, kitto* the kittiwake. **kitto-flixer**
a scarecrow. [both Eng and Ork forms are imitat]

kittie see KIT.

kittle1* to tickle. **kittly** ticklish [also Sc; ME
kytellen; ON *kitla*]

kittle 2 see KETTLE 1

kitto 1 see KITTICK.

kitto 2 see KIT 1.

kitty-come-hame the cry of the red grouse. The com-
plete song is:-
Kitty come hame (3)
Whit tae dae (3)
Tae beck (bake) (3)
Whit in? (3)
A buckyo-yo-yo-yo-yo.

kizz* the sound made to scare away a cat. [compare
Eng *pss!*; Norw *kyss*]

kla*, cla = claw. 1 to scratch. 2 a scratch.

klabbyclue a state of confusion. [compare Sh
kabbelow cabbage and potatoes mashed to-
gether]

klact verb. to seize hold of. noun. a firm hold [Sc
claught, a form of *cleek* see CLICK]

klaik-geese see KLEKK-GOOSE.

klaive the angle formed between the back rope and
the GEVEL. [see GEVELS; ON *klauf* cleft and
ON *klof* space between the legs]

klaivie a hollow in sandy links caused by drifting
sand. [ON *klauf* cleft; Faroese *kleyv* a hollow or
pass]

klakk a fishing bank. [compare Icel *klakkr* rock;
Faroese *klakkur* cliff]

klam* 1 to shut a door violently. 2 to press together
in a small space. [imitat]

klamp a patch on a boat. [Sc *clamp* a patch]

klams see CLAMS.

klank*, clank the sound made by a hen after it has
laid an egg. [imitat; compare ON *klaka*, of birds
to twitter; compare Norw *klunk* the croak of a
raven]

klanker, klankertony, klunkertony a big jelly fish
(*medusa*). *a scone and klanker* a scone and rhubarb jam (the jelly fish looks like rhubarb jam!).
[Eng *sea-nettle*; ON *klungr* bramble; ON *þrn* a
prickle; the jelly fish, nettle and bramble sting
or prick]

klap see CLAP.

klapwale a strap of wood along the outside of the
gunwale of a boat. [? *klamp* + *wale*]

klaran an anchor. [compare Icel *klára* a dung rake +
def article]

klash see CLASH.

klat see CLAT.

klatch, kleetch to slip up and down (of a badly fitting shoe). *tae go kleetch kletch* to go splish
splosh. [imitat]

klatter *in a klatter* broken up. [Swed dial *klatter* thing
in disorder]

klausen to be strongly attached to a someone. [ori-
gin unknown]

klavo, klowo a strap used for clasping together the
lower ends of the hames. [ON *klafi* a kind of
fork put on neck of cattle]

kleebo a slap. [Sc *clype*]

kleek a device used for making ropes out of straw.
[Sc *cleek* a hook]

kleester, klyster to smear, especially with mud.
[Norw *klysa* soft lump; Dan *klistre* paste]

kleetch see KLATCH.

klegg, cleg the horse fly. [ON *kleggi*]

klekk barnacle. [see KLEKK-GOOSE]

klekk-goose, klekk 1 barnacle. 2 barnacle goose. [the ancients believed that barnacle geese were born from barnacles; barnacles were also called SLY-GEESE; compare ON *klaka* to make a bird noise]

klemel, clemel† a soft stone used for moulding, mentioned in the Old Statistical Account (vol 5 p185). [compare Sh *klemel* soapstone; origin uncertain; compare OE *clām* clay]

klepp 1, kleppo 1 a lump of any soft substance. 2 a thick oat bannock. [ON *kleppr* lump]

klepp 2, clepp to walk noisily. [Eng clap]

kleppispur hermit crab. [ON *kleppr* lump with sense *soft lump* as in KLEPPY below; the reference being to the softness of the belly part; ON *sporðr* fish-tail]

kleppo see KLEPP 1.

kleppy a sea name for the halibut. [ON *kleppr* lump]

klepsy girs butterwort. [related to KLEPP 1; butterwort was added to coagulate milk]

klett, clett a rock. [common in coastal placenames; ON *klettr]*

klibber an old type of pack-saddle. **klibberbrods** old slippers. [Sh *klibberbrods* pack-saddle boards; the connection is not understood unless it referred originally to primitive wooden clogs; ON *klyf-beri;* compare Faroese *klyv* pack for a horse]

klick mill an old type of mill with a small horizontal water wheel. There is an example of such a mill near Dounby. The mill made a distinctive *click* in operation. [Norw dial *klikka* to tick]

klime to smear. [ON *kleima* to daub; see KLINE]

klimmer see CLIMMER.

klimper, klumper a boulder on a beach. [the essential meaning is *something round*; compare ON *klumba* a club; see KUNGLE for a word with a similar meaning and deriv]

klimse to be so thirsty that one can hardly open one's mouth. [compare ON *klumsa* to render speechless]

kline to smear butter on bread. '*Fa teu, brak and kline*' was an old invitation to start eating. **klino** a piece of bannock and butter. It was traditional for the herd to get a *klino* when any of cows were being served. [ON *klina* to smear; *kliningr* bread and butter]

klink 1 see CLINK.

klink 2 to strike a blow. [also Sc; Norw *klinka* to strike]

klink 3 verb. to rivet. noun. a rivet. [also Sc; Norw *klinke*]

klinkid see CLINK.

klinter, clinter *oot apae the klinter* out chasing girls at night!. [ON *klanda* to molest; ON *klandr* molestation]

klip see CLIP.

kliv the division in the hoof of a cow, pig, sheep etc. [ON *klyf* a splitting]

kliven tongs. **klivvens** the legs or the space between. [ON *klof* space between the legs]

klivvy 1 the place where a tide splits eg on a skerry. 2 a track or pathway up or down cliffs. [also CLIVOO; compare *Klivvith* a small geo on the Birsay coast; ON *kleif* a rocky ascent; ON *klyf* a splitting]

klogang 1 an area where sheep or cattle are wont to feed. 2 one's usual haunt. [the *Klogang of the Boons* is a placename on the island of Sanday; ON *klauf-gangr* tramp of cattle, literally of *cloven-footed animals;* in Westray and in Sh *klogang* is used, by extension, of one's usual surroundings; compare SUILKIE]

klokaman an old medicine man or charmer. [ON *klokr* cunning or clever]

klokk 1 the broad leaf on the tangle. 2 to cut off the leaves. [ON *klokka* a cape]

kloor*, cloor 1 a scratch, generally from a cat. 2 to scratch. **klooro** a rake used in seaweed harvesting. [ON *klóra* to scratch like a cat; ON *kló* claw]

kloot* see CLOOT.

klov, klow 1 a hoof, especially a cow's hoof. 2 half the hoof. 3 the cleft in the hoof. **bare klows** bare feet. **klov an ap** top to toe. [an example of the many reversed phrases in the dial; compare OOTSIDE-IN]. **klow-grund** cattle pasture. [ON *klauf* cloven foot; also transferred to humans]

klow see KLOV.

klowo see KLAVO.

klow-sheer an ear mark on a sheep. [ON *klofi* cleft; ON *skarð* notch or cut; such duplicated forms are found in ON; compare *hamar-klettr rock-rock*]

klumbung 1 an ill-shaped thing. 2 a clumsy person. [compare Norw *klump* a heap; Norw *bunga* a protuberance]

klump see CLUMP.

klumper see KLIMPER.

klumpies large loose boulders lying in the water. [see KLIMPER]

klunk 1 the sound made when swallowing. 2 *tae klunk doon* to swallow quickly. [Norw *klunk*]

klunker-tony see KLANKER.

klyers see CLYRES.

klyster see KLEESTER.

knab see KNAP.

knabbie a short piece of wood passing through the eye of a rope and used as a stall tether. [Norw *knabb* wooden peg]

knabsie a short, fat, active person [compare KNAPPY]

knap a knob, common in placenames e.g. the *Knap of Howar* is the name given to the original mound on Papa Westray which proved to be the site of the oldest domestic building in Europe. [ON *knappr* knob]

knap-for-naught a morsel of cake etc., so small as to be one mouthful [Sc *knap*, a mouthful]

knappy a well-built boy. [Sh *knab*; compare Swed dial *knabbe* a short well built person]

knark to crush with the teeth [a form of KNIRK]

knarp to bite [variant of Sh *knarp*, Norw. dial. *knurpa*, to chew]

knave see NAVE.

knave-kuithe a third year coalfish. [Sc *nieve*; ON *hnef* fist + KUITHE]

knave's lock a quantity of grain which was the due of the miller's servant, '*The laird got the mooter, the miller hid tae deu wi the knave's lock*'. [OSc *knave* a servant + Eng *lock* a handful of grain]

kned, knedge, knudge = to knead.

knep 1 a notch on a flail stick to which the leather band is attached. [Norw dial *kneppa* to join together]

knep 2 see NAP 2

knibby a button. [Cai *knib* a toggle; compare ON *knappr* knob]

knick 1 = knick. 2 to cut.

knicker 1 to neigh. 2 to giggle. [Norw dial *knikra* to laugh softly]

kniff, kniffie agile. [see NIFF]

knirdge 1 to press down hard. 2 the act of pressing down. [a form of KNED, KNEDGE]

knirk verb. of new footwear etc., to squeak. noun. a squeak. [Norw dial *knerka* to creak]

knitch a bundle of straw or heather carried in the arms. [OSc *kneck* a bundle]

knock to pound grain. **knockéd corn** bere which has been crushed; *kale and knockéd corn* was a popular Orkney meal. **knocking stone** a concave stone in which bere (barley) was pounded. [OSc *knok* to pound grain]

knoggelvi see NUCKLEAVEE.

knokk a bundle of carded wool. [compare Du *knocke* a bundle of flax and KNITCH]

knorro, knoro a lump, especially from a blow. [ME *knorre knot*]

knoop see NOUP.

knowe* a mound. [also Sc; Eng *knoll*]

knub a short club [also Sh Norw. dial. *knub(b)*, a log of wood]

knudge see KNEDGE.

knurl 1 the knuckle. 2 a large stone. **knurl bane** the knuckle bone. [ME *knorre* knot with dimin]

koather to caress or fondle. [see COTHER]

kobos to be *in the kobos* of hens, to moult. [the root sense of this word may be *block* or *stump* and may refer to the parson's nose which gets exposed in this condition; compare Gael *cibeni* rump of a bird]

kod see COD.

koilk a concave in the bottom of a spirit bottle. [ON *kúla* a ball or knob]

kokk 1 = cock (haystack). 2 a heap of seaweed.

koldroit a worm. [origin unknown]

kolf to work hard with a spade etc. [? a metathetical form of ON *kljúfa;* literally to split open (the earth), hence *klofi* a deep trench]

koll, kull *the koll o the huid* the very middle of the night. [ON *kollr* head used here in the sense highest point]

kolo 1 a cry of victory in a childrens game. [see KOOERLY]

kolo 2 a call to a dog. [see KUIL]

koly, *koly-lamp* the old lamp shaped in the form of a small saucer which held fish oil, the wick being the inside of a reed. **koly-ho** the lesser dogfish. The oil from this fish was used as lamp oil. [ON *kola;* related to KOL, charcoal through the idea of *burning*; see HO]

kolyie see CULLYA.

kongle see KUNGLE.

koo see COO

kooerly the cry of victory in a children's game (Hoy). [OSc *cour* to cower; Sc *coory* timid]

koofie any large oval shellfish eg *cyprina islandica*. [also Sh; ON *kúfr* heap]

koogild see COOGIL.

kooglie easily rocked or rolled about [see COCKLE and KUNGLE, related forms]

kooker to crouch over a fire. [Norw dial *kukra* to huddle up with cold]

kool-hoe see KOLY-HO

koolter back see COOLTER BACK.

koolter-neb see COOTER NEB.

koom see COOM.

koo-shell a kind of shellfish (*cyprina islandica*). [ON *kúskjel]*

koots a call to a pig. [see KUTCH]

Kork an Eday goblin who took up abode in Stronsay. [see WALTER RED and GIMP; ? a metathesis of ON *kreika* to limp; Norw *krake* dwarf]

korn-huggie see CORN.

kors see CORS.

kossel a pit where seaweed was collected. [the word probably originally referred to the heap of seaweed itself; ON *kös* heap]

korn *korns o butter*, the first appearance of butter in the churning process [see CORN]

koukan swallowing greedily. [compare ON *koka* to gulp like a gull]

kowed of an animal, polled. [Norw *kolla* to dock]

kown to whine. [ON *kveinka;* see KWINK]

64

kowisworth† see COO.

koy to exchange or barter. [origin uncertain; compare COSE]

kra 1 see CRAA.

kra 2 of waves to break. [compare Norw *krakk* waves in a tideway]

kraa-kruik a hand-winding device for twisting straw into ropes. [Sc *thraw-cruik*]

kraamill see CRAA.

krab, kraf, krav of a crop to go down after a strong wind and heavy rain. **kraved doon** of a person walking in a bent fashion. [Norw *krabbe*, Norw dial *kravla* to crawl, creep]

kraeno see KRANE.

kraig throat, but only in the phrase *tae pit ower the red kraig*, to drink down. [a pun on *red craig*, red cliff; here *kraig* is Sc *craig* neck or throat; compare Du *kraag*, neck]

krammy heavy drizzling weather. [ON *krammr* half-thawed (snow)]

krampis, krampies a mixture of oatmeal and refuse of melted fat kneaded into a dough then boiled. A similar Scots dish is called *cracklings*. [the basic sense is a soft mess, related to ON *krammr*; see KRAMMY above]

krane 1 see GREN.

krane 2, kraeno a small mussel which grows near the high water mark. [origin unknown]

krane 3 of a boat to keel over. [Norw dial *krengja* to turn upside down]

krang the flesh of a whale. [origin unknown]

krankie of a boat, easily capsized [compare KRANE 3]

krans a wooden tap on eg a brewing keg. [Sc *crann*; Du *kraan* water tap]

kranyo 1 a heap. [also KRONYO]. **2** a sickly woman. [essential meaning is twisted as in German *krank*, ill; compare Norw dial *krengja* to turn upside down]

krap the *krap of an eddy* its extremity. [Sc *crap* extremity]

krappen to compress eg fish livers. **krappen heads** stuffed cods' heads. [ON *kreppa* to squeeze]

krasho see CRAA.

krass to crush. [Norw dial *krasa* to crush]

krav see KRAB.

kreegle see KREEKLE.

kreekle, kreegle, kreetle to crawl about. [also Sh; the basic sense is to *go with bent back*; Norw dial *krekla* to creep]

kreesal of an animal, *lying in a kreesal* curled up as in sleep. [ON *krysja* to crouch]. **kreeso** in a disorder state (eg of clothes). [Norw dial *krysja* a confused heap]

kreest 1 to squeeze. **2** a complaining voice or a forced cry. [compare ON *kreista* to crush or squeeze,

hence *to force*]

kreestie-kringlick see KIRSTY KRINGLO.

kreetle see KREEKLE.

krepp tight (eg of clothes). [ON *kreppa* to squeeze]

kreppo 1 *tae go in a kreppo* to go with bent back. [Norw dial *kreppa* to stoop]

kreppo 2 an oatmeal bannock baked with fish livers as fat. [see KRAMPIS a related form]

krets '*Bi me krets*' an oath. ['by my creeds'; compare, *bi me faith, bi me certy* etc]

kreu see KRO.

kreul see KROIL,

kribble, kripple sheaves which occupied a certain unknown position in a stack. [? ON *kreppa* to compress]

krimmle *in a krimmle* bent down with age. **krimmled** of a horn crumpled. [perhaps a form of Eng *crumpled* but it may also represent a form of *crinkled*]

krimp 1 of material scanty. **2** of a boat close-hauled. [OSc *crimp* scarce, scant]

krinch a small bit. [Sc *crinch* a variant of Eng *crunch*]

kringle, cringle verb. to twist. *kringle in aside me* of a mother to a child in bed *cuddle in to me*. **tae kringle awa** to shrink through age etc. **kringled** of cloth, crumpled. **kringled teu** of cloth shrunk. noun. a round cushion. **kringle horned** crumple-horned. **kringle stuil** a cylindrical stool. **kringlo 1** a leather washer. **2** a little hillock. **3** a low straw stool. **kringlos** moving vapours seen above hills on a warm day (an old Sunday lady told the visiting doctor that it was a fine day for she could see the *kringlos*. When the doctor could not understand, her sister explained that it was the TEEBRO she was seeing!). **tae see kringlos** to see stars (after a blow on the head). **kringly headed 1** giddy. **2** foolish. [ON *kringla* a circle]

kringlo(s) see KRINGLE.

krint to grind the teeth. [variant of Sc *crinch* or *crinsh* to grind the teeth]

kripple see KRIBBLE.

kro, kreu, krue, creu* a yard, usually in the form PLANTIE-KRO or **kaly-kro** but earlier seemed to mean animal pen [ON *krókr* corner used in the sense of odd piece of land]

kroil, kruilyo, krull 1 a heap. **2** a messed up state, literally twisted. [Norw *krull* a curl]

kroilan failing in health. [see KRULL]

kromack see KRUMMO.

krome, crome* hoarse. [the sense is *seized up* or *pinched*; ON *kremja* to be pinched; compare Faroese *krim* catarrh and Norw *krauma* to speak with a whining voice; Sh *krimm* is to *clear the throat*]

65

kromo to tie the toes of geese to prevent them wandering far. **kromow** to batter, '*I'll kromow you*'. [related to Gael *cromag* a crook; compare Sc *crank* to shackle a horse]

kronglie misshapen. [see KRINGLE 1 and KRIMMLE]

krono a small detached stone outhouse. [ON *krókrinn* the nook or corner; the placename *Cruan* in Firth is an example

kronyo see KRANYO.

kroolter the gurnard. [? ON *kretta* to murmur; see CROOT; see also KROONER below]

krooner the gurnard. [also Sc *croon* to make a low murmuring sound; the gurnard makes a groaning sound when it is caught; the Norw name for this fish is *knurr* from knurra to growl]

kroose 1 a little dish or vessel. [ON *krus* a pot]

kroose 2 see CROOSE

kroot the raven. [imitat]

kroppen, croopen 1 bent in the back. 2 withered. [ON *kroppinn* shrivelled, shrunk]

kroppin-kuithe a kuithe stuffed with a mixture of oatmeal and livers. [see KRAMPIS and KUITHE]

krossick a starfish. [literally a fish in the shape of a *cross*; Norw *krossfisk*]

krove the carcase of an animal. [ON *krof*]

krow to crunch, especially with the teeth. [Norw *krølle* to crush; see KROIL]

krowo-shell a kind of ladle used in the process of making fish oil. [origin of first element uncertain; *shell* is ON *skál* a bowl]

krua a corner where two buildings meet at right angles, used for storing turnips, peats etc. [ON *krókr* nook or corner; compare KRO]

krubban of a work space confined or cramped. [compare Norw *krubbutt* narrow]

krubbick a small hammer for striking limpets off rocks. [origin uncertain; ?for *klubbick*, an unrecorded diminutive of English *club*]

krubbies the crooked spaces between the flagstones on a floor in the old days before the flags were squared off. [Sh *krubbet*; Norw *krubbutt* narrow]

krud see CRUD.

krue see KRO.

kruggle, cruggle 1 to crouch down. 2 to go bent. 3 to cram the body into a small space. [Norw dial *krukka* to huddle oneself together]

kruibo see KRUMMO.

kruik*, cruik 1 a crook, especially a hook in an old Orkney fireplace on which to hang pots etc. 2 a double knot used to tie the band of a sheaf, much more secure than a SOO'S TAIL. In the days of run-rig those who farmed adjacent strips used different knots to help identify sheaves after they had been scattered in a gale. 3 a North Ronaldsay

sheep mark. **kruik-tree** the beam from which the KRUIK was suspended. [ON *krókr*]

kruikle to crouch. [Eng dial *cruckle* to crouch]

kruilyo see KROIL.

kruit a slight impediment in speech. [see CROOT]

krull see KROIL.

krummo, kromack, kruibo see GROMO.

krummo-fu see GROMO.

krumpy bannock a bannock baked of oatmeal and fish livers kneaded together. [see KREPPO and KRAMPIS related forms]

kruncho a bundle of something tied together. [compare Norw *krumsa* the hand with the fingers bent inwards]

kruttle, cruttle verb. 1 to make a rattling noise. 2 to ripple of water or a ripple eg in a tideway. noun. a rattling noise. [imitat; compare Norw *krutla* or *krusla* to simmer]

kubby see CUBBY.

kucher to recover. [Eng *cocker* to revive in health]

kud poor oats. [origin uncertain]

kudgie of a man, dumpy. [Sc *gudge*; Eng *gouge*]

kuffy 1 applied to poor oats. [? a form of CHAFF; OE *ceaf* chaff]

kuffy 2 of a person fat. [see CEUF]

kuggle a form of KUNGLE.

kuil, koly, kully, cullye 1 to speak kindly to an animal, especially a dog. 2 to make too much of a situation. [Sc *culyie*; OSc *culze* to caress]

kuiller, queller a small tub, especially one without BOOLS, often used for storing butter. [ON *kolla* a pot without feet]

kuiserie, kulsary undue favouritism to relatives. [origin unknown]

kuithe, cuithe a one year old coalfish. **cuithin, kuithin** a coalfish of third year or more. [ON *koð* the young of a fish]

kuithin, cuithin see KUITHE.

kuits ankles. **kuitlan** knocking the ankles together while walking. **kuitos, cooticans** footless stockings. [also Sc; compare Du *koot* ankle]

kuitten noun. someone who is sensitive to cold. adj sensitive to cold. [origin uncertain; compare HUITEN and KOOTEN]

kuivy 1 1 **kuiv, kuvie, keuffy** 1 stump of a horse's tail. 2 a wooden block with grooves in it to guide strands in the rope-making process. 3 a sheep mark made by cutting off the tip of the ear. **kuivy-tangle** the largest tangle. [probably so named from its resemblance to the stump of a horse's tail; Norw dial *kufa* to dock or curtail]

kuivy 2 a little basket put over a horse's mouth to stop it eating when sheaves are being carted [ultimately related to CUBBY and KAVIT]

ku-kwacks a period of blustery weather in May. [Sc *cow quake*; so called because it supposedly induces a shaking illness in cattle]

kulkie the horizon. [? related to KOILK]

kull *the kull o the night* the middle of the night. [see KOLL]

kully see KOLO 2.

kulsary see KUISERIE.

kummick a coalfish a little older than a KUITHE. [compare Sc *cominie* a young coalfish; origin uncertain]

kummle† a mound. [found in placenames eg *Cumlaquoy* in Birsay; ON *kuml* related to Lat *tumulus*]

kumper a fish, either the fatherlasher or the short-spined sea-bullhead. [see UIKO]

kundie hole see CUNDY HOLE.

kungle, kuggle, kongle, cungle, cummle a lump of stone or rock. [compare Faroese *kongul* a lump of peat; essential meaning is *roundness*]

kunn to give (thanks) '*I kunn thee thanks*'. [also Sc; OE *cunnan*]

kunnin see CUNNIN.

kunno see CUNNIN.

kunyo a type of shellfish. [Norw dial *kung* sea snail]

kupp cunning, not easily cheated. [origin unknown]

kuppo a hollow in the land. [ON *koppr* hollow]

kurdy-murdy a state of confusion. [origin uncertain; compare KURRMULYO]

kurfufflit muffled up against the cold [origin unknown]

kurlo see CURL.

kurnow the mew of a cat. [imitat; today the cat would say *purmeow*; see KIZZ for exchange of a *p* and *k*; Sc *curmur* the purring of a cat and *curneow* a racket]

kurnudge a nudge. [perhaps a metathetical form of KNIRDGE but compare Sc *curriemudge* to beat good-naturedly]

kurre to coo [ON *kurra*, to murmur]

kurrivan see CURRIVAN.

kurrmulyo see CURRMULYO.

kurshow a form of KREESO.

kussack a calling term to a calf.

kutch, koots a calling term to a pig. [ON *kus* a call to a cow]

kuttack see CUTTY 1, CUTTACK.

kuttanoy see COTANOY.

kutto see CUTTACK 1.

kutty, kuttack see CUTTY 1, CUTTY 2.

kuvie see KUIVY.

kuy see KYEING.

kvenn† a woman. [ON *kvenna* woman]

kwack 1 to swarm with mites etc.

kwack 2 = quick; *in a quack*, quickly.

kwacko, whacko a quagmire. [Eng *quake* to shake]

kwark, kwarkie, quark, quarkie to swallow nois-

ily. [see WHARK]

kwarr to emit a rattling sound in the throat through difficulty in breathing. [ON *kvara* to rattle]

kweenack the female crab. [ON *kvenn* woman; see also KARL]

kwern = quern, a handmill for grinding meal or malt.

kwern-leather see LETHER.

kwerno the turbot. [from its resemblance to a QUERN; Eng *quern*; ON *kvern*]

kwick see QUICK.

kwill, quill, whullo, whull a small boat with bow and stern shaped the same. [Sh *kwilli*; origin uncertain; compare ON *hvelja* whaleskin]

kwink, quink 1 brent grose. 2 greylag grose. 3 the golden-eyed duck. [ON *kveinka* to whine; from the sound made by the wings in flight; Norw *kvinand* the golden eye duck]

kwinlo of horns twisted. [Norw *kvingla* to turn round]

kwint quick witted. [ME *queint* knowledgeable]

kwy 1, quoy 1 an enclosure, common in placenames. 2 to pen in. [ON *kví*]

kwy* 2 a heifer. [ON *kvíga*]

kye* cattle. [also Sc; OE *cy*; plural of *cu* cow]. **kye baest* cattle.

kyen see KEN.

kyerro a heap of stones. [Gael *carragh* stone pillar]

kyessel dried stomach of a calf used for making rennet an ingredient in cheese. [Norw *kjaese*]

kyest a heap. [ON *kostr*]

kyeter, ketter a term of abuse, only recorded in this taunt:-

> *Ketter-negger, hen beggar*
> *Beg the egg afore she laid her (it)*

[Sw dial *kältring* beggar, Norw *kjeltring* a scoundrel.

kyeug, kug to tug. **kyick** a sudden jerk or to make such a jerk. [Eng *tug* with *k* substituted for *t*, but see KIK]

kyinno see KENNO.

kyirk see KIRK.

kyirkéd of dust, swirling. [a metathesis of ON *kroekja* to wind round]

kyle see KILE.

kyne, kine 1 = kind. 2 soft, for example of the wool on the neck of the North Ronaldsay sheep.

kyolan moving or walking in a slow manner. [see KYOULT]

kyolks the muzzle of the old Orkney plough. [ON *kjalki* jaw]

kyolt, kyoult to carry something in an awkward manner. **kyoltas** a clumsy person. **kyolter** a clumsy movement in walking, '*She was gaan wi a kyolter*'. [ON *tolta* to amble]

kyoult see KYOLT.

kyso see KEESO.

L English l pronounced *ail*. Often missed out before *t* and *k* as in mat (malt), sat (salt), bak (balk). As in Scots, final double *l* often disappears eg BA, WA, CA, etc.

laaburro see LAWBORROWS.

laaginy *in a laaginy* in a state of stupor or laziness. [origin uncertain; compare Gael *lag* feeble, faint]

laagy see TISHALGO.

laamer beads amber beads [also Sc]. **laamered** yellowish in colour, used of the discoloured milk which comes from a cow about to calf. [Fr *l'ambre* amber]

labskoo stew. [Eng *lobscouse*]

lacer a lace, as in shoe lace [also Sc]

lachfasting† a legal prohibition. [ON *lögfesting*]

lacksy-daisy = lackadaisical.

lacky, lecko 1 the bowels of a sheep. 2 the third stomach of a ruminant. **tae cairry in the lacky** to carry eg a bundle of hay against the upper part of the body with the arms around. [ON *laki* the third stomach of a ruminant]

lade slime on tangles [ON *leðja*, mud, slime]

lade berry a rocky shelf used as a pier. [ON *hlað-berg*]

lady's hen see OUR LADY'S HEN.

laft* a loft. [also Sc; OSc *laft* to make a loft]

lagger to cover with any sticky substance. **laggered** covered with mud, paint etc. [compare Norw *laga* to pour liquid over; obs Eng *lag* to make muddy]

lagman see LAWMAN.

lagretman see LAWRIGHTMAN.

laigh to lower. [Sc *laich*; OSc *lauch low*]

laight a purlin. [Norw *lekte*]

laim see LAME.

laing a narrow ridge of land. [ON *lengya* a stripe]

laird a landed proprietor. **lairdship** the property of a laird. [also Sc; OSc *laird* a lord]

laith shame or disgrace, '*I think a laith o mesel.*' '*Hid's a laith o a craa (crow) that shites in hids ain nest*' is an old proverb. [Eng *loath*]

laivagan gossiping. [? Sc *laig* to gossip]

lake to trust. [? ON *hlíta* to trust]

lal a child's toy. [also Sh; ON *lalli* a toddler]

laldy* '*Gae hid laldy!*' said to a fiddler when you want him to play really quickly. [also Sc; ? OE *lael* a whip]

lamb = lamb. **lambing snow*** snow which falls in April at lambing time.

lame, laim pottery. [OE *lām* clay]

lamma† = lamb, an old form of address to a child.

lammar-spindle a contrivance for spinning horsehair into bridles. [origin uncertain; *lamer* a thong is recorded once in Sc]

Lammas* = Lammas. **Lammas beul** 1 a bed shared by a number of people, a common practice in the crowded town of Kirkwall during the LAMMAS MARKET (compare LANG BED). 2 used metaphorically of a flattened area in corn where lovers have been lying. **Lammas-brither/sister** a Lammas boyfried/girlfriend. **Lammas Market** the traditional market held in Kirkwall on the second Tuesday of August.

lamp to walk noisily. [Norw dial *lampa* to trudge]

lampered curdled. [see LAPPERED]

lampskar an old pot used for melting fish livers. [compare Dan dial *lampskaar* a kind of oil lamp]

landemaris† a boundary or boundaries. [also Sc; ON *landamaeri* boundary]

lander see LUNDER.

landit, lanyied of a cow striped across the back. [Sh form *lenget* is probably the same and more correct; ON *lengja* a strip]

landmail† rent. [ON *land* land; ON *mál* contract]

land side of a plough the straight side next the green as distinct from the board or mould board that turned the peat in a fur.

landskud† rent. [ON *land-skyld*]

lang = long. **lang bed** in the olden days weddings went on for days and at intervals the floor of the barn was covered with straw and everyone lay down to sleep side by side! (such beds exist in Norwegian mountain hostels today). **lang bolt** the bolt by which the shafts were attached to the cart. **the langer the lent** in the end, '*The langer the lent, I got aal me money back*'. **lang legged laroo** a daddy long legs. [origin uncertain]. **lang nebbid** of words, long (metaphorical use of NEB). **Lang Reed** the month of March [ON *langa hrið* long (difficult) time, but *hrið* also had the meaning *storm* especially *snow storm*; Shetlanders talk of stormy weather as a *ree*; compare Lat *tempestas* storm, related to Lat *tempus* time and STOOND]. **langsam** tedious, procrastinating [also Sc].

langer* = boredom [also Sc]. **langersom** tedious [also Sc].

lanter to hinder. **lantered** having someone in the house who overstays his/her welcome. [Sc *lant* to put in a dilemma etc from *lanterloo* an old card game]

lanyied see LANDIT.

lap a cut on a sheep's ear for the purpose of identification. [OSc *lap(e)* a flap]

lappered*, lampered of milk curdled. [also Sc; ON *hlaupa* to curdle milk]

lappie see LEPPY.

largis see LURGIS.

larikman see LAWRIGHTMAN.

larme to make a mewing noise [a corruption of YARM]

lass 1 girl. 2 maid servant. 3 a familiar form of address to a girl, a woman or a female farm animal. **lassie boy** an effeminate boy.

last the largest unit of weight in the old Orkney Standard. Twenty four MEALS made a *last* or 12 barrels of butter or oil. [ON *lest* a load or *hlass* cart load; compare OE *hlaest* which came to mean *a load of about 40000 pounds weight*]

lathowy of soup etc insipid. [origin uncertain; ? related to BLATHO]

lave the leavings. [also Sc; OSc *lafe*; OE *laf* what is left]

laverock, lavro* the lark. [also Sc; ON *laevirki*]. **lavro-high** a child's skipping game [*lark-high*]

lavrous see LAWBORROWS.

lawborrows, laaburro, lavrous† an injunction granted to prevent molestation or injury. [a Sc legal term; OSc *law-borch*]

lawman, lagman† the supreme justice in Orkney in Norse times; replaced by the term *sheriff* in 1541. [ON *lögsögu-maðr* lawspeaker]

lawmo, lummo hand, especially *big hand*. [ON *lámr* hand]

lawrightman, lagretman, larikman headman of a local court. [ON *lögrettu-maðr* member of a *logretu*; ON *lögretta* legislature, later *place of legislature*]

lawting† the chief annual headcourt held presumably initially at Tingwall in Rendall but in early records, in Kirkwall; after 1541 when Scottish sheriff courts were introduced *lawting* was used of any head court. [ON *lög-þing* public assembly]

lay 1 a lull in wave movement when a boat may safely approach the shore. [ON *lag]*

lay 2 1 = lay. 2 to weld or iron to replace loss by wear e.g. to lay harrow teeth, to lay the sock of a plough etc. 3 **tae lay oot/aff** to talk volubly e.g. '*He wis fairly layan oot o him*'. **tae lay at** to work hard. **tae lay in** to join with another in eg farm work. **lay thee with** do your best. **lay to (the door)** close (the door).

lay 3 frame of mind, *tae be on a good lay*. *on the lay o'd*, on the mind of it. [Norw *lag*]

lay 4 grassland. [Eng *leys* arable land under grass]

lay 5 a wrestle. [ON *leggja at jörðu* to throw to earth]

lay 6 1 = to place or put. 2 in rope making to wind the separate strands together, *tae lay a rope*.

lead 1 a swell in the sea. [ON *hljóð* sound]

lead 2 verb. 1 lead. 2 to cart (eg sheaves). [also Eng dial]. noun. a water channel as in mill-lead [also Sc]. **leadan** carting sheaves, '*I see Onston leadan the day*'.

lead-luss a lead sinker for a fishing line. [see LISS]

leap verb. 1 to parboil [also Sc]. 2 to shell (limpets etc) by plunging them in boiling water. noun. *a leap o haet* when a hot sun suddenly bursts

through the clouds. **leapéd** 1 overcome with heat. 2 scalded. 3 '*Me skin's aal leapéd*', used to describe the appearance of the skin after a bandage has been removed. **leapéd gibbo** hot buttermilk mixed with oatmeal in a kind of brose.

leaper a period of warm weather. [ON *hleypa* to leap with extended meaning curdle milk etc. see LAPPERED]

lear learning. **leardom** learning. [also Sc; ON *laerdómr*; OE *lár* teaching]

leavo in the game of hide and seek, the child called out '*Leavo!*' when he was hidden.

lecko see LACKY.

lee = lie, '*Hid's as big a lee as the keeng is a gentleman*'. '*If hids a lee hid wis lee'd tae me*' a qualification usually added to the end of a surprising piece of news.

leeb, leem used of poor crop, *just twa three leebs*. [Norw dial *lime* thin twiggy branches]

leed to listen. [ON *hlýða*]

leegeese barnacles on driftwood. [there was a belief held that the barnacle goose originated from barnacles; also known as SLYKEES, SEAGEESE etc]

leek a vigil held with the dead between death and the funeral. [also Sh *leek-wake*; ON *lík* corpse]

leekam, leetam a bad outcome, a let-down. [ON *líkamr* dead body, with extended meaning]

lee long live long, *the lee-long day*. [also Sc; ME *lefe long* literally dear long or very long]

leem see LEEB.

leen alone, '*He wis walkan by his leen*'. [Sc *lane*; OSc *his lane* etc]

leepéd see LEAP.

leepsy badly balanced. [a form of *lop-sided*; for *sy* suffix see BIGSY]

leero see LYRE.

leesom to make pliant. [Eng *lissom*]

leesome pleasant, agreeable. [OSc *lithe* to influence gently; OE *liðe* gentle, mild]

leet *never leet* don't say it to anyone. [also Sc and Sh; OSc *lete* to declare]

leetam a disappointment. [see LEEKAM]

leeter a little, somewhat. [coll Eng *leetle* little]

leethfu steady at work. [ON *líð*, help, assistance]

leetumpas one's usual condition or state of health. [a corruption of Sc legal term *legitima potestas*; see LUDGY POT]

leever, leevar rather. [compare Sc *leeve* willingly; archaic Eng *lief* dearly from OE *leof* dear]

leggan, leggin verb. '*Leggan thee plaet (plate) noo*', tilt it over on the rim to get the remains with the spoon. noun. 1 the rim of a barrel. 2 the contents of a barrel. **leggin-saw** a croze for cutting the groove in the leggin. [ON *lögg* the grove in the staves of a cask]

69

lempit see LIMPET.

lend, len* a loan. *tae hiv a len o* to borrow. '*Seeldoms (seldom) a len comes lauchan hame*' anything loaned often gets broken. [Sc *lend* a loan].

lendy bit* not at all! [compare FEENTY BIT]. **lends metters*, lendy odds*** it serves you (etc) right!

lenfu dreadful, '*Hid wis a most lenfu sight*'. [a contracted form of ILL-END].

lensho lying on haunches and elbows. [?*length + o*]

Lentran† spring time:-
> *In Lentran and the Lang Reed*
> *Naething bit water, kail and bere breed.*

a couplet about the hardships of Spring. [also Sc; OE *lencten* the spring; compare Eng *Lent*; for ending see FASTERN'S E'EN]

lepp to walk around clumsily or aimlessly. [compare Icel *lappa* to go heavily]

leppy, leppsy, lappie 1 a misshapen vessel, especially a bowl or cubby with one side higher than the other. 2 **leppy plate** a soup plate. [see LEEPSY]

lerblade, lerblading the cormorant. [ON *laer* thigh; ON *blettr* spot; so called from the white spot on its body near the thigh, this spot appearing only in the breeding season]

lergis a large unseemly mess (eg a lump of dough). [see LURGIS]

lergy filthy, *some lergy words kam oot o him*. [see LERGIS, LURGIS]

lerness a heap of wet dirt. [probably a corruption of LERGIS above]

lerp a mouthful of liquid. **lerpo** an unappetising mess of food. [compare Sw dialect *larpa* of a dog or child, to excrete]

lerrups strokes with a whip. [Sc *larrup* to thrash]

lest = verb. last. noun. substance 'Thir wis no muckle lest in that pair o shoes furtivver, the sole's come awey fae the upper already.'

let 1* abatement, with reference to weather, '*There's no let in this weather at all*'. [ON *létta* to abate]

let 2 = let. **let on*** to tell, but only used negatively in a clandestine conversation, '*Never let on.*' [also Sc]

lether the platform on which a *kwern* stands. [ON *lúðr* flour bin]

letten the sloping sides of a shelving rock. [ON *hlíð* slope with definite article suffix]

letter-fly any small moth found in the house. [in folklore it is said that to catch one is an indication that one will get a letter]

letto a trifling object. [ON *léttr* of little value]

leufer, luffer a bright patch in the sky. [ON *leiptra* to shine]

leufter of the sky to clear and form a bright patch. [ON *leiptra* to shine]

leure, lure the udder of a cow. [also Sc; ME *lure*]

levan uncooked bannocks eaten by people working far from home. [Eng *leaven*]

lew* lukewarm. [also Eng dial; ME *lew* warm]

ley 1 a creek where a lobster pot may be set or a net for catching a seal. [Norw *laegje* a lying place]

ley 2 a boat shelter, usually unroofed [ON *leggja*, to pace]

lib to castrate. **libbit** castrated [also Sc OSc *lib*, ME *libben*, id.]

lice = lice. **lice and nits** *a lice and nits jersey* a jersey knitted in a mixture of grey and white wool. [compare Sc *pepper and salt*]

lick 1 to thrash. 2 in a contest, to soundly beat. **licking** 1 a thrashing. 2 a trouncing [also Sc]

lickie a small piece of wire hooked at one end and used for drawing the thread through the eye of a spinning wheel. [ON *lykkja* a loop]

life = 1 life. 2 a living creature, '*There wisna a life tae be seen*'. 3 a fish on a line or in a net. [ON *líf* person, literally *life*]. **life corn*** a temporary and involuntary twitching of the eyelid (Eng *lifeblood*). ['corn' is used here in the sense smallest part; see CORN and GRAIN; the sense is therefore 'little bit of life']. **lifeless** = lifeless. '*Thir lifeless thit's faaltless*', an old proverb, 'They are lifeless who are faultless'.

lift 1 = lift. 2 a swell in the sea. **lifter** one of a gang of men who in the Springtime would go round farms and lift undernourished cattle to their feet. *gan apae lifting* or *nearly on lifting* starving hungry (like cattle which need to be lifted). **liftings** *in liftings*, of a weak animal, held up by a sling, to keep it on its feet [see LIFT]

light* *tae light on* to attack, '*The boy lighted on him on the wey home*'. [Eng *alight*]

lighter*, lyter = litter, used also of chickens, *a lighter o chickens*. [OF *litiere* a bed, later transferred to the young in the bed]

lighter-pin a pin for raising the upper stone of a mill, for making it lighter.

light-loaden of a girl, giddy. [?Eng *light-laden*]

ligny, linglay, linyo a calm spot on water. [ON *lögn* calm]

like adj, adv. 1 = like. 2* alike, '*My thir (they're) aafil like*' (speaking of brothers for example who look alike). 3* looking, '*My thir (they're) aafil like,*' referring to the same brothers who are shabbily dressed! 4 **Whit like*** or **Whit like the day?*** 'How are you?' or 'How are you today?' a common Orkney greeting 5* so to speak, '*Anywey at the back o dinner time I gid roond tae the byre like..*[also Sc]. **the like** such a thing; '*Ah'm never seen the like*'. **liken*** likely [also Sc] '*He hid clammered so high he wis liken tae fa*'.

lilder verb. to saunter. noun. a saunter. [probably a

70

form of DILDER; perhaps a relic of an original DILDER-LILDER]

lilypee a soft drink. [origin unknown]

limiter a cripple. [also Sc *lamiter* and *lamiger*; related to Eng *lame*]

limmer an unpleasant term for a woman. [also Sc; origin unknown]

limpet, lempit 1 a limpet. 2 nickname for an inhabitant of Stronsay.

limpit exhausted [? Eng *limp*]

limro phosphorescence on objects in the open air and caused by unusual atmospheric conditions. Old Jamie Spence of Queena in Birsay saw a ball of *limro* rolling down the hillside in that area. [ON *ljómi* brilliance]

lin, link, lint to rest for a short while, '*Lin thee a minute*'. [ON *linna* to stop or OE linnan]

linglay see LIGNY.

link 1 to walk purposefully, *tae link along*. [also Sc; Norw dial *linka* to toss or bend the body]

link 2 see LIN

links* sandy ridges near the sea. **links goose** the shelduck. [also Sc; OE *hlenc* ridge]

linn a plank laid across the gunwales near the stern of a boat. [ON *hlunnr*]

linner a strong gust of wind. [see LUNDER]

linny pin the pin at the end of a cart axle to keep on a wheel [Sc *lin-nail*, OE *lynis*, linch]

lint see LIN.

lintie* the linnet. **lintick** a dimin of *lintie*. **lintie-white** the linnet. (*lintie* + *twite*) [OF *linette* so called from its habit of feeding on flax)

linyo see LIGNY.

linyo-been haunch bone. [ON *lend* loin; ON *bein* bone]

lion shaft of the horse mill, the long shaft which goes into the barn.

liper see LYPER.

lippan of a bucket etc full to the *lip*. [also Sc; compare BRIMMAN]

lippen*, litten to expect. **lippen on** to chance upon. [also Sc but with an additional meaning *to trust* which is not recorded in Ork; ON *hlíta* to trust]

lipper* verb. 1 to spill over the edge (of water in a bucket etc). 2 to jump up, of little waves in a tideway. noun. a ripple in a tideway [OSc *lypper*, noun and verb, ripple]

lirk* a fold. [also Sc; origin uncertain]

lispund an old weight standard (approximately 28 lbs or 12.5 kilograms). [ON *lífspund* an abbreviated form of *Livlandsk pund* the pound weight used in Livonia]

liss a fragment. [ON *flís* a splinter or chip with loss of initial *f*; usually negatively, *no a lisso o maet in the hoose*.

lit alas! *Oh lit, Oh lit!* [see ALITTLE]

liter, lyter = loiter.

lith 1 1 a joint in a limb. 2 a limb. **lithy** broken, of a crop with broken stems after a storm. **lithy girs** horsetail grass. [ON *liðr* joint, limb]

lith 2 in a sheep's fleece the gap between the old fleece and the new. [ON *hlið* gap, space]

lithe, lye the pollack. [also Cai; ON *lyrr*]

lither to spill over, to overflow. [Norw *lidra* to make sideways movements but see LIPPER]

lithie see LITHY 2.

lithy 1 1 a gap in the breakers when a boat can more safely approach the shore. 2 a period of calm in the midst of a storm. [ON *hlið* space or interval]

lithy 2, lithie a piece of wood fixed firmly across the corner of a byre and to which a cow band was attached. [an ancient word; ON *laeðingr* was the charmed fetter with which the wolf Fenrir in Norse mythology was bound! Related words today are ON *liðr*, joint, Norw *led* link;]

lithy 3, lith a small sheaf of straw. [related to LITH 1 in the sense of section of a stack]

litten see LIPPEN.

liv* the palm of the hand. [Sc luif; ON *lófi*]

livan lane the only one. [*living* + Sc *lane* solitary]

live 1 = to live. *livan hair* red hair.

live 2 the rear piece of the old Orkney plough to which the mould boards were attached. [ON *lófi* palm of the hand]

liver = liver. **liver bannos** bannocks baked with fish livers in them. **liversoakie** a young coalfish gutted, filled with livers and roasted. [ON *sugga* a sow (a fat thing); compare MOOGELDIN]. **livery folds** food prepared with fish liver [see FOAL]

livering, lyveran a mixture of meal, water and salt. [compare Norw dial *livr* a soft thick mass]

liversoakie see LIVER.

loaded = loaded. *loaded wi the cowld* having a heavy cold.

loba, lubbo coarse hill grass. [also Sh; Norw *lubben* thickly growing, leafy]

lock* a quantity or number, '*My there wis a lock of folk there*'. **lockman†** in old records, a hangman. [also Sc; related to Eng *lock of hair*; LGer *lo(c)k* an amount; the hangman was given a quantity of grain for performing his service]

loff (plural **loff**) = a loaf of bread [*bread* is used only to describe bannocks eg bere bread, flooery bread, oatbread]. **loffie saps*** a kind of pudding made of bread soaked in warm milk and sweetened with sugar.

lokéd a *lokéd mist* a thick mist. [Eng *locked*]

lokkars* goodness! '*Lokkars me!*' '*Lokkars daisy!*'. [a corrupt form of obs Eng *lack-a-daisy* alas the day]

long leggéd laroo see LANG.

Long-Reed see LANG REED.

lonyo, lonyou, loyo cow dung. [Norw *lo*, cow muck]

loo the core of a horn. [Norw *lo*]

lood, loodan, luid humour, in the sense, '*There's a poor lood on him the day*'. [ON *hljóð* sound]

loofer an animal shelter. [ON *hlífar* shelters; compare *Livaness* a Sanday placename]

loom 1 of the sky to brighten. **loomie** *loomie bottom* dark and light spots on the sea bottom in shallow water. **loomin** twilight. [compare MoIcel *dagr ljómar* the day breaks; ON *ljómi* to shine]

loom 2, loomie the red-throated diver. [ON *lóm;* see RAIN GOOSE; ON *hljóma* to sound]

loon a boy. [also Sc; formerly in Sc had also a worthless connotation; compare MDu *loen* a stupid fellow]

loons marshland. (common in Orkney placenames as *The Loons*). [ON *lón,* sea loch]

loop to jump. [Sc lowp]

loopacks small jumping insects found under stones at the beach. **looper** a sheep which has jumped over the wall from the beach on to the arable land (North Ronaldsay). [Sc *loup* to jump; ON *hlaupa*]

loopie 1 see LUPPY.

loopie 2 a small bit of pasture almost surrounded by cultivated land. [Eng *loop* + *ie*]

loopsie heavy featured. [origin uncertain]

loordy '*Loordy bit o me*' I certainly will not.... [a form of Eng *Lord, compare* FEENTY BIT]

loot 1 verb. to bend down. noun. a stoop, '*He wis gan wi a loot*'. **tae loot and lift** to bind sheaves. [ON *lúta*]

loot 2 to jump. [a corruption of LOOP]

loots, louts milk which has gone sour. [ON *hleypa mjólk* to curdle milk; compare LAPPERED]

loppened powerless with cold, chiefly of hands. [Norw dial *loppen* numb]

lorry to dirty. [ON *lortr* excreta]

loshans me goodness me! **losh seks** goodness me! [a minced form of *Lord*; also Sc]

loss = 1 loss. 2 to lose, '*Don't loss your money noo.*'

lotherfoo peaceable. [origin uncertain; compare obs Du *lodder* pleasant]

lothivar a filthy mess, especially the vomit of a cat. [Norw *lo*, cow muck +? neuter definite article; ON *vergr* soiled or dirty; compare Sh *varg* a dirty mess]

louden bad or wicked, angry, given to foul language. [see LOOD, LOODAN]

louse† to redeem land. [ON *leysa* to loose but also to redeem or purchase (land)]

louts see LOOTS.

lovanentie goodness me! [also Sc; ? a corruption of *Lord defend thee*]

love = to love. **lovesam** sweet natured, *a lovesam bit*

a bairn.

lowe verb. to burn with a flame. noun. a flame. **tae pit lowe tae** to set on fire. [also Sc; ON *logi* a flame]

low picko see PICKO.

lowrie 1 the pollack. 2 a small cod. [ON *lȳrr* pollack]

lowse verb. 1 to loosen. 2 to unyoke a horse. adj. loose [also Sc]. **lowse weather** unsettled weather. **lowsing time** time to unyoke the horse hence, by extension, time for a period of work to end.

lowter a lump of mud. [ON *lortr* filth]

loyo dung or excrement. [see LONYO]

lozens panes of glass. [also Sc; a form of Eng *lozenge* from its shape]

lubbo 1 see LOBA.

lubbo 2 a meal measure made of bent grass. [see LUPPY]

luck = luck. **luck penny** a sum of money given for luck [also Sc.] **luck stone** a small red sandstone charm which was tied to the old Orkney plough [see DIAN STANE] **lucky** 1 = lucky. 2 big in size e.g. speaking of a jacket [also Sc]

lucker a small portion, especially of food. [see LOCK]

lucky see LUCK.

Lucky Minni a witch [also Sc], a name formerly used to frighten children. *Lucky Minni* was a legendary female who lived on Malcolm's Head in Fair Isle. [ON *lokkr* a lock of hair but probably with an earlier unrecorded meaning *rag*; evil creatures in northern mythology are generally ragged, hence the evil giant *Loki* and the related verb *lokka* to allure; *minni* on its own would also have had the same meaning; compare the name of the Norse giantess *Menia* and *Men-glöð* a fairy woman. Old Norse *men,* only recorded as a necklace is clearly related to rag in the sense of dangling. In Birsay there was an expression, *as long as Lucky Minni sat in Foozber, seven year o Yule days* meaning a very long time. Since there were 13 days in Yule, *seven year o Yule days* would be approximately 200 years. **Lucky Minni's oo** (wool) bog cotton. The white socks worn formerly by the Orkney bride were traditionally knitted from this material.]

ludgy pot '*Ah'm in me ludgy pot*', I'm in the best of spirits (Westray). [Sc *liege poustie*; OF *lige poesté* sound in mind and body; compare LEETUMPAS]

ludo-ludo an expression used when hearing surprising news. [? a corrupt form of *Lord defend you*; compare LOVANENTIE]

lue applied to fields or parts of fields in North Ronaldsay e.g. *lint-lus*. [ON *ló* meadow]

72

luely softly. [origin uncertain]

luffer a lull in a storm. [see LEUFER]

lug* 1 the ear. *'He's no chaet for lugs'* he has big ears. *'I widna gae hid lug room'*, I wouldn't listen to that. *'He's fairly layan ap his lugs'* he's listening attentively to something which does not concern him. 2 that part of a bucket to which the handle is attached. **lugget*** a slap on the ear with the palm of the hand. **luggy** a kind of peat spade so named from the projecting foot rest. **luggy-kep** a cap with projecting parts which cover the ears. **luggy box** a lobster box in the sea. [origin uncertain; perhaps because it had handles or *lugs*]. **lug-hitch** a hitch around a cow's ear and horns to stop it pulling. **lugsky, earsky** one of the pins stuck into the old side plough to act as a mould-board to turn over the furrow. [OSc *lugg* ear]

luid see LOOD.

luirkyan, luiskyan a great mass of something. [see LURKY]

luirl to sneak away as if trying to avoid notice. [Norw dial *lura* to sneak away]

luirtiss, luittoo a mess of excrement etc. [Norw *lort* filth]

luiskyan see LUIRKYAN above. [interchange of *r* and *s* in the Indo-European languages is common eg Eng *hare*; Ger *hase* or ON *hreysi* or *hreyr* a cairn]

luittoo see LUIRTISS.

luk = look. *tae luk aboot* to take heed, *'Thoo better luk aboot thee beuy'*.

lum chimney pot or vent [also Sc]. **lum hat** a top hat like a chimney. [origin uncertain but probably related to ON *ljóm*, light; the connection being that chimneys originally acted as skylights and smoke vents; compare Gael *àrlas* chimney, related to *leus* light]

lummo see LAWMO.

lump 1 = lump. 2 *lazy lump* a contemptuous term for someone, especially a young person. 3 a huge wave, *'A great lump o water cam ower the starn'*.

lunder, linner 1 to strike heavily. 2 to walk noisily.

3 a heavy blow. [also LANDER]. 4 a gust of wind. [Sc *lounder*; Sc *lewder* a heavy wooden bar]

luppack a spoon, chiefly a horn spoon. [origin uncertain but compare Du *lepel* spoon]

luppy, loopie, lubbo a small woven basket. [ON *laupr* basket]

lurdane see LURIDAN.

lure pig lard. [*saem* was the usual word; Cai *lure* edible offal; see LEURE]

lurgis, largis, lergis verb. *'Lurgis hid oan'* lay it on thick, of paint etc. noun. a filthy mess. [see LUIRTISS]

luridan, lurdane a type of brownie or fairy which, in the 17th century was believed to live on The Mainland of Orkney. It was a house spirit which at night helped the family with domestic chores. [Sc *luridan* a stupid person; OF *lourdin* heavy dull-witted person]

lurky 1 a big horn spoon. 2 a dinghy. [Sh *lurkie* a large clumsy boat which fits the deriv much better; ON *lurkr* a club]

lurt 1 a lump. 2 a lazy person. [see LUIRTISS]

lusker a tramp or beggar. [obs Eng *lusk* a lazy fellow; see SOHOD]]

luss see LISS.

lussin a dimin of LISS.

lustoo look here. [*Luks-thoo* the dialect form of imperative *look!*]

lye 1 see LITHE.

lye 2 green slimy growth found on the seashore. [ON *slý*]

lyken† in good condition (eg of a cow). [Sc *liking* appearance or condition]

lyper, liper 1 a mass of sores. 2 a state of filth. 3 to cover with dirt. [also Sc; OSc *lippir* a leper]

lyre, lyrie, leero 1 the manx shearwater. 2 a nickname for the people of Walls on the island of Hoy. [ON *líri*]

lyter see LIGHTER.

lyth see LYE 1.

lyveran see LIVERING.

M English *m* pronounced *aim*.

maa 1, meh* 1 of a sheep, to bleat. 2 a bleat. 3 an enticing call to a lamb. [imit; compare Eng *baa*]

maa 2* a sea-gull. [more usually WHITEMAA; Sc maw; ON *már*]

maa-bag stomach of a fish. [also Sc; ON *magi* stomach]

maagle see MAAGS.

maags, mogs, moags* verb. to walk with difficulty through deep mud. noun. thick mud [a contraction of MAR and -GIS; see MURGIS]

maak* = make. **tae maak weet*** to rain. **tae maak (fur) home** to head home. **tae maak on** to pretend. '*Maak thee supper*'* Have your supper. **a makking o tea** sufficient quantity of tea for one infusion. **maaky up*** a tune composed on the spur of the moment.

maalie a marble. [a clipped form of Sc *marley* a marble made from red clay (marl) hardened in the fire]

maalo, mailo, mallock, mallow a kind of seaweed *(zostera marina)*. [compare *Mallow Banks* off East Burness, Sanday; Norw *marlauk* literally *sea leek*]

maan see MAINS.

maas to fix the riding rope of a boat to the stone anchor. [essential meaning is *to knot* as in Norw *maske* a stitch in knitting and Sc *mask* to make a netting stitch]

machle see MAFFLE.

mad 1 = mad. 2 angry. **mad for*** keen on, '*He's aafil mad for this snooker on television*'. [compare Eng *crazy about*]

madrom anger. [in Sh the word means *happiness*!; a corruption of OE *wodrome* madness which is also recorded in Sc; ON *oðr* furious or mad]

madwallie of strong construction. [Eng *made* + WALLIE]

mae† a sand dune or stretch of sand. [only in placenames; ON *melr* sand; see MESGAR]

mael* = meal. **maely tattie** a potato which bursts its skin when boiled and has a *mealy* consistency.

maelskorn a very light meal, '*That wis just a maelskorn*'. [ON *mál* meal; ON *korn* used here in the sense of small particle]

maes = mess. **hundamaes** 1 a great quantity of dirt. 2 much ado about nothing [ON *hundr* dog]

maet* 1 meat. 2 food. 3 to give food to animals, *tae maet the kye*.

maffle, machle, maggle to trudge. [origin uncertain but probably related to Sc *bauchle*]

magdom 1 shape. 2 trace in the sense of *trace left behind*. **a magdom o a man** an apology for a man. [OSc *makdome*].

maggie-hunder-legs* centipede. [compare Sc *Maggie-mony-feet*; Norw *tusenbein* thousand legs]

maggle, meggle see MAFFLE.

magse see MAAGS.

mahon *as lazy as a Mahon soldier* extremely lazy. [Sc *Mahon* (a form of Mahomet) the Devil; compare Eng *lazy devil*]

maigrament excitement. [late ME *megrim* pain from OF *migraine*; earlier Lat *hemicrania* a severe headache; compare Sh *maigrament pain*]

mail† rent. [ON *mál* contract; see LANDMAIL]

mailing† a holding of land paying so much MAIL. [ON *maeling* measurement]

mailo see MAALO.

main = main. strength of will or patience, '*He didna hiv the main (or mains) tae wait*'. **mainless** 1 purposeless. 2 impatient.

mains, maan 1 = main. 2 the strongest part of a tideway.

Mairch = March.

mairch a boundary. **mairch stone** boundary stone. [also Sc; Eng *march*; ON *merki*]

maisan see MAITHE.

maise, maizie a straw basket used for transporting materials on horseback. [also Sc; ON *meiss* basket]

maisk 1 shy. 2 needing to be coaxed to eat. [see MUISKAN]

maister see MESTER.

maith a maggot. [also Sc; ON *maðkr;* OE *maða*]

maithe, maisan, meeo, meeth, meethe, meethis* a point on land used by fishermen to establish their position at sea. [also Sc; ON *mið* literally *middle* but also meaning *mark* or even *fishing bank*]

maize a puzzle. [Eng *maze*]

maizie see MAISE.

mak see MAAK.

makly *a makly buddy* a friendly person. [ON *maki* a fellow, equal]

malicefu sickly or in poor health. [Eng *malease* + *ful*]

mallduck see MALLIMAK.

mallie see MAALIE.

mallimak*, mallduck fulmar petrel. [also Sc and Eng dial; Du *mal* foolish; *mok* gull; the fulmar petrel cannot get airborne without a breeze of wind unless it jumps from cliffs etc hence its name *foolish*]

mallock see MAALO.

mallow see MAALO.

malonconie ailment. [Eng *melancholy*]

man = man. **man-buddy*** a man. '*I don't think there's a man-buddy aboot the hoose at aal*'. [see BUDDY]. **manfierdy** of a woman of marriageable age. [see FERDY]. **men-folk** = men (plural of *man-buddy*). **Men's Ba** a ball game played by male adults in Kirkwall. [see BA]

man-cog, mant-cog a bride's cog. [Sc *maun* a two handled basket; OF *mandé* basket made of wooden slats]

manse* the dwelling house of the minister of a church. [also Sc. OSc *manse* mansion]

Mansemas† the feast of St Magnus traditionally celebrated in Orkney and Shetland on 16 April and 13 December. **Mansemas Hill** in Rousay probably commemorates the site of an old fair held in that region on Mansemas Day. [compare *Georgemas* in Caithness]

Mansie 1 the popular form of the personal name *Magnus*. 2 in Caithness a nickname for an Orcadian, *a boat load o Mansies*.

mant to stammer. [also Sc; Gael *manntach* stammering]

mant-cog see MAN-COG.

mantelpiece a form of mantelplace. [see PIECE]

manyirpo a big well grown individual. [Norw *yrpa* stout or thick]

mar 1 clay or mud. **marpow** a pool where such clay is found. [Faer *mar(r)a* mud; Swed dial *mar* morass]

mar 2 1 = mar. 2 to annoy or inconvenience. [also Cai]

mardroo the sea-lace. [ON *marr* the sea + DROO]

mark, merk 1 an old Scots coin of high value, originally worth 2/3 of £1 Scots. 2 the smallest standard of weight, approx 500 gms. **markland** formerly land to the value of one mark.

market = 1 market. 2 a fair e.g. Lammas Market. **market 'flu** a hangover (after attending the fair!)

marksten see MAIRCHSTONE.

marool the angler fish [also Sh; ON *mörulfr*]

marpow see MAR 1.

marracked *shit-marracked* utterly exhausted. **piss-marracked** very drunk. [also Sc. a deriv of MIRACULOUS]

marros likeness e.g. a farmer might have two cattle, one the *marros* of the other [also Sc; OSc *marrow* to associate with]

marsgrim, marskamo, maskamo the angler fish. [ON *marr* the sea and probably ON *skraemi* monster; a reference to its odd appearance; compare *sea-devil* an alternative Eng name]

marskamo see MARSGRIM.

maskamo see MARSGRIM.

masthead = masthead. *orders fae the masthead* something which has to be done. [perhaps stems from the whaling days in the NORWAST when the captain climbed the mast to give orders]

matlo a fly, especially a blue-bottle. **sharny matlo** a dung fly. **horse matlo** a horse fly. [ON *maðkr* maggot; ON *fluga* fly]

matrass = mattress (the emphasis is on the last syllable)

mattie-man early morning mist at sowing time [origin unknown]

mattle to toddle. [see PATTLE]

maud plaid. [also Sc; OSc *maldy* cloth of mixed colours; possibly a metathesis of *medley*]

maun must, '*The neck o the monster maun hae been 30 feet high!*'. [also Sc; ON *munu* must]

maundom good physical condition. [ON *magn* strength]

mavis the song thrush. [also Sc; OF *mauvis*]

ma-we, mawey the stomach. [ON *magi* stomach; Dan *mave*]

maxy (the)* myxamatosis in rabbits; **maxy** adj. a rabbit with myxamatosis, *a maxy rabbit*

May = May. **May-bird** the whimbrel, a spring and autumn migrant, nesting in late May/early June. **May-term** traditionally (and legally) the Scottish year was divided into four terms. The May term and the November term are best known because it was at these times that contracts ended and people could move house or FLIT.

me 1 = me. 2 my, '*Tak me claes here*'. [common in Eng dial]. 3 myself, '*I think Ah'll go and wash me afore I go tae bed*'.

meadowswift† an old term for the division of meadowland among the tunship farmers. [ON *skipti* a sharing; see INSKEYFT]

meal, meil a measure of weight. [ON *maelir* measure]

mean 1 = mean, *as mean as tea in a tinnie, as mean as cat shite* very niggardly.

mean 2 ridge of a house. [ON *moenir*]

means metters '*Serves you (etc) right!*' [compare LENDS METTERS; perhaps *ill-man's metters* where *ill-man* is Sc *devil*]

meantime for the meantime. [commonly used in Orkney and also throughout Eng dial]

meedow 1 = meadow. 2* a stretch of marshy ground where at one time hay was cut. **meedow hay*** hay cut from a meadow [also Sc]

meek of milk cows, to increase yield. [ON *mikla* to increase]

meely follies the plant milfoil or yarrow.

meen a moan. *tae mak meen*, to make a moaning noise. (the indefinite article is omitted; compare NOISE).

meeo 1 1 a midge. 2 a house fly. [ON *mý* midge]

meeo 2 a form of MAITHE.

meesk see MAISK.

meet past part **mitten***. = meet. *tae meet in ends wi* to meet by chance.

meeter, metter 1 = matter. 2 pus in a boil or pimple.

meeth see MAITHE.

meethe see MAITHE.

meethis see MAITHE.

meg paw of an animal or flipper of a seal. [Sc *maig*;

75

Gael *môg*]
meggle see MAGGLE.
meh see MAA 1.
meil see MEAL.
meith to set out boundary marks. [also Sc; see MAITHE]
melder 1 to dry grain in a kiln. 2 kiln-dried grain ready for grinding. [ON *meldr* flour]
mell 1 to smash clods of earth in a field. 2 a mallet used for this activity. 3 the mallet used with a knocking stone. **mellin** *no wan mellin* not a single fragment. **mellit** the hand. [compare Sc *mell* heavy fist; but also *mallet*; the hand is referred to as a *mallet*, a *breaker* or *pounder*; ON *melja* to pound or crush; related to MELDER above]
Men's BA see MAN and BA.
mense a quantity of something, *a mense o cars.* [also Sc; a contraction of Eng *immense*; compare NORMOUS]
menye a company or social gathering. [also Sc; OSc *menzie* a multitude; OF *meyné* a dwelling]
mercy = mercy. *'Mercy!*'*', an exclamation of surprise, more usually with an additional word such as: *'Mercy me!' 'Mercy seks (sakes)' 'Mercy goodness (me)'.* **merciment** a small gift for a poor person.
merk 1 marrow in a bone. [ON *mergr]*
merk 2 see MARK.
merkie-pin that part of a plough to which the plough-share was fixed (in the old Orkney plough). [ON *mark* mark, with a sense *position*]
merkister a field boundary. [also Sh; Faer *merkisgarður*; ON *merkigarðr* a dividing wall of fence]
merly of clouds gleaming. [ON *merla* to gleam]
Merran Da's Cat* *'He's tin ap wi ither company like Merran Da's Cat'. Merran Da* must have been an old word for a witch. A mound (now flattened) in Sanday was called *Kro Merran Deem* and the belief was held that a witch was buried there. *Lucky Merran* was a Shetland witch; compare LUCKY MINNIE)
merry = merry. **merry Andrew** a show off, *'He's a real merry Andrew'.* **merry-begot** an illegitimate child. **Merry-Dancers** 1* aurora borealis or the Northern lights [also Sc]. 2 a nickname for the people of the parish of Stenness. *'He was on his merry pins'* he was dancing with glee.
merter to bruise. [see MURDER]
mervy easily broken. [Sc form of Eng *marrowy* full of marrow; compare CARVEY for a similar change in pronunciation]
mesgar 1 a small basket used as a muzzle on a horse. [ON *meiss* basket; ON *gerð* harness]
mesgar 2, **misgar** a hollow in the sands. [ON *melr* sand; ON *skor* a rift; see MAE]

messagate see MESSIGATE.
messages* shopping, *'I always go for messages on a Thursday'.* [also Sc; a special usage of Eng *message]*
messan undersized potatoes. [Sc *messan* a small dog or insignificant person; Gael *measan* lap dog]
messigate, messagate, messiegate 1 the right-of-way to a church. [also MESTRAGATE; only in place names]. 2 any path. [ON *messa* mass or *messu-dagr* mass-day; ON *gata* path]
mester 1 = master. 2 a landlord. 3 headmaster of a small school. 4 mastery, *'He hid the mester o him in the fight'.* **mesterfu** overbearing. **Mester-Fiend** the devil. **mester-hoosal** master of ceremonies (at a wedding for example). **mester pens** 1 long feathers in the cock's tail. 2 a duck's curly tail. **mester-ship** a huge vessel about which many tales are told in Orkney legend. The reader might not be aware that the first two men who landed on the moon were Orkneymen. They were two sailors who were reefing the sails in a storm and were thrown on to the moon when the top gallant mast of the *mester-ship* struck it!.
mestragate see MESSIGATE.
met 1 a measure. 2 a boundary stone between kelp allotments. 3 portion of shore dyke in North Ronaldsay which it was one man's duty to maintain. [Sc *met* or *mett* is used in similar senses; ON *met* the weight of a balance; Faer *mát* measure]
metal 1 = metal. 2* hard rock, especially *road metal.* [also Sc; now also used in Eng]
methis see MAITHE.
metter see MEETER.
metticks*, **mettos, mettoos** 1 a plant or weed, sand-sedge, growing on sand dunes with thick roots running along underground. 2 couch grass. [Sc *muttyached* matted together]
metting 1 a grain of corn. 2 a tea leaf. 3 *no wan metting* not one little piece. [Norw dial *mata* to form seed]
mettly-crab a crab which was pulverised and given as medicine to sick cows. [ON *matr* food; ON *matleiði* loathing for food]
mettos see METTICKS.
midding = midden. [also Sc and Eng dial; ME *midding*; Dan *mödding* an abbrev form of *mögdynge* a heap *(dynge)* of dung *(mög)]*
middle 1 to gossip, *'I saa them middlan fornent the shop'.* [special development of Eng *meddle*; compare Sc *middle* to associate with]
middle 2 *tae tak oot a middle* to take out a finish in ploughing.
middle-end the middle room in a three roomed house [compare BEN END and BUT END]

76

midger the fatty membrane surrounding small intestines of an animal. [Eng dial *midgerum*; OE *mycgern* fat about kidneys]

midla† the middle rigs in the old tunship system of land tenure. [ON *meðal middle*; found in compounds]

mighty* a remark indicating surprise: also '*Mighty me!*' '*My mighty*', or '*My mighty be here*'. [Eng *Almighty*]

milanter, milander to thwart or impede. [Sc *ma* prefix + LANTER]

mild see MYLDO.

milderings crumbled biscuits etc. [see MULDER and MULDRO]

mildo black peaty earth or mould forming on a dunghill. [Norw dial *mylda*]

mildrew see MILDROO.

mildroo, mildrew phosphorescence. [ON *möru-eldr;* see MIRACLES]

milk 1 = milk. **milk cellar** a small room off the kitchen of a farm house used as a dairy. **milk gruel** porridge made with milk. **Milk Gruel Day** Shrove Tuesday when oatmeal bannocks were eaten. **milk pot** a milk jug.

milk 2 = milt, the roe in a male fish.

millar a scree slope at the base of a cliff. [ON *melr* gravel bank; see MULLER]

millcoorse = mill course.

millifelamul showing pronounced family characteristics, *like mother, like daughter*'. [ON *milli* between + ?]

milling the very smallest particle [Eng *mill*]

mim putting on airs. [also Sc; imitat]

mimmy-feeblick, bimmy feeblick a common daisy. [see BAIM FLOOERS and FEEBLO]

mimp to speak in an affected manner. [see MIM]

mind 1 = mind. 2 recall '*Dae yi mind that veet that kam here wance?*' 3 remind '*Yi mind me o the time o that ferfil snow*. **mind on** remember '*Mind on and git that things fae the toon tae me*'. **mind and no** take care you don't '*Mind and no fa wi that eggs noo*.' **tae be aff the mind o** to have changed one's mind '*Ah'm aff the mind o flittan noo*.' **minding** no in me minding not that I can recall. **mindless** forgetful '*That's wan mindless thing*'[also Sc; compare HANDLESS].

mine's = mine, '*Whars shoes is this?*' '*Mine's*' especially in children's language. [also Eng dial]

mingse to mix. [ON *menga* to mix; perhaps confused with Eng *mix*]

minn skill in doing something. [ON *mennt* skill]

minnie an older woman. [children's language; see LUCKY MINNIE]

mint 1 to aim a gun at someone (but with no harmful intention). 2 to pick at food in an indifferent way. '*Stop mintan at that and eat hid up*'. 3 to

mention. **ill-minted** especially negatively, *no ill-minted* with no evil intention. [OE *myntan* to intend]

minwit common sense. [Eng *mind* + *wit*]

minxter = mixture

miraacles mockery [? Eng *miracle*]

miracles phosphorescence eg on fish or on objects (even human beings!) in peculiar atmospheric conditions. [Eng *miracle* confused with ON *möru-eldr* phosphorescence]

miraculous 1 = miraculous. 2 very drunk. [also Sc; compare MARRACKED]

mire snipe the snipe. [ON *mýrisnípa*]

mirk, mirky dark coloured. [ON *myrkr*]

mirking see MIRKNING.

mirkles, mirkyals the edible leaves growing at the base of HONEY WARE. [Faroese *mirkjallur* the midrib of the same plant]

mirkning, mirking twilight. [ON *myrkna* to grow dark]

mirky see MIRK.

mirkyals see MIRKLES.

mirly applied to the sky-covered with light, high-floating cirrus clowds. [Sc *merlit*; OF *merelé* chequered]

mirr* to tingle eg of a leg which has been 'sleeping'. [Norw dial *mirra* to tingle]

mirren see MOORHEN.

misackered badly injured. [also Sc; a form of Eng *massacred*]

misanter, mislander an accident. [OSc *mysawenteure*; OF *mesaventure*]

misca* 1 to miscall. 2 to speak ill of someone [also Sc]

Mischief the Devil.

miscone dried cow dung. [ON *myki-skán*]

misfoarded to come to grief, especially of a boat. [ON *mis-ferð* mishap]

misgar see MESGAR.

misgleam, misglybe to neglect. [ON *misgleyma*]

misglybe see MISGLEAM.

mislander see MISANTER.

mismorrow to mismatch [see MARROS]

miss 1 = a miss. 2* a loss, '*Whit a miss Bella's gan tae be in the shop*'.

mister† need or necessity. [also Sc; OF *mestier* need]

mither* = mother. **mither naked*** stark naked, *naked as at birth*. **Mither o the Sea** the spirit of the sea, in folk mythology. She invariably won the Spring battle with TERRAN and thus ensured the return of Summer and the cycle of life. **mither's bairn*** a spoilt child.

mitten see MEET.

mittle to injure severely eg to hack someone's shins in a game of football. [EME *mutile*; Fr *mutiler* to mutilate]

77

mixture = mixture. **mixter-maxter** a jumble. **mixture o mercies*** '*In this draaer (drawer) I keep a mixture o mercies*' a number of odd things. [also Sc].

mizzle fine drizzling rain with a slight fog. [? a running together of *mist* and *drizzle*]

moags see MAAGS.

mock = mock. **mocksome** given to mimicry.

mod a small quantity [also Sh ON *mót*, mark or stamp]

modren modern. [compare PATTREN]

mogs see MAAGS.

mogy, moogan, muogsy 1 a mitten. 2 a stocking foot worn as a slipper. [origin unknown]

mollygrant a lament, dissatisfaction. [also Sc; a form of Eng *mulligrubs*]

moniment 1 monument. 2 a mean disreputable person. [also Sh]

month, munt (plural **month** if preceded by a numeral) = month. [compare 'EAR]. **monthly cloot** sanitary towel

moo see MOOL IRON.

moogan see MOGY.

moogildin, mudyoleen an ungutted coalfish roasted on hot embers. [in Sh a *moogildin* is a small coalfish stuffed with fish livers and fried; ON *magi* stomach; ON *galti* a pig; the reference is to fatness of the belly; compare LIVER-SOAKIE, BERGILT, SOO-FISH etc; in Sh a mature coalfish is called a 'belly'.]

mool see MULL(S)

mool-iron, moo the foremost part of an old Orkney plough. [ON *múli* literally *snout*]

moor 1* of snow to drift. 2* a thick blinding snowstorm. *moored wi the cowld** having difficulty in breathing because of a heavy cold. [Icel *mor* dust; Norw *mure* coal refuse; compare SMOOR and SMOOK]

moor hen, mirren* the red grouse.

moorish in olden days all the bones left over from a meal were kept and dried beside the fire; these were thrown on to the kiln during the last firing of the beremeal and this imparted a *moorish* flavour to it [probably a yeasty flavour; ON *morkna* to decay; see MURTEN]

moorit of wool, reddish brown. [ON *mó-rauðr* yellowish brown]

moor(s) silver-weed, a plant with long trailing roots. [ON *mura*]

moortag a small dark featured child. [Sh *murti* very small; ON *murti* a small fellow]

moose = mouse. *better a moose in the pot than no maet at aal* an injunction to be satisfied with what is available. **moosefa** a mousetrap. [Norw *musfelle*; ON *fella* mouse-trap]. **moosie-haak** a kestrel. [compare Dan *muse-hog* sparrow-hawk].

moose-pea purple vetch. **moose-wab** a cobweb. [also Sc; particularly big grey (dusty) cobwebs; may be derived from Norw *smuss* dirt or filth; see SMOOSH]

moosened musty (of hay, bread etc). [see MOZE]

moosket, muisket, muisky a dull colour. [Norw *smusket*, a dull colour]

mooten to grow mouldy [compare MOOSENED]

mooter 1 the meal kept by a miller as payment for grinding corn [also Sc; OF *molture* from Lat *molitura* a grinding]

mooter 2 verb. to kiss. noun. a kiss. At barn dances in olden days, when the fiddler played a few high notes above the bridge and called '*Mooter boys!*', it was an invitation to kiss one's partner [a variation of SMOOTER]

mooth* = mouth. **moothie*** a mouth organ. **moothless*** having little conversation, *an aafil moothless cratur.*

mootho a hollow in sandy links. [ON *múðr* mouth + *o*]

mootie the stormy petrel. [see ALAMOTTI; also Sh; Norw dial *mutt* a small creature]

moozie of the weather damp and overcast. [see MOZE]

moppy, moppit a child's word for a rabbit. [also Sc; OSc *moppe* to nibble]

morefare preferable, '*Hid wid be morefare if yi cleaned up yir room*' it would be better etc. [Eng *more favoured*]

morn (the)* tomorrow [also Sc]. **morn's morning (the)*** tomorrow morning. **morn's night (the)*** tomorrow evening. '*Here the day and awey the morn*' said of an unreliable character. **the night afore the morn** the evening before the Kirkwall Lammas Market day. [ME *morn* a variant of *morrow*]

morrow see MYRO.

morrowless without a match [see MARROS]

mortal 1 = mortal. 2 *dead* drunk. [also Sh]

mortasheen glanders, a disease of horses. [Sc *mortichein*; OF *mort d'éschine* death of the spine]

mortbrod a wooden memorial plaque. There is a fine example in St Magnus Cathedral. [Eng *mort* death + BROD]

mortcloth a cloth covering a coffin on the way to the grave. It was usually hired out for funerals. [Eng *mort* + *cloth*]

mose see MOZE.

moss 1 = moss. 2* moorland. **peat moss*** a piece of ground where peat can be cut. **upper moss** the *upper peat*. **buddum moss** the lower peat in the peat bank. [ON *mósi* moorland]

mostlings* for the most part. [Eng *most* with old suffix *lings*]

mother-worship see WURSUM MITHER.

mouch a moth. An old Orkney verse runs:-
Jerusalem is a bonny piece
Nae mouch or moosewab there
Hid's streets are laid wi baeten gold
Oh gin I wis there
[also Sc; ME *moghe*]

mouchless feeble. [Sc *machless*; OSc *macht* strength, power]

moy-foy destruction. *gin tae moy-foy* in a state of complete ruin. [ON *mola* to crush; Sc *fulyie* dirt; see MUMFOIL]

moze, mose verb. to become mouldy, of damp clothes etc. noun. rot in hay or timber. **mosy** partly decayed. [also Sh; compare Gael *musgan* dry rot in wood]

muck 1 = to clean out a byre [also Sc]. 2 to clean out or tidy up anything 3 to spread dung. **muck-hole** the hole at the end of the byre through which dung was thrown. [ON *myki* dung]

muckafy to make dirty [Eng *muck* + *fy*]

muckle* 1 big. 2 much, especially in the negative sense *no muckle*. **muckle needle** a darning needle. **muckle preen** a large pin for fastening a shawl etc. **Muckle Supper** a harvest home feast. **Muckle Water (The)** an old name for the Harray Loch. [common in placenames; ON *mikill* great, large]

muddy-crab a species of hairy crab found in deep waters. [Gael *mogach* hairy or shaggy]

mudge to move. *'Hid'll no mudge wan bit'*. [also Sc; a running together of *move* and *budge*]

mudgo, mudgick a form of Eng *midge* + dimin.

mudyoleen see MOOGILDIN.

muero forky tail (Westray). [an extension in meaning of MYRO]

muffle 1 = muffle. 2 a fingerless glove.

muggafisty drizzly. [see MUGGROFU and FEESTER]

muggaty-fue see MUGGRO-FUE.

muggrofu*, muggaty-fue, muggry misty, drizzling weather. **muggrafu** a dowdy colour. [ON *mugga* soft drizzling mist; Norw *fokk* drifting (snow)]

muggry see MUGGROFU.

muggy the stomach of a fish. [ON *magi* stomach] .

muif verb. to give out hot air. noun. close, oppressive heat. **muify** sultry weather. [Sc *muithy*; ON *móða* a mist on a fine day]

muir hen see MOOR HEN.

muiskan, muisky 1 shy. 2 to act in a shy manner e.g. *muiskan and laughan*. [see SMOOSK]

muisket see MOOSKET.

muisky 1 see MOOSKET.

muisky 2 see MUISKAN.

muith a tooth. *'He didna hiv a muith in his head'*. [? an extension of Eng *mouth*]

mulder 1 = moulder. 2 to crumble. **muldro(o)** a crumb, *'The biscuit's in muldroos'*.

mullack a piece of wood fixed on each end of the keel of a boat to clamp the stern or stern post to the keel. [ON *múli* with the sense *a projection*]

muller a pebbly beach. **mullery** pebbly [Norw dial *møller-bakke* shingle bank]

mull(s) 1 of an animal, lip(s). 2 jokingly a person's mouth. 3 a headland (**mull** as in Mull Head, Deerness). **mullsan** pouting. *'He's fairly hingan his mulls the day'* he's in a bad temper (compare TRUTMULLED). [ON *múli* a muzzle, a jutting crag]

mully fustered smashed to pieces. [ON *melja* to crush; see FLEEST]

mullyo verb. to gather gleanings into wisps of corn. noun. 1 a small bundle of straw gleaned off the harvest field. 2 a watcher employed in olden days to ensure that no one took corn from a neighbour's RIG. [Gael *muillean* a truss]

mulyered broken into pieces [compare MULDER]

mumfoil *'He made a mumfoil o his biscuit'* he crumbled it down. [see MUMMY and MOY-FOY]

mummel = mumble.

mummy small fragments, *'The cup just gid in mummy'*. [also Sh; Norw *molma* a soft granulated mass]

mump 1 to twitch the mouth like a rabbit or a toothless person. 2 to grumble. [also Sc; Eng dial *mump* to munch; see MOPPY a related word]

munger-hoose a taboo term used at sea for a church. [ON *múnkr* monk; ON *hús* house; Munkerhoose was the old name for St. Boniface Church in Papay]

munt see MONTH.

munted = 1 mounted. 2 improved in position eg after getting a sum of money [also Sc].

munyo strength. [ON *magn*]

muogsy see MOGY.

murder, merter to bruise, *'Me legs were aal murdered'*. **murdered blood** congealed blood. [Sc *martyr* to *martyr* or torture]

murderer a device for catching deep sea fish.

murdowser to take advantage of one. [origin unknown]

murgis 1 a mess eg of soft mud. 2 a noisy crowd of people. 3 a heavy cold. [see MAAGS]

murl, mirl to crumble. [also Sc; compare Faroese *morla* to crush in small pieces]

murled of animals spotted in the face. [see MIRLY]

murly round, like a small pebble, used also to describe a small faced child. [Sc *marley* a marble]

murmell 1 of a baby to make cooing noises. 2 to grumble or lament over. [OSc *murmell* murmuring]

murment lament over a trifling matter. [Sc *murn* to

mourn + MENT]

murr 1 verb. 1 of butter in a churn to form into small particles. 2 to separate eg small potatoes from large ones. noun. 1 a small fragment. 2 an undernourished object eg a potato. 3 a confused mess (of e.g. weeds). [Icel *mor* fine dust]

murr 2 to drizzle. **murry** of weather damp and drizzling. [see MOOR]

murred see MURTEN.

murten, murred of grain to grow mouldy. [ON *morkna* to become decayed]

musk 1 the arm or tentacle of the Sand Gaper fish (*mya arenaria*). [Gael *mùsgan* razor fish]

musk 2 a small fragment. [Norw dial *musk*]

mussa 1 a white spongy moss. 2 a lichen. [ON *mosi]*

mussa-kruppan cotton grass. [Sc *moss-crops*]

mutch a type of head covering formerly worn by women. [also Sc; related to Ger *Mütze*]

mutchkin jeck a mug, holding three quarters of a pint, also applied to mugs of similar size. [obs Du *mudseken* such a measure; see JECK]

myldo, mild a type of bream, the gilthead. [origin uncertain]

myre-snipe see MIRE-SNIPE.

myro(o), morrow an ant. **myroo nest** an ant hill. [Norw *maur* ant]

my sall a form of *upon my soul.*

mystical 1 = mystical. 2 in a mysterious or round about manner, '*He spoke in a mystical manner*'.

N Eng *n* pronounced *ain*; *n* preceding a *b* is pronounced *m*; see IMBY

na 1*, na na* = no (emphatic form of *no*, frequently pronounced with a tremor in the voice to give a sound not unlike the bleat of a sheep!) [also Sc; OSc *na*]

na 2* not (but only after auxiliary verbs), '*He didna see me*', '*I widna trust her*', etc. [also Sc]

naafil awful, dreadful, where AAFIL (q.v.) picks up the *n* of the preceding indefinite article, '*Whit a naafil wey o working*'. In some cases the *a* of the indefinite article is completely lost, '*Naafil o folk here, min*'; the indefinite article *an* is normally never used before a vowel in Orkney dialect, AAFIL being, apparently, the sole and unaccountable exception.

na nae noo an exclamation of surprise '*Goodness me!*'. [compare Sc *na* and *noo*]

nabal 1 mean or stingy. 2 a fool. [*Nabal* is a miser who appears in Samuel 1, Chap. 25]

nabsie see KNABSIE

nacket 1 small and insignificant. [see NACKOES]

nacket 2 a mischievous child. [also Sc; OF *nacquet* ball boy in tennis]

nackoes very short corn. In Westray grain planted in the first week of May gives *nackoes* in the second week, corn and in the third week SLUSH. [Sh *nakk*; ON *hnekkja* to check]

nae = no. **naebody, naebothy** nobody. **naethin** nothing [also Sc]

naeslin 1 nuzzling. 2 fitting together well (of shapes). [related to Eng *nuzzle*]

nag verb. = to nag. noun. a gnawing pain.

nail 1 = 1 nail. 2 the middle finger used as a measure by knitters from the tip to the knuckle; to the first joint is *half a nail*, 11 cms; the Eng nail length is 6 cms. 3 a nasty character trait.

nail 2 = finger nail. **nail-cowld*** extreme pain, particularly in the finger nails after prolonged exposure to cold.

nain only in the combined form *me-nain* my own. [the original was *mine own* but the *n* of the *mine* has been transposed to form the first letter of *own*, compare NAAFIL]

naitran *naitran and rainan.* [see NATTER]

naked = naked. **bare naked, mither naked, bollock naked** stark naked. **naked truth** evidence, '*There's the naked truth*' You can see for yourself.

nakeharein a beating or scolding. [see NICTIONS and NIZZIN]

nammonie a little while. [compare Sh *namin* a little bit in the sense *portion* but also *time*; ON *naumr* short with respect to time]

namse a gulp, '*Wan namse and that would be doon*'. [ON *nema* to snatch]

nanty neat and tidy. [see NINT]

nap 1 1 a knob. 2 tassel of a cap. 3 **the napp o the hass** Adam's apple. [ON *knappr* knob]

nap 2 verb to knock. noun a knock. **napper** a stone breaker's hammer. [imitat]

nap 3 1 a plough rein. 2 a horse or cow halter. [compare Sc *knypin* a short rope used for tying boats together in harbour; Norw dial *kneppa* to bind tightly together]

nap 4 to nibble at each other (of horses). [ON *gneypa* to pinch]

nap 5 *tae tak the nap aff somebody* to tease them. [also Sc; Eng *nap* woollen surface on cloth]

nap 6 oatmeal and milk mixed to the consistency of

dough and eaten uncooked, the traditional snack taken to the sea by fishermen. [compare Sh *neb*; ON *knappr* knob; from its round ball shape; Irish slaves in Iceland called a similar snack *minn-þak*]

nappa a seal. [ON *knappr* knob; a reference to its round shape; compare Norw *kobbe* seal; related to Norw *kubbe* chunk]

napper see NAP 2.

nappy see KNAPPY.

narbegan, near-begaan stingy. [Sc *near begaun* nearby + gone]

narlings nearly. [compare MOSTLINGS]

narsh bitter or rancid. [also Sh; a form of NISS]

nask 1 to steal. 2 to nibble at or snatch. [Norw *naske* to chew]

natter verb. 1* to chatter. 2 to drizzle. [also NITTER]. noun. a chat* *'They wir hivan a natter ootside the door'*. [Norw *gnadre* to grumble]

navar a toggle or button. [ON *knappr*]

nave*, neiv 1 the fist. 2 a handful. 3 the handgrip of an oar. [ON *hnefi* fist or handful] **nave-kuithe** see KNAVE-KUITHE.

navesan groping with the hands eg a young child in its food. [see NIVSAN]

nave's lock see KNAVESLOCK.

near 1 near. 2 nearly. **nearaboot*** almost, *'Good! he nearaboot dung me doon wi his byke whin he cam roond the corner'*. **near-begaan** see NARBEGAN. **nearhand** close at hand [also Sc] **nearmost*** nearest [also Sc]

nears kidneys. [also Sc; ON *nýra*]

neavie the horns of a CLIPPER, a kind of saddle. [ON *nef* nose; Norw *nibb* point; in Sh such horns were called *nibis*]

neb* beak. *pickan for neb* used of chickens just about to hatch. **nebbid moose*** a shrew. **neb-cloot** a handkerchief. **goose-neb** long nosed pliers.

neddo's craas little black clouds on the horizon portending wind or bad weather. [*cra* is probably a metaphorical use of *crow*; origin of *neddo* unknown]

neeblance short rich grass favoured by geese, sheep etc. [Eng *nibblings*]

neebor* 1 = neighbour. 2* one of a pair [also Sc], *'Here's wan shoe furtiver, noo whar's the neebor o har?'*. **neeborless*** odd, *neeborless shoes*.

needles = needle. **needles and preens** an example of many inverted phrases found in Orkney. The normal form is 'pins and needles'. [see OOTSIDE IN and PREEN]

neef to pay attention. [origin uncertain]

neef-naffs small things. [compare Eng *knick-knacks*]

neem = name. *the neemless thing* toothache.

neep* noun. a turnip [also Sc]. verb. *tae neep* to give neeps to, *'Ah'll just go and neep the kye first'*.

[OE *naep* turnip]

neese to sneeze. [also Sc; ON *fnýsa* or *hnjósa*]

neest, neester, neist to drizzle. [ON *gneisti* a spark]

neester 1 see NEEST.

neester 2 1 to snigger. 2 of a door to creak or of a new cheese to squeak. [Norw *gnistre* to creak; Norw *knistre* to giggle]

neist 1, neisting, nist, nyst a spark. [ON *gneisti*]

neist 2 see NEEST.

neist 3 next. *neist coat* a petticoat. [also Sc; OSc *neste*; ON *noest*]

neisting see NEIST 1.

neitch, nitch, nitchoo, nidgick a tied wisp of straw similar to a WINLING. [also Cai; ME *knyeche* a small bundle]

neiv see NAVE.

netral* = natural. **netral girse** natural grass.

netting wire* = wire netting. [an example of many inverted phrases in Orkney dial; see OOTSIDE IN]

nettle kale nettles. [nettles were used for cooking in Orkney at one time; OSc *netl caill*]

netty 1 dexterous. 2 tidy. [Norw dial *natig* dexterous]

Neuar-day* New Year's Day. **Neuar-time*** New Year time. The first few days of the New Year. [the dialect form does not have a possessive as in Eng; contrast *the morn's morning* which has a possessive in the Orkney dial but is absent in Eng 'tomorrow morning'; in Orkney, days of the week also had a possessive eg *Friday's night* = Friday night]

neuch to nibble. [ON *gnaga*]

neud-mirk see NUID-MIRK.

neuk = nook. **neuk bed** a bed set into a wall. **neuk (in the)** of a woman in the final stages of labour. **neuk o the back** the wall at the back of a stove or grate.

news = news. **newsan*** gossiping.

next = next. **next night*** tomorrow night, *'Ah'll come ower next night'*.

nibbet of clothes scant, especially close-cut. [ON *hneppa* to cut short]

nibbie 1 a toggle. 2 a bit of wood used for a button. [ON *knappr*; see NAVAR]

nibblowy hillocky. [related to ON *knappr* knob and Eng *nipple*]

nibsy stout, especially of a boy. [Sh *nib* a small knob + *sy*]

nick 1 *the nick o the tide* the turn of the tide. [ON *hnyggja* to push back]

nick 2 verb. 1 of a bone or joint to crack. 2 to twist (and hurt) the neck. noun. a crack. [ON *kneikja* to bend back with force]

nick 3 to impede or thwart. [ON *hnakkja* to thwart]

nickaparl with full power. [*parl* a form of PIRL 2;

81

for *nicka* see NICKYTOBAR]

nicker see KNICKER.

nickum* a little brat. [Sc *Nick* or *Auld Nick* the devil]

nickysnarl a bad tangle on a piece of thread. [also Sh; Norw dial *nokkesnur* a bad tangle on a spun thread]

nickytobar† a word formerly used among children for fast skipping. [Sc *nick* to beat; Sc *tabour* to beat]

nictions a scolding or punishment, '*Thoo'll get thee nictions the night*' [see NICKYTOBAR]

nidder to dwindle away. [see NITHER]

niddle, niggle 1 to fiddle with something. 2 to annoy someone by so doing. 3 to spread dung in turnip drills. 4 to walk with short steps, to mince along. **niddled** dirty, with too much fingering. [Sc *niddle* to work quickly; imitat of short jerky movements]

nidgick see NEITCH.

niff clever, nimble, able. [ON *naefr*]

niggle see NIDDLE.

nilded* mouldy. [see BLUE-NILD]

nile* the plug used for the NILE-HOLE which drains water out of the boat. [ON *negla;* related to Eng *nail*]

nile-hole* see NILE.

nimms*, nimm-nimms good things to eat, used only by children when looking at tasty food or by a parent encouraging a child to eat, '*Come on noo bairn, nimm nimms.*' **nimmy goods*** an expression used by a mother when feeding a baby solid food. [compare Eng *mmm!*].

nineteen 1 = nineteen. 2 the traditional duration of a farm lease [also Sc]. Nineteen (years) represented three courses of a six year rotation, the final year restoring the original cropping. It is recorded in Clouston's *The Orkney Parishes* that, at one time, the farm of Tormiston in Stenness was let for *nineteen nineteens* 361 years.

nint something small. [compare Eng dial *nunty* of dress scrimp, scanty]

nip* nippie* 1 nip. 2 a small quantity (especially of whisky) [also Sc]. 3 a sharp coldness, '*There's a nip in the air*'. **nipcake** a scolding, '*She'll get nip-cake when she gets home*'. [*nip-cake* is probably the same as *nipped-doons*, hence a sarcastic use of the phrase]. **nippéd-doons** bread or bannock broken down into milk. **nippit** mean. **nippy** of the air, cold or frosty.

nirk see KNIRK.

nirled stunted in growth. **nirlie** small. [see KNURL]

nirls chicken pox. [also Sc; the essential meaning is *lumps*; see KNURL]

niroo a corn or small callous on the foot. [see NORO]

nirp, nyrp to find fault. **nirpéd, nyrpéd** cross grained, contankerous or stingy. [see SNIRPET;

loss of initial *s* is common in the Germanic languages]

nirr 1 a disagreeable taste with food. [Norw *nissen*]

nirr 2 to grumble. **nirren** a crabbed sort of person. [see NYIRR]

nirr 3 to purr. [see NYIRR]

nirt a small particle. [also Sh; really a little knot; compare Norw *knart* knot]

nismeat a sheaf of oats half-thrashed fed to a horse instead of oats. [see NIZZ]

nissan *sittan nissan* said of someone sitting in the corner of a room contributing nothing to the conversation. [probably with the originally meaning *to hum a tune through one's nose*; Sc *nizz* nose; compare NUE]

nist see NEIST.

nit = 1 nit. **nits and lice** see LICE AND NITS. 2 a small mischievous person.

nitch see NIDGICK.

nitchoo see NIDGICK.

nither* 1 neither. '*Hid's nither tae me or fae me*' it makes no difference. **nither the wan nor the ither**, neither. '*He hid (had) two boys and nither the wan nor the ither hid (had) time for the sea so he selt the boat.*'

nither 2, nidder of a grain crop to wither away. [ON *niðra* to bring low]

nither-end* the posterior [also Sc; ON *niðr* low]

nittbold stunted, especially of a calf. [perhaps for *nittpold?*; ON *gnit* a nit, see POLT]

nitter to drizzle. [also Cai in the form *nyatter*; see NATTER]

nittret, nittery ill-natured, cross. [Norw *gnadre* to grumble]

niver, nivver = never. **niver a ken I** I don't know. **nivver-spaek*** frequently said in reply to an obvious statement. [approximately the Eng equivalent of *Well do I know it!*; Eng *never + speak*]. *nivver wis hid ither* a reply to a statement indicating in a disparaging way that things have not changed. '*Hid's a naafil maes aboot that ferm.*' '*Niver wis hid ither!*.'

nivsan petting. [see NAVE and NIVVLE]

nivvle to grip hard. [ON *hnefa* to grip; Norw dial *knevla* to squeeze]

nizz, nyse to half thrash a sheaf. **nizzin** a severe reprimand. **nizz-meat** a sheaf which has been partly beaten. [ON *knosa* to bruise]

nizzend of food tainted. [ON *knissa* or *hnissa* bad flavour]

nizzet jocularly the nose. [Sc *nizz* nose]

no* 1 = no 2 not. '*Ah'm no gan*', I'm not going. Often used in dialect to express an opposite meaning e.g. '*Hid's no a ill day,*' It's quite a nice day. '*Hid's no aisy (easy)*', It's difficult, a common expression usually with the meaning 'We are/he is etc. passing through difficult times'. '*Whit wae this form filling and wark hid's no aisy min.*' **tae ken no** not to know, usually '*I ken no*' I don't know.

noaran arguing. [see NORY]

nog, nogg the long rockers at the end of cradle for rocking with the foot. [see NUGG]

nogal a large chunk of something. [see NUGGLE]

nogg see NUGG.

noise = noise. used for some unaccountable reason without the indefinite article in the presence of a sleeping child, '*Don't mak noise*'.[compare MEEN]

noler a snub (particularly to one who has offended you). [Sc *knool* to beat or strike; *knoolt* dejected]

noo = now [also Sc]. **noo and sae*** in indifferent health or condition. [also Sh; *now so*; compare Eng *so-so*]. **noos an dans** = now and then.

nood to nod off to sleep.

noops hair. '*Snog thee noops*', 'Cut your hair'. [*noop* here is really head as in ON *knappr* head of a pole; see NAP 1]

nor* = or. '*Hid was far bigger nor hid's noo*'. [*or* is normally used for *than* in such a situation; also Sc]

Noraway, Norraway Norway. [OSc Norroway]

Norie the puffin. [the correct term is TAMMIE NORRIE]

normous* '*There was normous o folk there*'. [a corruption of *enormous*; compare IMMENSE]

Norn the old language of Orkney. **nornaway, norny** 1 cantankerous. 2 old fashioned. [ON *norroena* the Norse language; the extended meanings of this word tell us succinctly why the old language - indeed any language - dies out; it became unfashionable to speak the language and those who continued to do so acquired, in the eyes of the majority, inferior characteristics, a kind of social bullying to conform]

norny see NORN.

noro*, niroo, nurro a lump, *a noro o a lump*. [Sc *knur*; ME *knorre* a knot]

Norraway see NORAWAY.

Nort* = north, '*The wind's gin roond tae the nort*'. [also Sh]

Norwast (The) 1 North West. 2 the Davis Straits, Greenland. [a term from the whaling days]. **Norwaster** a special type of sea-chest used by Orkneymen who went whaling to the *Norwast*.

nory 1 the cormorant. [for possible derivation see TAMMIE NORRIE]

nory 2 ill-tempered. [literally *knotted*, related to NORO; compare however Gael *narrach* crosstempered]

notice 1 = notice. 2* to take care of [also Sc], '*I could never get awey fae the hoose fur noticing me owld mither*'.

notion* 1 a liking [also Sc], '*I think he his a notion in her*' speaking of a man attracted to someone of the opposite sex. 2 whims or caprices, applied to people or animals, used for example when a horse will not stand still, '*Hid's just notions she's tin*'.

notty a piece of tangle cut into a ball and used as a missile for a sling. [ON *knöttr* ball]

nousneedle a bone needle about 9cm long used for sewing the lacing round the mouth of a cubby etc. [ME *nouche* a collar]

noust* a scooped out hollow near the beach where boats are left in the summer. [in Sc the form *oust* is found with loss of initial *n*; ON *naust*]

nout 1 cattle. **nout-beul** an enclosure for cattle. There was formerly a *nout-beul* in Hoy across the valley from the Dwarfie Stone. 2 a fool. [also Sc; Norw *naut*; ON *naut* cattle]

noutan see NOWTAN.

nouty ill-tempered. [see NOWTAN]

November term see MAY TERM.

now = new. **nows*** news.

nowp to chew vigorously. [a form of Sc *mowp* to nibble or munch]

nowtan, noutan muttering loudly to oneself. **nouty** ill-tempered. [ON *gnyðja* to mutter]

nuck no. [? related to Norw *neigu* indeed not]

Nuckelavee a sea monster which features in Orkney legend. [ON *nykr;* ON *haf* the sea; see also NUGGLE]

nue to hum a tune to oneself. [a similar form is used in Sh; ON *gnýja* to sound]

nugg 1 1 the pin on a boat to which the oar strap was fixed. 2 the projecting knobs of the main bearers at the back of a cart. [Norw *knugg* a protuberance]

nugg 2 *nugged ale* ale warmed by immersion of a hot poker. [also Sh; origin uncertain; Norw *knag* a peg; ? originally used for stirring]

nuggle 1, nogal a lump. [ON *knykill* protuberance]

nuggle 2 the water horse, a fabled animal associated with water. It often grazed on the banks of burns and lochs and when someone was tempted to have a ride on its back the animal galloped into the water and drowned its rider. [see NUCKLEAVEE]

nuid-mirk pitch dark. [ON *niða-myrkr* pitch darkness; Faroese *nið a* blackness of night when no moon is shining]

nuither to hum a tune. [ON *gnyðr* a murmur]

nulla, nurlay† the lowest rigs in a tunship when the system of rig-a-rendal was in operation. [ON *neðarla* lower down]

nurlay see NULLA above.

nurro 1 a lump. 2 a bunion. [see NORO]

nyaffle to bite at ineptly. **nyafflins** chewed fragments of food. [Norw *gnavle* to chew slowly]

nyaggle to chew laboriously at something. [YAGGLE with an initial *n*]

nyamsy long-jawed. [related to GAMSY long-jawed; an *n* has been picked up as in NYARM]

nyarg to argue persistently or to grumble. [related to Norw *knark* a crabby old man]

nyarm* 1 to yowl (of cat). [compare ON *jarma* to bleat (of sheep) but used on the Mainland of Orkney for the mew of a cat; *yarm* has collected an initial *n*; compare NYAGGLE, NYAMSY etc]

nyavse to chew away at something, '*He wis nyavsan at a bone*'. [Norw *jafsa* to snap at with the mouth + initial *n*]

nyesnawie the smell of mildew. '*Hid his a kinda nyesnawie wey wi hid*' [ON *hnissa* bad smell, especially the odour of cooking; see NIZZENED]

nyirr to growl. **nyirran** hopping mad, literally growling. [ON *knurra]*

nyow* to mew. '*Peety help them thit baroos the cat's dish for hid's aye nyowan*', said of anyone who harps on about something which everyone would wish forgotten. (Pity help those who borrow the cat's dish for its always mewing). [imitat; compare KURNOW]

nyrlan cowld bitter cold. [Sh *nirl* a cold biting wind, a cold wind makes one curl up; related to KNURL]

nyrp see NIRP.

nyrpéd see NIRPéD.

nyrr to have a *nyrr* at someone is to have a feeling of anger on account of some wrong or fancied wrong. [see NYIRRAN]

nyse a form of NIZZ.

nyst see NEIST 1.

O English *o* pronounced approximately as it is in Eng.

o* 1 of [also Sc]. 2 when *o* is used to designate a farmer eg Willie o Spurdagro, the *o* might represent the original ON *á*, at. [compare Criste Aelingklact the earliest recorded form of the surname Linklater]. 3 in telling time, '*Hid's five meenits o two*'*, '*Whit o clock is hid?*'* What time is it?

oam see AEM.

oat-fowl a small unidentified bird mentioned in the 1795 Statistical Account. [probably the *snow-bunting*]

ob see AB.

ober 1 responsibilty. 2 impudence, self confidence. [ON *ábyrgð* responsibility]

obstrapulous* = obstreperous. [also Eng dial]

odal see UDAL.

odder, odder steen a door lintel. [ON *ofdyri]*

oddle*, oddler a sewer, more specifically the channel which runs through the middle of a byre. **oddle-hole*** the hole in the end of the byre through which the urine is drained away. [Norw *aale* cattle urine; OE *adela* filth; hence Eng *ad-dled* egg; see OOLER for another form and related meaning of this word]

oddmal of animals, poor looking. [see UDMAL]

ofhend(t)† a legal term meaning to *alienate property*. [ON *afhenda* to hand over]

ogang† a perambulation of a boundary. [ON *á-gangr*, a going round; ON *á* had a variety of meanings, one of the less common being 'around']

ogude† profit or benefit. [ON *ágóði]*

oily-bogie a nickname for the people of Burray. [Eng *oily* + ON *belgr*, skin bag; whole animal skins were used for holding oil etc; a reference to the fatness or greasiness of the inhabitants!; compare GRUELLY BELKIE]

oily-cruisie see CRUSIE.

oily-voil† old pronunciation of *olive oil*.

oires poorly drained clay soil. [ON *aurr* clay or mud]

oisie an expression used eg when lifting a child up in the air, '*Oisie! Oisie!*'. [ON *hoza* to raise; see OOPSIE]

olas '*He'll no come olas wi his wark*', he won't get on with his work. [origin unknown]

ombisman† in old records, a procurator or agent. [ON *omboðs maðr]*

omo confusion, hopeless disorder. [see OOMO]

on = on. '*My whit a seas on the day*'* there's a heavy sea running. 2 at, *gan oot on the night** going out at night e.g. of a farmer attending to a calving cow. **gan on the night** of young men going after the girls very late at night. **on a time** now and then. **on-pit** 1 an inversion of PIT-ON. 2 clothing, '*Anything will deu for an on-pit*'. [Sc *put-on* to dress]

onca, oncall, onnekarl† a small tenant farmer who helped the landlord at busy times of the year and in this way paid for the rent of his property. [Norw *onnekar* literally *season man*; compare ON *onnungr* labourer]

ongelid a strong gale. [ON, from an assumed *andar-gul* breeze; modelled on *andar-gustr* breath of

84

wind which we find in Sh *ongast* head wind]

on-mannan of a woman forward in nature. [origin unknown]

onmark see AN-MARK.

onnekarl see *ONCA.*

on-plush something coming on suddenly which upsets one. [also Sh where it has the other meaning *sudden gale*; ON *and-blástr* gale; see ONGELID]

ony = any. **onyeen** anyone.

oo 1 = wool [also Sc], '*O aye a hae a ae oo*' reputedly said by an old lady who affirmed she was knitting a jersey in one colour of wool 'Oh yes, I have all one wool'. '*He pays no black oo for that*', its bred in the bone.'

oo 2 to coo. [imitat]

ooby part of the old Orkney kitchen. [a form of OOT-BYE; see INBYE]

ood a sheep mark, the wool tied in a little knob on the forehead. [the first element of ON *auðkenni* sheep mark; literally *easy-know*]

ooled, oolie forlorn or sorry looking. [ON *ugla* owl (from its solitary behaviour)]

ooler, uiler 1 small, *a lot o ooler dirt*. 2 a small potato. [Sh *oller* mud; Norw *aale* cattle urine]

oolie see OOLED.

ooma pitiful. [ON *ú-magi* a helpless individual]

oomin a slight hint (of something). [the essential meaning is a *glimmer of light*; ON *húm* twilight]

oomo, omo, umo noun. disorder or confusion. **in oomo** broken up. [a clipped form of URMAL]

oon 1 a strip of field cut by a scythe. 2 a group of three people cutting side by side with a HOOK. 3 as much as will make a sheaf of corn. [Norw dial *one* a strip]

oonenyafoo see INGANAFOU.

oonwandan see UNWANDAN.

oopsie-cassie = oopsie daisie.

ooran *tae sit ooran* to sit dozing or dreaming. [Norw *ore* doze or muddle]

oorie noun. drizzle. adj. bleak (by extension). [ON *úr* drizzling rain]

oot* = out [also Sc]. **oot-aboot*** out and around, '*Wi the fine weather grandad can go oot-aboot again and that's lightsome for him*'. **oot-aboot-toed** splay footed. **oot apae the day** late in the day. **oot-be-tald** of behaviour, beyond belief. **ootbrecks** marginal land. **oot-fa** light grains and seeds separated from grain by winnowing. **oot-feeted*** splay footed [ON *út-faetr*]. **oot-had** endurance. **oot-mouchted** tired out, exhausted. **oot-o-dykes** outside the tunship wall. **oot o the wey** * = out of the way. *no oot o the wey* of price, reasonable, '*£2 for that piece o maet is no oot o the wey*'. **oot-owld** extremely old. **oot-run*** a piece of outlying grazing. **ootside-in*** =

inside-out. [an example of the many reversed forms in the Orkney dial; the Eng form is more logical since it is possible to see the inside when it's out but not the outside when it's in!; see NETTING-WIRE, HEADLIGHT etc for other examples]. **oot-tak*** substance, '*Thir's no muckle oot-tak in that*'. **oot-takker** the person who takes the peats from the tusker operator. **oot-toed*** splay footed. **ootwailings, ootwalls** the leavings in the sense of 'what has not been selected'. [see WALE]. **oot-winter** to keep cattle out all winter [also Sc]

ooteny see OWDNY.

ootenyafu out of sorts. [see INGANAFOU]

oot-fa 1 see OOT.

oot-fa 2 ebb tide. [compare ON *útfall*]

oot o traip see TARP.

ootrug an outward undercurrent. [related to Norw *utrykking* a pulling out]

open = to open. **open roads (to)** to cut passages with scythes etc in a field of corn to allow the reaper or binder to work.

opgestrie† the custom by which, in Orkney and Sh a UDAL proprietor could, with the consent of his heirs, transfer his property to another in return for lifelong support. [from an assumed ON *uppgefster* one who surrenders himself to another]

or 1 = or. 2* than, *bigger or*. [see also NOR used in this sense]. 3 before, '*I doot hid'll rain or night*'.

Orcadian (pronounced Urcadian). 1 a native of Orkney, particularly a native living in Orkney; (of people of Orkney descent living outside Orkney, the tendency is to speak of *Orkney folk, Orkneyman, Orkney wife* etc). 2 the dialect of Orkney. (*Orcadian* is never correctly used as an adjective, always *Orkney* as in *Orkney chair, Orkney cheese* etc). [not a native word but developed from *Orcades,* the Latin word for the islands]

orafu greedy. [see ORROFU]

orgil a burn or glen. [ON *ár-gil* stream channel; compare the placename *Orgil* in Hoy]

oro 1 a little child. [see URRIE]

oro 2 mad. **oro gyte** mad. [see GITE; ON *óra* to rave]

orra odd, occasional. **orra-boy** a boy employed occasionally. **orra-hoose** a shed. **orra-man** a man who does occasional work. [also Sc; *orra* a reduced form of Sc *oweraa* over and above]

orrible a strong rush of water in a stream, a rapid. [ON *ár-bylgja*]

orrofu eager for news. [ON *óra* to rave!]

orrowed wedged. [Norw dial *årette* a wedge]

Orkney (pronounced Ortney) = noun. Orkney. adj. having origin in Orkney. **Orkney chair** the mod-

85

ern name for a straw backed chair, formerly known as a STRAA BACKÉD STUIL. **Orkney folk** native born islanders living <u>outside</u> the islands (compare ORCADIAN). **Orkney cheese/butter** etc., dairy products made on the farm [ON *Orkneyjar*, Orkney Islands, based on an earlier Celtic *Orc*; adj. *Orkneyskr*]

ort 1 to distribute wastefully. 2 to work energetically but in a wasteful manner. **orter** worry or trouble, '*My whit a orter her family's been tae her*'. [ME *ortus*; LGer *ort* leavings]

orva-kuithe a large coalfish. [see HARVA-KUITHE]

oshit a dingy grey colour. [see USHAT]

osmal see USMAL.

ossigar* in ossigar 1 of hens, moulting. 2 of a person, down at heel. [ON *af-skurðr;* literally a *cutting off*; the Sh form *nossigar* picks up the **n** of the phrase **in ossigar;** the *s-k-r* form meaning *to cut* is also found in Breton **diskar** to moult]

ossle-tree the wooden axle of a cart. [a form of Eng *axle*]

othy the smallest pig of a litter. [Norw dial *odda* a bit left over; compare PEEDIE-ODDIE]

otterbow *an otterbow thing* something ill-shaped. [origin uncertain]

Our Lady's hen *the lark* in Orkney but elsewhere *the wren.* [the three dark spots on the bird's tongue are supposed to represent The Trinity; the thief who steals a lark's eggs will acquire three black spots on the tongue too as a punishment]

ouse see OWSE.

outbrecks see OOTBRECKS.

outher '*Yi'll hiv tae outher him*', you'll have to find out the source of his information. [origin uncertain]

oven = oven. **oven-pot** a shallow three-legged pot buried in hot ashes and used for cooking [also Sc]

over a nonsense word in a child's counting out rhyme. [also Sc; perhaps Celtic for number 8]

overly kind or generous. [ON *ofrligr* excessive]

owch see EECH.

owdny huge in size (eg of a house). **ooteny** a large number of cattle etc. **ownie** of a house large in size. [Sc *noityon* a lump with loss of initial *n*]

ower 1 = over. 2* rather, '*Sheu wis standan ower closs tae the fire*'. **ower-cammo** of horses striking down with their forefeet. [see KAME]. **ower-end*** to set on end. **ower-faamer** to make helpless. [Norw dial *f(j)åma* to go about in a dazed manner]. **ower-gaen** 1 over-run, '*Me gairden's ower-gaen wi weeds*'. 2 over bearing. **ower-hank** (having) advantage over. [probably a form of *upperhand*]. **ower-kemmle** to knock over. [compare Sh *kuml* a form of WHUMMLE]. **owers** 1 what is left over. 2 more than is required. **ower-skelly, owskelly** a windy day with bright clouds against a contrasting background. [ON *skjöldóttr* of cattle, dappled]. **ower-weel** 1* satisfactory, '*Oh hid's ower-weel*'. 2 **ower-weel hid*** that's alright by me. 3 **ower-weel kent*** well known, in a disparaging sense, '*Hid's ower-weel kent that he's the faither o the bairn*'. verb. **ower** to overcome, to get over, *Wir owered the 'flu for a mercy*'

owld* = 1 old. 2 a disrespectful term for anyone regardless of age, '*There's owld Garson gan tae the hill*'. **owld mare's milk** a mixture of eggs, sugar and whisky. **Owld Neuar Day** (Old New Year's Day) the 13th of January. **Owld Christmas Day** the 6th of January. [Orcadians, like the Shetlanders persisted in keeping the Gregorian calendar (although it was officially abolished in 1753!). *Owld Neuar Day* continues to be remembered among the old people]

owmuth* a delegate. [ON *umboðs-maðr* a steward]

ownie see OWDNY.

owse, ouse* to bale water out of a boat, etc. [ON *ausa*]

owsen = oxsen. [OSc *oussin* oxen]

owse-room† the starboard side of a vessel [ON *austrrúm* the space where the bilge pump was located.]

owskelly see OWER-SKELLY.

owtchistis† in old records a form of OUTSKIFT. [see SKIFT]

oxter* the armpit. [also Sc; OE *oxta*]

oy a grandchild or a nephew. [Gael *ogha*]

oyce*, uiss a small salt water lagoon trapped behind a shingle spit. [ON *óss* river mouth; most of the Orkney lagoons are also stream mouths eg *The Oyce* in Firth parish]

P the letter *p* pronounced as in English.

paal to move slowly, '*He wis cairryan as much as he could paal under*'. [also Sh; Norw dial *pala*]

paalo, paalo whal, pallo, pallack, pellack a por-

poise. *as fat as a pallack* very fat. **pallo** bulky and clumsy. [OSc *peloka*]

Pace 1, Paes Easter. [also Sc *Pace eggs* Easter eggs; OF *pasche* ultimately from Hebrew *pasah* to pass over]

pace 2, pes* = pace. The distance of one step, still used as a measure of distance among older people. [one of a number of Orkney words which do not change in the plural e.g. *fower pace*; compare HORSE]

paction a collusion. [OSc *pactioun* an agreement]

pad scc PADDY.

paddle, paedle the lumpsucker fish. [also Sc; origin uncertain but compare ON *padda* a toad; Dan *havpadde* lumpsucker, literally sea frog]

paddo*, paddock 1 a toad. 2 a term of abuse used as in Eng *toad! **paddo-saets** toadstools. [also Sc; ON *padda]*

paddy, pad a young suckling pig. **paddy-tang** a type of seaweed favoured by pigs. [compare Norw *patte-gris* a suckling pig; *patte* here refers to the teat of an animal]

pae, pi on, upon '*Pit hid pae the table.*' [= APAE but compare similar contracted form in Norwegian *på*, on, upon]

paece = peace. 1 '*Tak paece on thee*', calm down. 2 '*Sit a-paece!**' sit still. [*a* = in; compare Eng *asunder*; Ork dial *a-geldro*]

paedle see PADDLE.

Paes see PACE.

paet* 1 = peat. 2 a block of peat. 3 the furrow turned over by the plough. **paet bank*** a place from which peat is dug. **tae cut paets*** (Eng to cut peat). **three paet deep*** the depth of three standard peats. **paet-skyo** a shed for storing peat. [see SKYO]

paiks a threshing, '*Thoo'll get thee paicks the morn*'. [also Sc; OSc *paikis* a thrashing]

pair = pair. **the pair o them**, both (used disrespectfully); **none o the pair o them**, neither (also used disrespectfully; see NITHER)

pale a water-tap. [also Sc; Fr *pelle* shutter of a sluice; Lat *pala* spade]

pall = pawl. verb. to take a good firm grip as in tug of war etc. noun. 1 a support. 2 a puzzle. **palled** to be at a loss as in, '*Ah'm palled for news*' [also Sc]

pallack see PAALO.

pallan see PILLAN.

palled see PALL 1.

pallo see PAALO.

pallowy, polly of an animal thin. [Sc *palie*; related perhaps to PELL; *owy* adj suffix; compare NORNAWAY]

palmer the cormorant. **palmer** something unusually big e.g. *a palmer o a duck*. [Sc *palmer* to go about with a shuffling gait; originally to walk like a pilgrim who carried a *palm* as evidence that he had been to the Holy Land]

pan 1 = pan. 2 the layer between the new and old

wool on a sheep's back. **pan drop** a hard round white mint-flavoured sweet [also Sc]. **pan loaf*** a loaf made in a sealed tin or pan [also Sc].

pand see PANT 1.

pangse to walk with difficulty. [Norw *bangsa*]

panshite, panshine* '*Whit a panshite he was in*' a state of excitement. [in Eng and Sc dial; origin uncertain]

pant 1, pand the vallance which covered the spaces between the legs of a bed. [also Sc; OF *pandre* to hang]

pant 2* a joke, '*He did hid just for a pant*'. [a reduced form of *pantomime*]

pan-tree, paun-tree a bar hanging in the chimney of old fireplaces. [OSc *pane* a wall plate]

panyal a boggy part of a field [a corruption of DANYEL]

pap, pappo* 1 a teat [also Sc]. 2 **the pap o the hass** uvula. **tae gae the pap/pappo** to breast feed. [arch Eng *pap*]

parago, paragray wool of mixed colours, like LICE AND NITS. [obs Eng *paragon* a mixed worsted material]

paralytic* dead drunk. [Eng *paralysed*]

pargis, pirkas see FARGIS.

Parisian barm baker's yeast said to have been brought to Orkney from France by a soldier baker in the Napoleonic Wars. During the 1st World War, Jolly's Bakery in Harray supplied Parisian Barm for the bakeries of the Grand Fleet in Scapa Flow.

parly = parrel, an old type of wooden traveller used on the mast of a boat.

parochin† parish. [also Sc; OSc *parrochyn*]

partan* the edible crab. *as fu as a partan* absolutely full. **partan-taed** in-toed. [Gael *partan*]

parteeclar 1 = particular. 2* excellent, especially *just parteeclar* speaking of the weather, a well completed job etc. 3 excellently, '*He's gittan on parteeclar efter his operation*'.

paska lazy or listless. [? a form of POOSTED]

past = past. '*He wis nine past in November*'* he had his ninth birthday in November [also Sc]. **pit hid past*** put it away.

pasters the ankles of a horse. [Eng *pastern*]

pat see PIT.

pattle verb. 1 to walk with short steps. 2 to move like e.g. the fins of a fish. 3 to kick and sprawl while lying on the back. noun. a small long handed spade for cleaning a plough. [also known as a PATTLE-TREE; in Sc takes additional form *spattle*]. **pattle-tree spinner** a nonsense phrase to describe someone who is busy about something. **pattled*** trodden down e.g. of a damp piece of grass so that mud can be seen through it. [OSc *patyl* a ploughstaff]

pattren* = pattern. [ME patron]

patty a call term to a pig. [see PADDY]

paun-tre see PAN-TREE.

pavie verb. to strut, to put on airs. **in a pavie** in a state of worry or excitement. [also Sc; OSc *pavie* a caper]

pech to pant. [also Sc; imitat]

pee small, as in *pee-ting* something very small. [a clipped form of PEEDIE + TING]

peed, peetie a call to a calf. [see PEEDIE]

peedie* small. [also Cai]. Probably the most common dialect word. The popularity of this word has grown this century and has almost eclipsed PEERIE; as an illustration of this, the small 'sea' to the west of Kirkwall appears on Ordnance Survey maps as the Peerie Sea but today is invariably called the Peedie Sea. **peedie-oddie*** very small. [see UDDY]. **peedie-breeks*** a little child. **peedie end*** the room in the Orkney two-teacher school in which the infants are taught. **peedie finger*** little finger. **peedie gren** a small quantity. **peedie meenit** a very short time, '*Just wait a peedie meenit.*' [*peedie* is used especially by children and for small living things; the origin of *peedie* and *peerie* is lost in the Nordic languages but it seems that it is one of a group of words meaning 'something budding, growing or shooting out from a point', the initial root having lost an initial *s*; examples are Norw *pita*, a small object, Far *petti*, a little piece, Norw *pir*, small mackerel, Far *pirra*, a little object, Ork *pirrens* young girls; further removed are Ork *picka*, the blenny, ON *píka*, girl, Eng *pig*, originally meaning the young of swine; the lost *s* is retained in Norw *spedbarn*, baby, *spedkalf*, sucking calf and *spir* another word for small mackerel. Eng *spit*, *spire*, *spike* etc., referring to points also retain the *s*]

peekit 1 = picked. 2 off colour [also Sc]

peelo a fragment. [Norw *pile* a particle]

peen the pointed top of a hammer. [also Sc; Eng dial; EME *pen* the pointed end of a hammer]

peenie* an apron. [a form of Eng *pinafore*; also Sc and Eng dial in the form *pinny*]

peeps the time signal on the radio, '*There's the peeps, hid's six o'clock*'. [imitat]

peerie formerly the most common word for small in the dialect, it has gradually been overtaken by PEEDIE this century but remains firmly fossilised in placenames e.g. Peerie Sea. **peerie-folk** = fairies. **peerie-laird** = a small landholder. **peerie cubit** a measurement of 38 cm. The cubit was an old measure, from the elbow to the tip of the middle finger, approx 45cm. **peerie-orrie** very small. [see URRY]. **peerie-snippo** the dunlin. [see SNIPPO]. **peerie-whaup** the whimbrel. [see PEEDIE]

peese 1, piss a coaxing term to a dog. [also Sc; compare Norw *kiss* call used to attract cats or cows and Ork *kiss* used to scare cats]

peese 2 of children to beg persistently in a family situation. [a form of PEESTER]

peesel a close look at something [origin unknown]

peester 1 verb. to squeak. 2 to groan or gasp. noun. suppressed laughter. [Norw *pistra* to make a small noise like a mouse]

peetch to reserve for oneself (only in children's language) [origin unknown]

peetie see PEED.

peety = pity. *tae think (a) peety o* to pity.

Pelkie the devil. [for PELTRY (the ragged one), compare Eng *ragman*, the devil; see also PEOLU; compare ON *trefla-kolla* a witch where *trefla* is a deriv of *trefill* fringe]

pell a rag or a dirty matted piece of hair hanging from an animal [Sh *bell* as in *dillbells*]. **pelliehog** a poor ragged sheep which has barely survived the winter. [see PELTERS]. When March was cold and bitter they had a saying in Sanday:

Mairch said tae April,
'If yi'll lend me days three,
Ah'll mak a' thee pelliehogs tae dee
(die)'.

[*hog* here is Eng yearling sheep]

pellack see PAALO.

pello a surface peat to which the grass still clings. [Norw dial *pela* to pare turf with a spade]

pelt 1 see PELL.

pelt 2 1 = pelt. 2* a blow, '*She got a right pelt on the side o the head*'. **pelter** to hit with stones.

pelters* 1 rags. 2 dung clinging to an animal's coat. **peltry** hanging in rags. [Faroese *pjöltur* a rag]

pen dung but only of hens as in **hen-pen.** [also Sc; (dung from) the hen-pen where *pen* is used in the sense of enclosure]

pen-gun a type of pea shooter made from a pen or quill. A piece of turnip is stuck in each end, one piece is forced in with a stick and the compressed air forces the other out, pop-gun style.

pennied dappled, *a pennied mare*. [Gael *peighinneach* spotted]

penny 1 = penny. 2 money. *anything tae mak a penny* anything to earn money. *every penny's a prisoner* he's tight-fisted. *he's no wantan a penny* he has plenty of money. **penny-for-the Pope*** at Hallowe'en the children of Stromness go round with their turnip lanterns using this phrase as their begging slogan. The use of the word Pope suggests that the custom is pre-Reformation. **pennyland** an old land division based on SKAT, a system of taxation. Eighteen pennylands went to make up an urisland. In the

1880's a pennyland varied from 4 acres on the coast to 8 or 9 inland. **penny-wadding** a wedding to which guests brought food and drink. [also Sc; also known as an IN-PIT WEDDING]
Peolu the Devil. [Sh *pyoli-man* a ragged person; see PELKIE]
pepper 1 = pepper. 2 a skipping rope turned as fast as possible.
perjink* prim. [also Sc where we find the additional form *perjinkety*; origin uncertain]
pernickety* precise. [also Sc and Eng dial; origin uncertain]
pes see PACE 2.
peswisp a tangle (of eg wool). [Sc *peasewisp* a wisp of pease straw]
Peter's thoom black marks behind the gills of a haddock. [St Peter's thumb]
pettican feats of strength. [a corrupt form of PRETTIKIN]
peuchis tripe, stomach of a cow etc. [? ON *poki* bag influenced by Sc *haggis* stomach]
peule = pewl, *peulan an greetan* whining.
peunkie a belch of air from the stomach. [imitat]
pewrl to fret or whine [a corruption of *pewl*]
peuy see POY.
pewther see PUTHER.
pick verb. 1 = pick. 2 to move slowly e.g. in walking or doing a job, especially *pickan awa*. 3* to tap lightly eg on a window. **pickan for neb*** used of chickens just about to hatch. **pickéd*** of the hands chapped through working in cold weather. noun. **pick** a light tap. **picko** 1 the old name for the children's game popularly known as TIG. In **high picko** the child had to be touched on the body, in **low picko** on the legs, in **relievy picko** a child had to stand still when touched but could be relieved in a number of ways. 2 (haily)-**picko*** hailstone.
picka, picko the blenny (Stromness). [Sc *pickie* the young of the coalfish etc. see PEEDIE]
pickie small, as in *pickie-laird* a small landowner. [see PEEDIE]
pickie-turds the magpie, only in a children's rhyme:-
Tell-pye pickie turds sittan on a tree
Tellan doun the peerie burds, one two three
[Eng *pick* + *turds]*
pickanairish affected in behaviour. [origin uncertain]
Pickie-dyke see PICKS.
pickiefeer a quarrel. [Sh and Sc *pikkifield* etc; origin uncertain]
pickie-terno a tern. [also Sc; the last element is Eng *tern*; *pickie* refers to the pointed beak of this bird]
picko see PICK.
Picks* = Picts. **Picky Dyke** any prehistoric earthen wall. **Picks' hoose*** a general name for what

appears to be any prehistoric dwelling. [It is difficult in the local dialect to sound the letter *t* after a *c* unless it is followed by a vowel; compare *acs* for *acts*. It is even difficult sometimes when there is a following vowel; *actually* is sounded *aculy*].
pidro 1 a slight touch. 2 the game of TIG. [ON *fiðra* to touch (with a feather)]
piece 1 = piece. 2* a piece of bread. 3* packed lunch. 4* a distance, *'He lived a piece awey'*. 5* used frequently instead of place e.g. *'Whar piece are yi gaan?' 'Ah'm no gan tae get a car for I hiv no piece tae keep hid'.'Thee pipe's on the mantelpiece'.* **piece-time*** break time or interval in the Orkney school. [see PIECE 2]
pie-hole a hole in leather etc to allow a lace to pass through. [also Sc; origin uncertain]
pig a large earthenware jar. [also Sc; ME *pygg*]
pight 1 a Pict. 2 a little mischief maker, *'Thoo're a peedie pight'* [the sense is *spirit*, many of the pre-historic structures in the Orkney landscape being credited to the *Pights* or Picts]
pike 1 to work away persistently at something. 2 to walk feebly, *to pike away*. [a form of PICK]
pilder to run slowly and feebly. [Norw *pilte* to run or scurry influenced perhaps by DILDER]
pile 1 = pile. 2* crowd, *'Beuy whit a pile o folk wis there'*. [see also HEAP]
pilk 1 to shell. [also Sh; Norw *pilka* to scrape]
pilk 2 a small light-built boy. [Sh *pilkin*; ON *piltr* boy]
pilkya a state of distress. [Sc *pilget* a quarrel; origin unknown]
pill* the penis. [Norw *pill*, Eng (Shak.) *pillicock*]
pillan, pallan a partan with a soft shell. [origin unknown]
pillersho 1 a heap of small insignificant objects. 2 a little trout. [Norw dial *pilar* a kind of small fish; Norw *kjøe* small trout]
pilter the movement of small fishes when breaking through the surface and making a ripple. [Norw *pilte* to scurry]
piltick* a second year coalfish. [also Sh; origin uncertain; may relate to ON *piltr* boy or to PILTER]
pin verb 1 = to pin. 2 to move quickly. **pin-leg** a wooden leg. **pinning** a small stone used to plug a gap in a wall.
pinch = to pinch. **pinchan** disappointing.
pingy pinched looking. [? a form of Eng *pinched*]
pinkie* the little finger. [also known as WINKIE. compare Du *pinkie*; the word *pinkie* is used in Sc with a variety of *small* associations; the original meaning seems to have been a tiny point of light as in Eng *blink*]
pink-peenk the sound made by water dropping in a bucket etc. [Eng *drip-drop*; imitat; compare

89

TEENK-TANK]

pinksy dressed in fine clothes. [OSc *pynk* to decorate clothes by cutting + *sy* adj suffix]

pinno a point of rock from which a man fishes. [Norw *pinne* a point]

pinnovvers a trifling matter. [origin unknown]

pinstrae the stalks of crested dogstail grass. [Icel *punstra* windlestraw]

pintle the penis. **pintill-fich†** in a 16th century charter, razor fish. [OE *pintel* penis]

pipes = bagpipes. '*He's tunan his pipes*' said of a child crying.

pird of an animal to jump in the air with all four feet off the ground. [ON *spretta* a spurt or bound with loss of initial *s*]

pirkas see PARKIS.

pirl 1* a little ball of sheep, rabbit etc dung. **pirlie snaa** snow which falls in round shapes. [also Sh; Norw *parle*]

pirl 2 to turn round lightly. **pirlan** the spiralling motion of e.g. a rope running over the gunwale of a boat. [also Sc; practically any consonant and the vowel *i* in front of *rl* will give a word 'to turn' in the Ork dialect]

pirn-taed in-toed. [the essential meaning is 'turned in,' see PURM]

pirr a state of excitement, '*Whit a pirr she's in the day*'. **pirry** of an animal e.g. lively. [PIRR, BIRR and related forms exist throughout the Teutonic languages referring to *turning*]

pirrens children, used of girls rather than boys. [a form of PEERIE ANES little ones; compare Sc **weans;** see PEERIE]

pirrivee a flurry. [related to PIRR; compare Sc *tirrivee*]

piss 1 see PEESE 1.

piss 2 = piss. **piss cog** a wooden bucket, the equivalent of a chamber pot.

piss 3 a weakling. [Norw *pyse*]

pissle 1 to shell grain or to remove grain from straw e.g. a duck might be said to *pissle straes (straws)*. 2 to potter about. [Norw *pusle* to busy oneself]

pissocks slippers [origin unknown]

pit past tense PAT, POT, perfect tense PITTEN = (to) put. **tae pit mad** to make angry. **pit aboot** *pit aboot thee* wrap yourself up. **pit at*** to annoy, '*That pits at me*'. **pit by* by-pit** something temporary, '*Hid'll deu as a pit by*'. **pit doon** 1 to bury. 2 to take the boat from the house to the shore after the winter, '*Weel hiv tae pit the boat doon the morn*'. **pit fur*** send for, '*Pit fur the doctor at wance*'. **pit in*** '*Pit in thee hand noo*' an invitation to start helping oneself e.g. at a supper table. **pit on*** to make an excuse or such an excuse [also Sc]. **pit ower** of time, to pass, '*Ah'm never pitten ower a night like*'. **pitten***

perfect tense of PUT. (A pupil noticed another pupil's mistake and allegedly said to the teacher '*He's gin and pitten pitten whar he should hiv pitten put*'.) **pitten aboot*** upset or flustered.

pitten doon buried, '*Efter John wis pitten doon we gid ower and cleaned oot his belongings*'.

pitten tae, teu-pitten put to (a test), '*He wis right pitten tae, tae baet (beat) him*'.

pitcher 1 = pitcher. 2 a bucket.

pivver to tremble or quiver, especially of the lips. [Sh *pipper*; Norw *pipra*]

pizz verb. to fry. noun. the sound of a drop of hot water on a hot stove. **pizzan** very hot. [imitat]

pizzle-wisp a tangle. [a development of PESWISP]

pizzlo an entanglement. [see PIZZLE-WISP]

pizzo 1 see PIZZLO.

pizzo 2 peevish, awkward. [see PEESE 2]

plaasy, plaisy overbearing. [origin unknown]

place = 1 palace. 2 Birsay village, *doon at the Place* i.e. at the Earl's Palace in Birsay.

plainen† coarse linen. [also Sc; ? a deriv of Eng *plain*]

plainstones flagstones [also Sc]

plaisy see PLAASY.

plank† verb. to square land. noun. an old division of land, the equivalent of 1.33 acres. Commonly used in records at the time of the abolition of RUNRIG. *Westplank* is an alternative name for the farm of Lee in Birsay [compare Fr *planche* a strip of land and Eng *plank*]

plantie-creu* a yard for plants, usually **kaily-creu.** [also Sh in the form *plantie-crub*; see CREU]

plash a pool, specifically the clay lined dew ponds formerly used in Ork in areas where spring water was scarce; a slight earth tremor in the 1930's fractured the clay bottom of these pools and they dried up, never to be repaired. [OE *plaesc* a pool]

plashy *plashy showers* heavy showers. [imitat]

plat* verb. 1 to walk around with heavy feet. 2 to wash e.g. blankets with the feet by treading on them in a tub, *tae plat blankets*. noun. a fall, '*Whit a plat I got when me feet gid fae under me!*' **platties** home made slippers. [compare English *plod*]

platho a mess e.g. when rain has come through the roof of a house. [see BLATHO]

platsan plodding. [a form of PLAT]

platt *tae platt a pig* after killing, to scald a pig in hot water until the bristles came off easily. [Sc *plot*; see PLOUT]

platties see PLAT.

play 1 = play. 2 intercourse (*vulgar*). **play-drink** the last of the wort drawn off the malt, hence the weakest part of the browst. **playfer** a child's toy. In the 1930's a Birsay man went into a Dounby shop and asked, '*His thoo a playfer for a pullie?*',

90

Have you got a child's toy? [also Sc where it means playmate; *play* + Sc *fere* companion]. **playless** simply or easily '*I could do that playless*'.
pleed see PLEEP.
pleenk* weak tea or weak beer. [Sc *pink;* Norw *pink* weak brandy; probably meant originally a tiny spcck of light, then 'little substance'; see PLINKY]
pleep*, pleed, pleet, pleeter verb. 1 to make a mournful noise. 2 to squeek e.g. of a fatty sausage frying in a pan, *pleepan wi fat.* noun. **pleep** 1. a mournful noise. 2 a person who persistently talks about personal troubles or about troubles of the world in a mournful voice. adj. **pleepy** of a voice, mournful. **water-pleep** the snipe. [imitat; compare Sh *plee* of a bird to cry; Sc *pleengie* a seagull].
pleetran mournful, *a pleetran owld buddy* [see PLEESTER]
pleeshy of tea, week. [imitat]
pleester to whimper or whine. [compare PEESTER; Norw *plystre* to whine]
pleet see PLEEP.
pleeter see PLEEP.
pleetran see PLEEP.
plesky a small fault. [perhaps same as Sc *pliskie* a plight; origin of both words doubtful]
pleur 1 of a gull to cry. 2 of a child to whine. [imitat; compare PLEEP]
plick* 1 = pluck, *tae plick a hen.* 2 to pick (fruit). *tae plick at* to tease.
plicko* a torchlight [the operating button on early torches could not be held down for any length of time; Sh *plinkie* or *flicko*; the essential meaning is short/little flash hence Eng *flashlight*; related to BLINK]
plink to shine in sudden short bursts. [see PLICKO above]
plinkers *eye plinkers* eye lashes. [related to Eng *blink* and Sc *prink*]
plinkwir of a female, prim. [origin uncertain; see PRINKY etc for possibly related form]
plinky pale in colour. [originally a pale light; see PLEENK]
plirt a sudden fall or tumble. *tae sit in a plirt* to sit as if one had fallen. **coo's plirt** a cow pad. [imitat; compare Sc *ploutie*]
plitter* 1 to work (needlessly) in water, especially of children. 2 a watery mess or a mess generally. [related to PLASH and BLITTER; compare Dan dial *plutte* to dabble in water; see PLOWTER]
plitterytildran rattling e.g. of the latch of a door in the wind. [for *tildran* see TILTER, see also PLITTER a noise usually associated with water

but influenced by Eng *pitter* (patter)]
pliver, plivver the golden plover. **plivver pagick** the dunlin. [*plover's page*]
plook a pimple. [also Sc; origin uncertain; may be related to Eng *plug*]
ploot the foot. **bare ploots** bare feet. [see PLAT (verb)]
plother anything wet and soft like e.g. a cheese before it is pressed. [see PLATHO]
plout to plunge e.g. *ploutan blankets* treading blankets in the washing process. **plout-kirn** the old type of churn in which butter was made by *plouting* a stick up and down. Milk was used for this process and not cream, the churn being wide at the top unlike the cream churn which was narrow at the top. [also Sc; compare PLAT, PLATT and English *plod*]
plout-havie see HAVIE.
plowter 1 to walk about in mud or water. 2 to make a mess of a job, '*Whit a plowter yir makkan o that*'. [see PLITTER]
pluck 1 the internal organs of an animal. [also Eng dial; the sense is *what can be plucked out*]. 2* of hens to be **in the pluck**, to be in a moulting condition.
pluff a powder puff. [also Sc; compare LGer *ploffen* to puff]
plump also Sc. 1 = plump. 2* a sudden heavy shower, especially *thunder-plump.*
plunky a trick or an evil trick. [Sc; origin unknown]
plushney a catapult. [see SPLUSHNEY]
poag, poak to plod. [origin uncertain; ? Sc *pod* to walk with short steps]
pock* 1 originally a paper bag or hessian sack but now applied to polythene sacks as well [also Sc]. 2 a net for catching SILLOCKS (in this case the net was shaped like a bag). [ON *poki* bag]
podder see POTHER.
pogo a child's toy made from feathers tied together and released in the wind. [related to the movement in the air; see POAG]
pogsy fat bellied. [see PUGGY and PUGSY]
poindy of a person lean. [see PUNDS]
point = point. **points** 1 = points. 2 laces. Some types of leather lace are brought to a *point* with a fine wire wrapped at the end.
polly see PALLOWY.
polt a short dumpy person. **polty** 1 a small fat person. 2 the man who was lowered over the cliff to take bird eggs. He had to be small yet strong. [Norw **bult** chunk of wood]
pone 1 to pare off turf. [related to Norw *dial* panna roof tile]
pone 2† to take a vow. [Eng *depone*]†
ponge 1 = pounce. 2 to poke. [Sc *punce*]
pooch a naughty girl. [ON *púki* an imp]

poogs old working clothes. [? related to POAG]
pook of a sheep, to butt. **pooking** a thrashing, especially a mock thrashing. [Norw *buka* to strike]
pookan out of sorts. [Sc *poukit* literally plucked (in the sense *in moult*, of a fowl)]
pooko an unpleasant name for a woman. [ON *púta* harlot]
poolie a louse. [also Sc; origin uncertain]
poor = poor. **Poorsboard (The)** the former local authority institution for assisting the poor. **Poorshoose** = poor-house.
poorie an oil can. [a deriv of Eng *pour*]
poort a cry baby. [see PURDY 2]
poor wheeo the call of the golden plover. [see WHEEO]
pooshan poison. [OSc *pusoune*]
poost, poust energy or vigour. **poosted, powsted** having no energy and by extension, bewitched. [ME *pouste* power]
pooster = posture, position [also Sc] '*He pat hid in pooster on the wall*'.
poot a coaxing term to a pig and a cat. **pooty** a cat, especially **peedie pooty** used by a child when stroking a cat. [compare Dan *putte* call to a hen]
poother powder [also Sc]. [OSc *pulder*]
pootie a small cod. [OSc *powt*; Eng pout as in *eel-pouts*; see PEEDIE]
poots* to sulk. **pootsy*** pouting. [Eng *pout* with Sc dial suffix *sy*; compare BIGSY]
pooty a young pig [also PADDY]. **pooty-butties** false oat grass. **pooty-grice** pigs. [see POOT and POOTIE]
pop a speech impediment, *tae hiv the pop*. [imitat]
Pope see PENNY FOR THE POPE.
pose 1 a purse of money. 2 a store of money. [Norw *pose* a bag]
Post Office included because of the odd fact that it is the *off* of office which is accentuated and not the *post*.
pot see PIT.
pother, podder to swear or use foul language. [origin uncertain; compare Sc *peuther* to go drinking]
potree see POT-TREE.
potsker a piece of broken pot. [Eng *potsherd*]
pot-tree, potree a stick for stirring a pot. [see TREE]
potty* putty. [also Sc; Fr *potée* potful]
pounce big long meadow grass. [see PUNDS]
poundler see PUNDLAR.
pouskan walking in a breathless fashion. [see POOST]
poust see POOST.
povily listless. [Sc *pyauvie* an attack of sickness]
pow* a pool. [also Sc; OE *pol*]
powl 1 to wriggle like a fish. 2 to show signs of life, '*He never powled*'. [also Sc; origin uncertain]

powls bare legs and feet. [Eng *poles*]
powny* pony. [also Cai; OSc *powny*; OF *poulain* colt]
powsted see POOST.
poy, peuy *tae poy aboot* to potter around, *tae poy along* to move slowly along. [origin unknown]
pram-full full to overflowing. **prammed** crowded in with no room to move (e.g. in a bus). [Sc *pram* to squeeze]
preen* a pin. [also Sc; ON *prjónn*]
preenk to walk in a conceited fashion. [see PRINKY]
preeve 1 a trial run to see whether there are any fish present. 2 to make such a run. [ON *profa* to try; Norw *prøve fisken* to try for fish]
prequeer, purwheer plainly or clearly, '*I can see the Owld Man o Hoy prequeer the day*'. [also Sc; in John Barbour's poem *Freedom*, written perhaps around 1360, we read *Bot gyff he had assayit it, Than all perquer he suld it wyt..* (But should he try it (freedom), Then he would know it thoroughly); Fr *par coeur* by heart, which came to mean easily or thoroughly]
press 1 = press. 2* a cupboard. [also Sc; Eng *press* in the sense compress]
press-gang a body of sailors under an officer who had the power to impress men in the navy in the 18th and 19th century. [also Eng but *press-gang* features so prominently in old Orkney stories it is included here; OF *prester* to loan with the sense of *advance pay*]
pret action. [a special development of meaning of ON *prettr* trick; see PRETTIKIN]
prettikin a trick. *no a good prettikin* a bad habit. [ON *prettr* trick with Eng dimin *kin*; in Sh *prett* was also used with an extended meaning 'trial of strength'; see PETTICAN]
price = price. '*That's the price o him*'* that serves him right [also Sc]
pricks 1 = prick. 2 a V shaped wooden instrument on which a cod-line is wound. [from its sharp point]
prigging haggling. [also Sc; origin uncertain]
prinky conceited. [compare PLINKWIR]
printick a caper or prank. [? a nasalised form of PRETTIKIN]
prip two or three peats supporting each other. [related to Eng *prop*]
prip-tail a show off. [Sc *primp* a prig; *primp* is related to Eng *prim*]
prog 1* to pierce. '*Please sir, Trevor's just progged me wi a preen (pin)*'. [also Sc; compare ME *proke* to poke]
prog 2 prong, *a three progged fork* [see PROG]
prolie a little price or a windfall, something obtained for nothing, '*He's aff home wi a prolie*'. **proly** a feast on the sly; secret spoil etc. [related to Eng

prowl]
proper = proper. **proper spoken*** speaking Eng without a hint of dialect.
provag 1 = provoke. 2 showing off, '*Hid's just a bit o provag*'.
prowly sharp punishment or scolding. [? Norw *pryle* to thrash]
prullyans the entrails of a slaughtered animal. [Sh *prollaments* goods and *prolleks* fishermen's gear; origin uncertain; see PROLIE]
prullyo uproar or confusion. [see BRULLYO]
prummick provisions, especially for a sea journey. [see BRAM]
puckle 1* a small quantity. 2 a measure with two hands put together. [also Sc; ? related to Eng *peck*]
puddings 1* intestines. [also Sc and in NoEng dial]. 2* the intestines of the animal filled with meal etc. [compare Cornish *pot* a bag]
puddlies bare feet. [Sc *poddle* to walk with short steps]
pudyan a small gluttonous person. [origin uncertain; compare Sc *pudyal*; Eng *podgy*]
puffle to remove the husks from a boiling pot of KNOCKÉD-CORN. This was done with a band of straw. [related to Norw *puff* to push or shove; also Sc]
puggled* *fairly puggled* overcome by heat. [also Sc; origin uncertain]
puggy* a child's word for stomach. **pugso** a fat bully. **pugsy** having a large belly. [for *sy* suffix see POOTSY; ON *belgi* a bag; see SCOOR and GRUELLY BELKIE for related forms]
puilo a woman of ill-repute. [related to Norw *pjalt* tatters; see PELKIE and PEOLU related words]
puilt *puiltan and threshan*, working hard at threshing. [related to Eng *pelt* to throw from Lat *pultare* to strike or beat]
puink a whack. [compare PEUNKIE]
puirl see PEWRL
puldery (pronounced *pul-dairy*) the orchis. **pulderuck** bog asphodel. [a corrupt form of *valerian* a marsh flower]
puller an old type of oil lamp which required the wick to be pulled up rather than screwed up.
pullie a child, usually in the plural [see PELL; the essential meaning is *ragged*; compare HECKAPOLO and PELLIEHOG]
pull-mull sickly. [see PYULL; for *mull* see TRUTMULLED]

pulter to wash slightly. [Sc *plowter*; see PLOWTER]
pultis 1 = poultice. 2 a mess, '*Whit a pultis yir makan o that!*'
pulty fat or stumpy, *a pulty bit o thing*. [see POLT]
pund an enclosure for sheep etc. [Eng *pound*]
punder, pundler, pundlar, poundler, punlar 1 a large weighing beam formerly used in Orkney. 2 the human head (a stone the size of the human head was used as a counterbalance) [ON *pundari* weighing beam]
punds, pounce a coarse grass which grows on sandy links. **punded** straggling thin crop. **punyowy** of a crop, beast or person thin or lean. [Icel *pundur* bent grass; the suffix is an Ork adjectival form; compare NORNAWAY; GINNOWY etc]
punlar see PUNDER.
purdy 1 diarrhoea. 2 belching or rifting. 3 a nickname for a child, '*Come on purdy!*'. **purdo** a mess e.g. a sloppy pudding. **purdy-ribbon** indigestion [see REEPAN, a related word]. [Sh *purt* mess; Dan *purt* to fart]
purgas, purkis, pirkas a mess, especially of a mess of food. [PURDY + GIS]
purgis, purkis a small burden in a bag. [? a form of FARGIS]
purl to poke around e.g. in the ashes (or in the ear!). [related to PIRL]
purm* a bobbin. [Sc *pirn*; the essential meaning is 'to turn'; compare Sc *pirie* a spinning top]
purpie† old form of purple. [also Sc; OF *purpre*]
purr 1 to push out the burnt wick of the cruisie lamp. **purrin pin** a small pin attached to a cruisie lamp to assist in purring the wick. **purr** 2 to poke in ash etc, carefully as if to uncover something. [Sc *porr purr* to prod, poke thrust; Norw dial *pura*]
purwheer see PREQUEER.
pussie an animal or person with hair disordered and inclined to stand upright. [? bussy = *bushy*]
puther, pewther 1 to fuss about doing something. 2 to grope about e.g. in the dark. [also Sc; origin uncertain; compare Du *peuteren* to poke about]
putt* 1 verb. to nudge. *tae try a putt at a lass* to make advances to her. noun. a nudge. [OE *putian* originally to push and shove]
putt 2 '*Putt, putt!*' a call to a little pig. [see POOT]
puy to annoy. [origin uncertain; compare Sc *poy upon* to persuade strongly]
pyull to vomit. [origin uncertain; compare Eng *puly* sickly]

Q the letter *q* still pronounced *wh* by older people e.g. *wheen* for 'queen'.

quack 1 *'in a quack'* still living or alive. [ON *kvikr* alive]

quack 2 1 = to quake. 2 to swarm, *'The girnal wis just quackan wi mites'*. **quackoo, whackoo** a quagmire.

quar see KWARR.

quark see KWARK.

quarkie see KWARKIE.

quarrel† a quarry. There are a number of houses called *Quarrelbraes* in Orkney. [also Sc; ME *quarer*; OF *quarriere*]

queebeck the call of the grouse. [imitat, see KITTY-COME-HOME]

queller [see KUILLER]

quey a young cow before it has calved [ON *kvíga*]

quick = 1 quick. 2 infested. [also Sh]. **quick alive** swarming, alive. [see KWICK]

quiff a puff of wind etc. [imitat]

quilk = quilt. [see TWILT]

quill see KWILL.

quint see KWINT.

quite* = quit, *'Quite hid, min!'*. [see WHITE]

quoy*, why a piece of common pasture enclosed and cultivated, frequent in placenames. **quoyed in** closed in. The verbal form was in use in the 1940s when a gentleman spoke of the Germans being *quoyed in* at Stalingrad. [ON *kví* an enclosure for animals]

R the letter *r* pronounced as in English.

ra *tae tak a ra in* to shorten (a tether). [also Sh; ON *raxn* knot]

raa = raw. **raa-saithe** bait thrown into the sea to attract fish.

raan roe of a fish. [ON *hrogn;* ME rowne]

race 1 = race. 2* a short trip, *'I gid tae the toon a race'*. 3 the sweep of three scythes moving in parallel. Such a swathe was the width of a rig. 4 the shimmering movement seen in the air on a hot day, particularly on hilltops, caused by the upward movement of warm air [also known as TEEBRO etc and KRINGLOS]. **race-ca** the formula used for starting runners in a race.

raeoo, raew, rew 1 a cry (e.g. of a cat in pain). 2 a raucous mew (e.g.of a she-cat in heat). [imitat]

raes a knot, especially **runnan raes**, a slip knot [ON *raexn* a knot]

raew see RAEOO.

raffle* verb. to mix up. noun. a mix-up. *in a raffle like Stobie's draaers (underpants)* (Westray), in a mix up. [*Stobie* is a Scottish surname but the identity of the gentleman is unknown]. [Sc *raivel;* Du *ravelen, rafelen*; compare Norw *ruvla* to put out of order]

raft to cut, tear. **tae raft ware** to cut seaweed when collecting it for kelp. [ON *rífa* to tear]

rag 1, rugg, ruk a wet mist. **ruggy, rukky** drizzling. [ON *hraglandi* a drizzling shower]

rag 2 1 = rag. 2 a poor thin animal. **ragstones*** the stones set on edge on top of a wall. [perhaps from their ragged appearance]. **ragnail*** an agnail [also Sc]

rag* 3 a horizontal channel left in the wall of a house in readiness for an extension. [compare Sc **raggle** to cut a groove in stone ready for flashing and RAGLINS]

raglins* the top of the side walls of a house or the space between such and the roof. [also Sc; compare RAG 3]

rags to eat in a slovenly way. [origin uncertain; ? Eng *rag* to tear to rags]

raim curdled cream or milk. [also Sh; Sc *ream*; OE *ream* cream; compare ON *rjómi]*

rain-goose* the red-throated diver. Its song is:-
Mair weet, mair weet
Waur wedder Waur wedder
[from the belief that the call of the bird was a sign of rain]

raip* 1 = rope [also Sc]. 2 specifically the line, usually a piece of twine, stretched above the fireplace on which clothes etc were hung to dry. [also Sh and Cai]

raiso two peats propped against each other to dry. [compare Sh *race*; Norw *reis*; compare also ON *hreysi* a heap of stones]

rait† *rait and grait* right and proper. [ON *réttr* right + GRAIT]

raithe see RUITHE 1.

rake 1 * to stretch out the hands. An old invitation to eat heartily was, *'Rake in yir hand an dinna need a bidding'*. **rakster** 1 a stretch of poor ground. 2 a scolding. [ON *rekka* to stretch to; compare REX and Sc *reak]*

rake 2 to wander or prowl about. [ON *reika* to wander]

rake 3 to jerk (a fishing line) and catch the hook in the body of a fish rather than the mouth. [ON *rykkja* to jerk]

rakster 1 see RAKE 1.

rakster 2 *in a rakster* of anything which has gone to ruin. [ON *rek* wreckage]

ralligut a person who talks too much. [compare Norw dial *røl* boasting; compare RILLAGORY]

rally a swaying, staggering. [compare Norw dial *ralla, rulla* to roll, fall, walk unsteadily and RULLYIE 1]

ralyo a quarrel. [compare Sc *rally* quarrelsome and Norw dial *rál* scream or uproar]

raw-gabbéd speaking confidently on subjects about which one is evidently quite ignorant. [also Sh compare OSc *raw-mowit*; see GAB]

ram-gam see RAM-STAM.

ramist confused by drink, cross from lack of sleep. [also Sh; see RUMSE 2]

rammelgoforth a rash person. [Sc *rammle* to romp + *go forth*]

rammle-back* a bar in a chimney from which pots are suspended. [also known as RANTLE-TREE and AMMERS; Sc and NE *rannle balk;* compare Norw *rand* the beam near the fireplace between the long walls of the house; the essential meaning is *beam*]

ramp* 1 = romp. 2* to boil vigorously, *rampan and boilan*. **rampan*** restless, always on the move. [also Sh]

ramse* 1 rough in behaviour, e.g. someone pushing in through a door heedless of others. [Sc *rammish, rammis* crazy]

ramse 2 of butter, rank. [also Sc *ramsh*; ON *rammr* bitter]

ram-stam*, ram-gam headstrong or rash in behaviour. [also Sc; Sc *ramm* of uncertain origin + *stam* to blunder]

rand the border or edge of the heel of a boot or shoe [ON *rönd*, edge]

rander to reinforce a worn part of a knitted woollen garment. [Sc *ranter*; from OF *rentraire* to darn, mend]

randy a loose, disorderly, scolding woman [also Sc and in Eng dial.]

range to swill. **runge** a rinsing. [also Sc *reenge*; NE dial *rench*; NF dial *raincher*; from the same root as Eng *rinse*]

rango of a boat which returns from the sea without a catch, '*He's back rango*'. [origin uncertain; perhaps related to *rank* below]

rank of a boat, unstable. [also Sh; compare Norw *rank*]

rannel rubbish. [compare Sh *rantel* a rag; Norw *rand* a stripe]

ransel† to examine a house for stolen goods. **ranselman** an official who searched a house for stolen goods. [ON *rannsaka;* Eng *ransack, ransackle*]

rant* a convivial gathering, '*The bigger the rant the better the fun!*'. **ranty** very cheerful. [also Sc; obs Du *ranten* to rave]

rantle-tree see RAMMLE-BACK.

rantock a goosander. [only found in writing; per-

haps a misprint for *rautock*; compare RITTOCK]

ranty pipes a goose, in this ancient nonsense rhyme:-

As I sat in me cheerum-charum (chair)
Lukkan through me leerum-larum (window)
I see the ree-raa (?raven)
Bear me ranty-pipes awa,
I swore by me breeti-brattikin, (trousers)
If I hid me wheetie-whatikin (? gun)
I wad mak the ree-raa
Let me ranty-pipes fa.

ranyie, renyie an acute pain. [ON *rangr* awry]

ranyo a quarrel. [ON *rengja* to dispute; *rang-sattr* at variance]

rap a strip of arable ground. **rapaskift†** a division of land. [origin uncertain; compare REEVO]

rash = rush. *rashan (and rainan)** pouring with rain [also Sc]

rasper* *a rasper o a fart* a cracking fart. [compare MLoGer *ruspen* to belch; ON *rispa* to scratch]

ratch of a child, cheeky [a form of Eng *wretch*]

ratchel *ratchel nonsense* complete nonsense. **ratchelly** used as intensive, *ratchelly hungry*. [origin unknown]

rattin* 1 a rat. 2 a scamp or rascal. **rattin tail** a cord knitted by placing four little nails in the end of a cotton reel and levering the woollen loops through the hole with a pin. [also Sc; OF *raton* rat]

rattle = rattle. **rattle up*** to build with speed [also Sc]; several cottages in Orkney have this (not very complimentary!) name. **rattle doon** to demolish quickly.

rav a drizzle. [compare Sc *raff* a flying shower]

ravsy* badly dressed. [compare Norw *rave* torn clothing + Sc *sy*]

rawcheter* = rafter. [OSc *rawchter*]

rawley ugly. [Norw dial *raal* untidiness; see RULLY]

rawley-tongued using foul language. [? from RAWLEY]

raxward of a landlord making extraordinary demands. [Sc *rax* to stretch; compare REX]

ray 1 1 the corner of a kiln barn where dried oats were stored. 2 a recess in a barn for holding grain. [Sc and Eng dials *ree* an enclosure, sheepfold; ON *rá* a nook]

ray 2 *as mad as a ray* completely mad. [OSc *ra, rae* a deer]

red* 1 to comb the hair. **redder** a comb. [Norw *rede* to comb the hair]

red 2 the track on a beach along which a boat is drawn. [ME *rede* a trench or furrow]

red 3 1 = red. 2 poor quality rock used for bottoming roads, '*We'll need tae pit twa loads o red on the paet hill road*'. [from the reddish colour caused by the iron content; compare ON *rauði* bog iron

95

ore]. **redba*** the yolk of an egg. **red-loon*** *red-loon paet* a peat which burns leaving a red ash. [see LOON]. **red-tap** a red-haired person. **redware*** seaweed. **redware cod*** an inshore codling; they have a slight reddish colour. [see WARE]

red* 4 to clear out, *'We'll hiv tae red oot that owld shed ready fur the tatties'*. **redd haggis, reddins** the fatty layers covering e.g. pigs' intestines. These have to be cleaned off before, making PUDDINGS with them. [ON *ryðja* to clear, empty]

redd progress. [? OE *raedan* to arrange]

reddin slap the slit in a woman's skirt. [OE *raedan* to arrange; see SLAP]

ree* 1 adj. mad or furious [also Sc]. noun. the squeal of a pig. [ON *hrína* of a pig to squeal]

ree 2 *as poor as a ree* thin and emaciated. [ON *hrae* a wreck or ruin]

reed see LANG REED.

reef†, rife † of a festive occasion, plentifully supplied. [also Sc; Eng *rife* plentiful]

reek 1, reik* verb. 1 to emit smoke. 2* of a fire to send smoke into a room. 3* to emit a strong smell (e.g. urine on clothes). noun. 1* smoke. 2 stench, *'My whit a reek wi that owld cloot!'* 3† a house, literally a house with a fire, i.e. a dwelling house. **reek-hole** a hole in the roof of the old Orkney house through which the smoke passed. **reekéd** e.g. of a fish, smoked. **reekie brae** there are several such placenames in Orkney where fires were lit to send smoke signals e.g. to request a ferry. (e.g. *Reekie Brae* on Copinsay) [also Sc; ON *reykr* smoke; *rjúka* to smoke]

reek 2 an instrument for twisting straw into ropes. [basic sense is *to twist* as in Eng *wring*]

reel = reel. *reel o the barn* the last dance at an old Orkney wedding.

reemer a strip, border, e.g. a strip of seaweed left by the tide. [ON *rimi* a strip of land or perhaps Eng *rim*]

reen of a pig to squeal. **reenowy, reeowy** of a child whining. [ON *hrína*]

reeo a mixture of black and white wool. [Gael *riabhach* greyish, brindled]

reep *reep wi* to be coated with (slime). **reepan** slippery decayed seaweed. [ON *raepa* diarrhoea]

ree-raa† only in an old rhyme, ?a raven [see RANTY PIPES; ON *hrafn*, raven]

reesicky red-headed. [perhaps related to Eng *russet*]

reest* verb. to dry or cure meat by hanging in smoke. noun. where meat was hung to *reest*. [related to OE *hrost* a perch and ON *rot* the inner part of the roof of a house where meat, fish and stores are hung up; compare Sc *reest* a framework of

bars etc on which meat and fish are dried and Norw *røst* rafters; OSc *reist* to smoke, dry or cure; Norw *rista* grid iron]

reester* a bright roaring fire, *'My whit a reester yir pitten on'*. [? Sc *reeze* to burn brightly]

reetlawee, ruttlowy a description of poor uneven ploughland. [? Eng *rut* + dimin + *awee* suffix; compare NORNAWAY]

reeto, reetowy a thin scraggy animal. [ON *rytja* a shabby thing; related to *hrjóða* to strip]

reevis a strong gale, literally a tearing wind. [ON *rífa* to tear; compare SCREEVER]

reevle to talk unneccessarily. [compare Norw *ravle*]

reevligo adj. rash, hurried. **reveligo** noun. a rash uncouth person. [ON *rífa* to tear; compare Eng *in a tearing hurry*]

reevo a ridge in a cultivated field. [compare Norw *rave* strip]

reik see REEK.

relievy picko see PICKO.

rendall† verb. to allocate portions of land annually in rotation. noun. a system of land tenure in which land was parcelled out annually in scattered strips to ensure a fair distribution of good quality soil [a system of land utilisation which apparently has its roots in prehistoric times; see RIG]

renyie see RANYIE.

reshes* = rushes. [OSc, ME *resche* a rush]

reuan, ruan nodding as in falling asleep. [ON *róa* to rock backwards and forwards in a sitting position]

reul a young horse or pony in a poor condition. [see RULLY]

reult see ROOLT.

reumatiz rheumatism

reus, ruize to praise, commend. [Sc *ruise*]

reuthed *reuthed oot* poured out. [Norw *røyte* to shed; compare RUITHE]

reveligo see REEVLIGO.

rew verb. to whine. noun. a whine. [compare RAEOO]

rex* to stretch, especially of the arm, *'Rex in noo and mak thee supper'* a friendly invitation to help oneself. [Sc *rax*; OE *rakan*; compare Norw dial *rekkja* to strain, stretch out]

ribbon diarrhoea, only in PURDY RIBBON [ON *raep-in)*, (the) diarrhoea; compare SKITTER]

rice, rysos brushwood. [also Sc; ON *hris*; ME *rise*]

rickety buckie* a small snail which when pulverised (or cooked in milk) supposedly cured rickets. These snails were (and still are) found round St Tredwell's Chapel in Papa Westray.

rickle* something loosely made or built [also Sc]. **rickly*** tottering. [compare Norw *rygla* a small loose heap and *rigle* to totter]

96

riddle especially of a child to talk volubly. [compare Norw dial *radla* to chatter]

ridyan, rigand term of abuse applied to a woman. [variant of Sh *riggin*; of uncertain origin]

ridyet of an animal having a strip of different coloured hair along its back. [Sc *riggit*; ON *hryggr* (the) back]

ridyie a ridge of rocks running out into the sea. [ON *hryggr* a ridge; compare Eng *ridge*]

rif, riv a reef. [ON *rif*]

rife see REEF.

rift* to belch. [also Sc; ME; compare ON *repta*]

rig 1 a narrow field about 5 paces wide raised in the middle and sloping towards the edges, the ridge in the middle being caused by the method of ploughing. **rig and rendall†**, **rigga-rental†** an old system of joint land tenure. [in Sc also known as *runrig* or *rundale*; *run* relates to the RIGS running parallel; Sc *dale* a portion, share; compare OE *dael* a division]. **riggéd owsen** breaking waves, white horses. [literally 'striped oxen']. **riggin*** *the keel o the riggin* the flat of the back, '*He wis lyan on the keel o his riggin when I fand him*'.

rig 2 a pig of indetermined sex. [Sc *rig* a weakling; related to RIGGLIN]

rigand† a *rigand thief*, mentioned in a 17th. witch trial. [see RIDYAN]

riggaforaaser see RIGNAFORAASER

rigglin* an animal with only one testicle. [also Sc; compare Eng dial *ridgling*]

right 1 = right. 2* sound in mind (usually used negatively), '*That boy canna be right*'. 3* very: *right good*. **rights*:** '*I never got the rights o hid*' I never found out the truth.

rignaforaaser, riggaforaaser clumsy, stupid, '*Whitna rignaforaaser wey is that o workan?*' [perhaps RIGGIN AFORE RASS]

rill verb. to talk incessantly. noun. such talk. **rillagory** talking endlessly. [*rill* + ON *görn* guts; compare RALLIGUT; compare Norw dial *role*]

rim a strip of rocks or rocky grounds in the sense of an elevated ridge in the sea. [ON *rimi* an elevated strip of land]

rime of the sky to clear up. [OE *ryman* to open out; *ryma* to go away]

rimman 1 used as an intensive, *a rimman fool*. [Cai *ringan* fool; ON *remja* to bellow]

rimman 2 the horizon. [related to ON *rimi* a raised strip or Eng *rim*]

rimpis an ill-natured child. [? variant of Eng *rampage*]

rin of a pig in heat to rut. [ON *renna*]

rind to melt down (suet etc). [also Sc; Eng *render*; OF *rendre*]

rine the cross-shaped fitting which supports an upper millstone. [compare Sc *rind* a thin piece of wood; Eng = an outer skin]

ring 1 = ring. 2 a stone circle, the *Ring o Brogar*. [also Sc and in Eng local usage]

ringer goose* the shelduck. [from the ring like pattern on its breast]

ringit-quoy† a piece of enclosed common. [Sc *ringit* ringed; the original enclosures were probably circular]

ringle-eyed of a horse having too much white in the eye. [ON *hringeygr*]

rink* a twist, '*Ah'm gin me neck a rink*'. [OSc and NoME *wrenk*; a variant of Eng *wrench*]

rinker a knitted cap (from the idea of circle or ring). [compare Sc *rink* to encircle]

rinner, rinnick, runnick a small water channel or drain, especially in the byre. **rinner hole** a pit for collecting urine from a byre. [Sc *rin* to run; compare Norw *renna* a ditch]

rinyo a thin ill-thriving animal. [compare Norw *ringe* feeble, inferior and *rang* a very thin person]

rip 1 a head of corn, usually oats. In the olden days a farm servant who wanted work displayed a *rip* in his buttonhole at the Lammas Fair. [Sc *rip* a handful of unthreshed corn]

rip 2 1* a woman of doubtful reputation. [also Sc; from the idea of torn clothing; compare PEOLU]. 2 a slit on the ear, used as a sheepmark. [Eng *rip*]

ripe*, roop *ripe oot* clean out. [also Sc; OE *rypan* to rob]

ripper* *a ripper o a fart* one which rips or tears. [compare RASPER]

rippet a beast of small girth and long legs. [origin unknown]

ripping knife = ritting knife. [see RIT]

rispal† spare time (in which to do something). [OSc *respliet* an adjournment]

rissen of a person, to shiver or shudder. [compare Norw *risna* to shiver and ON *hrjósa* to shudder (with horror)]

risso a big stout girl. [ON *hryssa* a mare]

rissom a shred. **ruizement** a particle. [also Sc; ME *risom* an ear or head of oats]

rist a rocky ridge which cannot be ploughed. [compare Norw *rust* a ridge and HIRST]

rit* verb. to cut, slash. noun. a slit on the ear, used as a sheepmark. **ritting knife*** a very large knife not unlike a scythe but with the opposite edge sharpened, used in peeling the turf off banks and in making the horizontal cuts for the peats. [also Sh; Sc = scratch, groove, furrow; see FLAY]

rither = rather, in the tongue twister:-
Whither wid yi rither
Ur rither wid yi whither
Hiv a stewed soo's snoot
Ur a soo's snoot stewed?'

rittle 1 to mark off turf with a spade. 2 to plough in a scratchy way. [from RIT; compare Norw *reite* to dig furrows]

ritto 1 see ROOTO.

ritto* 2, rittock a black-headed gull. In some parts of Ork also a tern or a kittiwake. [ON *rytr* kittiwake; probably from ON *rauta* to roar (from the bird's noisy habits)]

riv 1 see RIF.

riv 2 the first appearance of dawn, *the riv o the dim* [ON *rifa*, fissure]

riva caisie a straw basket for carrying peats. [compare Sh *rivi* a coarsely-plaited carrying basket; ON *hrip* a carrying basket + CAISIE]

rive* 1 to tear. 2 to tear something away from something else, '*Rive hid min*' (e.g. when a piece of scaffolding had jammed). 3 *rive at something* to work hard at it. 4 *rive thee aff* an oath. **riving knife** a draw-knife, a large type of spokeshave used in boatbuilding. [also Sc; NoME rive; ON *rífa* to tear]

rivling* an old type of shoe made of untanned hide. [ON *hriflingr]*

rivvle 1, rivvle-pivvle rags or tatters. **rivlings** the frayed sleeve of a jersey. [ON *raefill* rag or tatter]

rivvle 2 stout, stumpy. [related to RIVVLE 1 or RIVE (in the sense of 'cut short')]

roary see RORY.

rock *no muckle tow on her rock*, not much flax on her distaff, not having much purpose. [also Sc; obs Eng = a distaff,]

rod spawn or spawning of trout. **roding** spawning. [OSc *raid* the spawn of fish]

rodshal, rodshally fat or stumpy. [perhaps a form of the personal name *Roger* used in Sc in the sense *big and ugly*]

rogg a sieve. [related to Norw *rugge* to shake]

roggy 1 a low straw stool. 2 a receptacle for holding rolls of carded wool. [essential meaning is probably 'to crouch down on'; Norw dial *ruka* to crouch; see CREEPIE for another illustration]

roith, rotht† 1 udal rights. 2 udal (land). **roithman**†, **rothsman**† applied to a member of an assize in 16th century Orkney. [literally *counsel-man* but this form is not recorded in ON; ON *ráðs-maðr* counsellor and Norw *rådmann* town official; ON *rað* counsel or advice]

roly-o-deich† a ball of oatmeal and water carried by fisherman as a snack. [= roll of dough; in the Icel *Landnáma* reference is made to Irish slaves using similar food at sea called *min-þak*]

rone* the down pipe from a gutter. [also Sc; compare Norw *renne*]

rone moose the shrew. [ON *rani* hog's snout (from its pointed nose); compare Ork NEBBID

MOOSE and Norw *spissmus* sharp-pointed mouse]

roo* 1, rou verb. to make a heap. noun. a disorderly or messy heap, especially *roo o shite* [also Sh; ON *hrúga, heap; Norw ruge* small dung heap]

roo 2 to pluck the wool off sheep. **rued** having the hair or wool removed. [also Sh; ON *rýja*]

rooan *rooan aboot* walking about in a daze. [compare REUAN]

roof 1 = roof. 2* a ceiling [also Sc; the roof and ceiling were at one time the same thing!]

rook* *as thin as a rook* very thin. [see ROOKLE]

rookery 1 a heap of stones etc. 2 an uproar. [variant of ROOKLE]

rookie a big lean cod. [see ROOKLE]

rookle, ruckle 1 a heap of rubbish. 2 a poor thin animal (or person), *a rookle o bones*. [? with the original sense *rattle*; compare SKOLDER]

rookler a big limpet of the type found high on the beach and of little use as bait. [dimin of ON *hrukka* a wrinkle; a reference to the texture of the shell]

roolt, reult, rult verb. to walk in slouching manner. noun. a slouching walk or rolling gait. [Norw *rulte* to waddle; related to DRILT with loss of initial *d*]

roop to steal, rob, '*Mercy the birds are just roopéd the stooks*'. [also Sc; variant of Sc *rook* to rob]

roose 1 see REUS.

roose 2 1 = rouse. 2 *tae roose aboot* to rush around.

roosk drizzle. **roosky** rainy, drizzly. [Norw dial *rusk*]

roost, ruist drizzle. [a form of ROOSK]

root verb. to make a loud noise. noun. a loud noise. [see ROUT; ON *rauta* to bellow]

roothiegong a rocky bottom in the sea where hooks are liable to catch. [perhaps ON *hryðr* scab + *gangr* a course]

rooto, ritto a lump on the head. [? Sc *rout* a blow]

rory*, roary of a colour, bright and garish. [also Sc; a special usage of Eng *roar*]

rose-beena the peony rose. [? a variant of *peony*]

rose-lintie the male linnet. [also Sc; Eng *rose* (from the colour of the plumage); Sc *lintie* a linnet]

rosen roasted. [also Sc; OSc *rossin*]

rosit* = rosin. **rosit ends** hemp thread prepared with *rosin* for sewing leather. [also Sc; OSc *rosate*]

rosk *to be rosk on*, to have a keen appetite for. [probably ON *röskr* vigorous]

rost 1* a rough tideway, e.g. Burgar Rost between Evie and Rousay. [ON *röst]*

rost 2 = roast, '*He cam oot in a rost o spots*' the body was covered with spots. **rostan*** used to describe severe instances of childhood illnesses such as chickenpox etc, '*Beuy she's just rostan wi the maisles*'.

rotchie a little auk. [also Sc; compare Du *rotje* pet-

98

rel]
rot-fat midden ooze. [ON *rotna* to rot; *vatn* water]
rothsman see ROITHMAN.
rotht see ROITH.
rou see ROO.
roult to shrug the shoulders. [a form of ROOLT]
roup* an auction sale. [also Sc; ON *raupa;* OE *hrōpan* to call, shout]
rous *tae rous herring*, to stir herring around in salt as part of the salting process [origin uncertain]
rout of a bull, to bellow. [see ROOT]
routh 1 1 a spell of time. 2 a spell of weather, good or bad. [see LONG REED]
routh 2 scab on a sore. [ON *hruðr]*
routh 3 abundance. [also Sc; origin obscure]
routh 4 that part of the gunwale of a boat on which the oar rests in rowing. [also Sh; ON *roðr* rowing]
routh 5 arguments and disagreements. [? ON *rauta* to roar]
routhcock† a barnacle goose. [probably originally a misreading of a 16th century text; *rout* = 'rood' (as in *rood-goose*) + 'hurrok' (as in HORRA-GOOSE]
routhurrok† a corrupt form of ROUTH-HURROCK. [see ROUTHCOCK]
rove 1 = rove. 2 to be delirious, rave. [also Sc and Eng dial]
row = roll [also Sc], '*Row thee sleeves up!*' **rower** a roll of carded wool ready for spinning. [also Sh].
rowers banks of cirro-cumulus cloud which look like rolls of carded wool. **row-head** the end of the mill-race where the water falls on the water wheel [also Sc].
rowt* see WORK.
ruan moving slowly as in old age. [see REUAN]
ruckle 1 see ROOKLE.
ruckle* 2 1 to wrinkle. 2 to shrug the shoulders. **ruckly** covered with wrinkles. [ON *hrukka;* Eng ruck]
rudd a small bag. [also Sh; compare Norw dial *rudda* a woven basket for carrying hay]
rudder a male crab, especially the partan. [compare Sh *rooder;* Faroese *ruðr* a kind of shellfish; ON *hruðr* a crust, scab (on a sore) and Gael *rudhag* a crab]
rudge 1 verb. of a boat against a pier, to rub and chafe. noun. the rattle of pebbles on a beach or of mucus in the throat. [Norw dial *ryda* to cough, gurgle; Icel *hryðja* to cough up phlegm]
rudge 2 1 to gather stones off the land. 2 to clear dung off pasture. [ON *ryðja* to clear]
rue 1 1 to talk nonsense. 2 to drizzle. [ON *hrjóða* to belch or vomit forth steam etc]
rue 2 refuse, generally of grain. **rue-klino** a piece of bread and butter given to a servant who had taken

the cow to the bull, bread made from poor quality grain. [see KLINO; ON *hroði* refuse]
ruff = rough. a shock of stiff hair. **ruffy** having bushy hair [also Sc]
rug to pull or tear vigorously. [also Sc; Norw *rukke* to tug]. *ruggan and kyeugan* pulling viciously.
rugface(d), rugfus fearsome looking. **rugfus** rough, rude. [? Norw *rygd* terror + Eng face]
rugg 1 a well built man. [ON *hrúga,* a heap; Norw *rugg* a large heavy person]
rugg 2, ruggy see RAG 1.
ruggy 1, ruggie 1 untidy in dress. 2 a nickname for the people from the north end of Sanday. [ON *rögg* shagginess]
ruggy 2 a big lean cod. [see ROOKLE]
rugras rough treatment. [origin uncertain]
ruilk to shrug the shoulders. [see ROULT]
ruim to talk a lot, chatter. [ON *ruma]*
ruim-rake to slander. [RUIM + ON *roegja* to slander]
ruist see ROOST.
ruithe 1, raithe 1 small potatoes. 2 the seeds of weeds thrown out in the thrashing process. '*Hid wis coman oot o his mooth like ruithe oot o the fanners*', he was talking nineteen to the dozen. [see RUE 3]
ruithe 2 of tangles, to shed blades. [ON *ryðja* to clear ground]
ruithy girs corn spurrey. [see RUE 3]
ruive a little metal washer used in the riveting process. [also Sc; nautical Eng *rove*; ON *ró]*
ruize to praise. [see REUS]
ruizement see RISSOM.
ruk see RAG 1.
rukky see RAG 1.
rully 1 a nickname for a North Ronaldsay person. 2 an old ewe. [ON *rolla* an old ewe; the essential meaning is *ragged*; related to TRULLS with loss of initial *t*]
rullyie 1 verb. to move in a clumsy way. noun. clumsy movement. [see ROOLT]
rullyie 2 a rough stretch of water. [ON *rugl* disturbance]
rullyo a heap of stones thrown on to the beach by the sea. [compare Norw *rulla* a bank of stones rolled together]
rult see ROOLT.
rummel 1 = rumble. 2 to scramble (eggs) [also Sc]
rumpis a noise, especially in the phrase *tae keek (kick) up a rumpis* [see RUMSE 1]
rumse 1 to rummage around. **rumse up 1** to shake up. 2 to make a noise [Norw *rumska* to shake]
rumse 2 to lie restlessly in bed. [ON *raumska* to stir from sleep]
run 1 = run. 2 a heavy sea, '*Whit a run is on the sea the day*'. **run on the night** to go out after girls

late at night. [compare GO ON THE NIGHT]

runch see RUNGE 4.

runcho* charlock, wild mustard. [Sc *runch* wild radish or wild mustard]

runge 1 the sound of the sea breaking on the shore. [also Sh; compare Norw *runge* to resound]

runge 2 see RANGE.

runge 3 a young lad, '*Gae the runge a hand wi the boat*'. [Sc *runchie* a coarsely-built person; see RUNK]

runge 4, runch to toss and turn in the bed when delirious. [compare RUMSE]

runk, runkly of a person or thing unsteady, '*Beuy I wad like tae see that gittan on tap o a runkly coo*', said by a farmer of a massive prize bull at the County Show! [Sw dial *runkla*, unsteady]

runnan* of a dog etc on heat. [Norw *lope* to run is also used in the same sense]

runnick see RINNICK.

runt* *a kale-runt* a cabbage stalk. [also Sc; origin uncertain]

runty-poid a shorn sheep. [possibly ON *rúinn* participle of *rýja* to pluck the wool off sheep; compare Sh *runin* a shorn sheep; *poid* is perhaps a form of PEED]

ruo see ROO 1.

ruse 1 = rouse, stir, awaken.

ruse 2 to speak well of. [also Sc; see REUS]

ruser 1 an energetic person. 2 a blazing fire, *a ruser o a fire*. [Norw *ruse* to rush]

rush 1 = rush. 2 a luxuriant growth (of e.g. grass), *a rush o gress*. 3 a (skin) rash [also Sc]

rusk 1 a handful of straw pulled out of a stack. 2 a protruding tuft of straw sticking out of a stack. [Norw *ruske* to tug]

rusked, ruskold of food slightly burned. [perhaps Norw dial *ro* red + *skjoldutt* flecked, streaked, scorched, singed]

russy-girs couch grass, horse grass. [ON *hross* a horse; see GIRSE]

ruttle coarse grass. [origin uncertain]

ruttlowy see REETLAWEE.

rycht† only in old records, law. [ON *réttr*]

rysos see RICE.

S normally pronounced as in English when in the initial position. If an *s* follows an *r* as in *worse*, the *s* is pronounced *sh*, hence *worsh*. If a word ending in an *r* sound is followed by a word with an initial *s*, the initial *s* is changed to *sh*, hence *more supper* becomes *more shupper*. Notice also '*Whar' sh that?*' = Whar's that = Who is that.

saa 1 ointment. [Sc saw; Eng *salve*]

saa* 2 = sow (seeds), *tae saa oats*.

saain a little gull. [ON *saeðingr* the common gull, literally *seed eater*]

saat = salt. **saatie backet** a container for salt. **saato** a swear word, '*The peedie boy cam oot wi a right saato*'. **saat pow** a coastal pool where formerly sea salt was extracted by evaporation. [see also SALT]

sabbéd* soaked. [related to Eng *sopping* (wet)]

sabble see SIBBLE.

sad 1 = sad. 2 of bread etc not rising, heavy [also Sc]

sae 1 = so. **sae-coman** 1 *gey sae-coman* not very good. 2 *a sae-comin wey* a peculiarity of behaviour.

sae 2, say a large wooden tub with LUGS through which a pole was passed to enable it to be carried easily. **sae-bink** a stone bench in the end room of a house on which the sae stood with the clean water supply for the household. **sae tree** the pole which was used to carry the sae. [ON *sár* cask; Norw *så*]

saegs*, segs rushes. It was believed that chewing *saeg* leaves was liable to make a child stammer or make him dumb. **seggie flooers** the wild iris. [Eng *sedge*; OE secg *sedge*]

saem 1 1 intestinal fat used in making mealy puddings etc. 2 liquid in which clothes are washed (Westray). [Sc *same*; OF saim *lard*]

saem* 2 1 = seam. 2 a parting in the hair. **saemer** the narrow flagstone which covers the gap between two roofing flags. [Sc *seam*; Eng *seam* (in sewing)]

sae track dee wa!† Keep your distance! an old admonition. [*sae* = take note; *track* Eng slang = to make one's way; *wa* = way]

saetro children's counting-out rhyme e.g. '*Eetle-ottle black bottle*' etc. [Sc *seater*; Welsh *saith* number 7 in children's counting out rhymes]

sain to make the sign of the cross. [also Sc and Sh; OE segnian]

sair = serve [also Sc].

saithe 1 the coalfish. [also Sc; ON *seiðr*]

saithe 2 bait thrown off rocks to attract fish. [compare Norw *sav* lobster bait]

sall a petty oath. [also '*My sall*'; also Sc *upon my soul*]

salor, salur, saller, siller, sellar, seller, sullar a small room leading off the living room and used for a variety of purposes. **siller door** the door into such a room. [Norw *sal*, small room off another]

salt = salt. **salted price** high priced [also Sc]. **tae weigh salt,** an old game of strength in which two people stood back to back and with arms interlinked tried to lift each other off the ground. **saly-backet** a salt dish [see BACKET] [see also SAAT]

salvendu, savandal, savandwal, sevandal of people or things strong, *'That's a sevandal job'*. [Sc *solvendie*; Lat *solvendo esse* to be solvent]

sal see SALT.

sam* = same. **sam as** 1 as if *'He lukkéd at me sam as he kent me.'* 2 even though *'Sam as he's me couseen, I widna trust him.'*

sameyn† joint possession. [ON *sameign]*

sand = sand. **sandbaa** a sandbank. [see BAA]. **sand greemy** sandy soil with a mixture of black earth as found in Sanday and North Ronaldsay. [ON *grómr* dirt]. **sandlark** the sandpiper [also Sc]. **sanloo, sinlick** the ringed plover. [ON *ló* plover]. **sanny-back** a kind of flounder.

sand = sand. **sand-paet** a poor quality peat dug from a shallow moor; such peats were used to place at the back of an open hearth fire; they were also burned and the ash used to manure the PLANTIE CREU [see YARPHA PAET]

Sandy oat a type of oat formerly grown in Orkney. [from *Sandy Tampson* an Aberdeenshire herdboy who is credited with discovering it]

san lavro a skylark. *tae jump san lavro height* to jump very high. [origin of *san* uncertain; the lark was a sacred bird in Orkney, the three spots on its tongue taken to be a sign of the Trinity; ?Latin *sanctus*, holy; see LAVEROCK]

sanloo, sinlick see SAND.

sap* a small quantity, *'Pit a good sap o milk in the bucket'*. [ON *sopi* small draught or mouthful]

saps* bread mixed with warm milk and sugar given to a child, *'Tak thee saps'* used jocularly to an adult, *'Eat up'*. [also Sc; Eng *sop*]

sark* verb. to cover the roof of a house with wooden boards prior to slating [also Sc]. noun. 1 a shirt. 2 the black membrane which lines the belly of a fish. **sarking*** wooden lining boards for a roof. [also Sc; ON *serkr]*

sarro an unpalatable mixture of food, e.g. cold porridge. [ON *saurr* excrement]

sastock† a piece of rough-hewn timber. [also Sh; Eng *saw* + *stock]*

sauney agreeable, generous, jolly. [origin unknown]

saut backet see SAAT.

savandal, savandwal see SALVENDU.

save heather shoots used for brewing heather ale. [ON *safi* sap]

Sawawan the devil. [Eng *sorrow* + *wan* = one; see SORROW and WALLAWA]

saw-bill the goosander, the red-breasted merganser.

[from its *saw like* beak; compare Sc *saw neb*]

sax = six(th). **saxherins†** a six oared boat. [also Sh in a variety of forms; ON *sexaeringr]*

saxburn the sixth water drawn from the grain when brewing. [see AFTERBURN]

saxhering see SAX.

say see SAE.

scad = scald [also Sc]. **scadoo** thin gruel, oatmeal scalded with hot water. **scad swine** more than plenty of something, *'No thanks that's scad swine'*. [= *scalded pig*; this is one of the first stages in preparing pork and the allusion is perhaps to having the whole pig]

scadman's head*, scar-man's head, scarriman's head sea-urchin shell. [ON *skalda* of hair to fall off; the sea urchin shells when washed ashore have usually lost their spines and are bald]

scafou compare SKATFU.

scail see SKAIL.

scale duck the shelduck. [see SKELDRO]

scamesome scheming. [Sc *skaim* scheme + *some*]

scar see SKARR.

scare see SKARE.

scarf see SKARF.

scarriman's head, scarman's head see SCADMAN'S HEAD.

scart see SKERT.

scart-hole see SKERT.

scat see SKAT.

scaw a barnacle. [also Sc; see SCAWED]

scawed scabby. [a form of Eng *scaled*]

Schalte† a Shetlander. [ON *Hjalti]*

schone† properly the seventh day (after the death of someone) when the estate was apportioned to the heritors. [ON *sjaund]*

sclack see SLACK 1.

sclateroo see SLATROO.

sclifter a splinter. [compare SKELFER]

scolder see SKOLDER.

scone 1 see SKON.

scone 2* a pancake [also Sc]. *as flat as a scone* absolutely flat.

sco a feeling of aversion or disgust [ME *skewen* to turn aside, Germ *scheuen* to avoid]

scoor, skoor* = scour. **scoor** the wab to wash a new cloth for the first time. **skoor the boggy and run** weak ale. [for BOGGY see PUGGY; Eng *scour* to purge]

scoots* diarrhoea, especially *tae hiv the scoots*. **scootie*, skootie** the starling. [from the mess it makes of its nest and surroundings; compare Sc **scoatins** birds' excreta and Sh **maas' skoots** seagulls' droppings]. **scoot** a little rascal [also Sc]. **scooty-allan*, scoutie-allan, skootie-allan** Arctic skua. [Sc *alan*; formerly known as *dirten-allan*; Norw *aale* cattle urine; see OOLER; ON

101

skjóta to shoot (out))]

scorie see SKORY 1.

Scotch = Scotch. **Scotch drum** a cylindrical thrashing mill drum with outside beaters.

scot lot scattered or wasted. [? Sc *scot and lot* municipal taxes]

scottie the oyster catcher (Egilsay). [ON *skjóttr* piebald; see SEA-PIE]

scouth, skouth *scouth o land* a stretch of land. [also Sc; ?a form of SKELF/SKELP]

scoutie-allan see SCOOTS.

scow, skow 1 a barrel stave. 2 a big gaunt woman. **scows** fragments. **tae lay in scows*** to shatter, '*Thir wis notheen bit the scows o the hen left when I got home*' (the rest had been eaten). [OSc *scow* a strip of wood]

scraik see SKREK.

scrat the first shallow furrow made by ploughmen when opening a rig. **scratto, scratter** 1* a pot cleaner made from heather. 2 a type of hoeing instrument also known as a SCUFFLER. **scratty** of an animal lean and not thriving. [OSc *skrat* to scratch]

screeve see SKREEVE.

screever see SKREEVE.

screwith a shrill cry, used of people or birds. [OSc *scry* a cry; ON *hví* the sound of a gull]

scrie see SKRY.

scrithan swarming. [ON *skriða* to crawl; see SKRIE]

scroblan scrambling round, on hands and knees. [origin uncertain; but compare SKRAVVLE]

scroovo see SKOVO.

scroulan scrambling through mud or filth. [possibly a form of SCROBLAN]

scrub = scrub. **scrubber** a flat stone etc dragged over a field to crush clods. **scrubby** mean.

scruffle to graze (the skin). [Sc *scriffle* to graze; related to SKRUFF 2]

scrunt, skrunt verb. *tae skrunt aboot* to rummage around. noun. a mean shabby person. **scrunty** mean. [also Sc; OSc *scrunt* something worn out or useless]

scud to strike with the hand, '*Answer noo or Ah'll scud thee doofie*' Behave now or I'll smack your bottom. [also Sc; origin unknown]

scuddlan claes working clothes. [OSc *scudle* to wash dishes]

scuffle* to destroy weeds between drills with a horse hoe. **scuffler*** the horse hoe used for this. [also Sc; compare Norw *skyfle* to hoe]

scumfish to disgust. [OSc *scomfyste* discomfited]

scunner*, skunner verb. 1 to sicken, disgust [also Sc]. 2 to loath. noun. an offensive smell. **scunnerous** disgusting. **(to) get a scunner*** to get more than enough of something. [probably related to Eng *shun*]

scuther in cooking to burn the outside of something before it is properly cooked. [OSc *skolder* to burn; related to Eng *scald*]

sea = sea. **sea-crow** the razorbill. [from its colour; in Sh refers to the *stormy petrel*]. **sea-cubbie** a straw or heather basket for carrying fish. [see CUBBY]. **sea-geese** barnacles which grow on driftwood. [compare SLY-GEESE]. **sea parrot** the puffin. [from its resemblance to a parrot]. **sea-pie** the oyster catcher. [Sc **sea-pyed**; see SCOTTIE] **sea-trow** a sea spirit. **sea-uiky** sea scorpion. [Norw *ulk*]

seam nail a nail used for joining together the boards of a boat. [ON *saumr* really a *sewing together*; the boards of some old Norw boats were actually sewn together]

seck* a sack. **secky*** made of sackcloth. **secky-bratto*** an apron made of sackcloth (see BRATTO). [ON *sekkr*]

see see SHA.

seed-furrs furrows in ploughed land shallower than the rest; these divided the land into rigs 4.5m wide, to guide the sower when sowing by hand [see FUR 2]

seek*, sic = such, '*Seek a like sight!*'. **seekan(a)*, siccana** such a '*Seekana sight Ah'm never seen*'. *Sic like usually taks up wi sic like* birds of a feather flock together. **sicansic** such and such.

seekensome* sickening.

seeldoms = seldom.

seelfu severe, *a seelfu pain*. [a special use of Sc *seelfu* binding, firm, hence *severe*]

seemicrow see SINLICROW.

seepan saturated with water, drenched. [see SYPE]

seestoo 1 Look at this! [also Sc; = *Sees thou?*]

seestoo 2 see SUISTO.

segs see SAEGS.

selkie 1 a grey seal. 2 the nickname for an inhabitant of North Ronaldsay. **selkie-folk** seals capable of transforming themselves into human beings. [also Sc; OSc *selich* a seal]

sellar, seller see SALOR.

selt perfect tense of *sell*

semmit*, simmet a vest. [also Sc; origin unknown]

servant = servant. **servant lass*** a young girl employee, especially on a farm. **servant man*** a farm labourer. [also Sc]

sess, cess a conglomeration of filth. [compare Sc *soss* a dirty wet mess, Norw *sos* matter in the eye after sleep]

sester, sesters* the channel in a byre draining away cattle urine, also known as the ODDLE or ODDLER [almost always used in the plural; compare Sh *sus* slop and SESS above]

sestuna Look!. [also Sc; = *Sees thou not?*]

set* verb 1 = set. 2 to plant (particularly potatoes)*,

'We set twa-three dreel o tatties last night'. 3 of the wind, to die down. noun. 1 the flaky material like dandruff in the hair of a horse. 2 the outer layer of the skin of a sheep, this layer coming off when the sheep is ROOED. **setting*** sufficient, a *setting o eggs* eggs to put under a broody hen; a *setting o tatties*, sufficient for one planting. **set up** verb. *'That'll no set him up'* that won't be of much advantage to him.

Setterday* = Saturday. *A silken Setterday affens maks a canvas Monday*, good weather on Saturday seldom lasts till Monday.

setting† a weighing standard formerly used in Orkney. It was the equivalent of a LISPUND and represented a sixth part of a MEIL. [ON *settungr* sixth part]

seuch *tae keep a calm seuch*, to remain unruffled. [Eng *sough* (of the wind)]

seugh a trench in which plants are kept before they are transplanted. **seuchar** the share of the old Orkney plough. [also Sc; nEME *sogh* a swamp]

seurtan of a pot, not boiling fast enough. [compare Norw *sarra* to simmer]

seut* = soot. *seuty salt's good enough for hairy butter* said of two equally bad things or people brought together. *wir roof drips seut* said when someone is listening in to a conversation. [compare Eng *eavesdrop*]

sevall a landing net for fish [Eng *save-all*]

sevandal see SALVENDU.

seven = seven. **seven 'ear (years) o Yule days** a very long time [compare Eng *a month of Sundays*]. There were thirteen days in Yule therefore seven years of Yule days would be approximately 200 years. *as long as Lucky Minnie sat in Foozber, seven ear o Yule days* an old Birsay saying. **seven lang and seven short** a very long time (? seven Yule day years + seven years) [the number 7 is significant in Indo-European thought e.g. there are 7 days in the week]

sgerter see SKELTER.

sha* verb. 1 = show. 2* to pass by hand, *'Sha me a hammer'* Pass the hammer, *'Sha me see the letter etc'* Let me see the letter etc. noun.* the part of a plant, especially a potato, above the ground. [also Sh; Sc *shaw*]

shabby lamp a primitive oil lamp. [Gael *siobhag* the wick of a lamp; Gael *siffin* a rush stem]

shack* = to shake. **shacking stanes** small flagstones built into the sidewalls of the barn thrashing floor about 70 cm high and projecting about 12 cm. It was on these stones that handfuls of corn were thrashed to make GLOY.

shackle 1 = shackle. 2 the afterbirth of an animal. **shackle bone** the wrist [also Sc]; from the 'knap o the shacklebone tae the knap o the shoulder'

was the *PEERIE CUBIT* a measure of 38 cms.

shadam a shadow. [Eng *shading*]

shady* a little, *'He's a shady better'*, *'Move hid ower tae the left a shady'*. [Eng *shade*]

shaef* see SHEAF.

Shaetland* = Shetland. **Shaetland grey** grey wool. **Shaetland soda** human urine kept in a graithtub for washing woollens and human hair. **Shaetloo** a Shetlander.

shaft* *tae shaft a nave* to shake one's fist. [see HAFT]

shag a bull not properly castrated. [also Cai; compare Dan dial *se.g.* a castrated boar]

shaggle 1 to walk in a feeble manner. **shaggly** loose jointed. [see SHOOGLY and SHUCHLE]

shaggle 2 to cut raggedly with a blunt instrument [Faer. *sjagla*, ON *saga* to saw]

shair of a boat, moving from side to side before taking up at anchor [origin unknown]

shaivle of a child to twist the face and say *'Nee, nee nee!'* as a taunt. [Sc *shevel* or *sheyle* to make faces; related to SHAVS, SHEB and SHEV; ON *skeifligr* twisted]

shald 1 a shoal in the sea. [also Sc and Sh; OE *sceald* shallow]

shald 2 = a shawl, especially a large shawl as worn to church by ladies in the olden days. [also Sh]

shalder the oyster catcher. [also Sc; ON *tjaldr*; the real meaning is *dappled*; see SKELDRO]

shance, chansh = chance. [also Cai]

shander to speak aggressively. [Sc **chander, channer** to make querulous complaint; OSc *channer* to grumble]

shangie 1 a hemliband. 2 loop in which lower end of a sprit (sail) rests. 3 a coil of grass packed round a jumper in a punching hole to prevent stones flying in the face. [also Sc; compare Norw *kjeng* an eye or staple (part of a door fixing)]

shankie the redshank

shankle to walk with long strides. [compare Norw *sjangle* to stagger]

shankum a man or animal with long thin legs. [Eng **shank + um**]

shard a hollow in sandy links. [ON *skarð* a cleft or cut; see CHARD]

share* 1 to grind (the teeth). [compare Norw *skjaere tanner*]

share* 2 past part SHORN*. 1 to cut peats, corn etc, *'Langskaill sterted tae share the day'*. 2 of milk to become sour. [compare Norw *skjør* curdled milk; ON *skera* to cut]

sharg* to nag. **shargin** ill humoured. [Norw *skark* to nag; compare Ger *schurgen* to vex or plague; the essential meaning is *to cut with the tongue*; ON *sarga* to hack]

sharger* a puny individual. *Hair and nails grow*

weel tae shargers, an old saying. [also Sc; OSc *sharg*; Gael *searg* a puny creature; ?related to SHARG]

sharn* cow dung but only used of cow dung sticking to something e.g. a shovel or trousers. [ON *skarn]*

sharp 1 = sharp. 2 of milk, sour. **sharping stone*** a whetstone [also Sc]

sharro 1 bitter. [also Cai; Gael *searbh* bitter]

sharro 2 a pain in the bowels with associated diarrhoea. [related to CHAR]

shaugly see SHOOGLY.

shaun a magic spell. [ON *sjón* sight; compare Eng *The Evil Eye*]

shavs to scowl. [related to SHAIVLE]

shay-gray of wool dark gray. [Sc *shela* of wool dark with a lighter tinge on top; ON *héla* hoar frost]

sheaf, shaef* 1 = sheaf. 2 a slice, *a sheaf o loaf*. [also Sc; ON *skífa* slice]

sheb, shev, *tae set a sheb* to pull a face (e.g. when on the point of crying). [related to SHAIVLE; ON *skelpa* a wry face; Shetlanders talk of 'setting a sleb' which may be a corrupted form]

shed† to dismantle. [also Sc; OSc *schede* to separate]

sheed a cultivated piece of land. In Sanday specifically a piece of land not big enough to be called a field. [OE *scēad* division]

Sheep-right Day that day on which native sheep were required by local law to be rounded up for counting, shearing, culling etc. [ON *réttr* law]

sheer a slit on an animal's ear as a mark of identification. **sheer moose** a shrew. **sheer tail** the tern. [Ger dial *scher-maus* mole; ON *skera* to cut; Eng *shear*]

sheer-bolts hip joints (jocularly). [origin uncertain]

sheer-maleens, sheer-mellins see SHELL-MALEENS.

sheld fowl the sheld duck.

shellmaleens, sheer maleens, sheer-mellins, shell-millings fragments [from the verb *to shell* (seeds); *millings* is a deriv of the Eng verb *to mill*]

shellweengs, shelvins the top boards of a horse-cart. [also Sc; OSc *shilwing*]

shepherd = shepherd. **shepherd's reed** mouth organ

sheriff 1 = sheriff. 2 a lead sinker used to slide down a fishing line and pull up a *lead* or *hook* that has stuck on the bottom of the sea.

shetlin a young sow having her first litter. [ME *shote* a young pig or perhaps Norw *syta* sow with *ling* dimin]

sheu 1 = sew. [Sc *shew*]

sheu 2 see SHU.

sheubros berries of wild thorns. [Gael *suibheag* fruit]

sheucher to sleep rough. **sheuchran** a tramp. [literally one who sleep in a ditch; see SEUGH]

sheul 1 a shovel, a spade. **sheully** having large feet (like a shovel).

sheul 2 = shuffle. [Sc *shuil*]

sheul bane, shool bane shoulder blade. [*sheul* is a form of shoulder]

sheully see SHEUL 1.

sheumit see SHUIMIT.

sheun see SHOE.

shev see SHEB.

shieldo a small protective porch in front of a house. [ON *skýla* to shelter]

shill 1 to remove the husks of oats. **shillans** whole kernel of oats. **shilling stones** millstones for *shilling*. [OSc *schele* to husk]

shill 2 a plough bridle. [Icel *sili* a strap belonging to harness]

shillacrack 1 a noise. 2 a noisy person. [ON *skella* to clash, *slam* + Eng *crack*]

shilpit* sour to the taste. [Sc = thin, puny; ? related to Gael *sealbhag* sorrel; compare SHARRO 1]

shine a party. [also Sc; see COOKIE SHINE]

shirpan see SKIRPAN.

shirree see SHARRO.

shirro a form of SHARRO.

shite (vulgar) = 1 shit. 2 mess, filth, unnecessary conglomeration, '*Tak aal this shite fae aboot the door; nobody can get in.*' **as weet as shite*** of a field etc., very wet. **a yap o shite** someone who talks incessantly. '*Shite a horse and stert a ferm (and fart a man tae work hid)*' an expression of exasperation. **as thick as shite in the neck o a bottle*** very stupid. **tae get a right shiter***, to be crestfallen, '*He got a right shiter when he saa me in the hoose.*' **tae lay in shite*** to smash to atoms. **shite-cairt†** old name for refuse vehicle in Kirkwall. **fill (full) o small shites** of someone who boasts about himself. [compare Gael *sgidean* a little contemptible man and Norw *skit-viktig* self important]. **shitmarrick(ed)** 1 exhausted 2 drunk. [see MIRACULOUS; compare Aberdeenshire **shit-deen** exhausted (vulgar)]

sho see SHOOS.

shoading† 1 footwear. 2 the metal hoop round a cartwheel. [Sc *shod* to furnish with shoes]

shobsy of clothes ill fitting. [? related to Eng *shabby*]

shochad see SHOCKET.

shock 1 = shock. 2* a (paralytic) stroke, *tae tak a shock*. [also Sc]

shocket, shocked the lapwing. [Sc *teuchat*; imitat; compare TEEO]

shod the brow or forehead, above the eye. [origin uncertain; see SHODDINGS]

shoddings, shods hair roots, '*He hid (had) a booick in the shoddings o his hair*'. [compare Sh *skoddin* the undergrowth of wool on a sheep; ON *skjóta* to shoot]

shoddo a large lump of anything. [origin unknown]

shods see SHODDINGS.

shoe = shoe. **shoon, sheun** 1 shoes. 2 boots.

Sholma see SHUIMIT.

sholt*, sholtie noun 1 a small horse, usually *Shetland sholt*. 2 a foreshore creature living under stones, the black sand hopper. 3 the common top shell. adj. from Shetland; quern stones were usually *Sholtie stones*. [ON *Hjalti* a Shetlander]

shoo 1, shue to *back water* with the oars. [also Cai and Sh; Sc *shue* to swing; OE *scūfan* to shove]

shoo 2 to sew. **shood** sewed. **shooer** one who sews [also Sc]

shoogly*, shaugly tottering. [Sc from *shog* to shake, sway; from ME; compare Norw *skakal* shaking]

shool bane see SHEULBANE.

shoon, sheun see SHOE.

shoos, shos the awns of bere. [Sc *shool, huil*]

shore 1 a strip of field mown by one man. [ON *skera* to cut]

shore 2 = shore. **shore-sparrow, shore-teeting** rock pipit. **Shoreocks†** an old (contemptuous) name for the inhabitants of Kirkwall who lived by the shore.

shorn see SHARE.

short = short. **short ago*** recently. [also Cai]

shos see SHOOS.

shot = shot. *tae hiv a good shot in* to be quite drunk.

shotty used of a sea when large breakers periodically alternate with moderate waves. [compare ON *bárn-skot* a swell]

shovance a bungling job, '*Whit a shovance he made o pittan on the door*'. [origin uncertain]

Show = agricultural show. **Showies** operators of amusement booths at the time of the agricultural shows.

shu, sheu = she. [ON *sú*]

shuchle to walk clumsily. [related to SHOOGLY and SHAGGLE]

shudder*, shuther 1 = shoulder. 2 the edge of a hill, *the shudder o the hill*.

shue see SHOO.

shug-shug a term used in speaking to a horse. **shuggy** a pet name for a horse. [compare Gael *sug* used in speaking to a lamb, *siug* a call to a calf and *suic* a call to a horse; related to Gael *sug* to suck; compare PADDY for a similar development of meaning]

shuimit, sheumit of a cow having a white face and a black body. **Sholma** a pet name for such a cow. [Icel *hjálmóttr* of a cow, 'helmeted']

shuislins rubbish. **shuizly** rubbishy. [Sc *shows* refuse of flax or hay; see SHOOS]

shuit to push. '*Shuit fae thee noo beuy*'. [ON *skjóta*

to push]

shuizly see SHUISLINS.

shut of walls to bulge. '*The wall seems tae be shuttan a piece min*'. [ON *skúta* to jut out]

shuther see SHUDDER.

shuttle a drawer or shelf in a chest. [also Sc; Eng = *shuttle*]

shyne to embarrass someone [? variant of Eng *shy*]

siar see SIE 1.

sib* related to one another, '*Oh yaas, thir sib*'. [obs Eng *sib* related; OE *sib* a relative]

sibbens a venereal sore [Gael. *suibheag*, raspberry, from the appearance of the sore]

sibble, sabble to sip. [compare Norw *sipla*]

sic see SEEK.

sicansic see SEEK.

siccana see SEEKANA.

sicker severe or harsh. [Sc = safe, secure; OE *sicor* from Lat *securus* firm]

side = side. **sideack** a loop on the side of the pannier basket carried by a horse, a form of 'side hank'. **side ditch*** the ditch alongside a road. **side dyke** the wall alongside a road. **sidelegs*** (to sit) with both legs on one side e.g in riding a horse. **sidelings*** to move *sidelings* i.e. crab fashion. [also Sc; compare Norw *sidelengs*]. **side plough** the old Orkney plough which had only one stilt and was driven by the ploughman from its left hand side. **sidyweys*** = sideways [also Sc], '*Pit hid in sidyweys*'.

sids the inner husks of oats. [also Sc and Sh; Eng *seeds*]

sie 1 verb to strain or filter e.g. milk or newly boiled potatoes, '*Mercy Ah'm forgotten tae sie the tatties and thir aal in a slester*.' **siar** 1 a strainer for milk. 2 a grid covering a drain. 3 the armhole of a garment. [ON *sía* to strain; also Sc]

sie 2 out of sorts. [origin unknown]

sie 3 a narrow, tar-soaked strip of cloth placed between the overlaps of the boards in a clinker built boat [origin unknown]

siffer, sifter to grope in the dark. [Eng *sift + er*]

sight 1 = to sight. 2 to examine newly born animals to determine the sex, also used of human beings indecently (a taunting threat among a group of young boys was the call '*Sight him!*')

sile 1 to strain or filter. [also Eng dial; Norw *sile*]

sile 2 part of a quern fittings. [called RINE in Papa Westray; Norw *sigle*]

sile 3 a young herring (no more than the size of one's little finger). [ON *sil* a kind of herring; Norw *sild* herring]

siller see SALOR.

siller door see SALOR.

sillock*, sillo a one year coalfish. [from the same root as SILE 3]

105

silly 1 = silly. 2 sick. [only recorded in the report of the Crofters' Commission; also Sh]

silt to hunger after a particular food. **silted** having a craving for, '*I wis right silted for a fresh herring*'. [ON *svelta* to hunger]

Silver Willie a top shell. [*silver* from its sheen + WILLIE]

simander to wander aimlessly. [? a running together of SIMMY and WANDER]

simean putting on airs. *simean aboot*. [a special development of SIMMY]

simman a home made rope of straw, horse hair etc. [ON *simi* a cord or rope; Gaelic *sioman* a straw rope is also from ON]

simmer the principal beam in a roof. [Sc and Eng *simmer*]

simmet see SEMMIT.

simmy to wander about aimlessly. **simyan** of a sick animal swaying about on its legs. [Norw *saema* to fumble about]

sin = sin. **sinfu** an intensive, *a sinfu lot*.

sinder-casten of a *rig* of land ploughed inwards from the furrow on either side. The furrow is thus thrown asunder. [Eng *cast* + *asunder*]

sindry* apart. *tae tak things sindry* to take things apart. [also Sc; OE *syndrig* apart]

sine to let drip or to strain off. [also Sc and Eng dial to rinse; Nor ME *sind* to rinse; compare SIE]

single = single. **singloo** a bundle of gleaned corn. *tae single neeps (turnips)* to remove the surplus plants leaving *single* plants about 15 cms apart. Weeds are removed at the same time.

sinkie* a small depression. [Norw *senking*]

sinlick see SANLOO.

sinlicrow, seemicrow a knotted mess. [SINGLOO + ON *krókr* winding]

sinlo, sinyo 1 *lyan in a sinloo* huddled together. 2 a tangled up mess. [a form of SINGLOO]

sinny fynnie the black guillemot. [a corruption of Sc *sittie-fittie*; perhaps because it sits on its feet?; see FOOTIE ARSE]

sinny-girs couch grass. [ON *sin(a)* a kind of rush]

sinyo see SINGLOO.

sipan soaking wet. [also sc; a form of Eng *seep*]

sipe = sip.

sire see SYRE.

sirp wet ground. **sirpan*** soaking wet, '*Me feet wis just sirpan*'. **sirpis** a soaking wet mess. **sirpo** a thick bran and oat drink for a cow. [Norw *sørpe* sludge or slush]

sirry the liquid which oozes from a midden. [also known as IPER; Norw dial *syra* seepage]

sisten a small quantity. **sistensation** the smallest possible quantity [Eng *sustenance, sustenation*]

sit = sit, perf. tense **sitten**. *sit teu* sit up at table, said usually to guests. **sitten*** an egg which has an embryo chicken inside it, '*I doot the egg's sitten*.' [also Sc]. **sitten on*** humiliated, '*When she didna get first prize, she wis right sitten on*'.

sitherip plough chains. [Eng *side-rope*]

sivvet a blow or a whack. [Sc *soaflet* from Fr *soufflet*]

skaa 1 see SKAAV.

skaa (only in the plural **skaas**) the small acorn barnacle found on rocks or on wood in the sea [ON *skán*, crust]

skaad-head* the shell of the sea-urchin. [see SCADMAN'S HEAD]

skaafy of a boat having a prominent rake at the bow or stern. [OSc *skaf* a light skiff]

skaav, skaa 1 to scrape, especially skin. 2 to hoe. [ON *skafa* to scrape]

skaddo only in *burstin-skaddo* a mixture of BURSTIN and boiling water. [*skaddo* is a deriv of Eng *scald*]

skafal of a person well built. [? compare ON *skapfelligr* well shapen in the face]

skaff 1 food, but used only jokingly. 2 headway or progress. [OSc *skaff* to scrounge]

skaffo see SKATFU.

skail 1 to scatter. 2 of a crowd to disperse. [ON *skilya* to separate]

skaithe fate. *devil skaithe* what does it matter!. [obs Eng *skaithe* to harm]

skaive a piece of hide suitable for making RIVLINGS. [see SKELF]

skaively*, skeffly* especially *skaively-feeted* walking with the feet out and in a clumsy fashion. [ON *skeifligr* awry]

skam verb. to damage, harm. noun. a spot or injury. **skam skatfaa** '*The ferm gid skam skatfaa*' completely to waste. [see SKATFAA; ON *skemma* to destroy]

skamy small. [ON *skammr* short]

skaoowaoo* twisted, off the straight. An old house near Dounby was built at an angle to the road and is locally known as *Skaoowaoo*. [a form of Eng *skee-whiff*]

skapie broad and flat. [origin uncertain]

skar to dislike or loathe certain foods. [see SKARR]

skare 1, skware, skyare clear and bright (e.g. of moonlight). [ON *skaerr* bright]

skare 2 a swathe mown by a scythe. [ON *skera* to cut]

skare 3 to join two boards together in such a way that the join is no thicker than the joined board. [Sc *skair*; ON *skara* to clinch the planks of a boat]

skarf*, scarf*, skarfie* the cormorant or the shag. **tae baet skarfs*** to beat the hands against the sides of the chest to warm them in the manner of the SKARF beating its wings to dry them. [see FLUIKS; ON *skarfr*]

skarps poor barren land. **skarpy** of land, barren. [ON *skarpr* of land, barren]

skarr*, scar frightened or nervous, '*An aafil skarr thing o bairn*'. [ON *skjarr* timid]

skarro, skirro a col or saddle in a hill. [ON *skarð]*

skarsum 1 applied to food loathsome. 2 very particular as far as food is concerned. [see SKAR]

skart 1 to strike a match. [OSc *skrat* to scratch]

skart 2 the cormorant or the shag. [also Sc; a corruption of SKARF]

skat an ancient type of tax levied in Norse times on landholders in Orkney and Shetland and still paid. **skatfaa** default in the payment of taxes and by extension, *ruin*. [ON *falla* in the sense *to fail*]. **skatland** land subject to *skat*. [ON *skattr* tax]

skate-rumple a nickname for an inhabitant of Deerness. [obs Sc **skate-rumple** tail of a skate (the fish); the probable meaning in this context is *lanky*]

skatfu, skaffo, scafou 1 greedy. 2 hungry. [ON *skattr* treasure + *full*; someone disposed to hoard treasure]

skatie-goo the Arctic skua. [see SCOOTY-ALLAN; Sc *gow* gull]

skatt dyk† ?boundary wall. [OE *scēad* a boundary + *dyke*]

skave to weed with a how. **skavan** hoeing potatoes. [see SKAAV]

skech queer. [ON *skeika* to go away]

skeeling goose the sheldrake. [ON *skjöldungr]*

skeenkle to walk in an uncoordinated manner. **skeenkly** lanky. [Faer *skinkla* to be loose in the joints]

skeet 1* 1 to squirt or shoot out. 2 to skim a stone over water so that it bounces off the surface. **skeeto** 1 the cuttlefish. 2 the sea anemone. 3* a squirt. [also Sc; ON *skjóta* to shoot]

skeet 2 verb. 1 to taunt. 2 to talk over confidently about something, *tae skeet at something yi ken nothing aboot*. noun. a taunt or a hurtful remark. [ON *skúta* to taunt]

skeeto see SKEET 1.

skeffly see SKAIVELY.

skegg* the beard or awn of the bere seed. **skeggs** woody fibrous material in a peat bank. [ON *skegg* beard or awns]

skeld the surf [see SHALD 1]

skelder 1 thin flaky stones. **skilter** a fragment. [Sh *skilder*; Sc *sculder* atoms; ON *skilja* (part. *skildr*) to separate]

skelder 2 see SKOLDER.

skelderack a scatter-brain. [see SKOLDER 1]

skeldro 1 the oyster catcher. [ON *skjöldóttr* of cattle, dappled]

skeldro 2 the shelduck. [ON *skjöldungr* sheldrake]

skelet see SKELF.

skelf 1 1 a thin piece of skin torn off. 2 a sharing. [OSc *skelf* a splinter; obs Du *schelf* a flake]

skelf 2, skelet a shelf; *the skelf o the bed* was the shelf at the foot of a box bed where children sometimes slept. [OSc *skelf*; compare ON *Hlið-skjálf* Odin's seat]

skelfer a thin piece of stone. **skelfery** easily split. [EME *skiffer*]

skeliment a board added to the top of a box cart to increase its depth. [SKELF 2 + *ment*]

skell 1 1 an egg-shell. 2 a *plate* used for lifting meal. [also SKELLO; originally a scallop shell was used for this purpose; ON *skel* shell but see also SKULLY]

skell 2 a clashing sound e.g. the waves breaking on the beach. **skelly** noisy: *a skelly day* when things are in turmoil. [ON *skella* to make a noise]

Skellat, Skellit, Skillet one of the smaller bells in St Magnus Cathedral. [OSc *skellat* hand bell; compare Du *skel*; Ger *Schelle* bell]

skello see SKELL.

skelly 1, skyelly of a sky when it is covered with bright white clouds. [see OWER-SKELLY]

skelly 2 see SKELL 2.

skelly-wheeter, skirly-wheeter an unhealthy looking animal. [ON *skella* to make a noise; see WHEET the plaintive sound made by birds]

skelp 1* *a skelp o land* a large extent of land. [also Sc; see SKELF 1]

skelp 2*, skyelp a smack with the flat of the hand. [also Sc; imitat]

skelter, skerpo, smerko, skertar, sgerter poor quality tangles. [see SKELDER]

skeo see SKYO.

skeolder see SKOLDER.

skep a round shallow basket made of straw. [also Sc; ON *skeppa]*

skerp see SKIRP.

skerpo, smerko see SKERTAR.

skert, scart an earmark used on a sheep. **scart** hole a sheep mark. [ON *skar* a cut]]

skertar see SKELTER.

skevandle, skvandle to wander around: '*Whar are thoo been skevandlan tae the day?*'. [compare Du *wandel* to walk about; Eng *squander* to roam; see SQUANDER]

skewen crooked, off the straight. [related to Eng *askew*]

skewhouses drying houses for fish. [see SKYO]

skibal see SKIVALT.

skibby a light passing shower. [see SKUB]

skiff the peak of a cap. [Sc *skip*; ON *skapt* a shaft shaped object]

skift† a land division referring to a broad ridge. [ON *skipti* division; see INSKEYFT and SHIFT]

107

skifter a very thin flake [see SKELF 1]

skigg to walk with an awkward gait. [ON *skeika* to go askew; compare SKYAIKY]

skiggan bright and clean. [ON *skyggǒr* bright]

skile, skyle to shelter in the sense of placing a protective shutter on the windward side of the old Orkney chimney which was positioned in the centre of the roof. [ON *skíla* to protect]

skillet see SKELLAT.

skilly skilful. [Eng *skill*]

skilt to squirt. [Sc *skilt* to move about quickly but perhaps a form of SKEET]

skilter 1 a fragment. [see SKELDER]

skilter 2 of lightning to flash. [Sc *skilter* to move hurriedly; Sh *skitter* to scatter]

skim to sneer at. [Icel *skimp* mockery or scorn]

skimmery having a scum on top, particulary a dirty scum. [Eng *scum*]

skimou a brownish pink colour. [see SKIRMY]

skimse, skrimse of a dog to go prowling around in search of food. [ON *skima* to look round restlessly]

skinnybreeks a shellfish (*mya arenaria*) so called from the appearance of its syphon. [*skinny* + BREEKS]

skint verb. to hurry: '*Skint thee noo!*' noun. 1 a short time. 2 a small piece. [ON *skynda* to hasten]

skio see SKYO.

skip 1 = skip. 2 to remove a garment.

skirin of a girl, attractive. [see SKYRAN]

skirl to make a shrill noise [also Sc]. **skirler** a strong gale. **skirlie*** a fried mixture of meal and onions. [imitat; compare Norw *skrelle* to resound]

skirlo* a small hand made wooden propeller which turns in the wind; also TIRLO [the basic idea is 'turning']

skirly-wheeter see SKELLY-WHEETER.

skirm 1 a thin flake. 2 a thin bannock or oatcake [see SKURM]

skirmy a light faded appearance. [see SKRIMINGS]

skirp*, skyirp, skerp 1 a large rip in clothing. 2 a flighty girl or tomboy. **skirpan, shirpan, skyirpan** especially in *skirpan clean* of cloth after it has been washed. [the word relates to the sound made by drawing the fingers along clean fibres e.g. newly washed hair; compare ON *skirp* to spit]

skirr to slide over ice etc. [also Eng dial; ON *skrida* to slide on snow shoes]

skirro see SKARRO.

skirry easily scared. [see SKARR]

skirvin noun. a miser. adj. mean or avaricious. [perhaps with an earlier meaning *wretched*; compare Norw *skarve* wretched]

skite a flat bit of hardwood nailed to the gunwale of a boat to prevent the abrasion by the oar. [ON

skíd a billet of wood]

skitoes home made slippers for the evening. [ON *skjóta* to shoot; Sc *skite* to slip or skid]

skitsy clumsy. [see SKUITSY]

skitter (the) 1* (vulgar). noun. 1 diarrhoea, esp *a dose o the skitter;* (the necessary accompanying definite article here is interesting; compare REEPAN) and Eng *the shits.* verb. to excrete diarrhoea. **skitter the slaps** to take home the last load of corn at harvest time. [see SLAP]. **skitter-brolty** the corn bunting. [compare ON *mýrr-skítr* snipe; ON *skítr* faeces]

skitter 2* verb *tae skitter aboot* to work in an unmethodical way. noun. *in a skitter* in a hurry, trying to do several things at once. [Sc *skilter* to hurry]

skivalt a thin layer of skin. **skibal** indecent exposure. [compare TALDERS]. **skoibal** untidy. [Sc *skybald*; ON *skífa* to slice; hence tatter]

skive 1 to pare a piece of wood. [ON *skífa* to slice]

skive 2 to deflect the wind on to winnowing grain. [see SKYVED]

skived see SKYVED.

skoibal see SKIVALT.

skol see SKULL.

skolder, scolder verb. to make a loud noise. noun. 1 noisy talk. 2 a strong breeze. 3 the screaming of seagulls. 4 the oyster catcher. 5 *a skolder o bones* a very thin person (a rattling skeleton). **skelder, skeolder, skyolder** especially in the phrase *tae go doon in a skyolder* to go down with a loud crash. [ON *skvaldr* noisy talk; Norw *skaaldre* to clatter or rattle]

skon a cake of cow dung. [ON *myki-skán;* the *Sconie Brae* placenames of Sanday are places where cow dung pads were dried for fuel]

skoo 1 a drying place. 2 a large empty, cold draughty house, *a skoo o a hoose* [see SKYO]

skooltie, skultan, skulty a large thin bere bannock. [Sc *scultie*; imitat from the sound made by the thin mixture; Sc *scult* to smack]

skoom 1 verb to skim. noun scum. [Norw *skum* scum and *skuma* to skim]

skoom 2 dusk. Speaking of a storm at twilight, a Birsay man said the moon was *just in skoom.* **skoomy** of the sky, darkening. [ON *skúmi* shade or dusk]

skoor see SCOOR.

skoosh *in skoosh* in pieces. [? a form of SMUSH]

skoot 1* verb. to jut out. noun. a jutting out. [ON *skúta* to project]

skoot 2, skout 1 the razor-bill. 2 the common guillemot. [see SCOOTS]

skootie see SCOOTS.

skootie-allan see SCOOTS.

skoovo see SKOVO.

skory 1, skorie, scorie a young seagull. A children's rhyme runs:-

Tammy Norie (or Betsy Gorie)
Catched a skorie
On the Peedie Sea,
He gid him a nippie
Apin the hippie
And than he let him flee

[also Sc; ON *skári*]

skory 2 a crowd or troop. [compare the old North Ronaldsay rhyme]:-

Come oot Green Gorey
Wi a thee skory
An follow me tae the sea

These words were spoken by the seal wife who returned to land to collect the cow and calves she owned. [ON *skari* a troop]

skothro a dried coalfish. [origin uncertain; see SKRATHAN]

skout see SKOOT 2.

skoutsy see SKUITSY

skouth see SCOUTH.

skovo, skoovo, scroovo the turf removed when a peat bank is flayed. [compare Icel *skaf* a scraping]

skow see SCOW.

skraable to rustle, especially of something which is very dry e.g. a sheaf. [? imitat]

skraal see SKRULLYIE.

skrae a shoal of sillocks. [see SKREED]

skraed covered with vermin [see SKREED]

skrae-fish dried fish. [ON *skrei*]

skraithaless, skrothaless 1 scandalous. 2 unusual. 3 astounding. 4 unreasonable. [origin uncertain]

skrall to bellow, scream or roar [Norw dial *skrolla*, to yell]

skrallyo see SKRULLYIE.

skran 1 = Eng dial *scram* a morsel, 'Thir wisna wan skran left efter they hid been there'.

skran 2 skinny or thin. [Norw dial *skram* skinny]

skrankie thin or emaciated. [Norw dial *skrank* thin]

skrat *a skrat o a sea* a little wave movement. [see SCRAT]

skrathan applied to any coarse looking living thing e.g. big coalfish or hens might be called *wild coorse skrathans*. [ON *skrydda*, shrivelled skin]

skratter see SCRATTO.

skrattie see SCRATTY.

skravvle to scramble. [ON *krafla*; influenced by Eng *scrabble*]

skreed*, skrythe, skry*, skro, verb to swarm. noun. 1 a swarm. 2 a crowd. **skratou** a number of anything small e.g. children, potatoes etc. **skrae, skruthy** swarming. [ON *skreid* a shoal; ON *skriða* to creep]

skreek, skreigh daybreak, *skreek o day.* [also Sc in a variety of forms; the equivalent of *cock-crow*; see SKREK]

skreeo a lean person or animal. [ON *skrydda*, shrivelled skin]

skreeve, screeve to make the small initial rut in ploughing. **skreever** a howling gale, literally a tearing or scratching wind. [also SKREEVIS; ON *skrífa* to scratch]

skreevis see SKREEVER.

skreigh see SKREEK.

skreim 1 to glimmer with unsteady light. 2 to vibrate [see SKRIME]

skrek, scraik verb. to talk with a high pitched voice. noun. a high pitched yell. [ON *skraekja* to shriek]

skreppo 1 any dry shrivelled up substance, *dried tae a skreppo.* 2 a small heap. 3 cow clap. 4 a ruin. [ON *skorpna* to shrivel up]

skrift, skrifty lean, hard grown. [related to Swed dial *skrift* skeleton]

skrime to see faintly, literally to see a gleam of. [ON *skrím* gleam; compare Norw *skrimsle* to catch a glimpse of]

skriman of a person sneaking, spying, underhand. [related to SKRIME above in the sense of *looking in a sly fashion*]

skrimings *the first skrimings* dawn. *the last skrimings* dusk. [ON *skrím* faint light]

skrimse see SKIMSE.

skrit to rend or tear [see SCRAT]

skrivver *a skrivver and klanker* a pancake coated with rhubarb jam (Sanday) [ON *skrifli* fragment; see KLANKER]

skro see SKRY.

skroa see SKRUE 1.

skrog 1 a tough root or old branch found in peat. 2 an animal or person with little flesh or bones. [related to Eng *scraggy* and Swed dial *skragg* something haggard or torn]

skroo verb. to stack sheaves. noun* a stack of sheaves. [ON *skrúfr* haystack]

skroolt verb. 1 to gnash the teeth. 2 to make a grating noise by the rubbing together of two rough surfaces, e.g. a boat *skrootlan* against the pier. noun. a scratching sound. [ON *skrölt* to jolt; compare SKROOTLE]

skroopan of a hen, the carcase. [Sc *scroban* gizzard; a confusion of Gael *sgrùban* gizzard and ON *skrokkr* carcase]

skroot see SKROOLT or SKROOTLE.

skrootle to make a grating noise, especially *skrootlan and skreetlan.* [Norw *skratte* or *skratle* to rattle]

skrothaless see SKRAITHALESS.

skrow see SKRUE 1.

skrue 1, skroa, skrow fragments, 'Whin I opened the biscuits they were aal in skrue'. [essential meaning is *broken pieces*; ON *skrjoðr* a shred]

skrue 2 dry, especially *as dry as skrue*. [related to SKRUE 1 in the sense small dry fragments; compare Eng *as dry as dust*]

skruff 1 *a skruff o hair* shaggy hair. [ON *skruf-harr* stiff haired]

skruff 2 1 a piece of coarse dry skin. 2 dry crust of bread. [ON *skrá* dry skin]

skruith a shoal of fish. [ON *skreið*]

skrull *in skrull* smashed to pieces. [Norw dial *skrell* a crash]

skrullyie, skraal, skrallyo 1 to swarm, especially *skrullyan alive*,' *His head wis skrullyan alive wi lice*'. 2 a crowd or swarm of something, especially lice. [Icel *skríll* mob]

skrult a scratching sound. [see SKROOT]

skrunt see SCRUNT.

skrupsy uncouth looking. [origin uncertain; Norw dial *skrubb* a harsh gruff person]

skruthy see SKREED.

skry, skro, scrie verb. to swarm. noun. a swarming mass of small living things* *a scrie o bairns* (also **skrying**). [compare Norw *skrei* a swarm; see SKREED]

skryme see SKRIME.

skub see SKUGG 4.

skuchle to walk clumsily. [Sc *shauchle*; Norw *skokle* to hobble]

skudder [see SKUTHER]

skugg 1 = scud. 2 *to go like skugg* to travel very fast. 3 a light passing shower.

skuglifeese to punish, a half jocular threat to children. [Sc *scud* to punish; the last element may be Sc *aveese* advice]

skuitsy, skitsy of the feet etc sticking out. [adj. form of SKOOT; see BIGSY for similar adj.]

skuity eccentric. [Sc *scoutie* worthless in character]

skuivle to walk clumsily. [see SKAIVELY]

skull 1, skol a box for holding a fishing line, a *lineskull*. [ON *skál* a bowl or *skjóla* a bucket; see also SKULLY]

skull 2 a disease of the mouth in young horses, characterised by the gums growing over the teeth. [Norw *skjol*]

skull 3 1 = scull. 2 to throw a small flattish stone over the surface of a flat stretch of water at a low angle so that the stone bounces repeatedly before sinking (also SKEET)

skullcap an unidentified wild flower.

skully 1 a child's cap. [Eng *skull-cap*]

skully 2 a little wooden bowl, usually applied to the bowl kept in a churn and used for lifting milk. [ON *skál* bowl]

skullyo a loud noise, *Good I heard this ferful skullyo and when I gid ootside here wis two cars head on* [O.N. *skella*, to make a noise]

skultan see SKOOLTIE.

skulty see SKOOLTIE.

skumfis see SCUMFISH.

skunface see SCUMFISH.

skunner see SCUNNER.

skunsin, skunsis thrifty. [origin unknown]

skunyal a measure used in net making to determine the mesh size. [Norw *skyndel* a weavers shuttle]

skups the male genitals. [ON *skopin*]

skurber poor barren soil. [Norw *skarv* stony mountain terrain; see SKARPS a related form]

skurm 1 rind on a cheese. 2 egg-shell. 3 dried up oatcake. **skurmy** having a hard skin (e.g. of bannocks). [also Sh; ON *skurn* egg shell]

skurro 1 a fissure in the ground or in a rock or cliff. [see SKURRO 2]

skurro 2 a gate. [ON *skarð* a breach or gap]

skurrock a stepping stone used e.g. when getting out of a boat. [ON *skör* a step]

skurt verb. to carry an object or bundle against the lower part of the body with both arms around it. noun. the lap. [Ice *kjalta* lap, the Ork dial form showing an original 's' which exists in Old Norse *skaut*, lap; in *skurt* an 'r' is substituted for 'l', a common characteristic of the northern languages; Gael *sguird* which is also possibly Norse has an identical meaning to the Ork word]

skutch a slight coating (e.g. of snow). [see SKUGG]

skuther, skwither, skudder verb 1 to scrape, '*I skuthered me shins against the wall*'. 2 to bounce a flat stone along the surface of a pool etc., [also SKEET and SKULL]. noun. a gale or shower. [a form of Sc *scudder*]

skutten white faced. [origin uncertain but may be related to ON *skyggðr* bright]

skuttle an egg shell, usually *egg-skuttle*. [Norw dial *eggja skutl*]

skutto a small division of land. [ON *skúta* to jut out]

skvandle see SKEVANDLE.

skware see SKARE 1.

skwin to slant. [compare Norw *skeine* to veer]

skwirly of a rock which does not split easily into flat strata but is filled with nodules. [compare Norw *svervel* an eddy and ON *hvirfla* to whirl]

skwirm to wither [? a variant of SKIRM]

skwither see SKUTHER.

sky 1 the mould board of the old Orkney plough. [Norw dial *skeid*]

sky 2 verb. to go love-making. noun. love-making. [also Sc; Eng *sky* (lark)]

skyaik to pout. **skyaiket** askew. **skyaiky** having an awkward gait. [ON *skeika* to go askew]

skyare see SKARE 1.

skyelly see SKELLY 1.

skyelp see SKELP.

skyelpan *skyelpan and runnan* running with difficulty. [Sc *skelp* to strike; compare Eng *hammer*

110

along]

skyirp see SKIRP.

skyko in the early part of this century, an old man who regularly visited a family in Sanday would greet them with the phrase *ap a skyko skorky willy*. [it may be a nonsense phrase but it is remarkably like Old Norse '*Judging by the clouds, it's going to rain*', a typical Orkney greeting!']

skyld see LANDSKYLD.

skyle see SKILE.

skyo, skeo, skio, skoo a roughly built hut of wood or stones for drying peats etc, formerly used for drying fish and flesh. [ON *skjá* a shed]

skyolder see SKOLDER

skyow-wow see SKAOOWAOO.

sky-pilot a fisherman's tabu term for a minister of religion.

skyran glittering of e.g. the sky. also applied metaphorically to a girl. [ON *skírr* bright]

skyte a bout of heavy drinking. [also Eng slang]

skyued of an indeterminate colour. [perhaps related to SKIMOU]

skyuik a sudden start, e.g. of a horse suddenly shying at an object in the ditch. [ON *skeika* to go askew]

skyuimet of a glance, sidelong, secret. [ON *skúmi* shade]

skyuimy of the sky when dark clouds above give way to a brighter sky below. [ON *skúmi* shade; see SKOOM 2]

skyved, skived askew. [ON *skeifr]*

slaa used of a mother who does not discipline her children '*She's kinda slaa wi her bairns*'. [ON *slakr* slack]

slack 1 knack. [ON *sloeg]*

slack 2 a col. [also Sc; ON *slakki;* see SLUNK, a dell]

slag 1 heavy motion (e.g. of the sea). [origin uncertain; perhaps related to SLAG 2]

slag 2 clumsy or ungainly. [ON *slag* a blow with extension of meaning]

slag 3 see SLAIK.

slaik verb. to cover with mud. **slaikie** slimy. noun. mud [see SLYK]

slairp see SLERP.

slaister* verb. to make a mess. noun. 1 a wet mess. 2 a bungling job. 3 a careless worker. **slaistery*** messy in the sense of *wet*. [also Sc; origin uncertain but perhaps related to Eng *slush;* Norw *slesk]*

slakie see SLAIK 1.

slap 1 a gate, especially a gate in a hill dyke. [also Sc; compare MGer *slop* gap; Sc *slap* to breach and Norw *sleppe* a fissure]

slap 2 = slap. **slap dab** slap dash.

slatero *, slatroo, slaterworm woodlouse, perhaps

from its slated appearance rather than its supposed habitat *among slates*. [compare Norw *skrukke-troll* wood louse where *skrukke* means *wrinkled;* the *o* is a diminutive]

slebbo *as slack as slebbo* hanging loosely. [Norw *slapp* loose; compare the phrase *as fast as funko*]

sled 1 a sledge used on a farm. 2 flat exposed bedrock. [OSc *sled* a sledge; Sh *sled* to slip]

slee see SLY 3.

sleek flattery [OSc *sleked*, plausible]

sleekéd* sly. [also Sc; Eng *sleek* smooth]

sleeven a thin boy. [?Sc *sliving* a slice; compare Sc *slype* a lazy fellow from *slype* a slice]

slerp * *a slerp o a kiss* a wet kiss. '*Gae hid a slerp o paint*' paint it, but don't be too particular. [also Sc; the main idea is 'unpleasant wetness'; see LERP]

slester see SLAISTER.

slestry see SLAISTERY.

slid *a great slid o a baest* an animal of huge bulk. [ON *slyðra* a flabby lump]

slide = slide. **slido*** a patch of ice made into a slide. **slidy** 1* slippery. 2 underhand. [compare Eng *slippery* (customer)]

slimen sneaking, unreliable. **slimsy** a *slimsy* caper, a mean trick. [Sc *slim* = 1 slim. 2 cunning; Sc adj. suffix *sy*]

slip = slip. *tae slip awey* to die. **slippy*** slippery. [also in Eng dial]

slip-me-laaver one who cannot be trusted to do any work properly. [Sc *slip-me-labour*]

slite* 1 smooth.2 level, '*The snow wis slite wi the dike.*' [ON *slettr* smooth]

slitter *in a slitter*, of clothes hanging in rags. [ON *slitri* rags or tatters]

slo see SLOO.

sloch see SLOUGH.

slock* 1 to extinguish a fire. 2 to quench a thirst. **slocking pint†** a traditional drink taken by tradesmen in Springtime when it was no longer necessary to use artificial light. [also Sc; ON *slökva* to extinguish fire or quench thirst]

sloo, slo, sloe the pith of a horn. [also Sc; ON *sló]*

sloond, slooan a lazy lout. '*I widna hiv that great hungry slooan takkan yir bit o piece*', in this instance, advice given by a neighbour referring to a visitor who often appeared at a house at dinner time. [also Sc; originally Sc *sleuth-hound* a type of bloodhound]

sloonky see SLUNKY.

sloopsy see SKRUPSY.

slot 1 1 slot. 2 *the slot o the breest* the depression below the Adam's apple. [also Sc; Eng *slot]*

slot 2 an unknown type of fish dish. [probably the same as Sh *slot* a dumpling of crushed fish livers and roe kneaded with meal; Norw *slo* fish

111

entrails]

slough, sloch the membrane round the intestines of a fish or the intestines themselves. [Norw *slo* fish entrails]

slubber to eat noisily, drawing in one's breath as one eats. [compare Eng *slubber* to gobble]

slug a lazy lout. [also Eng dial (now Eng *sluggard*); ON *slókr* a slouching person]

sluggermegullion 1 a lazy person. 2 an untidy person. [a form of Eng *slubberdegullion* a sloven]

sluggie 1 unripe. 2 half-filled. 3 bare, hungry or poor looking. [an extended meaning of SLUG]

sluiter to walk in a slouching manner. **sluits** old shoes or slippers worn down at the heels. [ON *sloðra* to trail along]

slumry of a fish, thin. [Norw *slumr* long weak stalks of grass]

slunk a hollow in sandy links. [Dan dial *slunk* a hollow]

slunky, sloonky long and lean. [Norw *slunken*]

slurk a noise made when drinking. [compare Norw *slurk* a noisy gulp]

slush = slush. *tae go slushan aboot* to tackle something in a slipshod manner. **slushy** 1 slovenly. 2 of crop broken down by wind and rain.

sly 1 1 green slimy growth on rocks where freshwater runs into the sea. 2 alluvial mud. 3 the issue from an animal in heat. [ON *slý* slimy ground]

sly 2, slee an iron band or collar. [a form of Eng *sleeve*]

sly 3 = sly. **slygoose** the shelduck, from its secretive nesting habits. [the word *goose* was often applied to birds other than geese; compare EMMER-GOOSE the great northern diver]

slyk 1 alluvial mud. 2 green slimy algae found on the sea shore (*ulva*). [Sc *sleek*; MLGer *slick* mud]

slykees barnacles. [also known as KLAIK-GEESE; in Sc *claik-geese* are barnacle geese; it was popularly believed that barnacle geese were born from barnacles]

slype a stroke with anything wet such as a wet towel. [imitat]

sma* = small. **sma breid** rolls or COOKIES. **sma drink** used negatively, '*He's no sma drink*' he's very important. **sma hunner/hunder** a hundred, as opposed to the bigger hundred of six score [see LONG HUNDER]. **small laird** a small land owner. **sma-tings** odds and ends [compare Norw *småting* something small]. **smaaly** not in very good health [compare Eng *poorly*]

smaffan small in stature. [Norw *småfengt* little]

smear verb. to spread butter. noun. butter. [ON *smjör* butter]

smeeo see SMOO 1.

smeerum fat bacon. [ON *smjör* butter]

smeetho cramps iron hard pan. [*smeetho* is prob-

ably a form of Eng *smith* blacksmith; bog iron ore was used by the medieval blacksmith]

smelt an oily patch on water caused by the use of mashed limpets for fish bait. [ON *smolt* grease on hot water; compare OE *smylte* calm, peaceful]

smerko see SKERPO and SKERTAR.

smero, smerow, smuiro 1 clover. 2 bird's foot trefoil. 3 possibly tormentil. A clover leaf was worn in the boot on market day to prevent the wearer being cheated. [ON *smári* clover]

smerslin, smurslin, smirlin the sand gaper, a shell found on sandy beaches (*mya truncata*). [also Sh; Icel *smyrslingr*]

smetters a contraction of LENDS METTERS.

smiddy* a smithy. [also Sc; OSc *smedye* smithy]

smirlin see SMERSLIN.

smikker = [a variation of SNIKKER]

smit* to infect [also Sc]. **smitsom*** infectious. [OE *smittan* to smite]

smitherin see SMUTHERIN.

smoke = smoke. **Smoky Tom** a cabbage stalk hollowed out, filled with tar and set alight.

smoly scorn or disrespect. [ON *smá* to disdain]

smoo, smeeo, smyoo verb. 1 of a dog to prowl around. 2 to laugh secretly [also SMOOSE]. noun. 1 a hole in a wall allowing sheep to pass through. 2 a covered drain. **smoothy** a hiding hole. **smoosie** inquisitive. **smoovin** sly. [ON *smjúga* to creep; *smúga* a gap]

smook* verb. of fine snow to blow around. noun. 1 fine powdery snow being driven around. 2 coal dust (Westray). 3 smithereens, *lyan in smook*. *tae go like smook*, to go very fast. [OSc *smuke* smoke]

smookit hidden, sly, untrustworthy [ON *smjúga* to creep]

smoor* 1 of fine powdery snow, to blow, especially in a whirling fashion, '*Hid's fairly smooran ootside noo*' 2 to choke, '*He's just smoored wi the cowld*'. 3 to damp down a fire. [also Sc; see also MOOR; OE *smorian* to suffocate]

smoose to go about slyly. [see SMOO]

smoosh see SMUSH 2.

smoosie see SMOO.

smoosk to smile in a sly manner. [Norw dial *smuska*]

smooter, smoots a kiss. [a form of Eng *smother*; also recorded as MOOTER with the loss of the initial *s*; compare SMOOR and MOOR]

smoothie a kiss. [dimin of SMUTHICK]

smoothy see SMOO.

smoots 1 see SMOOTER.

smoots 2 the sulks. [the essential meaning is *to stick out the lips*; compare Gael *smut* or *smuig* snout]

smoovin see SMOO.

smouch *smouch o a laugh* a muffled laugh. [related

to Gael *smuc* a nasal sound and Norw *smuska* to laugh secretly; see SMOOSK]

smud a small fragment. [a form of Eng *smut*]

smuggle verb 1 = to smuggle. 2* in the BA GAME, to conceal the ball and move it by deception towards the goal. noun* such a move.

smuggry see MUGGRY.

smuiro, smerow see SMERO.

smurslin see SMERSLIN.

smush, smoosh smoke or dust flying about. *aal in smush* completely broken up. [Sc *smuist*; Norw *smuss* dirt or filth]

smusk a snigger. [see SMOOSK and SMOUCH]

smutherin, smitherin 1 a small amount (e.g. of butter on bread). 2 **the smutherins o day** faint light in the sky at dawn or twilight. [? Eng *smothering*]

smuthick, smoothie a kiss. [Norw *smøyt*; see SMOOTER a related form]

smyoo see SMOO.

sna = snow. **snawy** snowy. **snawie-fowl** the snow bunting [ON *snae-fugl*; see also SNOW]

snack to be busy about something, *tae snack aboot*. [ON *snaka* to rummage]

snail see SNELL.

snailed see SNELL.

snaith see SNYTH.

snapper of a horse, to stumble. [also Sc; compare Ger dial *schnappen*; Norw *snuble* to stumble]

snarge, snargeo see SNEERKO.

snarl the string by which a BISMAR was suspended. [ON *snaeri* a twisted rope]

snarpy snappy by nature. [see SNIRPET]

sneck 1 organised, active, especially of a young girl. [Norw *snegg* brisk]

sneck 2* a door latch. [also Sc and NE; origin doubtful but perhaps *piece of wood cut off*; compare OSc *sneck* to cut; or imitat from ME *snacchen* to snap; compare Norw *klinke* a door latch]

snee to twist. [ON *snúa* to twist]

sneer 1 to take a sudden start, '*Hid tuk a sneer on the tether and ran roond in a circle*'. [ON *snara* to make a quick turn]

sneer 2 *tae sneer wi the cowld* to have a bad head cold. [also Sc; Norw *snorr* snot; OSc *sneir* a snort]

sneerko, snarge, snargeo, snirko a twist or knot. [? a development of SNEER 1; ON *snerkja* to wrinkle is an alternative possibility]

sneeshan, snysin the coot. [also known as the SNELLIE and the SNYTH; the bird is named from its bald patch; near related forms are ON *snoðinn* bald and Norw *snitte* to cut; see also SNY a white spot on a horse's face and SNELL; the *an* suffix probably represents *ing*]

sneeshin snuff. [also Sc; OSc *sneising*]

sneesteran inclined to make disparaging remarks. [Sc *sneist* to be scornful]

sneet 1 to blow the nose. [ON *snýta]*

sneet 2 see SNIT.

sneeter 1*, snutter to giggle, especially *sneeteran and laughan*. [Sc *snotter* to snuffle or *snuiter* to giggle]

sneeter 2 *sneeteran wi the cowld* with nose running because of a head cold. [ON *snuðra* to snuffle]

sneeter 3 of new cheese to make a squeaky sound when cut. [imitat; compare NEESTER]

sneevil a nasal intonation. [also Sc; OSc *snevil* to snuffle]

snell, snail a white strip on a horse's face. **snelld, snailed** used of a horse with a *snell*. **snellie** the coot. [compare SNY 2 a white spot on a horse's face; see SNEESHAN for deriv; Dan dial *snollet* bald is a closely related form]

sneud see SNUID.

sneuk see SNUIK.

sneuksie see SNUIK.

snib* 1 1 a catch for a door or window. 2 to open or close such a catch. **snibber** to make fast. [? imitat; compare SNECK]

snib 2 *tae snib tatties*, to break off the shoots to prevent them growing [also Sc ? a variation of Eng *snip*]

snickle a twitch for a horse, a loop of rope passing round a horse's nose and tightened with a short stick. It was used to restrain an awkward animal e.g. in shoeing. [a form of SNITTER]

sniddle to urinate. [imitat; compare Eng *piddle*]

snier to cut [origin uncertain compare ON *sneið*, slice]

snifter* 1 the beginning of a head cold. 2 a light shower. [ME *snyfter* to snuffle]

snikker a suppressed laugh [variant of Eng *snigger*]

snippack see SNIPPO.

snippit quick of speech. [Sc has related meanings; Eng *snip*]

snippo*, snippack a snipe. [ON *snípa*]

snirko see SNEERKO.

snirl 1 verb. of a rope to twist. noun. a twist. [Eng *snarl* to tangle]

snirl 2* to twist the face, especially, *tae snirl up the nose*. [Eng *snarl* grimace]

snirpet bad tempered. [Norw *snurpe* a disagreeable person; Norw verb *snurpe* to purse the lips]

snit, sneet especially *a snit o a thing*, applied derisively to people or things. [ON *snýta* a worthless fellow]

snitlan nosing around like a little pig. [origin uncertain; ? a deriv of SNOOT = snout]

snitter 1 a twitch for a horse. [compare Eng dial *snittle* (to catch with) a noose]

snitter 2 *his face was in a snitter* he was cross. [compare Sc *snipper*; Norw *snyrpa* to wrinkle]

snod to remove the husks and awns from grain. **tae mak snod** to make tidy; especially to trim a stack of sheaves after building by 'pruning' it roughly with the hay fork. **snoddy** a thick bannock, '*A cloddy fire's a snoddy fire*' ie it is the right fire to bake *snoddies* on. [the essential meaning is 'cut short'; compare CUTTACK; ? related to OE *snaedan* to prune]

snog to cut. '*Snog thee noops*' cut your hair. [see SNUG]

snoo see SNUE.

snooie see SNU.

snooter to grumble. [origin uncertain]

snorry-bone a child's toy, a whirligig. [a bone from the leg of a pig was used for this purpose originally; as it turned it made a buzzing sound; compare Norw *snurrebass* whirligig; Norw *snurre* to whirl]

snouan a lazy lout [corruption of SLOOAN]

snoury irascible, literally *twisted*. [compare ILL-SNORED]

snow = snow. **snowfang** snowdrift [see FANN]. **snowflake** 1 = snowflake. 2* a snowbunting.

snu, snuie '*Hid gid a snu across the road*', of an animal shying at something, also used of the twist of an animal's head. [ON *snuðr* twist]

snue, snoo, snuian a kind of seaweed. [ON *snuðr* twist; compare Eng *tangle*, seaweed with the sense *twisted* or *tangled*]

snug, snog 1 cut short, especially of hair. 2 trim and tidy. 3 held close and firm. [ON *snöggr*]

snuian see SNUE.

snuid 1*, sneud 1 a knot. 2 a twist, '*Whit a snuid's in the back o that sheep*'. 3 the twist used in making ropes or straw simmons. *tae tak a snuid* to sulk. [ON *snuðr* twist]

snuid 2 a ribbon formerly used by females for tying up their hair. In Orkney as in Scotland it was a symbol of virginity. The *snuid* was burned as part of the wedding ritual in a ceremony known as the *sweeing o the snuid*. [OSc; OE *snod* fillet]

snuid 3 the name formerly used by boys in Stromness for a short piece of fishing line. [Eng *snood* the gut used to fix a hook to a line]

snuie see SNU.

snuik, sneuk a whim. *in the snuiks*, in the sulks. **sneuksie** bad tempered. [Norw *snøkk*]

snull 1 to scold. 2 treat with contempt. **snulled** 1 not allowed to assert oneself. 2 broken in spirit. **snulka** a turn of ill-temper. [origin unknown]

snupie sour or cross-grained. [probably related to Eng *snappy*; compare Norw dial *snipen* cross]

snurt = snort.

snushan expelling air noisily through the nose, '*I widna trust a snushan bull.*' snushan and sleepan, sleeping noisily. [Norw *snase* to snort; Norw dial *snus(s)a* to sniff]

snutter mucus from the nose. [OSc *snotter*; MDu *snoter*]

sny 1 a slice. [ON *sneið*]

sny 2 a white spot on a horse's face. **snyed, snyst** of a horse, having a white spot on the face. [see SNELL and SNEESHAN]

snyiffle of cheese, a small piece. [compare Eng *sniff*; Sc *sniff* a small amount]

snype *tae tak snype* to take offence. [Sc *snip* to take offence]

snyse a muzzle used on a calf or foal to prevent it sucking its mother. [Norw dial *sneis*]

snysin see SNEESHAN.

snyst see SNY 2.

snyth, snaith see SNEESHAN.

soam strong, *a soam rope*. [a *soam* in Sc was originally a strong rope or chain; related to ON *saumr* a sewing or join]

soap = soap. **soapy blots*** soapy water in which something has been washed. [ON *blautr* wet]

soddan a knot or entanglement. [Norw dial *soda* a muddle]

sogy 1 = soggy. 2 a mixture of oatmeal and buttermilk eaten uncooked.

sohod a call to a dog when driving cattle, '*Sohod da luskers*' was a call to a dog to drive off tramps. [compare *soho* the OE call used in hare coursing from which the Soho placenames in Birmingham and London may be derived]

soind to die slowly. [a form of SWOON]

solan goose the gannet. [ON *sula*; the *an* suffix is either a form of *ing* (compare SNEESHAN) or; perhaps *and*, duck; *duck* and *goose* are often used synonomously in the Teutonic languages; the gannet is neither!]

soldier 1 = soldier. 2* a stalk of plantain, used to 'play soldiers'. [see KEMPO]

sole = sole. **sole-buird** the board or plank next to the HASSENS in a boat. **sole stockings*** stocking soles. One of many inverted phrases in the dialect. [compare OOTSIDE-IN]

some 1 = some. 2* extraordinary [also Sc], used by the young in Orkney in a peculiar way, '*He's some man!*', '*That's some good!*'. **somewey** 1* somehow, '*He wis gotten this car somewey*'. 2 somewhere, '*He wis been somewey and fa'n in tow wi this lass.*'

soo* 1 sow (pig). 2 two peats propped against each other to dry. [Sc *soo* an oblong stack of hay; from its resemblance to a sow's back; compare GILT]. '*The soo's run across hid*' something has been spoiled or ruined e.g. a relationship. **soo boat** a small boat used to ply between ship and shore and usually towed behind on a journey. **soofish** = sowfish, the wrasse. [also Sc; see BERGEL].

soo shell the truncated gaper shell. Orkney shells were given animal names by children who used them for farm games.

sooans* oat flour slightly fermented. The inner husks of oats are soaked for some days then strained and the resultant paste is used for making special scones. **sooan scones*** very thin pancakes made from *sooans*. **sooan sids** *sooan* seeds. [Gael *sughan* from *sugh* juice]

soogle see SUGGLE.

sook 1 dry conditions. '*Hid's makkan a fine sook the day*' usually associated with a drying wind. [ON *súgr* a draught of wind]

sook 2 verb. to strike a blow. noun. a blow, (also **sooker**), '*He gid him a right sook on the side o the head*'. [a variation of Eng *sock* in the sense of *blow*]

sook 3 1 = suck. 2 a call to a calf. **sookie** a child's comforting blanket or rag.

sook 4 a call to cattle when driving them to get them to move on. [see SUCK 3]

sook 5 to dry (fish). *sookéd fish* dried fish. [ON *súga* to dry up]

sookan 1 a straw rope made of a single strand and twisted with a KRA-KRUIK. [Gael *sugan*; compare *simman*]

sookan 2 a feeble person. [also Sc *soukin (bairn)* a suckling]

sooken a district or population thirled to a mill. **sookener** 1 one thirled to a mill. It is said that in olden days when the roof of the Mill o Bea in Sanday required thatching this announcement was made in the Cross Kirk, '*Ye sookeners o the Mill o Bea, come tae her the morn wi simmons and strae*'. **Sookener** 2 a nickname for an inhabitant of Burness parish, Sanday. [also Sc; ON *sókn* parish; see SUCKEN 1]

sooker see SOOK 2.

sookie see SOOK 3.

soolka see SUILKIE.

soon to faint (for lack of food or drink). [OSc *sown* related to Eng swoon]

soond 1 a fish's swimming bladder. [Eng *sound*]

soond 2* a narrow stretch of water. [ON *sund*]

soond 3* = adj. sound, especially *no soond* not of sound mind.

soople that part of the flail which strikes the grain. [also Sc; a form of Eng *swipple* related to *swipe*]

soor* = sour. **soored cuithes** coalfish gutted, split and left for four days to sour before being eaten.

soorick, sooro sorrel or dock. [ON *súra* sorrel; the *ick* suffix is a dimin]

sooth 1 = south. 2 across the Pentland Firth, especially *aff sooth*, on the Scottish mainland or in England. **Sooth Country*** originally the land across the Pentland Firth (as in Dennison's story) now used only as an adj. in *Sooth Country folk*, particularly English people.

Sorrow the devil (the bringer of sorrow). **Sorrow dor!** a mild expletive. [also Sc; see DOREEN]

sot* a form of *so* used by children in an argument e.g. Child A: '*Dis not*', Child B: '*Dis sot*'. [also Sc].

soud payment for goods in kind. [Eng *sold* pay from Lat *solidus* a piece of money]

soulka see SUILKIE.

souming the number of animals which can be supported by a certain amount of grazing. [OSc *sowmoys*; Lat summa *sum*]

sove, shove 1 = shove. 2 to push or strike.

sowany a native ram with only one descended testicle. [ON *sauðr* sheep; Sh *hwini* immature ram and Du *kween* hermaphrodite]

sowdan an insult, '*Yi lazy sowdan*'. [Sh *sowdan* a fat person; Eng *sultan*]

sowder* solder. [OF *soudre* to make solid]

sowled taken aback. [? Sc *sowl* to pull roughly by the ears]

sower to sow. [? a running together of *sow* and *scatter*]

spaek* speak. **spaekan proper*** attempting to speak a standard Eng but with affectation. **tae spaek in bye** to call in for a chat.

spaekalation a subject for gossip, '*Whit a spaekalation hid wid be if I wir seen oot wi yir wife*'. [Eng *speculation* with the obs meaning 'making conjectures about']

spaen to wean a baby or animal. [Sc *spean*; ME *spane*]

spaiter to use with care. [origin uncertain]

spalder of an animal, to sprawl [also Sc OSc *spald* to sprawl]

spang 1 a long step. [OSc *spang* to spring]

spang 2 *spang new* completely new. [Eng *span-new*]

spanky a *spanky o pens*, a feather duster. [Sc *spang* to grasp]

spann† an old legal measure of butter. [ON *smjör-spann* a measure of butter where *spann* had the original meaning *bucket*]

spare 1 a slit or opening in a skirt. [also Sc; Norw *spjerre* to tear]

spare 2 = spare. '*If wir etc spared*', God willing, '*We'll go tae the toon the morn if wir spared*'. An old story is told of the little boy who asked his mother if they would have cake to eat on Christmas Day. '*If wir spared*,' replied the mother. '*And if wir no spared*,' the little boy enquired, '*will we just hiv binnacks?*'

spark 1 = spark. 2 to spatter something with mud or

dirt 3 to fork dung out of a cart into a drill while the cart is in motion.

spaver a trouser fly. [also Sc; a form of SPARE]

spawl *black spawl* an old time disease of cattle, attacking the shoulders, supposedly brought about by too much running. [OSc *spauld* shoulder (of meat)]

speeder* spider. [also Sc; OSc *speidder* a spider]

speelings wood shavings. [see SPELL]

speer* to enquire. '*Yi'll hae tae speer the bung o the tar barrel*' a retort to an impertinent question. [also Sc; OE *spyrian*; ON *spyria*]

speet a stick on which KUITHES are dried. [a form of Eng *spit*]

speld, spell, spieldo a small piece of land. [see SPELDER]

spelder to split. [also Sc; Norw *spildre* to splinter]

spelkie verb. of a broken limb, to set in splints. noun. a splint. [Sc spelk; ON *spelkja*]

spell 1 a small bar used to keep the pulling chains of the plough apart and prevent them chafing the horse's legs. [Sc *spaid*; ON *spölr* bar]

spell 2 see SPELD.

spell 3 a spile.

spell 4* verb. to take a turn at work, '*Ah'll spell yi noo*'. noun. 1 = spell of time. 2 a period of hard work.

spellye see SPULLYIE.

spenye bamboo cane used for catching KUITHES and SILLOCKS. [with the original sense *Spanish* from the West Indies; also Sc in the sense *bamboo cane*]

speug a sparrow [Norw *spikke*]

speun = spoon. **speun cubby** a small container made of straw for holding spoons. [see CUBBY]

spew = spew. **spewings*** vomit, '*The bairns claes wis just covered wi spewings*'.

spick 1 pork fat. [ON *spik* blubber]

spick 2 poor cabbage. [ON *spík* spike]

spicko a big limpet. [possibly 'fat' limpet; ON *spik* blubber]

spieldo see SPELD.

spin of a cat, to purr, preserved in the old rhyme:-
Cat i the mill door, spinnan, spinnan
By cam a peerie moose, rinnan, rinnan
(the rest of the rhyme, like the fate of the mouse, is unknown!) [compare Norw *spinne* to purr, literally to make the sound of a spinning wheel]

spirl, spurl a spatula used in cooking. [a contraction of Sc *spurtle*]

spleet-new* brand new. [also Sc; compare Norw **splitter-ny;** the sense is *new as if split (open)* of a log for example]

spleuchan 1 a leather purse. 2 skin purses made by Red Indians. 3 an article of wood or wire hanging on the wall and having compartments for letters. [Gael *spliuchan* purse]

splint new completely new [see SPLEET NEW]

splushney a catapult. [also in the form PLUSHNEY; imitat., compare Sh *and-plush* a gust of wind]

spo to foretell. [ON *spá;* compare Sc *spae-wife*]

spoag 1* noun 1 a spoke of a wheel etc. 2 a leg. *tae spoag along* to walk stiff legged. [compare Eng pin for *leg*; a form of Eng *spoke*]

spoag 2 a jest. *tae cast spoags at.* [Norw *spok*]

sponses nostrils. [also Sc; Norw *spuns* a bung(-hole) in a barrel]

sponyalt a long legged boy. [origin uncertain ? related to SPANG]

spoor otter excrement. [ON *spor* track]

spoot* 1 spout. 2 razor fish. [also Sc; it *spoots* (spouts) water out through its hole in the sand. 3 a rain gutter under the eaves of a house. 4 lemonade. **spoot whale** a porpoise. **spoot ebb*** '*There should be a good spoot-ebb the night*', in the spring of the year the sea ebbs far out and allows *spoots* to be caught. **spoot girse** angelica, cow parsley, used by young boys for making water squirts. **spootricks** butter softened in the mouth before it is applied to bread. An old story known throughout Orkney tells of the herdie boy taking shelter in a house who was offered a biscuit and butter by an old lady. She gave him the choice of *toomspread* or *spootricks*. He did not know what spootricks was but looking at her dirty hands he decided that the new method could not be worse than butter spread by her thumb!]

spous energy or drive. to have *spous*. [related to POUST]

spout whale see SPOOT.

spraag to swagger [also Sh; origin uncertain; ?related to SPRAAGLE]

spraagle, spragle to flounder about when stuck in mud for example or to slither around like a cow on a slippery byre floor. [Sc *sprauchle*; ON *sprokla* to sprawl]

spraenge to sprinkle. [OE *sprengan*]

spragle see SPRAAGLE.

sprak a splinter of wood. [ON *sprek* a stick also used of small bits of driftwood]

sprangle to sprawl. [see SPRAAGLE]

spree 1 = spree. 2 to go courting. 3 of an animal to be in heat.

spret 1* verb. 1 to jump quickly, '*Whit a fleg I got whin this man spret oot o the ditch*'. 2 to burst, especially of a seam, '*Mercy Ah'm spret the erse o me breeks again*'. 3 to open the bottom of a pannier on a horse's back. noun. 1 a jump. 2 a wooden pin used to close the pannier on a horse's back. **spretto** 1 a turf of peat. 2 a footless stocking with a loop to fix over the toe next to the big

116

toe. [ON *spretta* to leap or of a seam to burst]

sprig a little nail used in cobblery. [ON *sprek* a stick]

spring verb. 1 = spring. 2 strain, '*Watch and no spring theesel wi liftan that weyt (weight)*'. 3 of milk in the butter making process to coagulate. 4 to burst. **springan** in a state of agitation to go to the toilet, '*My Ah'm just springan*'. noun. = Spring. *in the Spring o the 'ear (year)* in Springtime, (this is the only season referred to in this way).

sproll a rod of iron bent into a bow. Between the ends of this bow is stretched a piece of gut with fish hooks attached. [? Sc *sprewl* to sprawl from the shape]

sproosit spotted (of sheep). **sproostie** mottled. [? related to Ger *sprosse* freckle]

sprullyo a heavy fall, *tae go doon in a sprullyo*. [Eng *sprawl*]

sprunk see SPUNK.

spullyie 1 destruction. 2 anything destroyed. **spullyiereef** robbery, only recorded in this sense, '*Hid's weel kent she got her man by spullyiereef*' she allowed herself to become pregnant to her lover. [compare Sc *stouthrief* theft; *reef* is ON *reyfa* to rob, hence both elements mean approximately the same thing]. **spulyo** driftwood.

spulyaw a fight or quarrel. [OSc *spulye* to plunder; OF espuille *spoil*]

spunder verb. to run briskly or to gallop. noun. a run, '*Tak a spunder tae Jessie's for a gren o tea tae me will thoo*'. **spundery** long legged. [Sc *spinner*; a form of SPIN]

spunk*, sprunk a spark of fire. **spunkies** distant flashes of lightning with no sound of thunder (also known as WEATHER BLINKS). **spunko** an electric torch (also known as a PLICKO). [OSc *sponk* a spark]

spurl see SPIRL.

spurlwheep lean and hard grown [Norw *spirl* long thin figure; ON *óp* a crying probably in the sense 'moaning' here]

spurry 1 a footless stocking. [ON *spjörr* swathing band]

spurry 2 1 an earwig. 2 any fast moving insect. [Norw dial *spora* to run away]

spurry-girse cow parsnip. [related to Eng *spurrey*]

sputcher a wooden vessel for baling a boat. [origin unknown]

squander to stagger from side to side. [a special development in meaning of Eng *squander* to roam; see SWANDER]

square tree a game played in Sanday similar to pulling the SWEERIE stick but the stick was held aloft and the challenger was required to twist the stick and touch one end on the ground.

squirm see SKWIRM.

squizz to question someone secretly. [compare WHIZZ]

staan, stan noun. a loud earnest cry. adj. 1 *a staan race* running at full speed. 2 *the stan huid* the very middle of the night. [ON *standa* to last]

stab* a fencing post. [Eng *stob* pillar, post etc]

stabble to wobble, *tae go stabblan along*. [origin uncertain; compare Sc *stachle stacher*; ON *stakra*]

stack a tall column of rock rising out of the sea. [Faer *stakkur*]

stael* = steal. past tense STELT*. past part STELT*. (formerly STOWN†)

staff 1 = a staff. 2 a walking stick [also Sc.] When Lord Kitchener and his staff (assistants) were lost off Birsay in World War I, an old gentleman said he could understand the concern about the loss of this great man but he did not know why such a fuss was being made about the loss of his walking stick!]

staig a stallion. [Eng stag; compare ON *steggi* a male bird]

staincheon = stanchion.

stamman inclined to steal. [origin unknown]

stan see STAAN.

stand = stand. **standing stone*** a monolith [also Sc]. **standing bands** the chains or ropes for tying cattle in a byre

stane, steen a stone. '*He's liftan a stone tae brak his ain head wi*' what he is doing will ruin him. **staneputter, steenie-pouter** the turnstone. [OE *putian* to push]. **steenie-picker** the sand-piper. **steeniger, steenikyerro** a house or building in ruins. [see KYERRO]

stang 1 the point of a needle. [ON *stanga* to prick]

stang 2 part of the beam of the old Orkney plough. **stangigal** ill-thriving (of a calf etc). [ON *stöng* a beam]

stank 1 verb. to bury. noun. a ditch. [also Sc; OF *estanc* a pond from Lat *stagnum* pond]

stank 2 to drizzle heavily. [compare Norw **det stoenker** it is drizzling]

stap* = stop, to cram. 1 to pack in firmly, '*Stap hid aal in the barrel beuy*' sometimes used jocularly of food, '*Stap hid in beuy*'. 2 a dish consisting of cod's head stuffed with meal [also Sc]. *stappéd fill tae the tongue root* very full.

stappal 1 a short stout figure. [Norw dial *stapall*]

stappal 2 a stopper. [see STAP 1]

star 1 = star. 2 a speck on the eye. 3 a cataract

stark 1 = stark. 2 intense, furious (of e.g. a snowstorm), *a stark moor*.

starn 1* stern of a boat [also Sc]

starn 2 1 a star. 2 a small speck or quantity. **starned** of a horse having a blaze or star on its forehead.

starnlight starlight. **starnoo** an animal with a

117

white patch on the forehead. [also Sc; ON *stjarna*]

stash to finish. [origin unknown]

stathel a support for a stack. [OE *staðol*]

stathy steady. [compare *lathy* for *lady*]

stave = stave. *tae fa in the staves* to fall to pieces (like an old barrel)

steb* only in compounded forms *steb-mither*, *steb-sister* etc. [also Sh; a form of Eng *step*]

steck to walk determinedly, '*Whar are thoo steckan tae the day?*' [Sc *staik*; Norw dial *staka*]

steeding a group of farm buildings, *the steeding o Binscarth*. [Sc *steading*]

steek *tae steek the door* to jamb the latch of a door with a knife etc. [also Sc; OSc *steke* to shut a gate]

steel = steel. *no steel tae the back* dishonest.

steel-bow a form of land tenancy whereby the landlord provided the stock and implements which had to be returned at the end of a lease. [also Sc; Eng *steel* used figuratively; something strong or fixed + *bow*; see BOW]

steem-stan undecided. [compare STIMMIS]

steen see STANE.

steep a kind of peat with heather on. [compare Norw dial *styva* to pare (turf)]

steer 1 = steer. **steer-pin** a pin joining the stilt to the beam of the old Orkney plough.

steer 2*, **steero*** 1 confusion, '*Whit a steero we were in whin the visitors cam*'. 2 rotten rock on a quarry site used by children for marking slates or used in the smithy for marking iron. [OSc *stere* commotion]

steethe the foundation of a haystack etc. [ON *staðr* position (of something)]

steeve rigid [also Sc]. **steeve still** stock still. *tae go steeve on tae* to do directly. [OSc *steve* to strengthen related to Eng *stiff*]

stein-biter the lump sucker. [ON *stein-bítr*]

steine† a court or place of assembly. [see HIRDMANSTEIN; ON *stefnu-staðr* meeting place]

stelt see STAEL.

stem strength or vigour. [compare Faroese *stimbur* strength]

stensel† an iron bar fitted to a window. [OSc *stanchel*; Eng *stanchion*]

stent 1† a type of tax e.g. *butter stent* [Sc through OF *estente* valuation]

stent 2 limit. '*That's me stent for the day*'. [OSc *stent* limit; Eng *stint*]

sterk strong, robust [see STARK]

stewart† a sheriff. **Stewartry†** the area over which a Stewart had jurisdiction. The *Stewartry* of Orkney and Shetland existed until the 19th century. [OSc *stewart* a steward]

stick = to stick. *tae tak the stick** to refuse to move (e.g. of an animal). **stick in*** to persevere, to apply oneself [also Sc]. '*Stick in noo!*' eat up, a phrase used at table. [Eng *tuck in*]. **stickéd*** of a person, animal, the wind etc determined or perverse, '*That's a stickéd thing o coo that*'. **stickéd stoor** blinding snow which sticks to clothing.

stickle horn part of a cow horn fixed to the gunwale of a boat to prevent abrasion of the fishing line. [ON *stikill* the pointed end of a horn]

stig to walk determinedly, '*Whar are thoo stiggan tae the day?*'. [ON *stiga* to step]

stiggle poor straw or stalk of grain. **stigglin** poor quality crop. **stiggly** *stiggly straw*, of grain poor quality. [Norw dial *stikla* stubble]

stiggy a starling. [ON *styggr*, of birds and animals, easily scared; compare SKARR]

stilder, stildery see STILTER.

still-stand an example of an inverted phrase. [Eng *stand-still*; compare OOTSIDE-IN]

stilt 1 = stilt. 2 an elevated foundation for a corn stack (Birsay). 3 the handle of a plough.

stilter, stilder to totter. **stiltery, stildery** tottering. [Norw *stiltre* to stumble or walk stiffly]

stime* a haze. **stimmy** foggy. '*I couldna see a stime*' I could see nothing. **stiman*** '*He wis just stiman*' very drunk and walking as if blind. [compare Sh *stimba* a thick fog]

stimmis a quandary, as *in a stimmis* in a quandary. [also Sc; Norw *stim* disorder, tumult; related to STIME above]

stimless powerless, especially of numb hands. [see STEM]

stimmer 1 = to stammer.

stimmer 2 to stumble. [ON *stumra* to stumble]

stimmis see STIME 1.

stimmy to faint. [probably related to STIME 1]

stin to groan. **stinyan** groaning. [ON *stynja* to groan]

sting = sting. **stingy-bee*** a wild bee.

stinkie-buil wheatear. [Sc *stinkie* wheatear and stonechat; Icel *steindepill* wheatear]

stirk, strik a young ox or cow. [OE *stirc* calf]

stirling* a starling [also Sc]. **stirling snow** stormy, snowy weather in May when starlings congregate. [compare TEEICK SNOW, LAMBING SNOW]

stith† an anvil. [Eng *stithy*; ON *steði*]

stiv strong and stout [see STEEVE]

stivval solid and substantial. [see STEEVE]

stivven to freeze with the cold or congeal. [Norw *stivne* to stiffen]

stoak see STOOK 4.

stob verb. to dress or trim a stack with a fork to make the ends tidy. noun. remains of feathers on a plucked hen. **stobby** prickly. [OSc *stub* a stake

118

etc; a variation of Eng *stub*]

stock 1 a block of wood. 2 an old wizened person. **stock duck*** the mallard [Norw *stockkand*]. **stock owl** the eagle owl [also Sc]. **stock-whaup** the curlew. **stock, lock and barrel** an example of many transposed phrases in the dial. [Eng *lock, stock and barrel*; compare SOLE-STOCK-ING]

stockéd used of an animal with severe indigestion. [OSc *stokkit* obstinate]

stocking = stocking. **stocking feet*** '*He wis gan aboot in his stocking feet*' with no shoes on. [also Sc; compare SOLE-STOCKING]

stogal 1 strong and sturdy. 2 slow and stupid. [see STUGGAL]

stoing see STOND.

stoit to talk rubbish. [see STOT 1]

stokblind completely blind [ON *stokkr*, a log; ON *blindr*, blind; compare Eng *as deaf as a post*]

stoll to walk with difficulty. [Norw *stulle* to trudge along]

stomach 1 = stomach. 2* appetite, '*Ah'm fairly lost me stomach*' I have completely lost my appetite. **stomachless** having no appetite.

stond, stoing a tidal current setting in a certain direction. [ON *standa* to come from a certain direction (of the wind etc)]

stone 1 = stone. 2 a testicle. **stone-chat** a wheatear [also Sc]

stoo, styoo verb. to cut off, especially of hair. noun. a sheep's mark, the tip of the ear clipped off. **stoo and bits** a sheepmark. **stooed hemlin** half the ear cut off at a slant. **stooed rip** a slit made in the ear after the point has been cut off. [also Sc; ON *stýfa* to cut off]

stook 1 a sheepmark. [STOO + dimin *ick*]

stook 2† part of a church with its own altar. [a metaphorical use of ON *stúka* sleeve]

stook 3* a group of six sheaves set up in a field to dry. **stookie Sunday** the Sunday when the greatest number of stooks were to be seen in the fields. [also Sc and NE; OSc *stouk* a shock of corn; MLGer *stuke* a bundle of flax]

stook 4, **stookie, stoak** a straw *barrel* which held three or four sackfuls of grain. [ON *stokkr* trunk or chest but compare Gael *suigean* straw barrel]

stoon *Stoon fa me!* Goodness me! literally 'blow fell me!' [compare Eng *blow me*; ME *stund* to stupify]

stoondery walking in a clumsy manner. [see STUNDER]

stoondriment see STUNDER.

stoondy see STOUND.

stoop 1* 1 Be quiet! 2 You don't mean it! used as a reaction to an unbelievable piece of news. '*Stoop-cootch!*' a command to a dog to lie down.

[Eng *stop*; compare HOOP, West Mainland pronunciation of 'hope']

stoop 2 *door-stoop* a door jamb. *every stoop and roop* everything. **stoopéd bed** a four poster bed. [OSc *stoup* a post; ON *stolpe* a pillar]

stoor 1 verb. to move quickly* '*He fairly stoored doon the road*'. noun. 1 dust [also Sc]. 2 a mixture of oatmeal and water for quenching thirst.

stoories a mixture of oatmeal and buttermilk boiled together. [Sc *sturoch*; OF estour *tumult*]

stoor 2 strong and robust. [ON *stórr*].

Stoorworm (The) a sea-monster of Orkney folk-lore. [ON *storð*, (the earth, in poetry); *ormr* serpent; compare Old Norse *Storðar-gandr*, the world serpent also known as *Jörmun-gandr*]

stoot* = stout. **stootly** very, *stootly trowie* very ill.

stop 1 = stop. 2* to live or dwell, '*We stoppéd in a caravan till the roof wis mended*'.

storm-finch the stormy petrel. [also Sc]

stot 1 verb. to stutter. noun. a stutter. [also Sc; Norw *stote* or *stotre*]

stot 2* to reel about because of tiredness or drunkeness, '*He wis so drunk he wis just stotan along the street*'. [also Sc; OSc *stot* a bounce]

stot 3* a bullock. [also Sc and NE dial; compare ON *stútr* an ox, bull]

stouie a fisherman's buoy. [Sc *stoy*; Gael *stuthaidh* a marker bouy]

stound, stoond a mood or whim. **stoundy** moody. [also Sc; OE *stund* a period of time, a time of distress]

stounkie see STUNKY.

stoved *stoved in* bashed or dented. [Sc *stave* to hit with a stick, past tense **stove**, recorded also in Aberdeenshire]

stow 1 = stow (away). 2 shut up! [Eng slang *Stow it!*]. **stowed** satisfied, '*Me thirst's stowed noo*'.

stowers the tall reeds in Bea Loch, Sanday. [Eng dial *stower* pole. ON *staurr* a stake]

stown see STAEL.

stows the outline of a person or object, '*I saa the stows o him as he geed ower the hill*'. [see SKOWS]

strack see STRICK.

strae = straw. **strae buits** straw ropes wound round the legs to keep them warm, '*Yi canna draa a strae across thy baird the day*' he is in no mood for teasing. **strae/straa backéd stuil** the correct name for an Orkney chair.

strae-fuff see FUFF.

straffans rags. [see STRAPHAN]

straik 1 1 to stretch. 2 to lay out the dead [also Sc]. *tae straik graith* to stretch the harness, the name given to the ritual associated with ploughing the first furrow. In Birsay, urine was poured over the plough before ploughing commenced.

119

straik 2 1 to stroke. 2 to harrow. *straik o the harrows* once round the field with the harrows.

stram a state of excitement especially to accomplish some task, '*Whit a stram he was in*' [a clipped form of Sc *stramash*]

stramash a crash, a loud noise. [also Sc;.origin uncertain]

stramp verb. to tread or stamp [also Sc]. noun. a step, especially '*Ah'm no gan wan feet stramp*' I'm not going at all. [OSc *stramp* to tread]

strang adj. strong. noun. urine. [also Sc]. **strang bing** a vessel for holding human urine. **strang pig** a jar for holding human urine.

straphan 1 lining of the bowels. 2 thin skin. **striffan** a tough fibre in meat or vegetables [Sc *striffin*, a membrane, eME striffen]

straps = 1 straps. 2 braces

stravaig to wander. [also Sc; EF *extravaguer* from MLat *extravagare* to wander outside (the bounds)]

streamers† an old name for the MERRY DANCERS [also Sc].

strebogie an uproar, '*Whit a strebogie when her man cam home!*'. [origin uncertain; compare Sc *stramash* and similar forms]

streen (the) last night. [a corruption of Eng *yestreen* itself a shortened form of *yester-evening*; the use of the definite article *the* is modelled on *the day*, today *the morn*, etc]

street a jet of milk from a cow's teat. [compare Norw dial *stritla* to spray right and left]

streetle to go askew. [compare STREET above]

stret of an animal in poor condition, '*Feth that lamb's gey stret*'. **strett** tight (of e.g. a jersey across the chest). [OSc *strait* narrow, tightly drawn; ME; OF *estreit* narrow]

stretch = stretch. *stretch yir staff*, help yourself

streuntan strutting. [Sc *strunt*; Norw dial *strunta* to strut]

streunty anything long and thin or stretched out. [Sc *strunt*]

strick* = strike. past tense. **strack*.** perfect tense. **striken*.**

stridelegs* with legs apart, *tae sit stridelegs on a horse.* [also Sc; Eng *astride*]

striffan see STRAPHAN

strik see STIRK.

strikyar a gale of wind. [ON *strykr* gust of wind]

strill the starling. [a shortened metathesis of *stirling*]

string a narrow strip of water. [ON *strengr.* **The String** is the channel between Shapinsay and The Mainland]

stringer a strip of wood on which a boat seat rests. [ON *strengr* strip]

strip 1 = a strip. 2* a stripe [also Sc]. 3 a young fellow. **strippéd*** striped.

stripe to milk a cow. **strippings** last drops of milk from a cow. [also Sc and Eng dial; compare Dan and Swed dial *strippa* to draw off the last drops of milk]

strip-wind an addled egg. [compare Eng *wind-egg* addled egg with ON *stropað* bad egg; *wind* is used here in the sense 'turn(ed)'; compare WENTED]

striv the strain on a fishing line caused by the tide. [compare Norw *strev* striving, strain]

stromalty 1 difficulty. 2 a state of excitement. [? a corruption of Eng *extremity*]

stron a beach. [ON *strönd*]

stront, struint a long thin individual. [see STREUNTY]

strontamou a very sad person. [Sc *strunt* to sulk + *mou* = mouth; compare TRUTMULLED]

strood 1 a suit of clothes. 2 a set of sails. 3 a set of knitting needles, *a strood o needles*. [Sc has related meanings; ON *skruð* apparel, tackle or gear]

stroop* 1 the spout of a kettle or teapot [also Sc]. 2 jocularly a boy's penis. [compare Norw *strut* a spout or Norw dial *strupe* throat]

stroupie a teapot [see STROOP]

stroosh *in a stroosh* in a stressful hurry. [also Sc; origin uncertain]

struint see STRONT.

strunge rancid or generally disagreeable to taste. [Sc *strounge*; origin uncertain; compare Norw *strang* acrid]

studdle a small child. [ON *stuðill* a post; a reference to the shape]

studel a small frame used for winding up a fishing line. [see STUDDLE]

stugg to thicken a mixture. [compare Norw dial *stokka* to stiffen]

stuggal, stuggy of a person stout. [ME *stug* cut short]

stugger verb. to speak loudly to children. noun. a thick-set person. [compare Sc *stug* an intractable person; see STUGGAL]

stuggy see STUGGAL.

stuian a boat NOUST. [ON *stoð* landing place or berth with definite article suffixed]

stuil* 1 a chair. 2 a matted bed of grass or weeds. [ON *stoll* a chair, Eng dial *stool* chair]

stullyan walking feebly. [see STOLL]

stum dumb, mute. [compare Norw *stum* dumb]

stummer to stumble. [ON *stumra*]

stumsht stupified [also Sh; compare Norw. *stum, dumb*]

stunder verb. 1 to astonish. 2 to walk as if half asleep. noun. a whim, fancy. **stundery*** moody. **stundriment, stunderimp, stoonderment** a whim, irregularity, '*Best kens whit's happened the tractor, hid's some kind o stundriment hid's* *taen'*. [a form of STOUND]

stung dull or stupid. [see STUM]

stunky stupid, slow-witted. **stounkie** a stupid person. [see STUM]

stunyan groaning, *'The baest wis lyan stunyan in the ditch'*. [see STIN]

sturken, sturten to thicken, to congeal. [ON *storkna*]

sturt to gct underway. **sturtensome** easy to start, though used negatively, *'No very sturtensome'*. [Sc *sturt* to disturb; OSc *sturt* quarreling]

sturten see STURKEN.

stymie hole a cesspool. [origin uncertain; compare STIME mist ? hence vapour]

styoo see STOO.

styuilk a pejorative reference to a youth or man, *a muckle styuilk*. [Norw *stulk* a clumsy person]

such*, suck to bury young cabbage plants until they are ready to plant in drills; the *ch* is pronounced as in *loch*. [also Sc; ME *sogh* a furrow]

sucherin a small amount, a part payment in kind. [a form of Eng *succouring*]

suck* 1 1 a mess, a quagmire 2 a dirty person. **sucky** dirty. [Norw *søkkje*; ON *sukk* muddle, mess]

suck 2 straw or withered grass in a hen's nest in particular but also under an animal.(A VANMAN once said *'This weeman'll hiv tae pit a gren more suck in the nests fur A'hm gittan far too many broken eggs'* [origin uncertain; ON *súgr* a drying wind but also compare Gael *seac* to wither]

suck 3 = 1 seek. 2 a call to a dog to incite it to attack.*'Seek a haud!'* was another such call.

suck 4 see SUCH.

sucken* 1 1 exorbitant, *a sucken price*. 2 tied, bound or restricted in some way. 3 in debt. [see SOOKEN]

sucken* 2 1 sunk, *'His eyes wir just sucken in his head'*. 2 marshy, especially *sucken hole* used to describe the situation of a farm etc. [also Sc; compare DRUKKEN]

sucko a call to a calf. [Eng *suck* + *o*]

suckou a calming call to a cow while it is being milked. [compare SUCKO]

sucky see SUCK 1.

suddle to soil, especially clothes. [also Sc; MLoGer *sudeln*]

sugarally liquorice. [also Sc; OSc *sukker lagrace* liquorice]

sugg 1 a piece of hardened skin on the body. [Sc *sigg*; ON *sigg]*

sugg 2 1 to labour under a heavy load. 2 a fat woman. [Norw *sugg* a strong animal or person]

suggle 1 = suckle. 2 to draw liquid into the mouth by sucking. 3 to drink noisily.

suggse a mess in a byre. **suggsy** of a cow, dirty. [ON *söggr*, wet + GIS]

suggy wet, damp. [see SUGGSE]

sug-sug a call to cattle. [see SUCK 1]

suilkie 1 a mass of something with a hint of disorder. 2 one's usual environment. 2 the circle of the horizon as far as the eye can see. [Norw *sulke* to dirty or soil; 2 and 3 are ex tended meanings; the nearest Eng equivalent is *dump* or *stamping ground*; compare KLOGANG]

suisto 1 a violent noise or movement. 2 the noise made by something falling from a height. [Sc *souse*; MHiGer *sus* noise]

suistoo look! [Eng *sees thou?*; also Sc and Eng dial; see SESTUNA]

suit* = to suit. *'You suit that colour'*, that colour suits you.

suize to grasp. [? Eng *seize*]

sullar see SALOR.

sulvendo see SALVENDO.

sulyo a conglomeration of filth. [Norw *saula* mud, mire]

summer-whaup the whimbrel, also known as the MAY BIRD.

sun = sun. **sun-sitten** of eggs, addled and spoiled by the heat of the sun

superior duty feu duty. [another name for SKAT; OSc *superior* a person who has made a grant of land in feu to another]

supper = supper. verb. to feed cattle or horses at night [also Sc], *'Ah'll come in when Ah'm suppered the horse'*. **supper shaef** the last sheaf brought into the cornyard at harvest time.

suppose 1 = suppose. 2 to be required to, *'Yir supposed tae dae that'* [also Sc]. 3 even if, *'Suppose I hid (had) aal the money in the world I widna dae hid'*.

surgis a filthy mess. [ON *saurr* excrement etc. + GIS]

surt verb. to boil gently. noun. a thick porridge. **surto** 1 a winter well. 2 a bog [Norw *surre* to simmer; when applied to a well or bog, it means 'to bubble'; compare SUY]

surto see SURT.

suy to boil, especially *suyan and boilan*. [ON *sjóða* to boil]

swaa, swarr the sound of the sea in the distance on a fine day. [ON *svarri* to grumble]

swaar 1 see SWAA.

swaar 2 the middle of the night. [ON *svart-naetti* the black night]

swabble to walk through thick mud, *'He wis just swabblan in the neep field'* [origin uncertain]

swack* 1 of a person, fit or agile. [also Sc and Sh]. 2 weak from hunger. 3 of an animal, in good condition. 3 of a boat, unstable. [compare Flem *zwak*; Ger *schwach* weak]

swadge* especially in this sense *'Thoo'll hae tae swadge noo efter thee denner'* You'll have to sit

121

down and relax. [a form of Eng *assuage*]

swalkyan see SWALT 1.

swall to swell. [also Sc; OSc *swall* to swell]

swalt 1 1 to be starving. 2 to die or become weak. **swalkyan** starving. [ON *svelta* to die]

swalt 2 verb. to swallow. noun. a gulp. **swalty** a bellyful, generally of drink. [ON *svelgja* to swallow]

swander* a lurch, *'Good, the powny tuk a swander tae the wall'*. **swandery** unsteady, *'Watch that coffee table for the legs are kinda swandery'*. [see SQUANDER]

swankee *'Thoo'll git a good price fur that baest, I swankee'*. [a corruption of *'I'se warran thee'*; see SWARAN and WARRAN]

swap* 1 a gust of wind. [ON *sveipr* a sudden stir]

swap 2 1 the sweep of a scythe. 2 **tae swap aaks** to catch auks by sweeping a special net over the cliff face. [a form of Eng *sweep*]

swap 3 to match, especially of patterns or colours. [also Sc; Norw dial *sveipa* to resemble]

swap 4 to cast a fishing line. [ON *svipta* to throw or fling]

swaran completely or absolutely, *swaran free*. [Eng *sworn* under oath]

swarbie the black-backed gull. [Sh *swabie*; see SWARTBACK]

swarfarro black headed gull. [also known as RITTO; ON *svartr* black; the second element represents *tarrock* the tern or kittiwake; ON *svart-hofði* the black headed gull]

swarfish the spotted blenny. [see SWIRDO]

swarp a faint. [Sc *swarf*; ON *svarfa* to overturn]

swarral a large object. [related to Norw *svare* big or tremendous]

swart a large tangle. [Sc *swart-head* edible part of the head of a large tangle; see SWARRAL]

swartback the black backed gull. [ON *svart-bakr*]

swash* a quantity of liquid, *'Gae me a swash o tea'*. *'A great swash o water cam ower the side'*. [also Sc; imitat]

swathes the roe in male cod. [origin uncertain; perhaps related to SWILL 2]

swattle a dirty mess [also Sc]. *swattle o dirt* used for example to describe an uninteresting television programme. [a variant of Sc *swatter*; imitat]

swee 1* 1 to smart (e.g. of a hurt finger), especially from a burn. 2 of a crop on shallow soil, to burn. 3 to singe feather remains on a plucked hen etc. 4 **the sweean o the snuid** the ceremonial burning of the SNUID before the couple were officially married. [see SNUID 2] 5 to warm oneself in front of the fire. 6 **in a swee** in a stressful hurry. **swee-iron, sweeo-iron** a wire (with a wooden handle) heated red hot and used for making the holes in a calf-skin riddle. This type

of riddle was used for separating the SUDS from the meal after grinding on the quern. [ON *sviða* to burn or smart]

swee 2 of a kettle to sing. [imitat]

sweeg 1 of a barrel to leak. [Sc *sweege*; Norw dial *svikja* to leak]

sweeg 2 to bend or to pull at right angles on a rope. [ON *sveigja* to bend]

swee-iron see SWEE.

sweenkie see SWINKY.

sweenkle, swink when the stomach is full of liquid it is said to *sweenkle*. [Norw *skvinkla* to splash]]

sweeo-iron see SWEE.

sweep = sweep. **sweepings*** dust swept together in a pile. **sweepit, sweepid** the least little bit, *no a sweepit left*.

sweer lazy, reluctant or niggardly. [also Sc; related to Ger *schwer* difficult]

sweerie-stick, swera-tree a stick used in an old game. This trial of strength was called *pullan (pulling) the sweerie-stick*. The contestants sat on the floor facing each other with their feet against their partner's feet and pulled with both hands at a stick held at right angles to their arms. [also Sc; see SWEER]

sweero a box used when twining homespun wool. It had a wire across the top for holding reels. [probably Sc *sweir* lazy that is in the sense of saving work]

sweert used in this sense, *'Ah'm sweert tae layve yi'*. [OSc *swere* lazy or reluctant]

sweet = sweet. **sweetbed** in the process of making malt for brewing, the sprouting grain is piled in a heap and left till it takes heat. In this stage the grain becomes sweet to taste, hence *sweetbed*. **sweet-milk** cow's milk as distinct from sour milk.

sweetie-fole a kind of parkin biscuit sprinkled with sugar-coated carraway seeds. [see FOLE]

sweevle, sweevy a short sharp gust of wind. [also Sc; ON *sveifla* to turn]

Swelchie see SWILKIE.

swelt see SWALT.

sweratree a form of SWEERIE-STICK tree.

swero a winter well, one which dries in the summer. [see SURT and SUY]

swets the water in which SOOANS have been soaked, used to make a kind of beer. [OE *swatan* plural, beer]

swick* verb. to swindle. noun. 1 a swindle. 2 a swindler. [ON *svíkja* to cheat]

swilkie, swelchie a whirlpool; a famous whirlpool in the Pentland Firth is known as *The Swilkie*. [ON *svelgr*]

swill 1 part of a tether. Even hens were tethered at one time, the hen *swill* generally being made of leather, the animal swill, of wood. [a form of Eng *swivel*]

swill 2 milt in fish, especially cod. [Icel *svil* plural]

swill 3 1 = swill. 2* a quick wash, '*Gae yir face a swill*'.

swilter, swiller, switter to shake and splash (e.g. of water in a bucket). [compare Norw dial *skvitra* to splash]

swin see SKWIN.

swine = swine. '*They're aal the same swine-spik*' they're all the same flesh and blood. **swine-beads** the tall oat grass. [Eng *beads* a reference to the tubers; also known as POOTY-BUTTIES where POOTY is pig]. **swine-fish** the wolf fish. **swine-saem** pig grease, used in the olden days for styling the hair. [see SAEM 1]

swingan a *swingan drought* when everything dries very hard. [a form of Eng *swingeing*]

swingle-tree see SWITHER-TREE.

swink see SWEENKLE.

swinky, sweenkie verb. to wriggle. noun. an earthworm. [ON *svigna* to bend]

swird of a boat to turn. [Norw dial *svirra* to swerve]

swirdy, swirdo, swirdack 1 the blenny. 2 a poor emaciated cod. [ON *sverð* a sword; a reference to the shape]

swirly = verb. swirl. noun. a twist or knot in wood.

[Eng *swirl*]

swither-tree, swingle tree the large plough tree. [Norw *svidra* to swing]

switter 1 see SWILTER.

switter 2 to be in a flurry. [Sh *swider*; Norw dial *svidra* to move about restlessly]

swiz to buzz [imitat.]

swo the pain caused by a burn or sting. [Norw dial *svoda* an abrasion of the skin]

swy rope a swing. [ON *sveigja* to swing]

sye* 1 = scythe.

sye 2 see SIE 1.

syes* chives. [a form of CHIVES; Fr *cive*; Lat *cepa* onion]

syne since, especially *fae syne*, '*Ah'm never seen him fae syne*'. [OE *siththan* after that]

synsin the coot. [a form of SNEESHAN; *synsin* suggests that originally in Orkney dialect an *s* before an *n* was pronounced separately; *k* before *n* was formerly pronounced in Ork and continues to be pronounced in the Teutonic languages with the exception of Eng]

sype to drip or drain dry. [OSc *sipe* seepage]

syper to simmer. [an earlier form of *simmer* was *simper* of which *syper* is probably a variant; compare LAPPERED and LAMPERED]

syre, sire the grating over a drain. [Sc *syver*; ultimately related to Eng *sewer*]

T in the initial position normally pronounced as in English. Frequently omitted by young Orcadians when appearing in other parts of the word eg 'tatties' becomes *ta-ies* and 'watter' *wa-er*. The pronunciation of *th* in initial position varies as it does in Eng. The *h* is lost in some instances as in *tink* for 'think' and *toom* for 'thumb'. Formerly *th* was often pronounced *f*, for instance 'Thursday' is often found written as 'Fursday' in old documents. This pronunciation of 'Thursday' is retained in Shetland. *Thight*, the original pronunciation of Eng 'tight' can still be heard in Orkney. *T* followed by a long *u* is pronounced *choo* eg 'tube' is *choob*, 'Tuesday' is *Choosday* and 'tune' is *choon*. '*Tak the fiddle doon and gae's a choon min.*'

taas (the) a leather belt formerly used by teachers to punish children [see TAWSE]

tach tallow. **tachy** tallowy. [OSc *talch* tallow]

tack a lease or a tenancy. [also Sc; OSc *tak* a lease; compare ON *taka* tenure of land]

tacket* a hobnail [also Sc]. **tackety beuts*** hobnail boots. [a form of Eng *tack*]

tae* 1 = to. 2 for, '*Go and git some nails tae me*'.

'*Ah'll boil a egg tae his tea*'. '*Ah'm knittan a jersey tae Freddy*'. '*He works tae Swanbister*'.

taebeck the call of the red grouse. [imitat]

taen see TAK.

taft 1 see THAFT.

taft 2 to wave a fishing line up and down to keep the bait in motion. [origin uncertain]

tagfettle a bit of line attached in a loop to the head of a fishing-hook so that it can be readily attached to or detached from the *tome* of the fishing line. [ON *taug* string; see FETTLE]

taggowy tattered. **tagsy** untidy. [OSc *tag* a strip of cloth]

taik, tekk, thekk 1 verb. to thatch. noun. the thatch. 2 when a sheaf is withrawn from a stack and the twine has been cut by mice etc the sheaf is said to lie *aal in taik* as if it were laid out for thatching. **thekkid** thatched. **tekkal** a flat stone laid on the top of a wall on which the sloping flagstones or thatch rests. [ON *hella* flat stone; compare the Norw reversed form *helletak* slate roof; ON *þekja*]

taiken a pinch (e.g. of salt). [Eng *taking*]

tail noun. 1 = tail. 2 a tail shaped piece of land. verb.

123

to cut the tail off, especially turnips, '*We tailed twa three dreel o neeps afore denner*'. **tail girding** that part of a horses harness which goes under the tail. **tail pudding** a very fatty type of mealy pudding used to counteract the effect of alcohol. The fiddler who played at a wedding feast was traditionally met at the yard slap (gate) and had to eat a *tail pudding* to ensure that he remained sobre for a reasonable period of time. **tail sweepers** the last couple at the end of a wedding procession who, with besoms, removed the evidence of the party and prevented evil spirits following in their train. This couple were doomed to remain unmarried for a year. **Taily Day*** the second day of April. It was common throughout Orkney until fairly recently to pin a *tail* secretly on someone as a prank. In France a similar prank was played on April 1 when a paper fish was pinned on an unsuspecting undividual as a tail. If the ploy was successful the trickster would call '*Poisson d' avril!*', 'April fish!'. A similar custom prevailed in Iceland on Ash Wednesday, the first day of Lent, when it was the custom for women to pin a small bag of ashes and men a small bag of stones as a tail on someone of the opposite sex. If the bearer carried the tail unwittingly for three steps, or across a threshhold, the game was won.

taing, teeng a point of land. [ON *tangi]*

tait 1 a tuft of hair. 2 a small bundle of straw or bent grass. [Eng dial *tat* tuft]

taiver 1 to pick at food in an indifferent manner. 2 of a bird to shun its nest after the nest has been disturbed (usually DORT). **teffery, toffery** having a poor appetite. [Norw dial *te(i)vra* to play with one's food but compare TARROW]

taivers rags. [also Sc; Norw dial *tave*]

tak past tense TUK*, perfect tense. TAEN*, TIN, TEEN. 1 = take. 2 bring, '*Tak the teapot ben when yi come*'. **tae tak aboot** 1 to arrange or tidy (eg a stackyard). 2 to prepare a body for burial. **tae tak up*** of a fire to begin to burn more strongly. **tae tak oot** to take PEATS from the tusker operator and to set them on the bank. '*The frost's taen the air*' the air is very cold. **tae be taen** to die; in olden days it was taboo to use the name of someone who had recently died '*Him (or her) thit was taen*' was used instead. **tae tak paece** to settle down, '*I wish that bairn wid tak paece*'.

talders 1 the male organs. 2 rags. **talder-wallop** ragged clothes [compare Sc **tatter-wallop** a ragged woman]. **taldery*, tuiltry** ragged or unkempt. [compare Norw dial *taltrar* rags]

tale, teel = tale. *bi his tale* according to him.

tale-pie see TELL-PIE.

tallon tallow. [OSc talloun]

tame see TEM.

Tammie = Tommy. **Tammie-Noddie** 1 the puffin. 2 sleep in the eye. [also known as HENRY NODDY]. **Tammie-Norrie*** 1 the puffin. [also Sc; the use of first names among birds is common; compare *Jenny Wren; Tom-tit* etc; the second element is possibly related to Norw *knarr* or *knurr* to growl or grumble; compare Swed *kornknarr* corncrake]. 2 the sea-shell, fool's cap.

Tammie o Tirlybraes a legendary evil man whose name was invoked to scare naughty children. **Tammie reekie** a cabbage stalk hollowed out, filled with tar and set alight. [also known as a SMOKY TOM]. **Tammie-spinnle** a machine for making ropes. [Eng *spindle*]

tand 1 a spark of fire or live coal. 2 a hereditary trait. **tander** a hereditary trait. [ON *tandri* fire but only in poetry]

tanews the ears of the small black oats after they have been kiln dried. [see TINGVANGS]

tang* seaweed; *tang* grows above the low-water mark, WARE below. **tang cowes** seaweed fronds. **Tangie** a mythical sea spirit surrounded by a fire glow of phosphorescence. [may be a deriv of TANG but more probably confused with Sc *kelpie* a water demon; (Gael *cailpeach* a bullock); compare Sc *the red kelpies* St Elmo's fire]. **tangie** a seal, because of its association with *tang*. **tangie-spur** a small kind of seal. **tangsparrow** the rock pipit. **tang-whaup** the whimbrel [also Sc]. **tang whesser** a small seal. [ON *þang*]

tangvangels temples (of the head). [ON *þunnvangi*]

tanny* tawny. [OSc *tanny* brown]

tant 1 = taunt. 2 to turn the stomach [also Sc]

tanty 1, tanto very tidy or in good shape. [origin unknown]

tanty 2, tontie 1 tottering. 2 of a person, touchy. [origin uncertain; these words may be from different roots; compare TAUNTY]

taow 1 stringy roots. 2 tough beef. [ON *tág* root fibre; Norw dial *tag* sinew]

tap* = top. **the tap o the day*** noon. **tapo, tappiewhaesie** the shag, so called from the tuft on its head. [ON *visk* a bundle]. **tapmost*** highest. **tap square** apt to take offence. [compare Sh *tap square* of a boat top heavy]. **tappie-toorie** something which rises to a point or peak, specifically of a bonnet.

tappie* silly. [see TAUPIE GOAT]

tapsil-teerie a somersault. [Sc *tapsal teerie* upside down; compare Eng *topsy-turvy*]

tar = tar. **tarry fingered*** inclined to steal [also Sc; the fingers tend to stick to things like tar].

tara gott† that's that! [ON *þat er gort* that is done;

compare ON *svagort* so done]

tarf 1 rancid in taste. 2 rough (of sea or weather). 3 bad tempered. [ON *djarfr* bold, daring]

tarp, terp, traip verb. to argue. noun. a quarrel. '*He traipéd hid doon me throat*' he forced me to believe it, he argued with me. **oot o traip** '*He soon pat that oot o traip*' he changed the subject. **traipless** without argument, '*He did hid traipless*'. [Sc *threap*; ON *þrap* a quarrel]

tarpalyin* = tarpaulin. [the *y* sound placed behind an *l* is common in the dialect e.g. the surname Taylor is often pronouced *Taylyor*]

tarrock a tern or similar type of bird. [see SWARFARRO; a dimin of TERN]

tarrow to pick at one's food. [OSc *tarow* to be reluctant; related to Eng *tarry*]

tarry fingered see TAR.

tashed tattered, (of clothes). [OSc *tasch* a stain from Fr tache]

taste = taste. '*They never askéd me whether I hid taste or smell*' they offered me nothing to eat. **tasteless** 1 = tasteless. 2 irritating, '*Tae go home and then tae hiv tae go oot again so queek wis kinda tasteless.*' (Westray).

tasywisp see PESWISP.

tathery untidy. [see TALDERY]

tattie*, tatta potato. **tattie-bogle** a scare-crow. **tattie-chapper** potato masher. **tattie-shaa** potato foliage.

tattle* to handle with dirty fingers, '*Luk at me book, hid's aal tattled*'. [compare Sc *tattle* a lump of dung sticking to a fleece and Sc *taut* to mat or tangle]

taulter see TUILTER.

taunty, tontie huffy. [Sc *tant* to argue or dispute]

taupie-goat a fool. [Norw *tøpe*]

tave well, teeve well (only in placenames) several wells in Orkney are called *tave* wells or *teeve* wells and there is a marsh area in Birsay called *The Teeve*. [ON *djúp* deep: see DYUIVO]

tawas see TOOSE.

tawse a leather strap used for punishing children. [also Sc; Eng *taw* a piece of tanned leather from OE *tawian* to prepare]

tead a term of abuse. [a form of Eng *toad*]

tear = tear. **tear and wear*** wear and tear. [an example of many reversed phrases in the Orkney dial; see OOTSIDE-IN]

tedder = tether. **tether garth** a machine for making tethers from horse hair. **tether-herin** a tether made of hair [?Eng *hair* + EEN]. **teddrie-tail** an earwig.

tee the thigh. [a form of THIGH]

teebro, teedburn, teedburrow, tidburn, tidbirn, tidbrim heat shimmer which appears over the hills on a warm summer's day:-

Whin (when) yi see the teebro's flyan
Hid's a sign the grund is dryan
[ON *tiðr* quickly and ON *bragða* to flicker or brjándi flickering]

teefy* teefy bit, devil-a-bit. [ON *taufra-maðr* wizard]

teeick* see TEEO.

teeick snow see TEEO.

teek to entice. [compare Norw *tigge* to beg or beseech]

teel see TALE.

teended saddened eg by grief. [OSc *teyne* sorrow; OE *teona(n)* (to) hurt]

teeng see TAING.

teengs* tongs. [also Sh]

teenk-tank the sound of milk being squirted from the cow's udder into a pail. An old riddle runs, '*Teenk-tank under a bank, ten aboot fower*' the answer is 'a cow being milked'. [see also PINK-PEENK]

teeo*, teeick* lapwing. **teeick snow** snow which falls in March. [imitat; it is likely that the *o* and *ick* elements of this word are integral parts of the word rather than dimins; compare Eng *peewit*; Ger *kiebitz*]

teese a shout to scare off a dog. [compare KIS]

teet 1 quickly. [ON *títt*]

teet 2 to peep [compare KEEK]

teetan see TEETING.

teeter* to laugh in a secretive manner. [a form of Eng *titter*]

teet-gong heat shimmer. [see TEEBRO; ON *gangr* motion or activity]

teeth 1 = teeth. 2* a tooth; *Ah'm been tae the dentist and hin me teeth oot*,' an old lady remarked, '*All of them*?!' the visitor remarked in surprise. '*No, just the wan*,' was the confusing reply! **teethache*** toothache. **teethbrush*** a toothbrush. '*Feth I hiv aal me back teeth up*' I wasn't born yesterday.

teeting, teetan the meadow pipit. [related to ON *titlingr* sparrow]

teeve well see TAVE WELL.

teewallop-teeweep the call of the lapwing:-
Teewallop-teeweep
Teewallop-teeweep
I hiv an egg in me erse
And I canna get sleep
sound of a lapwing calling at night

teewhuppo a lapwing. [imitat; see TEEO]

teffery see TAIVER.

tefter 1 to idle. 2 to work to no purpose. [Norw dial *tavra*]

teind a tithe or tax [also Sc]. **teind penny, tent penny** in udal law a proprietor had the legal right to give away a tenth of his inherited property. This

125

was known as the *teind penny*. [ON *tíund* tax]

teistie see TYSTIE.

tekk 1 see TAIK.

tekk 2 a call to geese. [imitat; compare TIKKIE and KITTO]

tekkal see TAIK.

tell = tell, past and perfect tense **tellt**. **tae tell apin** to tell on, '*I wisna supposed tae go ootside bit the postman tellt apin me*'. **tae tell doon** to count.

tell-pie*, tale-pie a tell-tale:-

Tell-pie, tell pie sittan on the midden,
Pickan ap hen dirt and widna be forbidden.

[*pie* here is Eng 'magpie' used in the sense of 'chatterbox']

tem to stretch or *a stretching*, especially eg of a skin on a frame. [ON *þenja* to stretch]

tenor the cross-bar between the legs of a chair [also Sh. Eng dial. *tenor*, tenon]

tent see TEIND.

tepp* to dam water. **teppin** a dam. [ON *teppa*]

Term (the) = TERM DAY.

Term Day the day on which a farm labourer's contract began or ended, corresponding to English Quarter Days. The Term Days were Candlemas (2 Feb), Whitsunday (15 May), Lammas (1 Aug) and Martinmas (11 Nov).

terp see TARP.

terran, trooan irritable. **Terran** a mythical monster in Orkney folklore who annually battled with the spirit the *Mither o the Sea* in a duel known as the *vore tullye* and who was silenced until Autumn when he resumed battle in the *gore vellye*. In this encounter he emerged victor and ruled the seas for the winter months. [Norw *tyrren* angry or wrathful]

terry hatters* a children's playground game played at Firth School similar to *cops and robbers*. [origin unknown]

tether garth see TEDDER.

tether herin see TEDDER.

teu = to. **teu-fa** see TO-FA. **teu-name*** a nickname, usually a parish nickname; see MERRY DANCERS as an example]

teullyo see TULLYE.

teulter see TUILTER.

teultyir* in *teultyir* of a cow about to calve; also figuratively applied to women in labour. [essentially *to rock in the sense of moving off one leg on to the other*; see TILTER; compare TRIMSO]

teum*, toom, tuim verb. 1 to pour. 2 to defecate. 3 to empty. adj. hungry. [ON *toema* to empty]

teu-name see TEU.

teunt see TUINT.

teu-pitten 1 put or placed in a situation. '*Whit ither can a buddy deu when a buddy's teu-pitten*'. 2 angered.

thaft, taft rowing bench in a boat. [ON *þopta*]

than = then. '*He wis seen ahint the byre an than he gid tae the shore an that wis the last time he wis seen*'. **thanadays*** *in those days*. [OSc *than* then]

that = that. **that wans*** those; the plural form *those* is not used, '*Gae me that wans*'.

the 1 used instead of a possessive pronoun eg *the wife* instead of *my wife**. [compare Eng *the missus*]. 2 used frequently where Eng would miss it out e.g. '*Ah'm gan tae the kirk*', '*The bairns are awey tae the school*', '*John's for the toon*', '*He tuk tae the laughing*' (He started to laugh). 3 used derogatorily instead of a possessive, '*He wis standan there, the fag in the mooth*', '*The mither o him wis nivver home.*'. 4 as in 2, the definite article is frequently used before professions e.g. '*He works at the joiner wark*', '*He wrowt at the plumber wark a whilie*'.* 5 *the day, the morn, the night, the 'ear**. Eng today, tomorrow, tonight, this year. **the streen** last night [a corrupt form of *yester e'en* modelled on *the day, the morn* etc.]

thee* 1 accusative dative and vocative forms of familiar THOO, '*I saa thee yesterday*'. '*Ah'll gae thee some*'. '*Thee tak/Tak thee the shovel*'. 2 your, possessive pronoun, singular form, '*Come thee wiz*'. [ME *Come thy ways*]. 3 yourself, '*Sit thee doon*'.

theevnick a lapwing. [also Sc; imitat]

thekk see TAIK.

thekkid see TAIK.

them = them. **them wans*** sometimes used as accusative/dative plural of *that. Those* is never used. [see THAT WANS]

thick 1 = thick. 2 having a very close relationship, *as thick as horseheads*. [compare Eng as *thick as thieves*]

thight* 1 = tight. 2 tight-lipped. [ON *þéttr* tight; *tight* was formerly pronounced thight in Eng]

thing 1† an assembly. [see LAWTING]

thing 2 used of a small child e.g. *peedie thing*, 'bit a thing' etc. [see TING]

thingimur* = thingamagig.

think 1 *tae think long for** to long for. 2 *tae think tae** to have an opinion of '*Whit are yi thinkan tae this weather?*"

this 1 used for the definite article '*This Spences been in Birsay fur hunders o 'ears (years)*'. [Eng *the* was originally *this*]

this 2 = this. **this wans*** these. [see THAT WANS]

thistlecock corn-bunting. [the male of the species often chooses a tall thistle as a perch while he is singing]

thoo* you. nominative singular '*Thoo kens whit hid's like wi a hooseful o folk*'. [OE *thu*]

126

thorny-skate the skate (fish), so called because of the thorns on its back.

thraa* to twist, especially to *thraa the neck* the traditional method of killing a hen. **in a thraa** in a knot. **thraa-kruik** a rope making instrument.

thraan* perverse. usually ILL-THRAAN. [OE *thrawan* to turn or twist]

thrang, trang* busy. [also Sc; a form of Eng *throng*]

thrapple*, trapple verb. to choke '*Mercy he nearly thrappled me*'. noun. throat [also Sc] especially *tae weet (wet) the thrapple*' to have a drink. **thrapple hearse** hoarse. [origin uncertain; perhaps a form of Eng *throttle*]

thraws-spang a corruption of HAUSS-SPANG.

thrievlings triplets. [compare Sc *threeplets*]

thrift, trift 1 = thrift. 2 energy '*He didna hiv the thrift tae get aff his erse and help his owld mither.*'

through 1 = through. 2* during '*Through the day he wid sleep than git up aboot tea time*'.

thuddy of the wind, gusty. [see TUD]

thunderer a bull roarer. [imitat]

thwang a thong. [OE *thwang*; see DWANG a related word]

tial a fastening. [also Sc; EME *tyall*]

tibrick a young coalfish. [origin uncertain; perhaps related to TEEBRO describing their flashing movement in the water]

tice see TISE.

tidbrin, tidbrim, tidburn see TEEBRO.

tiddo call term to a lamb. [a form of KIDDO; compare TIKKIE and KITTO]

tide *a good tide o fish.* [ON *tíð* time with the special meaning *lucky time* [ON *tími* time or *good luck*; compare LANG REED and STOOND for extended meanings of 'time']

tie 1 1 = tie. 2* a persistent duty '*Ferm wark's an aafil tie*'.

tie 2 a small field. [found in placenames; ON *teigr* a strip of field]

tief = thief. **tief's knot** a thief's knot, a slip knot deceptively like a reef knot.

tiflin rummaging through boxes etc looking for something to complete a job. [probably a form of TIMPLIN; see TIMPLE]

tift* 1 of an injured finger etc, to throb. 2 of bones to ache. [also Sh; ON *þófta]*

tig 1 1 to beg. 2 to nag at someone. **tigsome** persistently nagging or begging. [Sc *thig*; ON *þiggja* to receive; Norw *tigge* to beseech]

tig 2* a children's game known in Eng as the game of 'catch'. **tig-tag** contentious rivalry. [also Sc; OSc *tig* to meddle]

tiggle to tease. [a form of TIG 2]

tikkie* a call term to hens. [a form of KITTO; see also TEKK]

tilder see TILTER.

Tildrin (Saint) the local name of St Tredwell. [origin uncertain]

tilt verb to struggle. *in good tilt* in good condition. noun 1 = tilth. 2 a struggle.

tilter*, tilder, toolter to sway or totter. **tiltery*, tuiltry** tottering. [OE *tealtrian*]

time 1 = time. 2* trouble with something or other especially bad weather '*Whit a time wir hin o hid*'. [see LONG REED for other illustrations of this relationship between *time* and *bad weather*]. **on a time*** now and then.

timmer = timber. **timmers*** the ribs of a boat. *tae be in the timmers o aathing*, a disparaging remark about someone who is involved in everything e.g. parish activities. **timmer-tuned** of a band, tuneless [also Sc]

timmer brittle [?like wood; see TIMMER]

timothy a downpour of rain. [derivative of ON *demba*, a pouring shower; see DEMPTION]

timple to fiddle with. [probably a form of Eng *tamper*]

timtairy perverse. [Sc *tamtarrie*]

tin see TAK.

ting = thing. **peerie-ting, peedie ting, pee ting** some small living thing, especially a child. **bit-a-ting*** used sentimentally of a small child '*The bairns fa'n and cut hidsel, the bit-a-ting*'. [compare Norw *ting* little (helpless) child]

tinglick only in a child's rhyme a tickle. [see KIRSTY-KRINGLO; dimin of Eng *tingle*]

tingvangs dust from bearded oats. [ON *tína* to winnow; ON *vaengr*, wing, i.e. husk]

tink* to think.

tinkler* a tinker. [also Sc; *tinkler* is an older form]. **tink*, tinkie*** pejorative forms of 'tinkler'. **tinkie's punishment** a game played by children. It consisted of grasping the four fingers of a partner and rubbing the finger tips firmly and quickly with the knuckles. [from *tinkle*, the sound of striking light resonant metal]

tinnie* a tin mug (perhaps a tin pail in the GODICK):-

> *Me mither pat me tae the well*
> *Better hid she gin hersel*
> *The string broke and the tinnie fell*
> *Whistle ower the lave o't*

tino, tyno a wooden skewer on which sillocks were dried. [ON *teinn*]

tinsal of a cow ready to give birth, *at the point of tinsal.* [on *þyngsl*, burden]

tint see TYNED.

tinter a trace. [a corruption of Eng *tincture*]

tippings last drops of milk from a cow. [related to STRIPPINGS]

tippy dressed in the height of fashion, especially *very*

127

tippy [also Sc Eng *tip*, extremity]

tiravee hullaballoo. [Sc *tirrivee*; origin uncertain]

tirl* verb. 1 to turn. 2 to upset by turning. 3 to poke in the earth. noun. 1 the wheel of the old click mill. 2 a spell of bad weather '*The Beltane tirls*'. **tirlo 1***, **tirlick** a small windmill made for a child. **Tirlos (The)** the wind generators on Burgar Hill. **tirlo 2***, **tirlack** a wrestling game in which a wrestler attempts to throw his opponent. [Norw *trille* to roll and *trill* a pulley]

tirr 1 see TIRVE.

tirr 2 a fit of temper [also Sc]. **tirry** angry. [compare Norw *tirre* to irritate]

tirran see TERRAN 2.

tirse* 1 verb. to pull in a determined way. 2 to struggle with a heavy load. 3 noun. a difficult pull. [a metathesis of ON *tríza* a pull]

tirso* 1 the dock. 2 marsh ragwort, especially the dried stem. 3 *sheu's nither a tirso nor a dochan.* fish aren't taking the bait. [uncertain; ? Lat *thyrsa* the stem of a plant; compare TISHALAGO]

tirve, tirr 1 to remove turf. 2 used intransitively too '*The riff's (roof's) tirvan*' the wind is removing the turf. [Scots *tirr*, ME *tirve* to strip]

tirvin a porch built to protect a door. It has a front but no sides. [a *turfed* (porch)]

tise*, tice to persuade. [a form of *entice*]

tishalago* coltsfoot. [also Sc; Lat *tussilago*; the Lat word is also used throughout Swed for this plant]

tislue a quarrel. **tislan** *a tislan thing* one who wants to create strife. [a form of TUSSLE]

tisso* 1 a kiss, used by a mother to a child. [a dimin of KISS]

tisso* 2 emotional stress. [Eng *tussle*; see TISLUE]

t'ither* *the t'ither*, the other, e.g. if you have four blocks of wood and you want to place them in two groups you would '*pit the wan wi the wan and the t'ither wi the t'ither*'. [also Sc; Eng *tother*; ME *tothir*]

titsam short tempered [also Sh: Sc *tid*, humour, a variant of Eng *tide*]

titter to shiver with cold or fear. [ON *titra*]

tittle 1 to annoy. 2 to amuse. [ME *tittle* to tickle]

titto strength or power. [Norw dial *tøte* (good quality) material]

Titto dimin. form of personal name *Kate* = Kitto

tivish to handle someone roughly. [origin uncertain]

tivisy ragged. [Norw dial *teve* a rag + Sc adj suffix *sy*; see TAIVERS]

tizzan* crying, especially *tizzan and greetan*. [imitat; compare Norw *tisse* of a child to urinate]

toddo's grund in a children's game, a sanctuary. [also Sc; ME *tod* fox; *grund* = ground; (there are no foxes in Orkney!)]

to-fa, teu-fa, tufal, tuffer a small addition to a house. [also Sc; the essential meaning is *falling or lean-*

ing towards; compare Eng *lean-to*]

toffery see TAIVER.

toft† originally an abandoned house site. [literally an *empty site*; related to TEUM; such sites were used over and over again; a common placename element in Orkney though if combined with an element often takes the form *tit* as in Crantit; ON *topt*]

tog a tail of barley or black oats. [variant of Sc *tag* a tail, loose ends]

toin, tunyie, twingyie to shrivel up. **tointy, tonyied** shrunk. [Norw *tvinne* to shrink]

tole not easily excited. [ON *þol* endurance]

tolfer see TULFAR.

tollan '*Hid'll be tollan him*' It would be to his advantage. [ON *þola* to bear or endure]

tomboy a small piece of wood fixed to the gunwale of a boat and over which the fishing line was drawn. [Norw dial *bøye* a cleft stick on which a fishing line is wound; for *tom* see TOME below]

tome, toom a fishing line. [ON *taumr* line or cord]

Tommy a puffin. [also Sc; see TAMMIE NORIE]

tong 1 see TANG.

tong 2 1 a tongue. 2 a tongue-shaped mark on a sheep's ear. 3 a *tongue* of land. **Tong-noo!** be quiet! **Had (hold) yir tongue!** 1 Be quiet! 2 You don't mean it! (a reaction to a piece of unbelievable news). [see STOOP 1 and 2]. '*He wis aye tongue afore teeth*' he spoke without thinking. **stappéd tae the tongue root** absolutely full up. **tongue tae the erse like a trump** extremely talkative, literally having a tongue stretching down to the backside like a Jew's harp. [ON *tunga* tongue]

tontie see TAUNTY.

tonyied see TOIN.

too, tuo, tuack 1 a tuft of grass. 2 a little knoll (a landscape feature in Sanday is called the *three toos*!). [TUO and TUACK forms are dimins; ON *þúfa*]

tooal see TOOL.

took*, tug a swig out of a bottle. [Sc *teuch*; Gael *deoch* drink]

tool, tooal = tool. **poor tool** a worthless person.

toolter see TILTER.

toom 1 see TEUM.

toom 2 thumb. **toomspread** of butter spread with the thumb. [Sc has *thoomit piece* a piece of bread on which butter has been spread with the thumb]

toom 3 see TOME.

toomal see TUMAL.

toon, toun 1 originally an administrative district, now a sub-unit of a parish and incorrectly called a *township*. 2 a division of a large farm (e.g. the Face o the Toon, the field immediately to the

north of the farm of Binscarth. 3 **the toon*** *gan
tae the toon* going to either Kirkwall or
Stromness whichever is one's normal service
centre. **toonland, townsland** the land of which
the toon (i.e. the district) was composed. [ON
tún enclosure]
toorie* a bobble on a bonnet. [also Sc; related to the
idea of *tower* or *heap*]
toose, tawas withered roots of grasses. [ON *tág* plant
roots with Eng plural]]
toosip, tusip withered roots of grasses. [related to
TOOSE above]
toot 1 1 to blow a horn. 2 to speak loudly or noisily.
[ME toute to sound]
toot* 2 the backside, especially when talking to a
child. [ME *toute* buttocks]
toota a call term to geese. [see TIKKIE for
comparision]
toot-moot, tut-mut a muttering. [also Sc; Sc *tout* to
mutter; *moot* is related to Eng *mutter*]
top see TAP.
topply liable to tip over. [developed form Eng *topple*]
torno a kind of skate, so called from the *spikes* or
thorns on its back. [see THORNY-SKATE]
torrow see TWARRO.
tosh friendly. [also Sc; origin unknown]
tot-bund of a man, having a mincing gate. [Sc *tot* to
toddle + BUND]
totum, tottem a spinning top made from a bobbin.
[Lat *totum* all, from its use in gambling]
toum noun. 1 a tall thin person. 2 poor quality oats.
adj. 1 empty. 2 hungry. [see TEUM]
toun see TOON.
tout 1 see TOOT 1.
tout 2 tae tak the tout to sulk. [also Sc; see TRUT]
tow 1 1 a fishing line. 2 a rope. [ON *taug]*
tow* 2 = tow. **tae fa in tow wi**'* to meet by chance,
generally used disrespectfully '*He fell in tow wi
a lass when he wis doon in London...*'
towie of crop neither wet nor dry. [see DOWIE]
tow-lowsin a thaw. [ON *þá* thaw, especially thawed
ground; dial *lowse* to loosen]
townit women's work. [Norw dial *tonad* to prepare
wool for yarn]
townsland see TOON.
tow-row an uproar [nonsense rhyme based on *row*]
toy a woman's cap, a type of mutch. [also Sc; perhaps related to Du *tooi* finery]
toyster see TUSKER.
traa* 1 suffering or trouble extending over a long
period of time. 2 a patch of rough water, *a traa
in the sea*. **i the traa** of food, becoming stale or
cooling off. [see THRAA]
traboond, traboon a blow which dislodges an object. [a form of rebound]

trachle* a difficulty. [related to Flem *tragelen* to
walk with difficulty]
tradad stylish, showing off. [origin unknown]
traheelso *tae knock traheelso* to knock head over
heels. [a nonce formation based on heels; compare HEELSDRO]
traip 1 see TARP.
traip 2 *in traip* of a construction, underway. **oot o
traip** out of order or condition. [origin unknown]
traipless see TARP.
tramins the ledge supporting the crossbeams of a
kiln. [ON *þrömr* edge; Norw dial *tram* a step]
trammel 1 = trammel. 2 the hinge of the flail.
trammy ragged. [Eng *thrum* a loose thread; originally the warp thread which made the loose end]
tramp 1 = tramp. 2 to wash blankets by treading on
them in a large tub; *trampan blankets* was at one
time an annual ritual. 3 to move quickly '*He wis
fairly trampan*' he was moving quickly by car,
motor-cycle, etc.
trams 1 the shafts of a cart. 2 jocularly *legs*. [OSc
tram the shaft of a barrow; LGer *traam* beam]
trance see TRANSE.
trang see THRANG.
transe, trance a passage or alley way. [also Sc; OSc
trans an aisle etc; perhaps originally Lat *transitus*
a passage]
transeerin a serious fall as from a horse '*I got a
bonny transeerin*'. [a form of Eng *trouncing*;
compare Sc *trounce* to smash]
trapple see THRAPPLE.
trasitten see TRAYSITTEN.
trass to crush down a crop by walking through it.
[origin uncertain; compare Sc *traissle*]
tratlebogie a gossip. [Sc *trattle* to gossip; see BO-
GIE]
travaig see STRAVAIG.
trave *a trave o dogs* a pack of dogs. [a special use of
trave or *thrave*, a measure of cut grain]
travellye 1 a catastrophe. 2 suffering or trouble of
long duration. **travulgence** a reprimand '*He'll
get a right travulgence fae me when he comes
home*'. [Sc *trevallie* a crash or a brawl; a form
of Eng *travail*]
travise a wooden partition between two animals in a
stable. [also Sc; a form of TRAVERSE]
tray, trey stubborn, especially of the wind '*When
hid goes tae the east hid's stickéd for that's a
tray airt*'. **tray-sitten** lazy, stupified, loath to
move, bewitched. [ON *þrá-viðri* a constant ad-
verse wind and Sc *thra* stubborn]
treb, treve, trebby dyke a prehistoric earthen ram-
part characteristic of the North Isles of Orkney
[ON *þrep* a ledge; Norw dial *trev* balcony in a
church]
tregellyie riff-raff. [Sc *tregallion* a form of

129

tree 1 a beam. [OSc *tre*; ON *tre]*
tree* 2 = three. *tree-neukety* three cornered.
treed = thread.
treeska resentful or difficult *'He's taen the treeska at me'*. **treesky** sulky, bad tempered. [compare Sh *trotska* a fit of sulks; ON *þrjózka* obstinate]
treest see TRIST.
tresh past tense TROOSH. = to thrash.
treve see TREB.
trey see TRAY.
treyan *tae go treyan aboot*, to go around as if suffering'. [see TRAA]
tribble, trivvle to grope with fingers for something. [Sh *trivvel*; ON *þrifla* to grasp at]
trift see THRIFT.
trig 1 complete, finished off. 2 of a man, neat looking. [also Sc; Sc *trig* to smarten up; ON *tryggr* faithful or secure]
trighan walking with a weary, tired gait. [origin uncertain]
trilka, truilkya *tae tak trilka* to sulk. [a form of TRITYA]
trill to run slowly (eg of a feeble horse). [compare Norw *trille* to spin, roll]
trilt, troult see DRILT.
trim* verb. to repair. [*trim* also has this meaning in Eng though *repair* would invariably be used today]. noun. humour or state of mind, *'She's in good trim the day.'* [a nautical metaphor]
trimse* to move impatiently off one leg on to another like a child needing to go to the toilet. **trimso** *in a trimso* in an agitated state. *gan in trimso* of a cow ready to give birth. [compare TEULTYIR; the essential meaning is 'to move off one leg on to the other'.]
trindly, trinluie *trindly-leggéd* spindly legged. **trinlicks, trinley pins** an old game in which wooden replicas of farm animals etc (each with a different value) had to be removed carefully from a heap without disturbing the others. [also Sc; essential meaning is *round stick*; compare Swed dial *trind* hedge stake]
Tring a Stronsay goblin. [see WALTER RED and KORK; origin uncertain]
trink*, trinkie a small ditch or cleft. [OSc *trink* water channel; relating to NF dial *trenque* trench]
trinky narrow or thin. [ON *þrongr* narrow]
trinley pins see TRINDLY.
trinlicks see TRINDLY.
trinluie see TRINDLY.
trinted of boots, clothes etc close fitting. [ON *þrongr* narrow]
trinyo a narrow passage between houses. [ON *þrong* a narrow place]
trip a pile of stones set up on a beach as a march or mark of division with reference to seaweed rights. **trip stane/steen** a stone set on end in the ground to mark a boundary or a march [see TREB]
trip-trap-truisky the game of *noughts and crosses*. In Harray the winner called *'Trip-trap-trullyo!'* on winning a game of noughts and crosses. [the usage must be ancient; compare Eng *tip-tap-toe*, Swed *trip-trap-trull* and Fr *tric trac*, a type of backgammon in which pegs as well as pieces are used]
trist*, treest 1 to squeeze or press down in the cheese making process. 2 to wring clothes. **tristic** a newly made cheese. [ON *þrýsta]*
trittle unending chatter [also Sc]. **trittle-bogie** a talkative person. [compare TRATLEBOGIE; imitat]
tritya *tae be in tritya* to sulk. [see TRUTMULLED]
trive = thrive *'Sae micht I trive!'* Upon my word!
trivvle see TRIBBLE.
trooan see TERRAN 2.
trooker a term of abuse applied to a female. [Sc *trucker* trader]
troose *troosed wi dirt* filthy. [compare Icel *tross* rubbish]
troosh see TRESH.
troot* = a trout. plural *troots*. **tae go tae the troots** to go angling. **trootie hoose** a trout trap built beside a burn e.g. at Tormiston Farm Stenness or Hybreck in Harray. **tae laek (leak) like a trootie hoose** used of a badly built dwelling. [see HORSE for other unusual plurals]
trot = throat.
troth* *'Bi me troth'* indeed!. [OE *troth* truth]
troult see DRILT.
trounce = trounce. **trouncean** restless. [? through confusion with TRIMSAN; see TRIMSE]
trow 1 through. **trow-geung, trow-dyeung** a church aisle, also used metaphorically of any passageway, *'Thoo're blockan the trow-geung'.* [also Sc; see also AP-TROW and DOON-TROW]
trow 2 to think or believe *'I trow thoo'll be takkan the peedie lass wi thee'.* [obs Eng *trow* from OE *treowan* to trust]
trow* 3 a troll. In Ork legend there were *hilltrows* and *sea-trows. Trow* came to be synonomous with the devil which was known as DROW. **trow tak thee** a curse. **trow glove** sea sponge *(axinell verrucosa).* This sponge is also associated with the supernatural in Shetland where it is called *Rann's Fingers.*
trowie noun. a troll. adj. **trowie* 1, trullie** sickly or ailing. 2 of quality, poor. *'That's trowie things o coorteens - thir all fa'an tae pieces wi the sun.'* **trowie-like*** having the appearance of being ill. **trowie-girse*** the foxglove. [also Sh: compare

Norw *trollheg* buckthorn]. **trowie-glove** the fox-glove. **trowie-spindle** mare's tail (grass). [dimin of ON *troll* a troll; see also TRULLIE]

trow-geung, trow-dyeung see TROW 1.

truck to trample down. [Norw *trakke*]

truff to exchange confidences '*They're busy truffan*'. [origin uncertain]

truffs see TRUMFS.

truilkya see TRILKA.

truint 1 narrow passage. 2 a drain. [origin uncertain; compare TRINYO and TRINK]

trull a nuisance, inconvenience '*Hid wis a bit o a trull when he didna come*'. [the sense is *delay*; see TRULLYIE, DRILT etc]

trullie sickly; recorded only once from Birsay. A servant lass at Swannay was very ill and when someone who had visited the girl was asked about her progress, the reply was, '*I doot she's kinda trullie, gullie*.' [see TROWIE]

trulls* 1 testicles. 2 matted wool or hair hanging from an animal. [the essential meaning is 'hanging' as in Norw *drolle*]

trullyie a heavy load. [compare TRILT]

trumfs*, truff(s) *trumps* in a game of cards '*Whit's truff the day?*' What news? [the original Eng form was *triumph*]

trumle = tremble.

trump a Jew's harp '*She's tongue tae the erse like a trump*' she's a very talkative person. [also Sc; OF trompe trumpet]

trumpie† the Arctic Skua. [probably ON *drumba*, log a reference to a stubby shape; compare BONXIE]

trunyie a heavy load. [origin uncertain; compare TRULLYIE]

truss to eat in a slovenly fashion. [see TROOSE]

trutmulled downcast. see TRITYA: [Sc *tut mou'd* having protruding lips; see MULLS]

tryllya aimless wandering. [see TRILL]

trystic *a trystic o kail* boiled cabbage with the water pressed out. It used to be supped with milk '*a trystic o kail and a err o milk*'. [see TRISTIC]

tuack see TOO.

tuction* rough treatment, '*Beuy that owld byke's hin some tuction*'. **tae mak tuction** to stir up trouble. [Sc *tuck* to beat a drum; through Fr from Lat *toccare* to strike a bell; the suffix is *Eng*]

tud a freak storm which periodically strikes the North-West of Marwick in Birsay. [Eng *thud* but compare ON *þjóta* of the wind to whistle]

tufal see TO-FA.

tuffer see TO-FA.

tug see TOOK.

tuggle 1 = toggle. 2 the pin which passes through two iron eyes on the side of the rowing bench, the purpose of this being to keep the mast up-

right.

tuilter, taulter, teulter to drag behind. [see DILDER]

tuiltry 1 see TILTER.

tuiltry 2 see TALDERS.

tuim see TEUM.

tuink a thump or crack, the sound of something heavy falling. [ON *dynkr*]

tuint verb. to pout or sulk. adj. peaked or pointed as e.g. of a badly made stack. [see TRUTMULLED a related word]

tulfar*, tolfer a floor-board in a boat. [ON *þilfar* deck boards]

tulliment, doliment to dance or jump, of stars but also of people. [Norw *tulle* to frisk or romp; the suffix is Eng]

tulliotan of stars, sparkling. [see TULLIMENT above]

tully a large kind of knife with blade fixed in the shaft. [also Sh: a form of GULLY]

tulye, tullye, teullyo, tullyo a struggle in combat; see HECK and TERRAN [related to TILT]

tulyies contents, presumably of a burden. [hence related to *tyoll*]

tumal†, toomal, tumail, tumult a field. Specifically the home field which was not part of the run-rig system. It always belonged to the adjacent dwelling as opposed to TOWNSLAND; now only in placenames apart from the compound HEN-TOOMAL. [ON *tún-völlr*]

tummle* = tumble. **tumlan Tammy** an old horse-drawn hay rake characterised by its '*tumbling*' motion.

tumult see TUMAL.

tune* 1 = tune. 2* mood '*He's in poor tune the day*'. [see LOOD for an older instance]

tunyie a form of TOIN.

tuo see TOO.

turkases heavy pliers as used by a blacksmith etc. [OSc *turkas* from OF *turcaise*]

turkey = turkey. '*No more sense than a sookan turkey*', very stupid

turn 1 = turn. 2 '*He his (has) a fine turn wi him*'* he is obliging and amiable. 3 '*The days is on the turn*'* daylight is lengthening. 4 '*Never turn hid*'* don't mention it to anyone. 5 **turned doon** applied to the loser in the game of SQUARE TREE. 6 '*He never does a hands turn*'* he is extremely lazy (in a situation where everyone would be expected to pull together). **tae deu the turn** to suffice [also Sc]. '*Hid's no muckle o a chair bit hid'll deu the turn*'.

turneep* = turnip.

tur-tur a call to a horse. [ON *trutta*]

tushtar see TUSKER.

tusip, toosip see TOOSIP.

tusk the blue catfish. [ON *þoskr*]

131

tusker, tushtar, toyster a peat cutting tool. [ON *torkfskeri*]

tusky stormy. [compare Norw *tuska* to clatter]

tut-mut see TOOT-MOOT,

twa* 1 = two. 2 a few, '*Ah'll gae thee twa eggs tae tak home wi thee tae thee tea*'. **twa-three, twartree*** a few [literally '*two or three*'; also Sc]

twal = twelve. **twal-cup*** a cup of tea at 12 o'clock. **a twal-munt*** a year, twelve months [also Sc]. **tae twal a coo** to milk a cow at noon [also Sh].

twang a thong used for tying a '*rivlin*'. [see DWANG]

twarro, twarrow, torrow a head-rig in a field. [ON *þverr* athwart]

twart-back*, twat-back cross-beam in a roof. [Norw *tverr-bjelke*]

twartlings crosswise. [see TWARRO; for '*lings*' see BACKLINGS]

twartree see TWA.

twarty bad tempered. [ON *þverr* perverse]

twat-back see TWART-BACK.

twathree, twatree see TWA.

tweeg* to pull. [a form of Eng *tweak*; OE *twiccian* to pluck]

tweestie, tweestoo homespun cloth of white and black, the thread consisting of a white and black twisted together. [a form of Eng *twist*]

twelp of a lapwing, to cry, *teeicks twelpan oot apae the brecks* [see TEEWALLOP]

twerny see TWIRN.

twilt* 1 quilt. [also in Eng dial]

twilt 2 to beat a person or animal. [compare Norw *dulta* to push]

twingyie see TOIN.

twirn 1 to shrivel up. 2 to twist the face. **twirry** of the face screwed up. **twerny** awkward. [related to ON dial *þverra* to shrink]

tyen see KEN.

tyinno see KEN.

tyke a dog. **vild tyke** a term of abuse. [also Sc; ON *tík* a bitch]

tyned, tint lost. [Sc *tyne* to lose; ON *týna* to destroy or lose]

tyno see TINO.

tynno, tyinno see KEN.

tyoll to carry a heavy burden. [related to TILT]

tyst*, tystie, teistie the black guillemot. [ON *þeist*]

U pronounced as in English.

ubby see OOBY.

udal, uthell, odal having no feudal superior, especially *udal tenure*. **udaller** one who owns udal land. [ON *oðal* ancestral property]

uddy small or insignificant. *peedie uddy, peerie-uddy* very small. **udmal, odmal** very small. [ON *oddr* spot etc.]

ue to hum a tune in a quiet self contented manner, usually *sittan uean*. [see NUE 1]

uen see UIN.

ugg 1 a distaste for food. **uggsome** 1 disgusting. [see AK and UIK]

ugg 2 only in *ugg-bone* the bone behind the gills of a fish. Also known as the PLOO BONE since this bone in the cod can be carved into a little toy plough. [ON *uggi* a pectoral fin]

uggy 2 of the sky threatening. [ON *uggr* fear]

ugmast the uppermost. [Sc *heaghmost*]

uigla earthworm casts. [? Sh *uggle* to soil; Norw *alka*]

uik to vomit [compare AAK].

uikowy, uiky of an animal, ill-thriving [see HECK]. **uikapurt** an ill-thriving animal [see HECKAPURDY under HECK].

uikname = ekename

uiko, uiky 1 a small fish, the bull-head or fatherlasher. *as saat as the sea-uiky* very salty [Norw *ulk*]

uiko 2 an angular field. **uiketty** angular or ill-shaped. [Norw *huken* bent]

uiky itchy. [see YEUK]

uiler see OOLER

uim, eum, 1* a hot atmosphere, '*My whit a uim in here*'. [Norw *ylma* warm air]

uim 2* mad, especially of a bull. Generally used of the male of a species but as Marwick points out never applied to a stallion. Applied metaphorically to people, '*He gid clean uim when the bairn didna deu whit hid was tellt*'. [ON *ólmr* savage]

uimater see AMITER.

uimist a contracted form of *uppermost*. [found in placenames e.g. *Uimest Hooses* in Stronsay; also Sh]

uimro greasy layer exposed when wool begins to fall off a sheep's back. [ON *hamr* skin; used especially of a peeling skin]

uin, eun 1 the smell of mildew. **uiny** having such a smell. '*Whit a uiny smell wi this cloot.*' [Norw dial *ulne* to become rancid]

uin 2 1 to hum a tune. 2 of an animal to groan in pain. [imitat]

uir to hum a tune. [see OORAN]

uirn to turn sick, '*Me stomach uirned on hid*'. [see VARR]

132

uirry trifling. [see PEERIE ORRIE]

uirs small particles or remnants, used especially of small potatoes. [see URRY]

uismal see USMAL.

uiss see OYCE.

uit an old pronunciation of EAT.

uitannion see OWDNY.

uitany see OWDNY.

uiter destruction, especially of animals trampling crop. [ON *ytri-* with the sense *utter*; the word for *destruction* has been lost; see UITER-ALD below]

uiter-ald extremely old. [ON *ytri-* outer; compare Norw *ut-gammal*, German *ur-alt* ancient]

uiter-kap a spider. [see ETTERCAP]

uivigar noun. 1 a sea urchin. 2 an ill-thriving animal. adj. unkempt or untidy, especially of the hair, '*Whit a uivigar yir in bairn!*' said to a young girl with long hair after she had been out in the wind. [OSc *ivegar*; Icel *igulker* sea urchin]

uiz a bright blazing fire. [see AIZE]

uizer a form of AIZER.

uldrawy of potatoes, small. [MULDER with loss of initial *m*; compare ULLERIE below; *awy* adj. suffix]

ulie† = oil. see [CRUSIE]

ullerie ground with an open bottom which does not hold water. [MULLERY with loss of initial *m*]

umbesettis† farms which had a special relationship with a *bu*. [also called ONSETTS; ON *ömbun* payment for service; ON *setr* settlement with Eng plural]

umboth, umbothman† an agent working on someone's behalf. [ON *umboð* charge or commission]

umman [see WIFE]

umo see OOMO.

unbatnafoo of an animal not thriving. [a negative form of ON *batna* to improve or recover + *ful*]

unbegun in the act of, '*I wis unbegun tae tak aff me claes when I heard feetsteps on the brig stones*'.

uncall see ONCA.

uncan see UNKAN.

unco very, extremely. [also Sc; OSc *uncow* strangely; OE *uncuð* unknown]

undeeman immense. [Sc *undeemous*; ON *udoemi* an enormous thing]

underfoud † a parish official with legal and administrative powers. superseded by the BAILLIE. [see FOUD]

under-hand in reserve. [Eng *in-hand*]

under-spey used of poorly drained land with an under ground spring. [Dan dial *spi* a spring; ON *spýja* to spew; compare Eng dialect *spew* a marsh]]

underwey 1 = underway. 2 pregnant.

unfaandoon in a state of imminent collapse, '*That owld hoose is just unfaandoon*'. [*un* + *fallen* + *down*]

unfaansindry* of a piece of equipment etc in a disintegrated condition. [see UNFAANDOON and SINDRY]

unfierdy not in proper order. [OSc *unferdy* clumsy]

uninyafoo slightly indisposed. [see INGANAFOU]

unkan* strange. **unkans, unkas** news, '*His thoo any unkans the day*'. [OSc *unkennand*]

unlaw † in old records a fine for contempt of court. [also Sc; OSc *unlaw*]

unless 1 = unless. 2 apart from, '*Thir wir fower folk there unless me*'.

unrynded of fat, unrendered.

unsamsied uncouth, even fearsome. [? ON *usoemr* unseemly]

unstowly of the weather, wild. [ON *ustöðuligr* unstable]

unwandan, oonwandan unexpected. [ON *aenting* hope or expectation]

uny see UIM 1.

up = up. **Up-the-Gates** that part of Kirkwall to the south of the Watergate, originally known as *The Laverock*. **Uppie** in the traditional BA' game in Kirkwall, someone born to the south of the cathedral.

uplay see UPPA.

upmak a deficiency payment in calculating a subsidy. [OSc *upmak* to make up for a deficiency]

uppa†, uplay in the old RIG-A-RENDALL system of agriculture, the *uppa* was the first rig in a sheed reckoning from the north or east according to the lie of the land. [ON *uppi* up]

uppie-killie-donkey a see saw. [see APACAILIE DUNKEY]

up-set *up-set price* the figure set up or established by the vendor as the selling price of a house etc. [also Sc]

upsides (wi) 1 attaining a certain level, standard, '*Ah'm upsides wi me wark noo*' I'm up to date. 2 equal, '*Ah'm upsides wi him noo*'.

upstagang† a kind of upright loom formerly used in Orkney. [Norw dial *upstagogn*]

uptail to run away. [Eng *turn tail*]. **uptail-doon** upside down.

uptak an improvement in the weather. **queek in the uptak** smart in understanding what is meant [also Sc]

ur fine rain. [ON *úr* drizzling rain]

ure see URISLAND.

urgo bits floating in ale. [? ME *ortus* leavings]

uriscoppis† a purchase of the value of one ounce. [ON *eyris-kaup;* see URISLAND]

urisland, ure an old term for a unit of land valued at an *eyrir* that is an ounce of silver. [ON *eyris-land* land yielding a rent of an *eyrir*]

urmals fragments or small quantities. **urm** 1 undersized potatoes. 2 coal etc, dust. **urmy** small. [ON *ör-mul* small particles]
urmy see URMALS.
urrie, oro undersized. [see URRY 2]
urrigar not thriving. [a form of UIVIGAR]
urry 1 cow's udder. [ON *júgr*]
urry 2 very small [compare Icel *ör-* very small]
urter bare pasture. [ON *ör-tröð*]
ushat, oshit of wool, dingy grey in colour. [ON *mó-skjótt*, moor coloured with loss of initial *m*; see MOOSKET]
usmal 1, **uismal, osmal** of a woman big. [ON *ú-smar* big]
usmal 2 dismal, dark, often applied to the human face [also Sh compare Norw. *ysma*, hazy air]
uthell see UDAL.
uthy a smooth oily surface on the sea made by throwing out chopped up limpets as bait. [origin unknown]

V pronounced as in English.
vaaless see VARLESS.
vaam see VAMM.
vaan-kuithe see VATHAN-KUITHE.
vadmell see WADMELL.
vaer see VARR.
vaig to wander. [a clipped form of STRAVAIG; also Sc]
vaiper to saunter around aimlessly. [Eng *vapour*]
vair, vaer see VARR.
valess see VARLESS.
vamm, vaam an odour. [Norw *kvam* odour]
van = 1 van 2 travelling grocery van also known as the **motor van** or, earlier, **horse van**. **vanman** the driver of the grocery van who in the first half of this century and the latter part of the last century played a vital part in the economy of the islands not only by selling goods but also in buying farm produce, especially eggs. In the early part of this century they also bought wild birds' eggs; on one occasion the writer's mother as a child sold to the vanman twenty-one dozen lapwing eggs collected on the Rendall Moss.
vanda 1 value, especially negatively, *o little vanda.* 2 esteem or respect. [ON *vanda* to choose]
vandit 1 of a cow having stripes on the side. 2 used e.g. of a garment which has been badly dyed. 3 of a piece of knitting made from a yarn spun from more than one shade or colour. [ON *vöndr* a stick or wand; also used metaphorically in the sense of a *stripe* in a piece of cloth]
vanger *tae get the vanger of somebody* to get the upper hand. Also to *win the bangry* which has the same meaning. [ON *bang* hammering; Sc *bang* to overcome, hence Sc *bangster* victor]
vansome difficult to please. [ON *vandsame* difficult]
varbo a small tumour on an animal's hide caused by the larva of the gad-fly. Also known as AIKEL.

[Eng *warble*]
varden a companion spirit in the shape of an animal which accompanied the individual everywhere and moaned dismally if he was about to die. [it seems to be the equivalent of ON *fylgya;* ON *varðaðr,* Eng *warden* guardian]
varless, valess awkward or clumsy. [ON *vara* to heed]
varr, vaer, vair 1 appetite for food. 2 to have such an appetite; used negatively generally e.g. '*I couldna varr that fur dinner*'. [ON *varna* to abstain from; see also ARR and UIRN which have lost the initial *v*]
vashal a tub or barrel. [Eng *vessel*]
vathan-kuithe, vaan kuithe a three year old coalfish. [Norw dial *vada* to swim near the surface]
veallience a plain. [also Sc; ON *vellirnir* fields]
veck *tae veck the joints* to bend them and make them supple. [see VEEK]
veeat, viad a stretch of open ground or a quantity of cultivated ground under crop. [ON *viðatta* wideness or openness of a district]
veediment see VIDIMENT.
veegal, veekalty, veekny, veetel, veetn(e)y, vicany only in the phrase *oot o veegal* etc, '*This holiday is pitten the week clean oot o veekalty for me*'; the sense seems to be 'leaving one ignorant ' [ON *vitandi* knowing]
veek to veer. [ON *víkja* to turn]
veekalty see VEEGAL.
veekny see VEEGAL.
veeko a term of abuse. [see ILL-VEEKIT]
veel, veill a simpleton. [Eng *veal* originally calf]
veery-orms see EERIE-ORMS.
veet* pronunciation of *vet*, veterinary surgeon [also Sc]
veetel see VEEGAL.
veetny see VEEKNY.

134

veeze 1 1 to aim at something. 2 to study. [Sc *vissy* from Fr *viser* to aim at something]

veeze 2 to squeeze. **veeze-pin** 1 the wooden screw used to tighten the tension of the wheel band of the spinning wheel. 2 the peg of a fiddle. [a form of Eng *vice*]

veill a mischief maker. [see VEEL]

vellye 1 force or power, especially, *tae strik (strike) wi a vellye.* 2 tumult. [a clipped form of TRAVELLYE]

vellyeroo foolish, idle talk [see VILDRO]

velter to trudge heavily. [a form of Eng *welter*]

vennel a lane. [*The Vennel* the old name for what is now St Magnus Lane in Kirkwall; OF *venelle* a small street from MedLat *venella*]

venture = venture. **venteran** risky.

vert of a fish to leap, jumping through the surface searching for food. [Sc *vert* to turn over from Lat *vertere* to turn]

viad see VEEAT.

vicany see VEEGAL.

vickéd, vikket vigorous. [see VIKKEND]

vidge to move position, '*He wis vidgan for home*' he was making movements as if he intended to go home. [a form of Sc *fidge*; related to Eng *fidget*]

vidiment, veediment the smallest particle. [a form of Eng *whit* smallest particle; with Eng noun suffix *ment* as for example in *judgement* etc]

vikkend of a youth, well developed. [probably the same word as VICKED; ON *vígr* of fighting age]

vikket see VICKED.

vild vile. [see VYLDE]

vildro, vildroo, vilyero, villyero *tae go vildro* to go wrong, to go to ruin, to be scattered. [compare GELDRO; from an assumed *gvelder* to scream (of the wind) as in Ork and Sh *galdry* a big draughty house and Sh *vill* a squall of wind]

viny, vinie strong tasted, especially of game. [Eng *winded*; compare STRIP WIND]

vinya a little scheme or project. [ON *vinna* to gain by toil]

vire 1 to move or shift. [OSc *vire* to whirl; OF *vire* to turn]

vire 2 1 of a girl pretty. 2 of an animal well fed. [origin uncertain]

virr energy. [see BIRR]

visty, vista an outing. [Eng *visit*; compare ON *vitja* to visit]

vittle crop grown for cattle. [also Sc; a form of Eng *victual*]

vizzie of a cat to prepare for a pounce. [see VEEZE 1]

vizzie-hole a peep hole. [see VEESE 1]

voar, vore springtime. [ON *vár*]

voe a bay or inlet of the sea, now only in placenames as in *Ronsvoe* now St Margaret's Hope Bay [ON *vágr* bay]

vokish fond of display in dress etc. [Sc *voky* proud; origin unknown]

voldro see VOLO.

vole-grun used of old earthen dividing walls or balks, *vole-grunn dykes* [ON *vallar-gróinn* turf-covered]

volo, vole-moose, voldro the Orkney vole. [in the *volo* and *voldro* forms the *o* is a dimin; in the northern languages words ending with an *l* consonant often picked up a *d* and *r*; compare SPELL, SPELDER]

vonna a loud powerful voice. [origin unknown]

vooer a lover. [Eng *wooer*]

vore see VOAR.

vose-mither the core of a boil. [Faer *vágsmóðir*]

vuigny worthless rubbish (eg chaff). [origin uncertain; ?*winded*, winnowed; see VINY]

vylde filthy or objectionable. [also Sc and ME; a form of Eng *vile*]

W pronounced as in Eng. Formerly as in Sc where a *w* was followed by an *r* there was a tendency to insert another vowel eg 'wrong' was *wirang* and wrinkled *werinkled*. As in Sc where when a *w* is followed by an *h* the *h* is always sounded. *Qu* is still pronounced *wh* in certain parts of Orkney. [see WHANG for an old example of this]

wa* = wall. **wa head** the top of the wall. In the olden days, a celebration was held when a new building reached *wa head height*. **tae stand tae the wa*** of a door to be wide open, '*The door wis standan tae the wa*'.

waal* a well. '*Her tail's in the waal*' she is pregnant (but unmarried). [OSc *wall* a well in placenames]

waan 1 aptitude. [ON *vandi* custom or habit]

waan 2 hope. **waanly, wanlie** offering hope, '*This luks a waanly bit for fish*'. **waanyaless** ill-thriving. [ON *ván*]

waar, war* worse, '*Ah'm feeling waar the day*'. '*He's gan bi the waar*' He's getting worse, '*He's tin a waar wey*'* he has taken a turn for the worse. [ON *verr* worse]

waar-cowe see WARE.

waarin† goods, wares. [ON *varningr*]

135

wab = web. **wab o the wame** the fatty tissue surrounding the stomach of an animal [see WAME]
wabbit*, wappéd tired. [also Sc; apparently a corruption of Sc *wobart*]
wach see WAFT.
wad 1* = would have. '*I wad comed if hid (it) hid (had) been a bonny night*' I would have come.
wad 2 to wade. [ON *vaða*]
waddie a ford. [ON *vað*]
wadding* wedding [also Sc]. **wadding walk** in the olden days the wedding company walked to the manse for the marriage ceremony and the party was led by a fiddler followed by people sweeping the path.
wade 1 the draught of a boat. [a special usage of Eng *wade*]
wade (a) 2 mastitis in cattle or sheep. [Sc *weed*; OE weden *delirious*]
wadmell† standard home-woven cloth. [ON *vaðmal*]
waersay see WARSHIE.
waethorn see WAITH-HORN.
waff see WAFT.
waffle 1 to twist, used especially of wind and rain beating down growing crop. 2 to flutter in the wind. **waffly** shaking; *a poor waffly buddy*. [ON *vafla* to swing or flutter; see WEEFLE]
waft*, waff, wach 1 a hint of a (generally unpleasant) smell. 2 a signal. Before the days of the telephone, people used signals to communicate at a distance e.g. a sheet might be displayed in a prominent position or a CUBBY placed on top of a high pole, such signals having a pre-determined meaning. (see REEKIE BRAE for another instance). [NoME *waffe* wave, blow; variation of Eng *wave*]
wag = wag *tae tak the wag o* to make a fool of [also Sc]. **wag-at-the -wa*** a clock with the pendulum suspended below the body, also known as a Dutch clock.
waiko, wecko a kittiwake. [imitat]
wail to separate e.g. small potatoes from large ones or little peats from the larger peats. [ON *velja* to choose or pick out]
waith-horn, waethorn, waithie originally a piece of horn with a groove in it fixed to the gunwale of a boat and through which the fishing line ran. [ON *vaðhorn*]
waiveran-laif the broad leaf of the greater plantain used to draw boils etc. [a form of Eng *waybread* plantain]
wakative easily aroused from sleep. [a form of *wakeful* with Eng adj *ative* suffix as in talkative]
wakkéd matted, especially of a woollen garment, '*Me jersey's all wakkéd under the airms*'. [also Sc; Eng *walk* to full cloth]

wald 1 to brandish or aim. 2 to command or control, *He nivver hid right wald o his legs*. [OSc *wauld* related to Eng *weild*]
wale 1 a gunwale. [ME *wale* a ridge]
wale 2, wall to grab. [see WAIL]
Wallawa the devil. [ME *walawai* an exclamation of sorrow, the equivalent of 'Woe is me!'; compare SORROWAN]
wally* 1 huge. 2 substantial. **Wallyman** the devil. [Norw *veldig*, enormous]
Walter Red, Warty Red, Wattie Reid a hobgoblin in Sandwick folklore. This name is attached to holes and depressions in the Orkney landscape e.g. 1 on the Brough of Birsay. 2 the dip in the hills between Leeon and the Hill o Heddle and known as Stenady (spirits also lay in hill saddles in Iceland and Norway [ON *vaetr* goblin + *hreða* goblin]
wame the belly or lower stomach. [OE *wamb* womb]
wammelan moving slightly. [OSc *wamble* to totter]
wanboona a curse, '*Wanboona apin thee!*'. [Faer *vanbøn* to curse]
wand 1 = wand. 2 a horse's penis [also Sc]. 3 a bamboo rod used for fishing kuithes [also Sh]. '*He laid aal his wands in the watter*' he tried his hardest.
wanfine *tae go tae wanfine* to come to a bad end. [ON *van* a negative prefix used here as an equivalent of 'ill'; see ILL-END; *fine* is Lat *finis* end; also found in the expression, *tae come tae fine*; see FINE]
wanheel a curse. [Norw *vanhell*]
wanjoy noun. sorrow. adj. bringing sorrow, '*That bairn's a wanjoy thing*'. [Eng *joy* with the ON *negative* prefix van; see WAN forms above]
wanlie see WAANLY.
want 1 = want. *tae want home* to want to go home.
want 2 verb. = want, to lack, '*A man came intae the shop wantan a leg*' caused much amusement because of its ambiguity! noun. a defect, particularly a mental defect* '*He his (has) a kinda want aboot him*'. [obs Eng *to lack*; also Sc; ON *vanta* to lack]
wantrivan ill-thriving. [see WAN forms above]
wanwort trifling or valueless. [also Sc; see WAN forms above]
wap*, wip, wup past tense **wappéd** verb. 1 to turn e.g. the cranking handle of an old car. 2 to throw or to strike with a blow '*He wappéd hid doon*'. 3 to bind with e.g. a bandage. 4 to toss the arms about in walking, '*There he goes wappan along the road*'. noun. **wap 1** a cranking handle for an engine. 2 commotion, '*Whit a wap's in the duck hoose, there must be a rat among them*'. **wap organ** barrel organ [also Sc; OSc *wap* to wrap, Norw *vippe* to swing]

136

wappéd 2 see WABBIT.

wappin steine† an assembly for the purpose of counting weapons of war. [ON *vapna-stefna*]

war see WAAR.

ward to wish. **weel warded**, well deserved [? a clipped form of Eng *award*]

ware*, waar seaweed growing below the low water mark (*tang* grows above), '*The ware time is a sair time*', an old saying meaning that it was a laborious job to manure the land with seaweed in Spring time. **ware brack** seaweed breaking loose and driving ashore in the spring and autumn. **ware cowe** a piece of seaweed. **ware sea** a heavy sea which casts seaweed ashore. **ware pick** a bent pick for gathering seaweed. [OE *war* seaweed]

wark* 1 = noun. 1 work. 2 on goings, especially *wild wark* violent on goings. 3 a fuss, '*A lot o wark aboot nothing*'. 4 other things in addition, '*Whit wae this drinking and wark, bae Monday he doesna hiv a penny tae himsel.*' **wark lumes** joiners' tools. [OSc *werk lum*]

wark 2 a violent cholic, *the wark*. [Sc and Eng dial; ON *verkr*]

wark lumes see WARK 1.

warl wealth. [contraction of *world's wealth*]

warp a pull with an oar. [a special use of Eng *warp* to twist]

warran = warrant, '*I'se warran*'. '*I warrant thee for hid*' I'm certain that's true. '*He'll no be aback o askan, I'se warran*' I'm certain that he will not be too shy to ask.

warshie, waersay 1 unwell. 2 having a craving for a particular food. [Sc *wersh* feeble; ME *werische* sickly]

wart 1 a landmark on a hilltop. [common in placenames; ON *varða*]

wart 2 a pull with an oar. [a form of WARP]

warty girse sun spurge. [the milky fluid from the hollow stem supposedly cures *warts*]

Warty Red see WALTER RED.

wash = wash. past tense **wush** '*I wush aal day yesterday and got aal me washing dry*'.

washy a small cod. [compare Eng *wishy-washy*]

wassle verb. to wrestle. noun. a wrestle, though as a noun usually in the plural *the wassles*. [a form of Eng *wrestle*]

wassum an untidy bundle. [see WAZZIE and WEESKO]

wast west [also Sc]

wat to know, '*Sae weel I wat*' well do I know that. [OE *witan*]

watch 1 to watch. 2 to see, '*I watched his daeth in the paeper*'. **watchman**† in those days when SKARFS were killed for food, the task of the hunter was to catch first of all the skarf which remained awake while the others were sleeping. It was known as the *watchman*. If this was successful it was very easy to capture the others.

water = water, pronounced 'watter' as in Sc. *tae wade the water* or *tae be through the water* referring to passage through life's troubles, '*Wir been through the water and we ken hoo deep hid is*'. **water-arro, water-arvo** common chickweed. [ON *arfi* chickweed]. **water-berge** see BERGE. **water-blot** rinsing water. [see BLOTS]. **water-furring** constructing a shallow furrow in a field to carry off excess water. [see FUR]. **water-hen*** a moor hen. [in Ork *moor hen* is reserved for the red grouse]. **waterings** a watering hole for cattle in the old days. **water-pleep** the snipe. [see PLEEP and HORSEGOKK]. **water-traa** heartburn. [see TRAA, THRAA]. **watery-pleeps** the redshank. [see WATER-PLEEP above]. **watery-wagtail** the wagtail, so called because it is supposedly a sign of rainy weather if it comes near the house.

wather see WEATHER.

wather gauge see WEATHER.

wather-moose see WEATHER.

wattle† an old tax, originally an obligation to entertain a king or his stewards. [ON *veizla* obligatory reception]

Watty Red see WALTER RED.

wauch a large draught (of ale etc). [also Sc in the form *waucht*; origin uncertain; perhaps a form of QUAFF]

wauld to move with a heavy gait. [OE *waeltan* to roll]

wazzan the gullet. [Eng *weasand* windpipe; OE *wasēnd* gullet]

wazzie 1 a band of twisted straw used as a horse collar. 2 a round flat straw cushion formerly used by stone breakers etc. 3 a cylindrical stool. [related to Norw *vase* to tangle]

weary 1 = weary. 2 annoyance, irritation. *That's the weary o'd*. [also Sc].

weather, wather = noun. weather. verb. to set to windward of. **weather-banked** of a sailing boat having the passengers or cargo placed so that the vessel has made a deliberate list to windward. **weather blinks** distant flashes of lightning in the sky too far away for thunder to be heard. [also known as SPUNKIES or WILD FIRE]. **weather-kind** a cloudy sky betokening a rainstorm but which is unlikely to materialise. [a special usage of Eng *kind*; also used in ON postfixed as in the Orkney example, but only of men or beasts e.g. *sauð-kind* sheep]. **wather-moose** a twitch in the eye. [also known as a LIFE CORN; ?*weather-muscle*, a portent of (bad?) weather; ON *mús was* used metaphorically of

137

biceps muscle]. **wather gauge, weather gauge** a barometer, *tae get the wather gauge o somebody* to get the upper hand. **weather-mooth** a point on the horizon from which clouds apparently radiate indicating the *mouth* from which the weather is coming. The clouds are in fact parallel and appear to radiate because of perspective. *'Keep yir weather eye winkan/liftan'* be on the alert. **weather-set** weather bound.

wecko see WAIKO.

wee 1 see WHEE.

wee 2 small. [also Sc; very rarely used in Ork where the words PEEDIE and PEERIE are universal; ME *wei* a bit]

weedow = widow. **weedo-wife** widow. **weedow-man** widower

weefle to shake. **weefle-hole** a contemptuous term for a person [*hole* = posterior]. **weefly** shaky, *'Me legs are kinda weefly'*. [see WAFFLE]

weegaldie-waggaldie unsteady. [a form of Eng *wiggle* with a reduplicated element]

weegings see WEEKINGS.

week the corner of the mouth, generally in the plural, *'Clean thee weeks bairn'*. **tae be doon i' the weeks** to look sad [ON *munn-vík* the corner of the mouth]

weekings, weegings a dimin of WEEKS. [see WEEK above]

weel = well. **weel-at-himsel** of a man or animal, grown stout. **weel-bodden** having plenty. **weel said** it's truly said, *'Hid's weel said he's no tae be trusted'*. **weel-hung** of a male animal having large testicles, used jocularly also of humans. **weel-willied** kindly disposed [also Sc]. **weel workan** industrious.

weeman* = women, used as a plural of wife (*wan wife, two weeman*). **tae go tae the weeman** to go courting.

weeng see WING.

weengle 1 to swing around, particularly of a child balancing his chair on two legs, *'Stop weenglan on that chair beuy!'* **2 tae weengle something oot o somebody** to wheedle it out. [Norw *vingle* to walk uncertainly]

weenkly unstable, bending. **weenkle-wankle** *'He wis walkan weenkle-wankle'*. [see WEENGLE]

weeo a kittiwake. [imitat of its call; compare Sh *weeg*; ON *hví* a call imitating a gull's cry; see also WHEEO]

weese allan† the Arctic skua. [OSc *wheese*; OE *wesan* to ouse; see SCOOTY ALLAN]

weesk*, wheesk verb. 1 of a door or a mouse, to squeak. 2 to whisper. 3 of a fawning dog to make a high pitched whine. noun. a squeak. [imitat. compare EESK 1]

weesko, weeskal, weeso, weeslo, wheeso, wisoo a tangled mass of threads. [ON *vísk* a bundle]

weester to squeak. [compare WEESK]

weet* = wet. **tae maak weet*** to rain.

weh verb. to make a moaning noise as if in pain; *'A ferfil wehan soond kam fae ahint the press.'* **weh** noun. a moaning noise [from the sound, compare WEOW]

weigh 1 = weight. 2 a standard weight formerly used in the kelp trade approximating 500 kg. **tae weigh salt** to stand back to back and with the arms linked lift each other alternatively off the ground until one of the pair gives in.

weight a tray made by stretching a skin over a wooden frame. [Sc *wecht*]

welbestow dinner. [Sc *stow* to fill the stomach with food]

well a tide race. [ON *vella* to well up]

welt *tae go at full welt*. [OSc *walt*; ME *walten* to throw; compare PELT]

wented of food, tainted. [OSc *went* a turn or change]

wenyarn small or stunted. [origin uncertain]

werchie 1 of the weather miserable, damp, cold. 2 weak tea or tasteless soup. [ME *werische* insipid or sickly; see also WARSHIE]

wersy porridge without salt. [see WERCHIE]

whaak a stammer or stutter. [imitat]

whaal-backs long unbroken waves moving shorewards. [Eng *whale* + *back*]

whaar see WHEER.

whack = whack (to beat). **whacker** outstanding in size etc., *'Beuy that's a right whacker o a baest'*. **whackan** big.

whacko 1 nothing at all, *'Whit wis in the box?'* *'Whacko!'*. [origin uncertain]

whacko 2 a quagmire [Eng. *quake* + dimin. *o*]

wham a trick. [see WHIM-WHAM]

whamsy out of sorts. [Eng *qualm* + *sy*]

whan *'Bit oh whan, oh whan?'* Dearie me! [also Sc in a variety of forms; Gael *ochan*]

whang a term of abuse applied to a woman. [Sc *quean*; OE *cwene* prostitute]

whanner see WHINNER.

whanter-nap 1 a trick or dodge. 2 a silly notion. [a corrupt form of OSc *cantrip* a magic spell]

whar* 1 who, *'Whar's that gaan along the road?'* Who is that going along the road? [ON *hverr* who]

whar 2* = where. **wharon** = whereon but used as a noun, *'He had wharon'*, that is *'he had something to live on'*. **wharpiece*** where?, *'Wharpiece are yi gan?'*.

whark* to cough up, *tae whark and spit* [imitat]

whasapavaaraa *as much as to say*. [origin unknown]

whasay a story of doubtful origin. [also Sc; Eng *whosay*]

whass a whim. [see WHASSIGO]

138

whassigo* 1 insincere talk. 2 an excuse. 3 a fancy or craze. [must have as its original meaning *a blast of wind*; ON *hvass* of the wind fresh, sharp; ON *gjóla* a gust of wind; compare Sh *gandigo* with similar meanings and Eng *wind* empty, insignificant talk]

whaup* a curlew [also Sc]

wheble to speak with a weak, squeaky voice. [Sc *wheeple*]

whee, wee to neigh. [ON *hvía* to whinny]

wheeble to quibble. [with *wh* for *qu*; also Sc; imitat]

wheek* to snatch, '*Beuy afore I could deu anything he wheekéd hid ot o me hand*'. [Sc *wheech*; imitat]

wheel 1, wheeld to rest, especially *tae wheel doon*. [ON *hvíla;* see WHEELIECREUSE]

wheel 2 = wheel. **wheel-gut** the long small bowel of a sheep formerly used as a driving band on a spinning wheel. **wheel-spow** only in *tae go wheelspow* to turn a cartwheel. [? *wheel spoke*]

wheeliecreuse 1 a place where a funeral cortege rested. 2 a churchyard. [see WHEEL + plural form of Ork dial CREU enclosure]

wheenk to toss the head or jerk the body expressively, especially *tae wheenk and laugh*. [Norw dial *vinka* swing to and fro]

wheeo the story is told from Rendall of a father and his son working in the peat hill. A golden plover passed overhead with its characteristic note which the father interpreted as *poor wheeo, poor wheeo*. The father turned to his son and said '*Poor enough, God knows*'. [ON *hví* cry of a gull; *poor-wheeo* may be a lost name for the golden plover; compare the North American nightjar called the *poorwill*; likewise, *wheeo* may be a lost word for a sad mournful person; compare PLEEP]

wheer*, whaar to wheeze, '*The cowld's gin doon on his breest noo and he's just wheeran*'. [imitat; compare Eng *whirr*]

wheerny 1 a rumour. 2 a gentle breeze. [see WHERN]

wheery a peculiarity or trait in a person, generally an unpleasant trait. [from Eng *queer*]

wheesa-cramps, wheesacrapes out of sorts through body ache or ill-humour. *to be in the wheesacramps* to be ill. [first element relates to ModIcel *kveisa* shooting pains; Eng *cramp*]

wheesh a call to a horse to turn to the right.

wheesht see WHEEST.

wheesk see WEESK.

wheeso see WEESKO.

wheesp a rumour. [origin uncertain]

wheest*, wheesht 'Be quiet!'; also '*Had yir wheest*'. [archaic Eng *whist*! be silent]

wheetle the sound made by a duckling. [see WHEBLE]

wheeve a cough. [ON *kvef* catarrh]

wheisa-girse ground-elder. [ON *kveisu-gras*]

wheiso-baylin a whitlow. [ON *kveisa*]

wheou the sound made by the wind whistling through the chinks of a closed door. [compare WHEWAN]

whern 1 to make quick body movements. 2 to cast a glance around. [the main idea is *turning*; related to Eng *quern*]

whess* to pant. [compare ON *hvaesa* to hiss and Eng *wheeze*]

whesso goutweed. The roots and leaves were boiled and used as a poultice in case of gout. [compare WHEISA-GIRSE]

whet see WHITE.

wheu a swathe mown when cutting with the scythe. [imitat]

whewan of the wind howling round corners. [Eng *whew*; imitat]

whewl to howl. [ON *ýla*]

whid a peculiarity of temper. **whiddy** 1 of a wind changing direction. 2 of people or animals temperamental. [ON *hviða* a gust of wind]

whigaleerie strange notions or actions. [Sc *whigmaleerie*]

whigget a lump (of e.g. cheese or bread). [origin unknown]

whilberty of a garment short. [origin unknown]

while*, whiley* a length of time [also Sc], '*He wis a while in Canada*'. **whill** until, '*Bide there whill I come*'.

whill see WHULL.

whilter a shallow rocky piece of ground. [Sh *hulter*; ON *holt* dry barren stony ground]

whilyo-markit a cow's ear marked on the tip at birth. [ON *hvel* wheel; a reference to the curved shape]

whimen of a person undependable. [see WHYME]

whim-wham a trick. [a reduplicated form of Eng *whim*]

whin 1 gorse. [also Eng]

whin 2 hard stone, especially, *blue whin* hard sandstone bedrock bluish in colour. **whinny** of a field, stony. [origin uncertain, also Sc]

whin 3 to dry up hard. **whinnery** very hard. [Sc *win* to dry out]

whinner, whanner 1 a blow or a knock [also Sc]. 2 of a strong wind to roar in the chimney. [imitat]

whinnery see WHIN 3.

whinshoo see WINCHOU.

whint clever or crafty. [OSc *quent* clever]

whinyan also Sc. 1 = whining. 2 of a dog howling.

whinyo a girl of low repute. [see WHANG]

whirgal a large neck on a horse. [see WHUGGAL]

whirlygigger 1 = whirlygig. 2 a small boy's penis. An old lady who had seen a new born child in a

139

nearby house was asked whether the new arrival was a '*boy or a lass*.' '*Hid (it) hid (had) a whirlygigger furtiver*,' was the reply!

whirny 1 of bread dried up. 2 of a face wrinkled. [a methathesis of WHINNERY]

whirr to dry up. [origin uncertain; see WHIRNY]

whiss 1, whizz to whisper. [ON *kvisa* to whisper]

whiss 2, whizz 1 = quiz. 2 to ask questions of in a forthright (and inquisitive) manner.

whit* = what? **whit wey** how. '*Whitwey deu I get oot o here noo?*' **Whit wey hid**?, Why not? e.g. '*Ah'm no gan tae the toon the morn efter aal*'. '*Whit wey hid?*'. **whit a** a curtailed form of *whit a lot o* e.g. '*Whit a kye in the mart the day*,' what a lot of cattle in the mart today. '*Whit o'clock is hid?*' What time is it? **whit time?*** when? '*Whit time are yi gan oot?*' **whitan** what, '*Whitan man is that*'. [see WHITNA]. **whit-like*** how?, especially in the common social greeting '*Whit like the day?*' How are you today? **whitna*** what? as in, '*Whitna man is that?*' [more common then *whitan*; a short form of *what kind of*; also found in Eng dial]. **whitnafura** what kind of? '*Whitnafura jam is this on the table?*'. [compare Norw *hva for* what].

white* = quit. past tense WHET. '*White hid noo!*' stop it at once. '*Ah'm whet gan tae the sea noo - Ah'm too owld beuy!*'

whitemaa a seagull. [ON *hvít-máfr* common gull]

whitherward awkward or perverse, *the wame's the waur that his the whitherward mester*, the 'stomach has the worst of it if it has an awkward master'. **witherwart** lurching, unsteady. **witherwas** *tae go witherwas* not going the way it was intended. [obs Eng *whither* in a contrary direction]

whitna see WHIT.

whizz 1 see WHISS 1.

whizz 2 see WHISS 2.

whome a half-built stack. [see WHUM]

whonk to turn suddenly. [see WHEENK]

whuff a puff of smoke. [compare Eng *whiff*]

whuggal a lump of e.g. cheese. [origin uncertain; compare WHIGGET and WHIRGAL]

whull, whullo, whill [see KWILL]

whum a covering of sheaves temporarily placed on an unfinished corn stack. **whummle** to cover an unfinished stack with sheaves which will run water. [Norw dial *kvelm* a truss of hay]

whumble to turn upside down. [OSc *quhelm* to turn upside down]

whummle 1, whumble of the sky to darken. [a variant of HOOM]

whummle 2 to poke in the ear. [Eng dial *wimble* to bore into]

whump a sudden start or a toss of the head in impa-

tience. [compare Dan dial *hvimpe* of a horse to toss the head]

whunyo, whinyo a girl of low repute. [see WHANG]

whup verb. 1 = whip. 2 to snatch*. noun. a snatch*, '*He whuppéd the knife oot o me hand*'.

why 1 see QUEY.

why 2 see QUOY.

whyme to sneak around furtively like a dog. **whymowee** looking down in the mouth. [ON *hvima* to move the eyes as if frightened]

wi see WITH.

wicht a shrew. [OE *wiht* creature]

wid* = would [see also WAD]. **widna*** = would not. '*I widna say*' I tend to agree with you. [compare DOOT]

wife* 1 = wife. 2 = woman. [the plural of *wife* is *weeman*; 'woman' is used only vocatively and familiarly in Ork dial when it is pronounced *wumman* or *umman* '*Come on umman!*' = Come on dear!]. **owld wife** 1 used of a man who gossips and shows excessive interest in other people's affairs, '*He's just a owld wife*'. 2 a hag or witch; **tae free the owld wife** an expression used at sea when fishing cuithes. After three cuithes had been landed the fisherman had *freed the owld wife*. [the meaning appears to be 'to have got free from the old wife', i.e. to 'break the spell'; compare Icel *komast frá kerlingunni* to escape from the hag, which also meant 'to have caught three fish']

wifflo = snag, '*Me wool's gin in a weeflo*'. [see WAFFLE]

wight 1 = weight. 2 blame, '*Thoo'll hiv tae tak the wight for hid*'.

wild = wild. **wild duck*** a mallard. **wild fire** lightning without thunder.

wilk* 1 = whelk. 2 the nickname of an inhabitant of Wyre.

Wilkie a spirit which inhabited certain mounds in Westray and which was periodically given an offering of milk poured through a hole in the top of the mound. [ON *fylgja* female guardian spirit]

will to lose one's way, also **tae go will**. **willan** wandering in the mind. **willsome** speaking of e.g. a hill, '*That's a willsome hill*' i.e. a hill with no paths where it is easy to get lost in the dark. [ON *villa* to lead astray]

Willie* 1 = Willie. 2* child's name for penis. **Willie-long-legs** daddy long legs or the crane fly. **Willie-wabster** a spider. **tae work Willie Hay's wark** to be up to mischief (Westray). [also recorded in Fife with a different meaning]. **Willie Heron** the heron.

will-ness, wull-ness dizziness. [ON *villa* delusion related to WILL above]

wilsome see WILL.

wimbrods the boards of the horse clibber (part of a pack saddle). [Eng *wing* + *boards*]

win 1 = win. 2* to succeed in reaching a goal, '*I couldna win tae the toon fur me car broke doon*'. '*The door wis locked and I couldna win in*'. 3* to defeat, used reflexively, '*We'll win yi*'. [contrast BAET = BEAT, sometimes not used reflexively!]

winchou see WINSHOO.

winco granny a little old woman. [see WINKIE]

win(d) a pleasure or delight, '*He's workan his hardest, hid's a win(d) tae see him*'. '*Hid's just a win(d) o him*' of anyone who has acted meritoriously. [OE *wyn* joy]

wind 1 = the wind, '*Ah'm heard the wind blowan afore*'* I don't believe you will do what you say you will. 2* air, '*I must pit some wind in me tyres*'. **wind bird**, **wind cuffer** the kestrel. [from its habit of hovering in the air when searching for prey]. **wind-blether** a sea-shell. **wind-feeder** a shower which brings with it an increase in the wind's strength. **windrift** ruin or destruction '*Hid's a gin tae windrift*'. [compare A-GILDRO, AVILDRO]. **wind-skew** a board with a long stick attached to it, used to change the draught in the open central flue of the Old Orkney house. **windthrush** the redwing. **windy** a call by schoolboys when a player of the opposite team kicks a ball out of play, sarcastically suggesting that the breach has been caused by the wind. **windy-whistle** an acute pain in the front teeth occurring naturally or caused by inhaling air rapidly through them.

winder* verb. (sometimes reflexive) = to wonder.'*I winder tae me if he's any happier*'. '*I widna winder bit he's gin home*' I think he's gone home.

wind-feeder see WIND.

windling, winling an armful of hay or straw tied with its own ends. [ON *vindill* a wisp]

window = window. **window-sole** window-sill.

window-cubby a small cubby used in winnowing corn. [OE *windwian* to winnow]

wing, weeng = wing. *on the weengs o the wind* of stock, depleted.

winge see WINYA.

winkie the little finger. [also Sh; from an original *winkie-pinkie*]

winling see WINDLING.

winshoo, whinshoo, winchou a contrivance for rope making. [Eng *winch*]

wint* = wont. '*He's wint wae that*', '*He's ower-weel wint*'* He's (too) accustomed to having the best, said of a child over fussy about his food etc. **tae pit somebody in a bad wint*** to introduce someone to something he/she should not experience,

'*Don't gae the bairn wine, hid'll pit her in a bad wint*'.

winter = winter. **winter-muck** to apply manure to the fields in the winter.

winya, winge destruction or ruin, '*Hid's all gin tae winyo*'. [see WIND, WINDRIFT]

winyaless frail or weak. [Norw dial *vinn* energy, push + less]

wip see WAP.

wipple *in a wipple* in a confused state of a rope, tether etc. [see WUPPLE]

wir*, **wur** our. [also Sh and Sc], '*This is wir youngest son*'. **wiroos** our house. [a running together of '*wir*' and '*hoose*'; also Sh]. **wirs*** ours. **wirsels*** ourselves [when a Marwick lady was asked her opinion of incomers she replied, '*Thir (they are) grand folk, just like wir-sels.*'

wird see WORD.

wire-grass couch grass.

wiring, wirroo the strip of wood in a boat which supports the seat benches. [also Sh and Cai; Du *wegering*; ME *weyr*]

wirk* past tense ROWT, WROUGHT, WROWT, WIROUT, WIRROWT. 1 to work. 2 to be employed (at), '*He wrowt at Gorn a whiley*'*. 3 of ale, to ferment. 4 **tae wirk a sock** to knit a sock. **tae work the creels** to fish lobsters. **tae wirk a wark*** 1 to be busy about something, '*Whit a wark he's wirkan doon there at the corner*'(he was building a house and there was a sign of much activity). 2 to make mischief* '*Whit a wark that young fulloos were wirkan at Edwin's last night*', they were playing Hallowe'en pranks. 3 to behave in an odd way*, '*Every time I stert me car hid splutters an wirks a wark.*' **wirkeen** working; *tae go fae wirkeen*** of machinery etc to break down. **wrought*** pronounced 'rowt' and commonly used for the past tense of WORK, '*He wrought at the cheese factory for 'ears (years)*'.

wiroos see WIR.

wirout see WORK.

wirran a wren. [a form of Eng *wren*; compare OE *wrenna* or *werna* wren]

wirroo see WIRING.

wirrowt see WORK.

wirs see WIR.

wirsels see WIR.

wirt = worth. *no muckle wirt* useless.

wisoo see WEESO.

wit to examine, especially *tae wit a duck* to feel a duck to see if it has an egg to lay. [ON *vita* to know]

witchuck a sandmartin. [imitat]

wite to blame. [also Sc; OSc *wyte* blame; OE *witan* to blame]

141

witgate freedom or licence. [Sc *withgate* related to ON *viðganga* admission]

with, wi 1 = with. *'Lay thee with/woath!'* do your very best. [compare Faroese *leggia saer við* to exert oneself]. 2 by, *tae go wi the bus, car etc* to go by bus, car etc*. **wi** used only vocatively, *'Gae me a box o matches wi thee'*. [a clipped form of *wi thee hand*; this latter form is still used in North Ronaldsay]

wither the barb of a hook. [Sc *witter*; OE *wither* against, in the sense of contrary direction; MDu *wederhake* barb]

witheron a rogue. [see HUTHERIN]

withershins in an anti-clockwise direction, *'Hid's bad luck beuy tae turn the boat withershins'*. [OSc *widdersyns*]

witherwart see WHITHERWARD.

witherwas see WHITHERWARD.

withy, withie noun. gallows. adj tough. **withiefu** mischievous. [OSc *widdy* the gallows rope; originally made of willow]

witnesbirtht† evidence. [ON *vitnis-burðr*]

wittance knowledge or awareness, *'I had no wittance o that'*. [Sc *witting*; ON *vitand* knowledge]

witter to guide or inform. [also Sc; ON *vitra* to make, to know]

witty = witty. used negatively, **no witty*** crazy.

wiz = ways only in *'Come thee wiz'*, 'Come this way,' used particularly as a warm invitation to a visitor in the sense 'Come in'. [also Sc; compare ME *Come thy ways*]

woath *lay thee woath* hurry. [see WITH]

wodset† a mortgage. [also Sc; ME *wedsette* to pledge]

woggie-kattie-mattie naughts and crosses. [origin unknown but must be an ancient form; see TRIP-TRAP-TRUISKY!]

woople wrap up a bandage etc. [see WAP 1]

word, wird = word. 1 **tae hiv words*** to have an argument. 2 **tae come intae words** to get round to talking about something, *'I don't ken whit wey hid kam intae words'* I don't know how we came to speak of it.

worm (the) toothache. [from the belief that it was caused by a worm]

worry to choke. [also Sc; OSc *wery* to strangle, to be choked]

wrak, wrack† seaweed, wrack. **wrack and waith** flotsam and jetsam. [OE *wrack*; ON *vrek*]

wring† [see YEARIN]

wrought see WORK.

wrowt see WORK.

wuff a shrew. [origin uncertain but probably a form of WICHT]

wullness see WILLNESS.

wumman, umman = woman, a familiar form of address, *'Come on wumman'*

wummle a gimlet. A rhyme used in tickling a child is:-

> Haet (heat) a wummle, bore a hole,
> Whar piece, whar piece
> Just there, there there

[Eng *wimble*]

wun past part of WIN.

wup a journey up and down with a plough *'Mercy I hid done only two wup when the rain kam on'*. [see WAP 1]

wupple, wipple to roll up and wrap round. [see WAP 1]

wur* our. [also recorded in the form WIR]

wursam-mither the core of a boil. [also Sc; OE *worsm* or *worms* pus; see VOSE-MITHER]

wush see WASH.

wusp, wuspal an entanglement of thread, wool, fishing line etc. [see PESWISP]

Y the letter *y*

ya*, yaa* Yes, *'Are yi gaan the morn?'* 'Ya'. [also Sh]. **yaas and naes** the ins and outs of a story, *'Tell me the yaas and naes o hid'*. **yaase*** yes, *'Yaase min'* Hello. [Norw *ja* yes]

yaager 1 1 a horse. 2 a strong man. [ON *jálkr* gelding; *Jálkr* was also a by name of Odin]

yaager 2 of dogs, to tear with the teeth. [see YAGGLE]

yaase yaas. [see YA]

yaavel, yaval *yaavel land* land sown with a cereal crop a second time, consecutively. [also Sc; see AWALD]

yack an Eskimo (from whaling days) [also Sc; ?Norw *jåkig*, simple]

yackie thunder any unusual noise. [Sc *yachis* a sudden noise]

yackle 1 molar tooth. 2 to chew, *'He's cut all his yackles'* he wasn't born yesterday. [ON *jaxl* molar tooth]

yagg 1 the inferior stone which lies below the *red* and immediately above the *blue whin*. [origin unknown]

yagg 2 to argue. [ON *jag* a quarrel]

yagger a pedlar. [also Sh; Du *heringjager* a herring-fleet tender; these Dutch vessels traded all commodities in Shetland and Orkney]

yaggle* 1 to chew laboriously at something or to work laboriously at something. 2 to make a mess of cutting something (eg cloth), '*Yir makin a naafil yaggle wi that blunt shears*'. [Norw dial *jagla* to chew; related to YACKLE]

yakster thick barm. [ON *jöstr* yeast]

yalder 1 of a frightened dog to yelp. 2 to chatter. [see YOLDER]

yalpan *yalpan stane* a loose paving stone. [Sc *yalp* a form of 'yelp' from the sound of the moving stone]

yam 1 = yam. 2 the large mussel (*modiolus vulgaris*) dredged up for bait. 3 an old type of potato grown in Orkney not unlike Kerr's Pink.

yammals, yamals, yammalds, yamils people of the same age, '*Me and Bob are yammals, we wir in the sam class at the school*'. [also Sh; ON *jafn-aldri* one of the same age]

yammel to mumble when talking like a toothless person. [compare ON *jamla* (slang), to grumble]

yammer 1 to whine or fret. 2 an outcry. [also Sc; ME *yamer*]

yap 1 verb. 1 to bark. 2* to talk incessantly. noun. someone who talks insistently*, **yap o dirt** or more strongly **yap o shite** a persistent talker.

yap 2 hungry. [Sc *yaup* a special development of ME *yepe* alert]

yard = yard. **yardsook** a strong drying wind at harvest-time which rapidly dries the corn in the yard. [see SOOK]

yarfa, yarfie peat peat cut with a heather crown, only one peat deep. Two cartloads of *yarfa peat* were burned and the ash used to manure the PLANTIE CREU annually. [ON *jarð-vegr* the earth; MoIcel *soil*]

yarg to nag. [Icel *jarga* to repeat tediously]

yark 1 1 the instep of the foot. 2 the space between the thumb and the forefinger. [ON *jarki* the outer edge of the foot]

yark 2 suspicious, afraid. [compare ON *argr* cowardly]

yark 3, yirk, yirg to jerk. [also Sc; ME *yerk* to pull tight]

yarm* 1 of a cat to mew plaintively. 2 of a sheep to bleat (North Ronaldsay). 3 to complain in a whining way. [ON *jarma* of sheep, to bleat, or of birds to cry]

yarp to complain. [also Sc; onomat; compare Norw

dial *jarpa* to jabber]

yarromang† a portion of land; possibly in this instance the collective amount of land held by an individual under the RUN-RIG system [ON *jarðar-megin*]

yass* North Isles form of YAASE.

yatter to chatter. [also Sc; compare Norw dial *jaddre* to jabber]

yaval see YAAVEL.

ydant busy, industrious. [also Sc; ON *iðinn*]

year = year (pronounced *'ear*). The plural of *'ear* (year) is *'ear* if it immediately follows a numeral e.g. *a hunder 'ear* but, *hunders o 'ears*. **yearin** produce of the earth. [ON *árangr* year's produce; ON *ár* year; OE *yēar* years (uninflected plural)]

yeask a squeaking sound made with difficulty, '*I wis so krom I could hardly mak a yeask*'. [imitat; compare YEESP, EESK, WEESK etc]

yeel see GEEL.

yeeld see YELD.

yeep the cheep of a chicken. [imitat]

yeesp to cheep or squeak. [see YEESK]

yeesteran squeaking. [imitat; compare EESK, NEESTER, YEESP etc]

yeird† earth. [ON *jord*]

yeld, yeeld barren. **yeeld kye** cows which have calved, have dried up and are not in calf, '*A yeld soo wis never good tae grices*' (metaphorical meaning can only be guessed at). [ON *geldr* dry of milk]

yellow, yalla, yilloo = yellow. **yellow fish*** smoked fish [also Sc]. **yellow gowan** marsh marigold. **yellow lily** yellow iris. **yellow yarling*** the bird, yellow hammer. [Sc *yellow-yoldring*; Eng dial *yowlring* = *yellow* + *ring*]

yern† the earth. [ON *jorð-in*]

yernings, yirnings, yirnam 1 rennet. 2 a nickname for the people of Orphir. It is said the name stems from an Orphir lady who made rennet commercially. [OSc *yirne* to curdle, a metathesis of ME *rennen* to curdle]

yertdrift drifting snow or a drifting snow shower. [see ERD(D)RIFT]

yetlin an iron girdle formerly hung on a CRUIK and used for baking. [OE *yēotan* to pour (metal); the original sense of *yetlin* would have been crucible]

yeuk to itch. **yeuky stone** a protruding stone at shoulder level in an old Ork house and used for itching the back. [OE *yiccean* to itch; compare Du *jeuken*]

yig a sharp pull or to pull sharply. [see YUG]

yildro see GELDRO.

yimmery shivery or off colour. [see YIVVER]

yin* that (common in the North Isles of Ork), '*My

whar's yin?' [OSc *yon* or ON *hinn* that]

yird 1 earth. 2 a slant to the earth like a ploughshare, *'Pit more yird on it'* an instruction to a blacksmith to make the plough sock take a better grip. [see YEIRD]

yirk, yirg to jerk. [see YERK]

yirn of cheese, to curd *'The cheese'll no yirn'*. **yirnam** see YERNINGS. [ME *rennen* to curdle]

yirpo a big hefty girl. [see MANYIRPO; Norw *yrpe* stout, thick object esp. a woman]

yivver verb. to shake. adj. **yivver, yivvery** 1 anxious for something. 2 anxious to do something. 3 healthy especially, *young and yivver*. [OE *gīfre*, desirous, greedy]

yog see YUG.

yoke 1 yoke. 2 the larger plough-tree. 3 a spell of work, originally the period of time when a horse was yoked.

yolder, yalder 1 to make a loud noise like a dog being hurt. 2 **yolderan and singan** with emphasis on volume rather than tune applied for example to a drunk person. [also Sh; ON *hjal(dr)* chatter]

yole a small undecked fishing boat with two masts and a jib. [a form of Eng *yawl*]

youp 1, yoop to cry. **yoopan and greetan** sobbing. [ON *óp* a shouting or crying]

youp 2 a one piece garment also known as a *BYRNE*. [see CHOOP]

yowe ewe [also Sc].

yuck an abusive term, *'Yon yuck!'*. [a special development in meaning of YEUK, itch]

yuffies see DUFFIES.

yug* 1, yog the large mussel. [? ON *aða]*

yug 2, yig verb. to pull or tug at something. noun. **yug** the leather tab on a boot used for pulling it on.

yuiko see UIKO.

yuink to drink in large gulps. [imitat]

Yule Christmas time [also Sc; ON *jól]*

Yule-girs the plant meadow-sweet. **Yule-skrep** a smack on the bottom [origin of *skrep* unknown] [ON *jóll* angelica; a wand of angelica makes a good cane!]

Z The letter *z* always pronounced *s*. *'We gid tae Edinburgh Soo (Zoo)'*

zeend† the numeral *1* used in counting sheep.